Richard Connaughton spent two years as Head of the British Army's Defence Studies, the culmination of a thirty-year career in the army, prior to early retirement in 1992. He now undertakes studies in the politico-military field on an international basis, and has published a number of books and research papers on contemporary matters relating to war, peace and defence. He lives deep in the Dorset countryside.

BY RICHARD CONNAUGHTON

Rising Sun and Tumbling Bear
Russia's War with Japan

The Republic of the Ushakovka
Admiral Kolchak and the Allied Intervention In Siberia 1918–1920

Military Intervention in the 1990s
A New Logic for War

Shrouded Secrets
Japan's War on Mainland Australia 1942–1944

Celebration of Victory

The Nature of Future Conflict

Descent into Chaos

MacArthur and Defeat in the Philippines

Military Intervention and Peacekeeping: the Reality

RISING SUN AND TUMBLING BEAR

Russia's war with Japan

RICHARD CONNAUGHTON

CASSELL

Cassell Military Paperbacks

Cassell
Wellington House, 125 Strand
London WC2R 0BB

Distributed in the USA
by Sterling Publishing Co. Inc.
387 Park Avenue South
New York
NY 10016-8810

First published in this edition 2003
by Cassell
This book is a major revision of the author's earlier
work *The War of the Rising Sun and Tumbling Bear*,
1988 and 1991.
This Cassell Military Paperbacks edition 2004

British Library Cataloguing-in-Publication Data.
A catalogue record for this book is available
from the British Library.

ISBN 0 304 36657 9

Printed and bound in Great Britain by
Cox and Wyman Ltd., Reading, Berks.

CONTENTS

LIST OF MAPS

PREFACE

'Much of the best history stems from serendipity,' said the *Economist* review of this book's first edition in 1988. This refers to the good fortune of my having been a member of the teaching staff at the Army Staff College, Camberley, at a time when the decision was taken to auction off to staff and students the library's duplicate books and papers. I found some very interesting books I wanted on the 1870–1 Franco-Prussian War but I also happened to notice volume after volume on a war about which I knew nothing – the Russo-Japanese War 1904–5. Curiosity got the better of me and I bid 50p (75¢) for each of the volumes on the latter war.

At the time, I was preparing for a two-year assignment to teach at the Australian Army Command and Staff College and packing was well advanced. The Librarian rang and said I had been successful at the book auction. I told him I would be down. 'Bring your car, you were the sole bidder for the Russo-Japanese War books and you have got the lot,' he said. I took them to Australia and in the process of scanning the volumes I was immediately struck by the similarities between what had happened in 1904–5 in Manchuria and what happened later in Europe 1914–18.

The book was published by Routledge in 1988. I did not set out to write an academic tome (there are few footnotes) and while I wanted to cover the spectrum from tactics to grand strategies, I also wanted to research the behaviour of the individuals involved – the man in uniform and the non-combatant. I was intensely aware of the danger of falling between a number of stools because national power was beginning to shift visibly in a way that it had not done for almost one hundred years. The exponential growth in technology and its effect on modern warfare was waiting to be fully tested at a time when the world was undergoing a tectonic shift in the way wars would be waged. In the early years of the twentieth century there was a discernible movement away from the concept of annihilation to attrition, from short wars to long wars, and from limited war to general war. Nevertheless, I gave myself a brief to tell the story of the war, its politics, its battles and its people. These limited objectives shielded the truth that I was writing about a major war in an area that at the time I was unable to visit.

In the year 2000 I received an invitation from the Chinese authorities to visit Manchuria, a Manchuria affected by one hundred years of population growth and development. Having said that, Port Arthur is a gem of a battlefield waiting to be rediscovered. Going there and deriving the benefit of *Fingerspitzengefühl* is essential in the writing of history. The Imperial Japanese Navy's insistence that General Nogi should concentrate not upon the eastern but upon the northern defences becomes transparently obvious and sensible when one stands on Wantai and finds that the view of the harbour is masked by an intervening feature, yet the view of the whole harbour from 203 Metre Hill is virtually unobstructed.

The original book was undoubtedly due for revision but the problem lies in determining what additional material to include in a one-volume history. There was some room for comment and limited analysis. There were wider questions deserving answers. Why was it, given that the war was witnessed by up to one hundred military observers who saw the pounding artillery, the deep trenchworks, barbed wire and machine guns, these lessons of the land campaign were apparently not learned in preparation for the First World War? Indeed, one of the greatest ironies of this war was that it arguably had greater impact upon the Second rather than the First World War.

The reason why the Japanese beat the Russians in every engagement on land and at sea is a worthy subject for a book by itself rather than through passing reference in concluding thoughts. This, the first defeat of a European power by an Asian power since the thirteenth-century invasion of the Mongols, did ring alarm bells, not only in St Petersburg but as far away as London, Paris, Berlin and Washington – and with good reason.

Richard Connaughton

CHAPTER ONE

THE EVENTS LEADING UP TO THE DECLARATION OF WAR

A milestone in the history of Russia's aspirations to gain a warm-water port on the Pacific coast occurred on 14 November 1860. The British and French forces had barely vacated Peking a week before when the Chinese ceded to the Tsar the eastern coast of Manchuria from the Amur River to the Korean frontier. This game of Russian bagatelle had taken almost three centuries to conclude. Russian tribes had been drawn initially into the vacuum created by the collapse of the Mongol Empire. Thwarted in the Mediterranean, unable to dominate the Kurds and Turks, squeezed south by the inhospitability of Siberia, they found in the mid-seventeenth century their new *lebensraum* at Kamchatka. Persistent efforts followed to achieve a dialogue with Japan, still enjoying her self-imposed seclusion, but these were continually rebuffed.

Russia's ultimate goal, a secure, permanently ice-free port, still eluded her. Vladivostok, 'Lord of the East', the new home of the Russian naval headquarters, was closed by ice for three months of the year. Her ability to use the new port effectively depended upon the attitude of Japan whose choker necklace of islands controlled both the Sea of Japan and the egress into the Pacific. To the north, the Straits of La Perouse were overlooked by the northern shore of Hokkaido and the Kurile Islands. Other than the Tsugaru Straits, a narrow passage between Hokkaido and Hondo, the main seaway lay to the south, the bottleneck of the Straits of Korea with the cork provided by the strategically placed Japanese island of Tsushima.

In 1861 the Russians invaded Tsushima. After a brief fight the island was taken by a force of marines. The British, not enjoying the best of relations

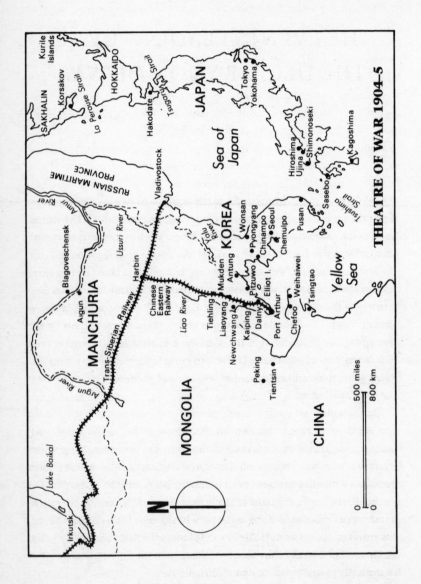

THEATRE OF WAR 1904–5

with Russia, sent a strong naval party to counter this aggression and backed it by vigorous diplomatic protests. As a result, the Russians withdrew, but not before the seeds of anti-Russian loathing were sown in the Japanese mind. Greater cause was yet to come.

Sakhalin had always been regarded by the Japanese as theirs. From early history it had been occupied by the Ainu tribe, but because of its northern aspect and inhospitable weather it was never settled by the people from the south. In new moves, Russia maintained that Sakhalin was hers by right of discovery, by right of occupancy by Siberians, and finally as part of the 1860 cession agreement. None of these claims had much validity but they did lead to a tenuous partition, establishing the Russians in the north and Japanese in the south. Russian pressure grew to such a degree that by 1875 Japan abandoned southern Sakhalin, having to accept the undisputed claim on what she already owned – the Kurile Islands. (The Kurile Islands were subsequently to be taken over by the Russians in the closing weeks of the Second World War when Moscow unilaterally renounced its non-aggression treaty with Tokyo.)

Japan's position at this stage of history is of interest. The world subordination of non-white tribes by white civilisations was almost complete. The Japanese were not as we know them now. Their interest was particularly defensive and inward-looking. They had no regional aspirations and, other than an incursion into Korea in the sixteenth century, had enjoyed for years their own form of splendid isolation. Although this indolence is not now recognisable, their national characteristic has remained constant, manifested by a fervent patriotism which, when provoked, releases an unstemmable national temper.

Her progress since Perry's arrival in 1853 had been remarkable, leading to a well-defined military and naval polarisation. The Japanese had already begun to admire the Prussian military machine as more closely akin to their own views than to any others. It was logical, therefore, that when the French were beaten by the Prussians in 1871 the Prussians should replace the French as instructors in an expanding army for which a new Conscription Act of that year had paved the way. The Royal Navy had always been popular with the Japanese and Nelson was much admired and studied. His philosophy of having a navy sufficiently strong to attack the enemy in their own ports was something the Japanese could both understand and copy.

Russia was gradually preparing Japan for the *coup de grâce,* and why not?

What had this most hungry and acquisitive white race to fear from a docile state? What had Russia, who had seen off Napoleon, to fear from these puny Asiatics? The humiliation of the Japanese over Sakhalin was not even noted as relevant by the Russians. To the Japanese it was yet another unacceptable loss of face. It showed that the only road to real independence was through military power. They prepared for war.

A weak China maintained suzerainty over the corrupt, bankrupt, feudal and defenceless kingdom of Korea; a Korea which was now taking on immense strategic importance. The fear of a Russian occupancy led the Japanese to determine two options for the future of Korea. Either she would be occupied by Japan or she should display her neutrality through independence. The first option was discarded, for Japan knew that the European states would not be averse to intervening, so she selected the second course and waited for the opportunity. Not long after, a Japanese ship off the Korean coast was fired upon and a number of sailors killed. Negotiations opened between the two countries with Japan treating Korea as a fully fledged independent state, ignoring the suzerainty claims of China. A game of cat and mouse then ensued.

The region's vogue for attempts at assassination, this time upon the King and Queen of Korea, gave China the opportunity to recover her sway by offering the threatened royal couple military protection. When it was gratefully accepted, China found herself once again holding the reins of power in Seoul. Anti-Japanese sentiment was never far below the surface and again came to prominence resulting in the legation being burned down. Not only did Japan demand reparations but, unprecedentedly, she sent troops to Seoul where their presence with Chinese soldiers held all the prospect for a major conflict. Eventually the danger subsided and by the Tientsin Convention of 1885, both parties agreed to withdraw their troops. It was also agreed that if either party's future interests required intervention, then the other party should be both forewarned and permitted to despatch a comparable number of troops. So passed another flurry, during which Japan gained a possible foothold into a country for which she had developed a growing interest.

Meanwhile, Russia had not been an idle spectator in the region. In 1891, as if to confirm her determination to dominate the Far East, she announced the single-track Siberian Railway Project. Hugely expensive, with no economic justification, and with the eastern terminus ending at Vladivostok, the Japanese had good cause to feel threatened. Their resolve not to be intimidated was hardening. There then occurred an act of incredible insensitivity. Arriving directly from the inauguration of the railway scheme at Vladivostok, Nicholas II, then heir apparent, came to Japan for a royal visit supported by no less than six warships. Of the six, one was the *Koreyetz* (Korea) and another the *Manjour* (Manchuria). As if to confirm the Japanese fear of the Russian peril, an otherwise respectable middle-class officer named Tsuda Sanzo stepped out from the crowd at Lake Biwa and attacked Nicholas with a sword. The small mark left by the sword on the Tsarevitch's head was soon to disappear but the psychological impact was not. Nicholas entirely misread the ensuing kowtowing and genuine embarrassment. In concluding that the Japanese were dangerous and unbalanced he spread abroad through the courts of Europe his own psychological propaganda against the Yellow Peril. He had not paused to wonder what the real cause of the attack was. Then in 1895, the year of the Tsar's accession, in Shimonoseki, Japan, the Chinese peace envoy plenipotentiary was shot in the face by a would-be assassin, confirming in the Tsar's mind his earlier impression. The anti-Japanese propaganda increased, presumably as a prelude to a 'preventive' advance by Russia.

The building of the railway moved on apace until it was decided at this stage in the events to abandon the 1,000-mile leg from Striekensk following the northern arch of the Amur River to Khabarovsk in favour of a direct route to Vladivostok through Manchuria. Accordingly, in 1896, a contract was drawn up between the Russo-Chinese Bank and the Chinese government which appointed the Chinese Eastern Railway Company to build the Manchurian link from Chita in the west, through Harbin to join the Vladivostok–Khabarovsk railway at Nikolsk Ussuriski. In this way, Russia had achieved a direct and cheaper route to the Pacific but, more importantly, an excuse to intervene in Manchuria if the railway were to be threatened.

Prior to 1896, however, China had already been at war with Japan. Once again, in 1894, a rebellion had broken out in Korea, the army was defeated and the King appealed to the suzerain power to come to his assistance. China responded, at the same time fulfilling the treaty agreement by informing Japan of the despatch of 2,000 troops to Seoul. The Japanese reacted, occupying Pusan and Chemulpo. By that time the Chinese had restored the situation in Seoul and on recommending a joint evacuation by the Chinese and Japanese armies, met resistance from Tokyo. Japan had grown very nervous of the weakness of Korea and saw the prospect of other nations intervening in what was coming to be considered by her an essential Japanese sphere of interest. She therefore asked China to initiate a number of reforms in Korea. The Chinese replied indignantly that the affairs of Korea were of no concern to Japan. So occurred the inevitable war.

It was a short campaign lasting eight months. At sea, a Captain Togo had come to prominence for his attack on a Chinese transport fleet in which 1,200 soldiers and sailors perished. On land, the Japanese launched a two-pronged attack. After the battle of Pyongyang on 15 September 1894 the First Japanese Army advanced north-west into Manchuria while the Second Japanese Army, which had landed on the Liaotung Peninsula on 24 October, joined forces on 6 March 1895 with the First Army to annihilate the Chinese at Tienchuangtai. With her navy routed and the Shantung peninsula occupied by a Japanese expeditionary force, the Chinese sued for peace. The peace treaty was signed at Shimonoseki on 10 April 1895. Under the terms of the treaty, the full independence of Korea was recognised, Japan gained Formosa, the Pescadores and the strategically important Liaotung Peninsula upon which lies the warm-water port of Port Arthur. Japan pocketed £25,000,000 at 1895 values and retained a foothold on the Shantung Peninsula until ratification. In all, Japan had a good war and was congratulating herself on her good fortune – that is, until the White Peril intervened.

Russia was not unnaturally mortified at Japan's success and determined that she should not enjoy the benefits of her spoils. After all, it was Russia's eventual aim that she should possess what she saw as the crucially important Port Arthur, not only because it was ice-free but also because she needed this foothold on the southern mainland of China in order to take advantage of what she foresaw as the impending collapse of China. However, the fact began to dawn upon Russia that she might not be sufficiently strong to attack Japan unaided. The Japanese had a reputation for stern, uncompromising defence. It still remained Russia's belief, supported by reports from the Military Attaché during the Sino-Japanese conflict, that Japan would never have the strength to attack a European nation.

An article appeared in the Russian newspaper *Novoe Vremya* on 20 April (reported in *The Times*, 22 April 1895):

> Russia cannot permit the protectorate over Korea which Japan
> has secured for herself by the conditions of the treaty. If the

single port of Port Arthur remains in possession of Japan, Russia
will severely suffer in the material interest and in the prestige of
a Great Power.

The Tsar and the Kaiser, his 'cousin Willy', both agreed on the dangers posed by the Yellow Peril. It was unusual, however, for Germany to take a direct interest in the area, but colonial aspirations were growing among important political personages. It was this intervention which had much to do with the Japanese Emperor's capitulation. There was no difficulty persuading France, who had major colonial interests in Africa and Indo-China, to join a coalition to confront Japan. *Le Temps* saw the situation as 'a constant menace for the interests of Europe'. It was 'a serious blow dealt at the rights of the immediate adjacent powers', and the article concluded that a European concert was 'now a duty toward civilisation'. So it was that the three European powers set out on a knuckle-rapping exercise to force this upstart Asiatic race to release her hold on her territorial gains. The eastern fleets of the three powers were reinforced and concentrated while Russia prepared the mobilisation of the army in the Amur region. On 20 April 1895 the objections were delivered through the respective diplomatic representatives in Tokyo. The Emperor was in no position to resist the demands of the Europeans and on 10 May 1895 was obliged to issue a withdrawal from the Treaty of Shimonoseki. 'I have', said the Emperor, 'yielded to the dictates of magnanimity, and accepted the advice of the three powers.' Although the Japanese fleet was fast expanding, it did not possess a single battleship and any one of the three opposing powers' fleets could have accounted for the Imperial Japanese Navy. Moreover, in 1895, the active component of the army numbered only 67,000 and the reserve was of little consequence.

As a sweetener for the retrocession of the Liaotung Peninsula and the loss of Port Arthur, Japan received £5,000,000 from China. There was, however, no sugar on earth sweet enough to assuage Japan's distaste and fury at this further example of regional bullying. Prisons began to fill with enraged Japanese patriots, newspapers were suspended and guards placed on printing presses. The volcano rumbled and then died down; for the time being. The total indemnity considerably exceeded Japan's outlay on the war. The profit was invested principally in a large contract placed on British shipyards for the most modern warships available. Having backed off, 'in the interests of peace', the jewel of Port Arthur was returned to the control of China.

Despite her disappointments in Korea and China, Japan's determination and confidence were growing. She had shown that she could organise against and defeat foreign armies. She had enjoyed the fruits of military success in the important regions of Korea and Manchuria. Whilst there, the military and political representatives were to cast envious eyes upon the economic possibilities of Korea and China and grew to covet the land. The pressure to colonise did not arise simply because the land was there or for a perceived divine right but out of an increasing need. It is also true that Russia shared this need for, large as her country was, much of it was useless; unarable, mountainous or frozen waste.

Japanese life was characterised by a burgeoning population with a massive expansion of her industrial and trade base. The population had grown from 34,000,000 in 1875 to 46,305,000 on 31 December 1903, but was still less than a third of Russia's. Over approximately the same period, Japan's foreign trade increased by a factor of twelve from 50,000,000 yen to over 600,000,000 yen, but again, she was still poor by comparison with Russia. During this period there had been a shift from rural to urban life reflecting the Japanese industrial revolution. By 1903, eighty-five per cent of Japan's export trade consisted of manufactured goods. The progress of agriculture was much less dramatic, failing now either to feed its population or to produce goods for manufacture. Japan became increasingly dependent on imports to feed her people while her ability to produce food for the home market went into an exponential decline. Japan's market both for the sale of her manufactured goods and the food baskets for her extra mouths was East Asia. Europe and America could not combine together in importance to Japan as could her own immediate area. If these markets were to be closed then Japan would surely be brought to her knees. Of the East Asian markets, none were more important to Japan than Korea and Manchuria. A conflict with Russia's own political and industrial aspirations was therefore inevitable; both countries were on a collision course, but only Japan knew that. She was soon to make necessity the mother of intervention.

The only crumb retained by Japan in the Yellow Sea was Weihaiwei on the Shantung Peninsula, since it did not form part of the Treaty of Shiminoseki but was rather a guarantee which was good until full reparations were paid by China. Germany too had an interest on the Shantung Peninsula. Indeed, even today, the town of Tsingtao has a brewery which produces large quantities of German-type lager beer. In 1897 two German missionaries were murdered. After lengthy discussions Germany was granted a ninety-nine-year lease of the land on either side of the entrance to Kiaochao Bay as well as certain trading rights. As a result of the German lease agreement, there developed among the other colonial powers an escalation of interest in the area.

In December 1897 a Russian fleet appeared off Port Arthur. After three months, a convention was agreed by which Russia was leased Port Arthur, Talienwan (a town which had interested Britain), and the surrounding waters. It was further agreed that the convention could be extended by mutual agreement. Russia clearly believed that would be the case for she lost no time in fortifying Port Arthur. A year later, in order to consolidate her position, she began a new railway from Harbin through Mukden to Port Arthur. It was at this stage that Britain negotiated the ninety-nine-year lease with China for Hong Kong's 'New Territories'. At the same time, in order to balance the position of the Russians across the Straits of Peichihli, Britain dispossessed Japan of Weihaiwei, securing an agreement for Britain to remain there as long as the Russians were at Port Arthur. Not to be left out, France made her own territorial demand for the lease of Kwangchouwan which was approved on 10 April.

Weak as China was, this scramble for her national territory by the despised 'ghost faces' led to the Boxer 'Rebellion', regarded by many Chinese as a necessary act of self-preservation. The seeds of the uprising had begun in Shantung in 1898 as a natural anti-Christian, anti-partisan action and followed the earlier murder of the German missionaries. Soon emotive circulars were to spread to Peking urging the masses to rise up to rid the nation of these 'foreign devils' before China was irrevocably partitioned and colonised. Chinese troops sent to reinforce Peking acquiesced with the nationalists and refused to intervene. The Japanese Chancellor and German Ambassador in Peking were murdered. On 12 June 1900 the legation area was attacked and besieged, resulting in those nations affected sending troops to raise the fifty-five-day siege of Peking.

The development of the railway was a contributory factor towards the Boxer 'Rebellion'. To many Chinese the railway represented the ascendancy of the west's materialism over their own spiritualism. The focus of attention was the conflict the new railways were to have with ancestral resting places. The placing to rest of remains depended on factors known as *fung shui*, literally wind and water.* It was not only auspicious but necessary that the departed were buried where these intangibles to western minds happened to exist. As a result, by western standards, Chinese burial grounds were haphazardly prevalent. Railway engineers could not avoid the multitude of cemeteries, being obliged to go over them or near them. As if the proximity of the line was not bad enough, the large mechanical engines wheezed their way throughout the countryside, polluting the all-important air with thick, acrid black smoke. It was not surprising that on 5 July the railway stations at Tiehling and Liaoyang were burnt. Russia acted predictably, mobilised and occupied Manchuria.

By 1902 order had been restored in Peking. The armed forces had been thinned out, reparations had been agreed and the 'rebels' punished. There then followed among the European powers a consolidation of their interests through a series of bilateral agreements. Encouraged by a mutual desire to see China and Korea retain their independence, Japan and Britain entered into an agreement on 30 January 1902. Japan had witnessed to her cost the power of even an *ad hoc* alliance and saw in this entente a natural development and display of her growing power. Britain's and Japan's concerns over Russia's strengthening position were increasing. Britain saw in the emergent Japan a convenient ally in the east, hence Britain's entry into this, her first alliance since turning her back on the rest of the world. The treaty was warmly welcomed in Japan providing a substantial boost to national pride. Under the terms of this agreement, if either nation was to go to war to protect its regional interests against a third power, the unaffected party would not only remain neutral but would also use its energies to prevent the conflict from widening. If the war was to be extended by the appearance of an additional power (they had France and Germany in mind), then the uncommitted country would come to the assistance of her ally. In effect the 1902 treaty facilitated Japan's acquisition of Korea and also strengthened Japan's resolve to chance her arm against Russia in Manchuria.

On 16 March 1902 a Franco-Russian declaration endorsed the principle of the Anglo-Japanese treaty but reserved their right to take action should

* A superficial explanation of *fung shui* would suggest that it is like the wind, which you cannot comprehend, and like water which you cannot grasp. However, according to an 1885 book of the Chehkiang Mission, the formulated system of *fung shui* has four divisions: Li, the general order of Nature; Su, her numerical proportions; Ki, her vital breath and subtle energies; and *Hing*, her form or outward aspect. The harmonising of these four factors would appear to constitute a perfect *fung shui* while anything less was considered to be the recipe for disaster.

either a third party intervene or the disturbances in China recur. This declaration was closely followed on 8 April by the Manchurian Convention between China and Russia. Russia confirmed her ultimate aim to evacuate Manchuria on condition that the railway and Russian citizens were protected by the Chinese. Russia reaffirmed the rights and independence of China.

It was agreed that Russia's withdrawal should be phased over three periods each of six months, handing back progressively predetermined areas of Manchuria. After six months the first assigned territory, the south-west of Mukden, was evacuated and returned to China. The anticipated second phase of the withdrawal from the remainder of the province of Mukden and Kirin did not occur. When the Chinese Ambassador at St Petersburg enquired as to why the move had been delayed he was fobbed off, being reassured that the matter was in hand. Eventually, twenty days after the withdrawal should have begun, Peking was presented with demands for concessions in Manchuria. There were seven in all:

None of the returned territory was in any way to be given to another power.

Mongolia's system of government was not to be altered.

No new ports or towns were to be developed or opened in Manchuria without informing Russia.

Foreigners serving in the Chinese government were not to exercise authority in northern Manchuria.

The telegraph line connecting the Liaotung Peninsula with Peking was to be assured.

On Newchwang being returned to China, the Customs' dues were to continue to be paid into the Russo-Chinese Bank.

The rights acquired by Russian interests or Russian people were to be continued.

On 29 April, encouraged by the protests and support of Great Britain, the United States and Japan, the Chinese government rejected the seven demands as an unwarranted interference in her domestic affairs. The leaking of these conditions by China had caused the Russians some embarrassment; so much so that the Foreign Minister, Count Lamsdorf, and the Russian Ambassador in Washington, Count Cassini, were to deny on 28 and 29 April the existence of such requirements. In Peking on 29 April, however, the Russian Chargé d'Affaires, Mr Plançon, was endeavouring to have each condition answered separately by the wavering and unwell Prince Ching. The Chinese Foreign Office showed all the signs of being overwhelmed by the will of the Russian bear. Japan now determined that there was no option but for her to deal directly with Russia.

At this point, it is necessary to turn back the clock to pick up another thread in the development of this story. The Korean assassins had persevered and, on 8 October 1895, had accounted for their turbulent, anti-reforming Queen. In July of the following year an uprising in the north prompted the King to seek temporary asylum in the Russian legation, from where he issued orders to dispose of the Prime Minister and two of his principal supporters. The King remained under Russian protection for two years, during which time the pendulum of power in that country took a distinct swing in Russia's favour. Russia seized this opportunity to strengthen her forces in defence of her legation, a move reciprocated by Japan in order to protect the telegraph line between Seoul and Pusan.

A further agreement between Russia and Japan had been signed in Tokyo on 25 April 1898. The agreement contained three understandings:

> The independence of Korea was assured; neither country would interfere in Korea's domestic affairs.

> There would be no appointment of military or civil advisers without discussion with the interested parties.

> Russia agreed not to hinder Japan's development of trade with Korea.

A Russo-Korean bank had been formed in 1897 and, across an entirely different bank, that of the Yalu, the boundary between China and Korea, a timber-cutting contract had been given to a consortium of Russian noblemen. The contract was not initiated until the Manchurian railway was completed. The manager of the logging company was a retired Russian officer who with his armed men, all ex-soldiers, began work in earnest in April 1903. This coincided with the arrival of Russians into the Yalu region, the acquisition of land and the establishment of a fort at Yongampo at the mouth of the Yalu River. Meanwhile large victualling contracts were being made, not only in the United States but also with Japan. Intelligence reports showed that Port Arthur was being heavily stocked with supplies while large Russian troop movements were observed across the Liaotung Peninsula heading for Korea. It was perfectly clear to the Japanese that Russia had no intention of honouring her agreement, treating the Japanese instead in a high-handed, contemptuous and arbitrary manner. A Japanese minister summed up the situation at the time: 'We do not want war, for it would cost us so much, and we have nothing to gain even if we win; but by keeping peace too long we may lose even our national existence'.

On 28 July 1903 the Japanese Ambassador at St Petersburg was instructed to represent his country's view that the drawing up of the seven demands did not represent a Russian relaxation of her hold on Manchuria but rather a consolidation. As if to confirm the Japanese assertion, on 30 July 1903 the Russian Admiral Alexeiev was appointed Viceroy of the Far East with supreme power to exercise diplomacy between Russian East Asia and neighbouring countries as well as command of Russian military and naval forces. Japan believed that the permanent occupation of Manchuria would be prejudicial to her own security and interests and would also constitute a threat to Korea, a sphere of interest she was not now prepared to share. Russia agreed to consider a draft treaty, which was presented at St Petersburg on 12 August 1903. There then followed on Russia's part much prevarication while she continued to strengthen her position in the Far East.

The situation was reached on 13 January 1904 whereby Japan offered to recognise Manchuria as being outside her sphere of interest and sought in return a similar statement relating to Russia's discontinuing interest in Korea. This proposal was by no means unanimous, being essentially a political rather than military idea. The army chief Yamagata Aritomo was implacably opposed to any concession likely to fuel Russia's wider ambitions. Japan requested an early reply to this proposal. By 4 February 1904 no reply had been forthcoming and on 6 February Mr Kurino, the Japanese Ambassador, called on the dumbfounded Russian Foreign Minister, Count Lamsdorf, to take his leave. Kurino explained to Lamsdorf that his government had decided to adopt such independent action as was deemed necessary to defend its established rights and legitimate interests.

Japanese patience had come to an end. The Russian Ambassador to Tokyo, Baron Rosen, had consistently warned his masters in St Petersburg that if Japan was manoeuvred into a corner she would fight. Much the same sentiment had been echoed by the War Minister, General Kuropatkin, who had resigned in a state of exasperation some months earlier. The Tsar did not want a war but was continually being assured by his closest advisers that

Japan would not under any circumstances fight. Nevertheless, when Mr Kurino left, an immediate signal was made to the newly appointed Russian Far East Viceroy, Admiral Alexeiev, at that time in Tokyo. The Viceroy had seen evidence of Japanese mobilisation and advised St Petersburg accordingly. After calling on the Japanese Foreign Ministry the Viceroy received confirmation that Japanese patience had been exhausted and that their ambassador had been recalled. There was no discussion of war and he signalled back that, in his view, Japan was bluffing. A more astute man might have formed another opinion but then, the Admiral had his limitations, owing his position more to the fact that his father was rumoured to have been Tsar Alexander II. It is possible that Alexeiev was not averse to war with a country which he believed would be militarily outclassed. There were certainly, at the time, those close to the Tsar who saw the possibility of a short victorious war as being an essential distraction to stem the tide of revolution which threatened three centuries of Romanov rule. The irony of the impending war was that both protagonists were about to fight for, and on, territory which neither owned. The Chinese, who found themselves caught between the two, suffered casualties and were dispossessed and humiliated.

On 6 February, while Mr Kurino was making his final preparations to leave St Petersburg, a small British steamer slipped quietly out of Port Arthur for the open sea. On board was the Japanese population of that city. In Japan, requisitioned trains and vehicles were assembling personnel and equipment at the port of Sasebo. The day before, Admiral Togo had opened his orders, 'to destroy the Russian fleet'. At 1 a.m. the imperial message was read to the naval commanders assembled on board the *Mikasa*. Thomas Cowen, a war correspondent with the *Daily Chronicle,* reported: 'In the evening the die was cast, the waiting ended and the tension relaxed. And Japan was glad – not glad to be at war, but glad to end the terrible strain, glad to know the worst at last.' In fact war was not to be declared until 10 February. Japan had a number of plans to execute before the formal declaration of war.

CHAPTER TWO

THE OPPONENTS

Japan had observed for some time the looming encroachment from the west. She responded by introducing conscription, which started to take effect in 1873. A conscious effort developed to restructure Japanese society, militarily, socially and politically. This was achieved by retaining the best of the home system – patriotism, industry and loyalty – combined with western technical skill and assistance. The previous tribal structure, with homage accorded to the feudal lord, was discarded, while the Japanese need to honour some higher being was diverted and channelled directly to no lesser person than the Emperor. The redundant retainers of the feudal lords, the Samurai, were encouraged into the services where their outlook and standards did much to raise the horizons of those lesser but willing mortals inducted into the employment of the Emperor.

The intelligence network was set up, officers sent abroad to study in military establishments and to return with ideas, books and pamphlets. All Japanese officers were obliged to be able to speak at least one language other than their own. By comparison, the Russian army had not one Japanese speaker in Port Arthur at the time of the siege. It was relatively simple, therefore, for the Japanese to select suitable officers to precede the army into Manchuria and Korea. Secretly and systematically the whole area to the east of Lake Baikal was surveyed and mapped. When war began, the Japanese had a more accurate knowledge of the Russian-held territory than did the Russians. That much they had learned from their studies of the Franco-Prussian War. The exceptional standard of the officer corps in staff and tactical ability was derived principally from the Prussian army and British naval systems. This was a vital investment from which Japan was to derive a worthy dividend. The Confucian dictum that 'one must make preparations before the rain falls' had been both well observed and actioned.

General Sir Ian Hamilton, whose *Staff Officer's Scrap Book* gives a valuable insight into the campaign, rated the Japanese soldier as better educated and more civilised than his beloved Gurkha, but not as physically strong. Both the army and the navy were imbued with a profound devotion to duty and a belief that to serve one's country was an honour but to die for it was the ultimate privilege. They were an indomitable and dogged people who fought with fortitude, at their best when under the most extreme difficulty.

These qualities were summarised by J. H. Anderson, an historian of the time: 'The training and "moral" were excellent, the war popular, the initiative was inculcated, and the men's bravery was hereditary – in short they retained the virtues of the barbarian without the defects of civilisation.'

At the outbreak of war, the Japanese military order of battle was approximately thus:

Active and reserve army	380,000
2nd reserve	200,000
Conscript reserve	50,000
Trained men of the National Army	220,000

The in-theatre trained troops totalled 850,000, with an untrained force consisting of the conscript reserve and those available for induction into the army amounting to 4,250,000.

On analysis, the effective strength would have been 257,000 infantry, 11,000 cavalry and 894 guns. The distribution of these assets was among the Imperial Guard, twelve infantry divisions each of 11,400 infantry, 430 cavalry and thirty-six guns, two cavalry brigades, and two artillery brigades. Batteries were established for six guns. The balance of 850,000 is achieved by adding thirteen reserve brigades, depot troops and the Formosa garrison. Most of the war commitment fell on those formations in being. Although four additional divisions and four reserve brigades were raised in 1904, no further formations were created, the pool of untrained troops being used to top up existing units.

Troops were combat-liable after twelve months' training but, as the war progressed, the liability changed to after six months. Divisions were to be fought as divisions unencumbered by a corps staff or corps troops. Garrison duties were conducted by reserve formations, leaving the best and sharpest teeth to fight the battle.

Russian drawing-rooms had resounded with laughter arising from reports of spies having seen Japanese cavalry going into the trot and riders being discarded over the whole line of advance. There may have been some truth in this, but also much exaggeration, which all fuelled a major under-appraisal of Japanese martial qualities. Although among the most intelligent, the Japanese cavalry was not the cream of the Imperial Army. They were trained principally for shock action, equipped with the 1900-pattern carbine and sword, but did not represent a high proportion of the military establishment. Even so, they had to satisfy the additional requirement of fighting on foot. Most of the Japanese cavalry engagements were fought as dismounted infantry, the horse being but an instrument to put them down at the desired place on the battlefield. Each man carried ninety rounds of ammunition, additional firepower being provided by the six Hotchkiss machine guns indigenous to each cavalry brigade. When the indifferent and 'overweighted' stock was taken into account, it was not surprising that standards were low.

Japanese artillery battalions consisted of three batteries. Both the field and mountain guns had the same calibre of 2.95 inches with a range out to 5,000 yards. Some batteries in the army artillery were equipped with 4.72-inch howitzers. The tactical employment of guns was superior to their effectiveness, particularly in relation to the second-generation Russian guns. Invariably a fire plan would precede offensive action. Fire and control were centralised at the highest level, missions being fired by less than a battalion only *in extremis*. Guns were set on reverse slopes or, where this was not practicable, earthworks were thrown up in front of the guns to conceal them from view and protect them from fire. Five of the infantry divisions and the artillery brigades were armed with the slow-firing Arisaka field gun which took either high explosive or shrapnel shells. All but one of the other divisions had the mountain guns, which had a slightly shorter range but proved to be more effective. The Seventh Division had two batteries of each type of gun.

The infantry were equipped with the modern 1900 .256-inch magazine rifle which was sighted out to 2,000 yards with the most effective range between 100–300 yards. The rounds were supplied in clips of five with each man having 210 (120 in pouches, thirty in his haversack, and an additional sixty on unit transport). This number would be varied in the light of future plans. Each soldier had a knapsack to which were attached a greatcoat and shelter tent. Inside he carried two days' rations and, in addition, some men carried entrenching tools. The total weight of what the British soldier would describe as the 'large pack' was 57 lbs. The equivalent to the 'small pack' was a blue holdall – the same colour as the winter-weight uniform. It was an open-ended blue drill sack sewn lengthwise down the middle. Normally it was carried empty, but often when it was required for the infantry to fight unencumbered by the large pack, the holdall was filled with reserve rations and ammunition and worn as a bandolier across the body with the two ends tied across the chest. At the outbreak of hostilities the machine gun had not been an infantry weapon. In the autumn of 1904, ten Hotchkiss guns were added to the division's inventory to be increased by March the following year to fourteen. These weapons were not distributed down to companies but were kept concentrated in two batteries of six guns and one section of two guns.

It has been said that tactics is the art of the logistically feasible; logistics being the gums which hold in place and regulate the teeth. As in so many cases, the success of a campaign was to turn on the ability to orchestrate logistic support and to attend to the detail in the unglamorous monotony of administration and routine. The Japanese supply system was better organised than the Russian and enjoyed the additional benefit of a short line of communication. In common with the current British system it was built up on a series of 'lines' of support; first line being unit resources, second line division, and third line higher formation. At first line, each soldier physically carried two days' rations with an additional day on echelon transport. At second line, the divisional transport column held four days' rations, while at third line the so-called magazine column drew from railhead, storage site or port of entry. Each division had its own transport battalion and while those soldiers underwent a shorter training period of three months, their recruitment followed the same pattern as the rest of the army. The gunners had the benefit of their own integral artillery re-supply train. An ambulance train dealt with casualties and, not unlike today's field ambulance, comprised a high proportion of doctors and medical attendants. Animal transport was relied upon heavily with the donkey preferred to the horse. Most of the supplies were manhandled from post to post along the main supply routes. One supply function was the requisitioning of Chinese carts and recruitment of Korean coolies. The Japanese had learnt that supplies and their transportation are equal and indivisible functions.

There is no consensus of opinion as to how many Russian troops were stationed in the Far East in February 1904. There is a variance between the British official account and the German official account. There is no doubt that Russia's trained army stood at 4,500,000. However, only six of the twenty-five European army corps played an active part in the war. It is believed that on 8 February 1904 the number of Russian combat troops available was: 60,000 infantry, 3,000 cavalry and 164 guns posted at Vladivostok and Port Arthur, with a portion at Harbin. By the middle of that month the figure had increased to 95,000: 45,000 field troops near Vladivostok, 8,000 at Harbin, 9,000 near Haicheng, 11,000 on the Yalu and 22,000 near Port Arthur. A corps consisted of two divisions and corps troops, yet a European corps and a Siberian corps were fundamentally different. The latter was smaller and less well organised. The Siberian division comprised 3,400 men and twelve horse artillery guns in two batteries while the field battery numbered eight guns. The Siberian infantry division did not exist when the war began but evolved from the expanding brigades. The Siberian corps not only had fewer guns than the Europeans but was also deficient in divisional cavalry. War began then with only two widely dispersed and disorganised Siberian corps. As the war progressed the harmony and efficiency of the Siberian army improved, and the number of corps increased to seven. They were to be joined from Europe by the First, Fourth, Eighth, Tenth, Sixteenth and Seventeenth Army Corps, each numbering 28,000 rifles and 112 guns. Three additional corps were despatched from Europe but were too late to take part in the war. It was none the less significant, therefore, that Russia embarked upon a more limited war than did the Japanese.

The emphasis was quite clearly placed on the ability of the Russians to mobilise quickly to reinforce. Vladivostok was ice-bound, so the pressure fell upon the new railway. With luck, a train from Europe would take fifteen days to cover the 5,000 miles but forty days was not unusual. It took, by rule of thumb, a month to deploy a battalion from Moscow to Mukden (Shenyang). Added to the difficulties was the high-handedness of nobility and generals claiming priority over their army who were relegated to sidings while the VIPs swept by. The sidings were used by returning engines, but not the rolling stock. It was not cost effective to return the empty wagons, which were destined to become either fuel or living accommodation.

An obstacle along the route was Lake Baikal because the railway had not been built initially around its southern end. The lake, the sixth largest in the world, is between twenty and fifty miles wide and 386 miles long, covering 13,200 square miles. It equates to approximately the size of Switzerland. The first severe frost of 1904 occurred on 2 January. Steamers or sledges plied across it depending on the weather but the thaw was most difficult to predict, in which case the soldiers marched the southern route while the supplies went across the water. If the ice persisted, then the men marched across.

Each year, usually during the months of February–April, a half-way house was established on the frozen lake. It was a substantial building made of wood, felt and brick. It offered temporary shelter for the privileged weary and limited sustenance of soup and coffee. The majority had to make do with rough shelters, a hurried meal and cursory treatment for such ailments as frostbite and influenza. In February of 1904, the need dictated that rails were laid across the ice of the lake and by 28 March over sixty military trains had made the laborious crossing. By September the Circum-Baikal link was completed, and by the end of the year the system ran nine to ten trains daily each way and had carried 410,000 soldiers, 93,000 horses and 1,000 guns. To put that in perspective, a European Russian army corps needed 267 railway trains with which to move.

The railways were spared the need for setting aside too much of the valued capacity on supplies. Other than tea, sugar, flour and oats, all other foodstuff was to be found locally. Cattle came from Mongolia, chickens, rice grain, corn and pigs were the subject of local arrangements. Coal for heating and fuelling ships' boilers was to be found in the region. The normal Russian procurement system was straightforward, a regional commander receiving funds with which to feed his men. This was not entirely possible in Manchuria and local purchase teams procured mountains of provisions. The operational and logistical planning was worked in tandem, the supplies and transport being orchestrated to produce the goods where the operational plan placed the troops. Transport vehicles consisted of four-wheeled wagons and two-wheeled carts found within the regimental transport echelon, the divisional supply column and special transport columns. At regimental and divisional level eight days' biscuits and six days' groats were carried. There was some pack transport and the special transport columns were formed at the outbreak of war – but then, very slowly. Russian plans were severely hampered by this acute shortage of transport exacerbated by an abysmal road system.

Russia's military thought had been moribund for years. The value of the bayonet, for example, had already come into question during the Franco–Prussian War of 1870–71. Seven years later the Russians were to fight the Turks and, as reported by the French observer, General Langlois, 'The two infantries charged one another in spite of theories to the contrary, and hand to hand fights were common enough for the Russian infantry to realise that the point of the bayonet was much surer than the bullet.' In peace and war, the Russians had their bayonets fixed as a matter of course. The bayonet, a cruel thin spike, extended their rifle barrels by some two feet. Not surprisingly, Sir Ian Hamilton was to describe the Russian soldier as the worst shot among the European quality armies. Aimed fire was therefore made difficult enough but their fire fight was also poor, being akin to the volley firing of the Napoleonic War. They were equipped with modern .299-inch calibre rifles sighted out to 3,000 yards, yet they were conditioned to fire in unison at short range on orders from their superior officer.

Both armies were to attack in close formation, but more so the Russians. From the mid-nineteenth century their tactic in the attack was to approach in echelon on a broad front, spurning the opportunity to use the flanks or to attempt anything which required an iota of co-ordination. Operations were preordained by detailed, specific and pedantic orders aimed at covering every contingency, except the unexpected. Orders were given at considerable length. Whereas planners today are encouraged to think 'two down', the issuing of orders two down, which occurred on occasions in the Russian army, by-passing the intermediate commander, led to confusion and chaos. Little wonder that companies and battalions surrounded their commander for an early indication of a change of idea. As the war evolved, the Japanese were to learn to spread out, but they were not at such great risk from aimed rifle fire. Their command and control system afforded greater flexibility than that available to the Russians. In mission-oriented orders, also known by the German term *auftragstaktik,* commanders at all levels were expected to use their own initiative within the framework established by a superior commander's concept of operations. In principle, *auftragstaktik* provided the more effective system yet, on occasions, action did founder due to inexperienced junior commanders not being used to making decisions in the fog and danger of war.

The majority of the Russian soldiers who fought in Manchuria were peasants from the east of their country who were nominally on a war footing. They were therefore hardy, brave, obedient soldiers accustomed to privation and, at the beginning of the war, the majority of Siberians were still motivated by loyalty to the Tsar. Spontaneous cheering and genuine warmth flowed through the Russian lines when the news of the Tsarevitch's birth was announced. Their lack of sophistication, education, flair and intuition separated them from a Japanese army well prepared to fight a modern war. The Russian soldier was a soft bear who took an alarming time to begin to hate his enemy. Once the war started the Russians were to maintain a genuine respect for the Japanese. General Kuropatkin described them as 'our brave foe'. When the Japanese sent the Russians their condolences on the loss of their flagship, an officer in Liaoyang responded by proposing and drinking a toast to the Japanese with the assembled company. They were kind, stoical, simple soldiers lacking fanaticism and leaders conditioned to fight a modern war. The average Russian soldier appeared confused in a war which he could neither cope with nor comprehend.

The very size of the Russian army demanded constant analysis and intelligence assessments. European armies had a grudging respect for the Russian soldier. His limitations were nullified largely by his numbers. The weak link in the Russian profession of arms was regarded universally as the officer corps. The prevailing British view of the Russian contingent during the Boxer Rebellion was summarised in 1901 by Colonel J. M. Grierson, who wrote in his reflections that they were 'lions led by asses'. He confirmed the admiration for the peasant soldier, yet observed that his officer was 'beneath contempt'. Observations of the Russian officers' performance during the Russo-Japanese War do not support Griersen's generalisation.

The officer corps was large, exceeding the then total strength of the United States' armed forces. The quality varied. The exploits of some rivalled the best that the Japanese were capable of achieving. For the most part, the regimental officer was brave, efficient and paternal yet not greatly gifted with intelligence. There was little qualitative difference noticeable between the regular and territorial officer, both adding to the homogeneity of the force. Their edge had been dulled by too long a period on low pay, in boring and indifferent posts with little prospect of promotion. On occasions their honesty was called into question, but this suspicion was fuelled from the Russian system of the commanding officer being responsible for the regiment's finance. While some may well have erred, it is not thought to have been common.

The first of two types of the General Staff were the educated graduates from the Staff College. For them, promotion was rapid but on merit. They were keen and zealous, although their critics will describe them as doctrinaire, safer with theory than practice. The second type, and one of the two least positive aspects of the Russian army, was the grace and favour afforded to the Guards officers who invariably found themselves in staff positions. Often effete, idle, preoccupied with social pursuit, promoted prematurely and beyond the level of their competence, they did little to facilitate the national war aims.

The crucial weakness of the Russian forces was the manifestation of the gerontocracy which evolved from the general rule of seniority being given precedence over talent. Many formation commanders were lacking in energy, having long since succumbed to sedentary lethargy. As a group, they displayed reluctance to make decisions and shoulder responsibility. Their ability to orchestrate formation tactics was invariably abysmal. They drank to excess, had little empathy with their soldiers, and lacked the flexibility to react to the changed circumstances of the modern war in which they found themselves embroiled. Confirmation is available in Story's book, *The Campaign with Kuropatkin*:

> When war broke out the chief commands were in the hands of
> generals of a departed generation. Many of them were igno-
> rant of the use of such ordinary instruments of modern warfare
> as wireless telegraphy, heliography, and flashlight signalling.
> I have known generals refuse permission for the erection of a
> heliograph apparatus on the ground that it was a mere toy.

As a microcosm of their society, they could not have demonstrated more clearly the reason why they, as a social group, were doomed.

A Russian soldier called to arms was liable for military service from his twenty-first to his forty-third birthday. This national service comprised four years with the colours, and fourteen years in the reserve during which time he would expect two training periods each of six weeks. After eighteen years he passed into the *Opolchenie* or militia.

There were few exemptions from military duty, although Cossacks, Finns and Christians in the Caucasus had different conditions of service. Muslims were permitted to pay a tax in lieu of service but could join in certain special cases. The soldiers filled the four components of the army: the field army brought up to wartime establishment from mobilised reserves; fortress troops filled in a similar manner as the field army but confined to garrison duties; depot troops and the militia which were responsible both for home defence and provision of reserves for the field troops. Approximately a hundred depot battalions were formed to sustain the front-line strength, of which half deployed to the Far East. Port Arthur, Vladivostok, Possiet Bay and Nikolaissk were manned by fortress troops comprising infantry, artillery and engineers. Port Arthur and Vladivostok each contained two East Siberian rifle divisions with each division comprising 11,400 rifles and between twenty-four and thirty-two guns. The lines of communication were protected by independent units. The highly sensitive railway systems, the Manchurian and Ussuri, were operated by special railway battalions initially provided by six East Siberian battalions reinforced from Europe during the course of the war.

The Russian cavalry comprised almost without exception Cossack troops. The word *Cossack* is derived from a Tartar word meaning 'bandit'. When cavalry was required in support of a division or corps, a suitable slice was detached from the cavalry division. Each division consisted of 3,400 sabres and lances with some divisions equipped with twelve horse artillery guns. The Cossacks were not to live up to their reputation, being of an inferior standard in comparison with European cavalry. Like the Japanese, they were trained to fight mounted and dismounted, yet their marksmanship imposed a severe limitation on their uses when on foot. The special terms of employment of Cossacks were that in exchange for a grant of land and freedom from taxation they were responsible, when called to arms, for the provision of their own horse, uniform and equipment. War for the Cossack had ceased to be cost effective, and this meant that these soldiers were not going to expose these items to unnecessary risk, particularly when the compensation was so paltry.

The war caught the Russian gunners in the midst of a re-equipment programme. A third of their guns were the new 3-inch quick-firing gun whose range of 6,000 yards bettered the Japanese field artillery. The issue programme escalated at the onset of war but, for many gunners, their training period was quite literally on the job and for real. At 13½ lbs the new gun's projectile was lighter than that fired by the 3.42-inch gun which still formed the bulk of the field artillery. Guns were grouped in brigades of between two and four batteries. Peacetime training had been largely neglected. Indirect laying had been hardly practised yet was quickly and widely resorted to, as was the use of gun pits.

The Russian infantryman had good claim to be the forerunner of the

Falklands yomper. His ammunition was supplied in clips of five rounds. He normally carried 120 rounds with an average of sixty-five rounds per man on the regimental carts. In this campaign each man carried, in addition, fifteen rounds in his kit bag with more in his blouse pockets so that it was not unusual for a soldier to go into action carrying between 200 and 300 rounds. His kit was carried in a waterproof canvas bag slung over his right shoulder and hanging down his left-hand side. In this bag he would carry two and a half days' supply of salt and biscuit. Over the left shoulder was his rolled greatcoat, a shelter tent sheet and occasionally a shovel. When his personal belongings and a kettle were added in, the weight of an individual's total kit came to 70 lbs. The infantry's firepower was enhanced by Maxim machine-gun companies which fired the same round as the .299-inch rifle. Although extremely effective, their value was not fully appreciated until later in the campaign and many divisions were never to receive their increment of machine-gun companies.

The effective support of the undertaking in Korea and Manchuria would not have been possible without command of the sea. That crucial factor was recognised by both countries. By 1902 Japan had a slight lead on the Russian Far East fleet but by 1904 Russia had spurred on her own notoriously lethargic shipbuilding industry to reach rough numerical parity. Her Black Sea fleet was still incarcerated by treaty to the confines of that sea, and the Baltic fleet with its own regional problems was thought to be too far away to influence events in the Yellow Sea.

Equivalence was numeric rather than qualitative. The Russian Far East fleet was already constrained from round-the-year training by being ice-bound in Vladivostok for three months. She also had a ragbag of a fleet with wide variations in armament, protection, speed and flexibility. Despite having its own shipbuilding industry, which Japan did not, the Russian navy had a high proportion of foreign-built ships under her flag, including vessels supplied from Great Britain, the United States, Germany and France. Architecturally there was an important difference between the two fleets. The Russians had a global interest, hence their ships needed large bunkers for large volumes of coal. Coal was carried at the expense of protection. The Japanese fleet was designed for localised operations, hence there was less need for large coal bunkers and the Japanese ships were better protected.

Russian naval manning policy was based on conscription which required seven years' active service with three years in reserve. In the main, the conscripts were found lacking in affinity, interest and tradition. It was not a happy service; the appointment of many officers was based seemingly on the criteria of who they knew rather than what they knew. Other than the notable Admiral Makarov, there do not appear to have been many among the senior naval officers who were highly regarded and respected by their men. It was not surprising that the discontent that was to be seen on the *Orel* should reappear with such dramatic effect on the *Potemkin*. At the outbreak of hostilities, the bulk of the Russian Far East fleet of seven battleships, six cruisers and thirteen antiquated torpedo boats was at Port Arthur; four first-class cruisers were supported by a number of torpedo boats at Vladivostok; and the American-built, first-class, protected cruiser *Varyag* with the gunboat *Koreyetz* were at Chemulpo in Korea.

The Japanese fleet suffered none of the Russian disadvantages. It was concentrated, with commonality being the keyword in its equipment and procedures. The six modern battleships and six cruisers, mostly British-built, were organised into two distinct squadrons by type. Of the smaller front-line vessels most were modern, well equipped and fast. Those other ships known not to be combat-worthy were given roles appropriate to their condition.

The officers were confident and enjoyed the confidence of their sailors. Most of the crew were conscripts serving eight years on active duty with four years in reserve. There was, however, a useful proportion of volunteers throughout the fleet. Unlike the army, the Japanese navy's tactical doctrine was not modified during the progress of the war.

CHAPTER THREE

EARLY NAVAL ACTION

During the first week of February 1904, events in Japan moved on apace. For Japan to have any prospect against mighty Russia, a pre-emptive strike against her fleet at Port Arthur, Dalny and in Korea was deemed to be imperative. The formal declaration of war would come only after the synchronised attacks on the Russian fleet. The flotilla was to sail from its base at Sasebo at the same time that diplomatic relations were to be broken off. No one questioned or moralised over the subject of pre-emptivity.

The final preparations for war were coming to a head, like the completion of a giant jigsaw puzzle. Troop trains sped through the night, troopships took up their predetermined positions already loaded with the provisions and munitions of war. On board his flagship the *Mikasa* on 6 February, the squat, unprepossessing Admiral Togo read his admirals the Emperor's message and after some champagne and enthusiastic *banzais* they separated to their various ships to set about their duty. A tumultuous farewell of assorted craft full of relatives and well-wishers joined the fleet as it slipped anchor. An array of lanterns was left bobbing in the wake of the departing vessels. Only two days previously, the British Ambassador had told a reporter that the Japanese were bluffing. Secrecy had been maintained with the press tightly gagged. In the early light of the morning, the flags on the *Mikasa* cracked in the cold wind as the fleet headed for the open sea.

When the war was over, the battleflag of the *Mikasa* was put into temporary retirement, to reappear in another war flying from the attack carrier *Akagi* at the pre-emptive assault on Pearl Harbor. Thus, we are provided with yet another instance of the lessons of war being overlooked or forgotten.

If war was to come, the Tsar wished it to be at a time and place of his own choosing. In the unlikely event that he was not to have the initiative, his rules of engagement were quite simple: Japan must fire first. The Japanese had a fail-safe rule in the event of meeting the Russians en route and that was quite simply to attack the enemy without question. They too agreed that they would fire first.

The combined fleet steamed to the west of the Korean coast, anchoring during the morning of Sunday 7 February at Lindsay Island to the south of Chemulpo. Here they made rendezvous with the cruiser *Akashi* tasked to watch for any Russian movement towards Korea. The message was of critical importance, for the fleet was at its first separation point. The information was that the Russians had not left Port Arthur. The way was therefore clear for the Japanese to land on the mainland of Korea without unnecessary complications. The sum of the Russian presence in Korea was the unprotected cruiser *Varyag* and the ageing gunboat *Koreyetz*, both anchored at Chemulpo. Three troopships, with 2,500 troops embarked, left the main body, escorted by the armoured cruiser *Asama*, 9,750 tons, the *Nanussa* and *Takachiho*, unarmoured and each of 3,700 tons, the 2,700-tons *Suma* and *Akashi*, and two torpedo boats. Their course was set for Chemulpo, the port of Seoul, where they had landed in 1894.

Togo sailed on with the main body for the new rendezvous point of Elliot Island some sixty-five miles east of Port Arthur. His fleet had been divided into three divisions. The first division, appropriately, had massive power among the six similar battleships. The *Hatsuse*, *Asahi* and *Shikishima* were sister ships at 15,000 tons with a common division speed of 18 knots. The *Fuji* and *Yashima* were sister ships at 12,300 tons. The flagship *Mikasa* displaced 15,000 tons with the average broadside for the first division at 4,000 lbs. Armoured cruisers made up the second division. All were in the region of 10,000 tons and capable of 24 knots. They were *Iwate, Izumo, Azuma, Yagumo* and *Tokiwa*. The third division comprised four fast but unarmoured cruisers, the *Kasagi, Chitose, Takasago* and *Yoshino*. Other ships were assigned to picquet duty but Togo's fleet also included fifteen 30-knot destroyers armed with the new Whitehead torpedo as well as some twenty makeweight torpedo destroyer boats.

Commanding the Chemulpo-bound flotilla was the forty-six-year-old Rear Admiral Uriu, a graduate of both the British and American schools of naval warfare. Already a proven and distinguished sailor, it was the diplomatic aspect of the forthcoming conflict which was uppermost in his mind as he sailed slowly eastward. Recent intelligence reports confirmed that at anchor in the port were not only the two Russian warships but also foreign warships protecting their respective national interests. The international fleet comprised HMS *Talbot*, USS *Vicksburg*, the French *Pascal*, the Italian *Elba* and, not unnaturally, a Japanese protected cruiser, the *Chiyoda*. The *Chiyoda* had come to be regarded as something of a fixture at Chemulpo during her ten-month sojourn in the port. Just before midnight on 7 February, however, without lights and with little sound, she slipped out to sea to make rendezvous with Admiral Uriu.

Three hours later *Chiyoda*'s captain reported to Uriu. His news did much to ease the Admiral's mind. The political brief that accompanied the captain gave guidance that since foreign warships were at anchor at Chemulpo it would be contrary to international law to attack the Russians in the harbour. If Russian ships were met outside the harbour, then they were to be attacked and sunk. During the course of the morning of 8 February other contingencies and plans were discussed as the Japanese continued their unhurried progress towards the culmination of the synchronised attack on the Russians.

The Japanese plans were to be made academic by the action of the Russian gunboat *Koreyetz*. That something was afoot was confirmed that morning by the absence of *Chiyoda*. The communication system was already in Japanese hands so it was determined that *Koreyetz* was to liaise with Port Arthur to gain an update on the political situation. Early in the afternoon, as the Russian ship sailed westward out of the harbour, she passed close by the Japanese fleet sailing eastward in the same channel. The Japanese fleet was not recognised immediately. The Russian guard of honour was quickly despatched to action stations as the rising sun emblems on the ships were discerned. The captain reversed course but in the confusion, and reflecting the prevalent trigger-happiness of the Russian fleet, two ineffectual shots were fired from this equally ineffectual gunboat. The Japanese now had the pretext upon which they were to reap a publicity dividend. They studiously ignored reference to their warlike presence, the earlier capture of a Russian ship at Pusan, and the loosing off of three torpedoes prior to *Koreyetz* opening fire.

Chemulpo is a deceptive anchorage. At high tide it appears an expansive harbour dotted with haphazard islands. Low tide sees an average drop of over twenty feet to reveal the reason why ships had to anchor in clusters three to five miles from shore. Mud. Lots of it, divided sparingly by tortuous little channels. *Koreyetz* returned to her original ice-free anchorage to the south of the lighthouse with the large *Varyag* on one side and the recently arrived steamer *Sungari* on the other. A hurried consultation ensued between the three captains. They did not know whether hostilities had commenced and consequently they were reluctant to open fire on the Japanese fleet now positioning itself inside the harbour. The warships anchored nearby, while the first of the Japanese troopships sailed into the inner harbour just off the town. It was 4 p.m., less than two hours to darkness.

At 6 p.m. on 8 February 1904, the first of the Japanese troops went ashore in sampans and lighterage brought by the troopships. New arrivals on shore gasped in amazement, 'It's not the Russians, it's the Japanese.' Bonfires were set up along the quay to illuminate the scene as the soldiers in their smart blue uniforms moved purposefully through the light fall of snow to be swallowed up by the dark shadows of the town. The deployment was quiet, mechanical and efficient. In many respects this occupation resembled what we now expect of the stereotype Japanese package tour. Guides led platoons through the town to prearranged billets for the night. While all this went on, the Russian crews looked on in amazement, while above them the barrels of their impotent guns protruded into the dark. By all accounts, they had become so neutralised by the total lack of information that they took on the role of the involuntary spectator; so much so that that night they did nothing, appearing to pretend they were not there – even washing was left out in the evening's cold breeze.

By 3 a.m. on 9 February the disembarkation of four battalions of the Twelfth Division had been completed without incident. As the morning arrived to eclipse totally the dying embers along the length of the quay, the Japanese fleet, with the exception of *Chiyoda,* left port. Concurrently, a letter from Rear Admiral Uriu was delivered to Captain Stefanov, the senior Russian. He was advised that a state of hostilities existed between the two countries and that the Russian ships must now leave the neutral port of Chemulpo. The ultimatum was copied through the various consulates so that if the Japanese fleet felt obliged to come into port to attack the Russians, then the neutrals had been warned to stay clear of the firing. The Russians had until noon to leave, but if in the event they should stay, firing would commence at 4 p.m. on 9 February.

A conference was quickly convened aboard HMS *Talbot*. Captain

Stefanov pleaded in vain that the other warships should either forcibly restrain the Japanese or escort the Russians out to the high seas. That morning a great deal of diplomatic decision-making was done at an unusually low and unlikely level. Captain Denis Bagly of the *Talbot* sailed out to meet Uriu with a letter signed by all the captains except the American, protesting the proposed violation of the neutral port of Chemulpo. He recognised his journey as forlorn but necessary. As he bade Stefanov farewell he advised him to go out and take his chance unless the Russians were prepared for the option of surrender. With the protest rejected, the Russians set about clearing for action, casting overboard anything superfluous, inflammable or liable to splinter. They would not surrender.

At 11 a.m., outgunned and outnumbered, the two Russian warships raised steam and left their anchorage. The harbour was littered with ships' debris, the hills filled as in an amphitheatre with thousands of spectators, while the ships' rails of the neutral vessels were lined by sympathetic sailors waving and wishing them luck. First the *Varyag* and then the old, slow *Koreyetz* steamed proudly past the non-combatant warships. *Varyag*'s band played 'God Save the Tsar' and then, each in turn as she saluted her comrades, the individual national anthems of the ships present. Across the length of the harbour spontaneous cheering broke out while the voices of the Russian sailors could be heard singing their national anthem as, with flags flying, they sailed out to meet the waiting Japanese fleet and what seemed to be certain death.

It was an unequal battle. The fast, American-built *Varyag* was encumbered and tied to the best possible speed achievable by the old *Koreyetz*. It was upon the more dangerous of the two that the *Asama* turned her 8-inch guns at a range of four miles. Soon the newly developed Shimose rounds were finding their target and then *Chiyoda*'s fire superimposed upon *Asama*'s to wreak havoc upon the luckless *Varyag*. The reporter Thomas Cowen produced a graphic description:

> Her decks were being torn and riven, and men were dashed
> down in mangled heaps all round each gun, for the guns had
> no shields to protect their crews. Like the furious windsqualls in
> the height of a hurricane came the bursting of terrible explo-
> sives all the length of the ship, shattering and burning and
> sweeping away men and pieces of machinery indiscriminately.

Soon there were not enough men left on deck to carry the wounded away. The captain on the bridge had great difficulty giving orders. A shell passed to his left, taking with it the corner of the bridge and the captain's runner. The next passed to his right, killing his bugler and removing the side of his own face. Most of the guns were disabled and then a shell struck below the waterline, listing the ship to port. Despite the flooding in the engine room and stokeholds, the men below decks stuck to their duty, manoeuvring the ship by the propellers after the steering gear had been shot away. The few guns left able to fire continued, but more in desperation than effect for the Japanese fleet was not to suffer any damage during the course of the one-hour engagement.

The captain ordered the ship back to port. Slowly she turned about, circled by the Japanese keeping up relentless fire like a marauding band of Red Indians. This manoeuvre left *Koreyetz* exposed for the first time. Unable to add to the fire fight due to her inadequate range, she attracted the attention of *Chiyoda*. The captain had already made the decision to follow *Varyag* when she was struck and set on fire. Then, as suddenly as the battle started, the noise stopped. The Japanese regrouped just outside the harbour to await developments while the Russians took up their original anchorages.

Much of the superstructure of *Varyag* had been flattened. Two of her four funnels were down, as were her masts. It was with difficulty that the ship signalled to the others in port for help to take off the wounded. As if to make amends for what appeared to be an earlier lack of solidarity, the *Vicksburg's* captain made available a recently arrived steamer. His offer was declined and the survivors were taken aboard HMS *Talbot, Elba* and *Pascal*.

The Russian captains decided that the three ships should be destroyed rather than fall into enemy hands. The old *Koreyetz* was not badly damaged, but she was no match for the pack waiting off the harbour entrance. So it was with humble reverence that the portrait of the Tsar was carried off the doomed vessels to be placed in safe keeping. At 4 p.m., two almost simultaneous explosions rocked the *Koreyetz*, sending two palls of thick black smoke and debris high into the sky. The fading sun was temporarily eclipsed by the smoke. When the sploshing and splashing noise of returning debris died down, the band of the *Elba* struck up the Russian national anthem. As the Russians took up the singing, the wounded struggled to their feet and across the bay sailors from many nations joined their voices with the Russians. It was a sad, poignant moment when many grown men wept unashamedly.

Varyag's departure was less dramatic. Riddled by shot and shell, she was already on fire. Accompanied by a few rumbles, her list to her damaged port side became progressively worse. At 6 p.m. she gave up the ghost as she rolled completely to port, the onrushing water extinguishing the flames with much noise and smoke. Then *Pascal*'s boat was launched for the *Sungari*. She was set on fire and burned throughout the night, sinking in the early morning of 10 February, the day Japan was to declare war on Russia. Meanwhile, out to sea the Japanese sailors turned landward and bowed in salute, not for the unfortunate Russians but to honour His Imperial Majesty. That is not to say that the Japanese were not honourable in victory. Some of the wounded were treated in the Japanese hospital at Chemulpo before receiving specialist treatment in Japan. Then, like their unwounded colleagues, they were permitted to return to Russia on parole.

CHAPTER FOUR

NAVAL ACTION AT PORT ARTHUR

Mizumo Kokichi, the Japanese Consul at Chefoo, stood on the deck of the British steamer *Foochow* as she edged herself carefully through the 400-yard wide entrance into Port Arthur harbour. He had arrived to supervise the mutually desirable business of evacuating Japanese nationals. It was the morning of 8 February 1904.

The naval dockyard was sited in a basin to the south of the old town between the fortifications on Quail Hill and Golden Hill. Opposite, the curl of the Tiger's Tail pointed like a crooked index finger at the main naval area of interest, apparently neglecting to declare its own role as the anchorage for the torpedo boats. At the very end of the finger was a lighthouse with a larger sister some nine miles further around the western end of the peninsula at Laotiehshan. The main disadvantages of the harbour were its small size and narrow access, described by *The Times* as 'the fatal germs of strategic death'. At low tide the Port Arthur channel out to the open sea was 6 metres deep. The *Novik* had a shallow draught of 5.7 metres and her ability to leave port at any time accounts for her being mentioned frequently in the accounts of naval activity. At high water, the channel had a depth of 8.7 metres. Battleships such as the *Pobieda*, *Poltava* and *Peresvyet* drew 8.3 metres of water so they could only enter and leave harbour during a brief period at high tide and in daylight. The Russians were notoriously bad at manoeuvring their battleships. It would take up to three days to move the Port Arthur fleet either in or out of harbour. It was normal practice therefore for the Imperial Russian fleet to anchor in the roadstead outside the harbour under the watchful fortifications on Golden Hill and Electric Hill. Here, in this exposed anchorage, the Russian fleet invited attack.

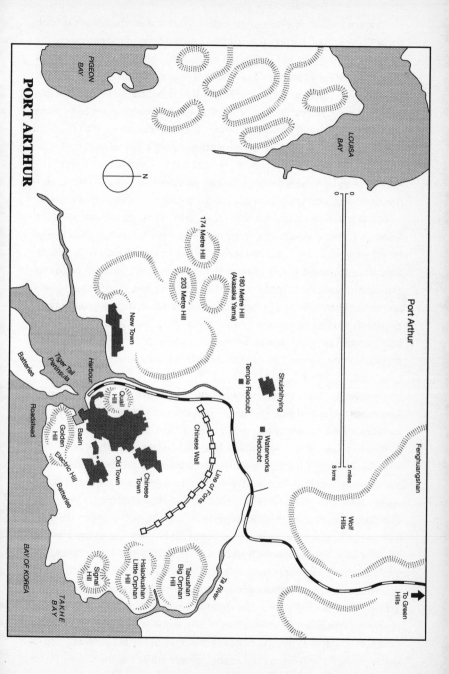

PORT ARTHUR

PIGEON BAY

LOUISA BAY

N

Port Arthur

174 Metre Hill

180 Metre Hill
(Akasaka Yama)

203 Metre Hill

New Town

Temple Redoubt

Shuishiying

Waterworks
Redoubt

0   5 miles
0   8 kms

Fenghuangshan

Tiger Tail Peninsula

Harbour

Quail Hill

Chinese Wall

Line of Forts

Wolf Hills

Batteries

Roadstead

Basin

Golden Hill

Electric Hill

Batteries

Old Town

Chinese Town

Signal Hill

Hsiaokushan
Little Orphan

Takushan
Big Orphan
Hill

Ta River

To Green Hills

BAY OF KOREA

TAKHE BAY

Kokichi took off in a sampan to make his final call on the Russian officials while his valet took particular interest in looking beyond the harbour to the open sea where the might of Russia's Far East fleet lay. The ships were set in three lines running east and west. The inner line comprised five battleships, *Petropavlovsk, Sevastopol, Peresvyet, Pobieda* and *Poltava*. In the middle line were the other two battleships, *Tsarevitch* and *Retvizan,* supported by three cruisers. In the southernmost line were three further cruisers with the duty ship, the *Pallada,* occupying the easternmost position. The valet took note of all this. He would have known too that the two picquet destroyers, the *Rastoropni and Bezstrashni* were patrolling twenty miles out to sea while similar small ships were safely ensconced in the harbour with their crews enjoying a general stand-down and run ashore. At about this time the captain of the Japanese gunboat *Tatsuta* joined the main Japanese fleet anchored at Round Island sixty miles away. He had made rendezvous previously with informants from the town who had reported that much jollification was to be expected in town that night. The fleet had returned from exercising off Dalny and was unlikely to sail again for a day or two. Satisfied, the valet put away his notebook. He had just completed his audit of the Russian fleet; a business being copied in many diverse forms throughout the various ports in the region. No normal valet, he was Commander Mori Gitaro of Japanese Naval Intelligence.

Port Arthur had changed significantly since being so named in 1860 by Lieutenant William Arthur, RN. The most marked difference was seen after the Russians leased the port from the Chinese in 1898. The old town to the east of the river was a slum that did not bear close inspection. There was, however, a rebuilding programme and a new settlement had been established on the western side of the river. The fortifications above the town were not as strong as they should have been. When he had been Minister for War, General Kuropatkin had frozen the funding for improving the town's defences since he had believed in the no-risk scenario. The money was diverted instead to smug little Dalny some forty miles to the north by rail. The fortress guns were not ready. The 10-inch guns on Electric Hill pointed impotently out to sea, their recoil mechanisms drained and their barrels smeared with thick grease to protect them from the rigours of the winter. This situation was repeated throughout the whole line of fortifications, few guns being in an operational state. As the day began to give way to the evening, army gunners prepared themselves for a night in town while the small duty crews cursed their bad luck. The light at the end of Tiger's Tail was illuminated and gradually the lights on the battleships below the forts were discerned.

The commander of the Russian Far Eastern Fleet was Vice Admiral Oscar Victorovitch Stark. The party he had planned that evening was entirely in keeping with his reputation as a fun-loving partygoer. Guests included Admiral Alexeiev, the Viceroy and Supreme Commander, his Chief-of-Staff, Vice Admiral Witgeft, and Stark's own deputy, Rear Admiral Prince Ukhtomski. Stark probably did not deserve his eventual fate. On a number of occasions he had pressed Alexeiev to permit him to prepare the fleet for war. The Viceroy refused, declaring such a measure to be premature and escalationary. Stark was no fool and suspected the Japanese. Surreptitiously he ordered his captains to prepare to repel torpedo attacks. So low-key was the instruction in relation to the Supreme Commander's known views that, in the event, nothing was done.

Port Arthur was a raucous town whose excesses surpassed anything seen elsewhere in the Far East. Sailors mingled with soldiers in the waterside pubs. In the main thoroughfare, Pushkin Street, Baratovski's international circus was performing as usual. There was an atmosphere of camaraderie in the air. The evacuation of the Japanese that morning had underlined for all walks of life the imminence of war. No one could enjoy a good night out quite like a Russian, particularly when those nights were likely to be numbered.

The business quarter, however, exuded an air of foreboding by its very tranquillity. The clanking of couplings and hiss of steam broke through the freezing air. A busy shunter went about its business preparing the morning's trains. Large unlit buildings stood incongruously nearby with what appeared to be a series of pyramids in silhouette. A light from a passing carriage revealed the buildings to be stacks of empty vodka cases and the pyramids to be coal stacks for fuelling the variety of winter fires and boilers. Two policemen stood under the light outside the building which represented Russia's regional interest, the Russo-Chinese Bank. The merchant Barwitz epitomised the middle class. He and his wife spent the evening entertaining a house guest to dinner while their new *amah* fussed around their restless four-year-old daughter.

At 7 p.m. Togo released his torpedo boat destroyers like greyhounds from a trap. The 1st, 2nd and 3rd Flotillas had orders to proceed to Port Arthur, and the 4th and 5th Flotillas were to make a simultaneous attack on any vessels found lying outside Dalny. The latter group was to confirm their earlier intelligence, finding only the *Foochow* hurriedly completing the last acts of evacuation.

The ten destroyers bound for Port Arthur carved through the calm sea at a sedate 20 knots. Successive waves coming over the bow began to build up a coat of ice around each ship. The temperature was ten degrees below freezing and the moon, in its last quarter, would not appear until daylight. Each ship had a crew of fifty and was armed with two 12-pounders, four 6-pounders and two torpedoes. At 10.50 p.m. the fleet bumped the *Rastoropni and Bezstrashni*. The Russians, obeying their orders not to fire, turned about to report the contact. Nevertheless, this chance meeting did much to lessen the intended Japanese blow. The leading Japanese destroyer turned to starboard to avoid the Russians while those destroyers bringing up the rear stopped to avoid detection. In consequence, the flotillas became separated and instead of a concerted hammer blow against the Russian fleet, what was to transpire was a series of uncoordinated opportune attacks. Just before midnight four of the Japanese destroyers were attracted to the glow from the searchlights and lighthouse of Port Arthur. Through the by now lightly falling snow the Japanese sighted the three ranks of ships. The cruiser *Pallada* saw the Japanese at about the same time but took them to be returning Russian ships. Not having radios, *Rastoropni* and *Bezstrashni* were still to report this danger at the port's door.

At 11.50 p.m. Captain Asai Shojero on board the *Shiragumo* signalled, 'Attack'. Turning to port, the destroyers increased their speed until the gauges indicated just over 30 knots. Each ship released its two torpedoes and then headed south. *Pallada,* one of the few ships showing any life, received particular attention. She was hit amidships, caught fire and keeled over. Next *Retvizan* was singled out. She was hit by the bow, exposing a hole through which a car could be driven.

The noise of battle had different effects on the two navies. It enabled the six disorientated Japanese destroyers to zone in on the earlier attack. They struck at 2 a.m. By the time they had released their torpedoes, the pride and most powerful ship of the Russian fleet, the *Tsarevitch,* had been disabled. The Russians were caught completely by surprise. The skeleton crews on the battleships did not know what was happening. They tumbled from their bunks to await orders. None came. When a ship is in action each individual has his own task, but when an attack comes unexpectedly, when a large proportion of the crew is absent, orders have to be given on the spur of the moment. It was too late. It was all over in two periods of five minutes. As the flagship *Petropavlovsk* winked out the signal for a situation report, the Japanese destroyers were on the open sea making their circuitous way to Elliot Island. They were of limited value against battleships in daylight. Instead, the Japanese battlefleet had steamed off to the south to make a wide sweep to approach Port Arthur from the west, with a view to arriving during daylight. Togo had no way of knowing what the torpedo destroyers had achieved. It did not matter greatly since the Russian naval threat to the Japanese landings in Korea and Manchuria had to be completely neutralised.

The sound of firing was heard by some in the town, but many were unaware of the attack until the morning. Those who did hear the commotion assumed an exercise to be in progress and thought no more of it. Daylight revealed that the three badly damaged Russian ships had reached shallow water before settling on the bottom. *Pallada* was on the western side of the harbour entrance near the lighthouse. The battleships *Retvizan* and *Tsarevitch* had stuck in the entrance which normally at low tide offered a gap of just over 100 yards. Their presence would not help manoeuvrability but their situation was to sow a seed of thought in Togo's mind.

Stark's staff briefed the Admiral, who took the news to the Viceregal Lodge. That which he had forewarned had occurred. Already those looking for a head were looking in Stark's direction. News of his party had spread and the reports became wildly exaggerated. He would have hoped the Viceroy might have supported his position and taken the blame upon himself. He was to be disappointed. In a tense but calm atmosphere the two admirals planned the next step for the undoubted return of the Japanese. The Viceroy sent a message appealing for calm while Stark ordered his fleet to make steam and get under way. On the jetties sailors caught lifts on boats back to their ships, the same craft that had brought in the dead and wounded.

Ships had barely reached full complement when the Japanese were seen again. At 8 a.m. a reconnaissance party of four light cruisers, the Third Division commanded by Rear Admiral Dewa, steamed some seven miles off the port without coming into range. Dewa saw the Russian fleet gathered under the protection of the forts. They had moved their positions but by only a few miles to the east. Dewa picked out the two battleships and cruiser aground. He sensed the Russians were in a state of shock and from his cruiser the *Takasago* recommended that the First and Second Divisions be brought up to consolidate the night's work. Togo was concerned about the firepower of the forts, but hearing that the enemy appeared unprepared and disorganised he decided to take the risk. Just before midday the Russians saw the Japanese fleet.

The lookouts in the forts sounded the alarm as they witnessed the Japanese bearing down on their own *Boyarin* making full speed towards the harbour and firing her stern guns to no effect. Chaos reigned in Port Arthur. Lighters had moved alongside the *Retvizan and Tsarevitch to* keep them afloat. Warships moved quickly to jettison inflammable material while enterprising coolies in sampans sifted through the jetsam for the more attractive souvenirs. Captains leapt about demanding to know why their ships were not ready, while all the time they could see the dark smudge on the horizon being blown towards them by the southerly wind in the clear blue sky. As the smudge grew larger, so did the frenzy of activity on the Russian warships.

At 12.15 the flagship *Mikasa,* leading the First Division, opened fire with her 12-inch guns. Only the large calibre guns were used as the three divisions steamed in succession from west to east. *Mikasa* took twenty minutes to pass. With the exception of the cruiser *Novik,* the Russians moved like ants around a nest beneath the forts' guns, endeavouring not to produce stationary targets. The *Novik* steamed out to meet the Japanese and was severely mauled for her pains. Also damaged was the flagship *Petropavlovsk* flying Stark's flag. The battleship *Poltava* was hit and the cruisers *Diana* and *Askold* were severely damaged. The damage was not all one way. The *Mikasa, Iwate, Shikishima, Fuji* and *Hatsuse* were hit. Fire from the forts became increasingly effective. Dewa's Third Division endured intense fire until ordered to withdraw by Togo. After one run, Togo called off his fleet to rendezvous with Uriu off Chemulpo. Casualties were evenly balanced, the Russians losing 150 killed and wounded and the Japanese 132. The pressing task for both sides was to repair the ships for the next round. Japan had at her disposal numerous drydocking facilities. The Russians had but one small dry dock at Port Arthur, with another still incomplete.

Some twenty 12-inch shells had fallen in town. The queues at the Quail Hill railway station were long and disorderly. The situation would have been much worse had the Chinese been permitted the use of the railway facilities. For many coolies there was no place to hide, so they fled instinctively into the hills where their frozen bodies were found in the ensuing days. The Russo-Chinese Bank had been hit. At the rear of the premises the local paper currency was being burned in open braziers while arrangements were made to move the coin northwards by rail. Lumps of coal covered the town like confetti. The Barwitzes' house guest returned to find that his host's house had been hit. Mr Barwitz and his wife, child and *amah* had been in the one room. Only the child remained alive, seated in the middle of the room surrounded by human remains. Her mother had almost disintegrated. All that could be identified was her long hair attached to the top part of her head, and a hand with rings on the fingers. The *amah* had more completely disappeared, adding to the pile of mangled flesh. In the corner was the intact body of Mr Barwitz with only his head shattered.

Those Chinese with money bought passage on the local steamers. The Norwegian steamer *Kumar* escaped successfully with a full complement of refugees; so too did the British-registered *Columbia* which made for the high seas, ignoring Russian orders to remain. Less fortunate were the British steamers *Fuping, Hsiping* and *Chingpong* of the Chinese Engineering and Mining Company. They and the German steamer *Pronto* were all fired upon by nervous Russian warships. Still bewildered, the Russians were working at cross-purposes, issuing contradictory instructions and forgetting what they had agreed. Invariably they would apologise, admit their 'mistake' and allow the vessels to proceed with their by now bloodied human cargo.

The Tsar was stunned by the news of the attack. He could not believe that Japan could initiate a warlike act without a formal declaration of war. Both he and the Emperor of Japan declared war on 10 February 1904. The rest of the world was by no means anti-Japan. The Japanese were masters of the psychological approach and secrecy. *The Times* summed up Britain's attitude to her ally by dismissing the pre-emptive attack as being quite normal for wars in modern times. The Americans were not so quick to embrace the Japanese sense of realism, yet they reluctantly fell in line behind a sympathetic President Roosevelt who had become the centre for Japanese fawning and attention.

The next few days were set aside for reflection and assessment. Togo was disappointed by the apparent lack of success of his torpedo attack. His real success, however, needs to be viewed in terms wider than that of pure shipping. In this action at Port Arthur, he had settled an old score and laid claim to his fleet's recognition as being on a par with the best in Europe. He had won command of the sea and at the same time almost completely demoralised his enemy. The Russians were quick to set about restorative work on the forts and to plan improvements under the army commander, General Stoessel. The fleet was moved into the crammed harbour as a matter of course on 10 February. The one exception was the still grounded *Retvizan* which took on the role of guardship. On 11 February a converted steamer, the *Yeneisei,* set about mining the approaches to the harbour. The sea was choppy and a mine was washed against the ship's rudder. She blew up. Eighty of the ship's company of 200 were saved, but the ship took with her the charts of the minefields laid so far. The cruiser *Boyarin,* sent out to investigate the loss of the *Yeneisei,* hit one of the mines and was subsequently abandoned. The Russians therefore had an additional problem which they would have happily foregone.

From their rendezvous at Chemulpo, Togo sailed his fleet back to Sasebo. He was deeply conscious of the veiled and implied criticism that he had failed to take the opportunity 'as Nelson would have done' of dealing a blow on the Russian fleet from which they would not recover. His friend and confidant, the Royal Navy Liaison Officer, Captain William Pakenham, excused him by saying that no one could have anticipated finding the Russians in such an unprepared condition. There was a deeper reason, however. The two warships being built in England had been embargoed once war was declared. Two additional ships had been secured by Japanese agents in Genoa, the armoured cruisers *Nisshin* and *Kasuga,* but with no naval dockyard of their own there were to be no more. Togo knew that the Russian Black Sea fleet would not be a threat as by treaty it could not now pass through the Bosphorus. There was a nagging outside possibility that the Russian Baltic fleet could be moved to reinforce Port Arthur and Vladivostok.

Togo toured his ships under repair in the Sasebo yard. This was an irreplaceable resource. If he was to retain command of the sea he would need to conserve his fleet. When he fought ship against ship he resolved to do so at the greatest distance, taking full advantage of his superior equipment, range and crews. His plan involved bringing superiority to the point of contact, thereby wearing the enemy down by a process of attrition. He cast his mind back to the previous year and to a theory put forward by Commander Arima Ryokitsu. He called for the officer to report to him immediately.

The fleet sailed again on 14 February after only two days in port. Still in the dry dock was *Fuji,* in need of further repair. With that sole exception the remainder of the fleet was back at sea, good as new, despite being hit many times by the Russians. Their shells were not as effective as the Japanese ammunition. Shimose was a newly developed powder which gave the Japanese shells great velocity, extremely effective on impact.

Other than a brave attack by two Japanese destroyers, the Russians had been left undisturbed since the first major confrontation. The Japanese had not been idle, however. While in Sasebo, Togo discussed with Commander Ryokitsu the latter's plan formed in 1903 of blocking the entrance to Port Arthur, thereby virtually turning the harbour into a lake. A special order soliciting volunteers for a hazardous mission was met by a response from 2,000 sailors, with some applications written in blood. Only seventy were needed, fourteen to each ship, and the vacancies were spread around the ships of the fleet.

The attack was planned originally for 20 February, but had to be postponed because the weather was too rough. It was essential that the conditions were right since the placing of ships at night, under fire and in the glare of searchlights, would be difficult enough without having to contend with a gale. Some doubted that the enterprise would succeed under any circumstances. The steamers were very old, capable of only 10 knots, and had large holds suitable for the volume and variety of coastal trading. What was needed were reinforced ships, and certainly those with a large number of watertight compartments.

The evening of 23 February was cold but calm and fine. After much lauding and honouring of the volunteers, who were not thought to have much prospect of returning, the five ancient steamers set course for Port Arthur. Two cruisers confirmed that all looked quiet in front of the harbour, while the little fleet headed inexorably onward, led by five torpedo boat destroyers.

Just before first light on 24 February the lookouts in the forts and the stranded guardship saw at the same time the sedate convoy calmly heading for the harbour mouth. A Russian supply convoy had been long awaited. As soldiers and sailors examined the unlit flotilla in the poor light there was much teeth-sucking and shuffling of the feet, while all the time the ships moved closer. Four searchlights moved from one ship to another. The decision to open fire was taken by the captain of the *Retvizan* whose booming guns lighting up the morning sky were closely followed by those in the forts.

Once detected, the steamers were too slow to run the gauntlet. The crews were blinded by the searchlights as the seaward guns of the *Retvizan* and those in the fortress fired into their rusty sides with consummate ease. The lead ship, *Mokoko Maru,* formerly of Kawamura and Company, reached the furthest until stopped by *Retvizan* at point-blank range on the eastern side of the entrance. The others sank progressively further back. The volunteer crews abandoned ship. Their casualties had been one killed and three injured. The majority made their way out to sea to be picked up by destroyers, while a few whose lifeboats sank beneath them were taken prisoner. It had been a disappointing failure.

The Russians had not unnaturally assumed that they had been subjected to a night frontal assault by Japanese warships. That the enemy should sail straight into the harbour rather than stand off seemed entirely in keeping with the impression the Russians were forming of Japanese recklessness and unpredictability. It was certain that the invaders had been sunk, and, since it also seemed obvious that nothing less than battleships would sail into the teeth of a modern fortress, that five battleships had gone under. No one had noticed that the Russian ships and forts were not subjected to returning fire.

Alexeiev was desperate to receive good news. When the first report reached him he signalled the Tsar the details of this great naval victory, eulogising the crucial role played by the damaged but game *Retvizan*. Meanwhile, at the harbour entrance, the wrecks were being examined by searchlight. They did not look like battleships. When daylight came, all was revealed. A second signal was sent hurriedly from Port Arthur to the Tsar.

The Japanese had done their homework well. The Russian fleet had been accounted for. In Vladivostok, under the command of Rear Admiral Jessell, lay the armoured cruisers *Gromoboi*, *Rossiya*, *Rurik* and *Bogatyr*. Rear Admiral Kamimura's cruiser squadron and torpedo boats were deployed as a reaction force in the vicinity of Tsushima. Picquets were established to patrol the gaps between the Japanese islands to report movements. The Russians, however, lacking in daring and inventiveness, were inhibited by Alexeiev's order that they were not to steam more than one day from port. The sum of their efforts to date had been the sinking of two unarmed Japanese merchantmen. This action created a furore in the Japanese press, deprecating in the strongest possible manner this 'attack of fiendish depravity and savagery'. The war with China in 1894 had begun, however, with the sinking of a steamship by Togo. The Chinese Eastern Railway Company, formed by Russia as a means of dominating Manchuria, had soon lost ten of its seventeen new steamships, either sunk or captured, as were ships under foreign flags trading with Port Arthur. Pressure was gradually and consistently being applied upon the Russians.

The gunboat *Manjour* was the one loose end of the Russian fleet. At the outbreak of war she took refuge in Shanghai, anchoring off the Customs quay. A Japanese task force led by the cruiser *Akitsushima* waited in international waters, threatening to come upstream to force the Russian ship out. The threats were to have little effect upon her captain, an old Etonian named Crown. Like others of his genre, he was most persuasive, being able to articulate international pressure to prevent a recurrence of the fate which befell her sister ship, *Koreyetz*. Although the ship avoided the unequal fight, she could not escape the full effect of the international rules under which she sheltered and, despite much stalling by her commander, was eventually dismantled. The officers and crew were repatriated, except for Crown who decided to take the battle to the enemy. Disguised as an Englishman, he took passage to Japan.

St Petersburg's view of the severity of the situation was reflected in the announcement of two new appointments in February. The former Minister for War, General Kuropatkin, was appointed Land Commander, Manchuria. He left St Petersburg on 12 March, arriving at Harbin on 28 March. At the time, the naval situation was more pressing and, on 8 March, Vice Admiral Makarov arrived at Port Arthur to replace the tired, uninspiring and unfortunate Stark. The news of these appointments and the officers' subsequent arrivals gave the Russian forces a much needed confidence boost. Here the government gave a clear display of their commitment by appointing arguably the two best officers for the respective posts. Their lack of perception was in placing both these go-ahead commanders under Alexeiev, whose ego far outstripped his energy and competence.

At the time Makarov left his previous command, the fortress of Kronstadt, he received news of the cruisers *Askold, Bayan* and *Novik* being damaged. The following day, two Russian destroyers, *Bezstrashni* and *Viestnitelni,* were intercepted by the Japanese while returning to port. The latter was unable to outrun her pursuers and was destroyed in Pigeon Bay. The new commander was therefore confronted with the picture of accumulating losses without having engaged the enemy. He had already determined that this situation would change and that the no-risk scenario would go with Stark. Makarov was a sailor's sailor who believed actions speak louder than words. He would not give an order which he would not be prepared to carry out. He was still superbly fit and his highly developed mental state was reflected in a series of valuable naval inventions. A noted naval tactician, a copy of his book was already in the cabin of his adversary, Admiral Togo.

During the interregnum period of the handover and takeover, Stark continued to fly his flag from the *Petropavlovsk*. Makarov hoisted his on the recently repaired *Askold*. The sight of this flag flying from one of the much respected cruisers provided a new impetus and resolve. *Retvizan* and *Tsarevitch* were soon to join the ranks of the battleworthy. Destroyer flotillas were sent out in search of the Japanese. On the morning of 10 March, the blockading Japanese flotilla was set upon by the Russians. The Japanese were taken aback by the insistence of the Russians in taking up the fight and while this was conducted with more enthusiasm than skill, the message passed back to Togo was that for once the enemy had shown resilience and were prepared to do battle.

At the beginning of the war much had been made of torpedoes by both sides. They were to be proved disappointing. The weapon which did have a profound effect, however, was the mine. The Japanese persistently used their destroyers to lay mines at night. The Russians would take bearings on these activities and at high tide the next day would use grappling hooks to clear the field. Invariably their adversary would lay mines ten feet below the surface, yet there were a number of imponderables. The weights would sink into the mud and variations in the sea bed would produce an array of mines at different levels. Even when all things were equal, the twenty-foot tide range in places meant that a ship sailing out on a high tide could pass over a mine and hit it on returning when the tide was on the ebb. The rough weather, a feature of the region, was responsible for releasing a significant number of mines which floated on the surface with the current.

During the night of 10 March the Japanese attempted a ruse. One flotilla of four destroyers approached the harbour and paraded outside to entice the Russian destroyers to come out. In keeping with their new-found confidence, six Russian ships tore after the Japanese flotilla which had by now turned about and was heading in the direction of Laoteshan. A second flotilla moved in and mined the water at the harbour entrance which the outgoing Russian flotilla had used. It was 4.30 a.m. A lookout in the fort saw the Japanese destroyers below. Coming under fire, the Japanese aborted their activity and headed out for the open sea. Meanwhile, the Russian destroyers, now some ten miles out from their home port, heard the sound of firing from the forts and reversed course. The four Japanese destroyers positioned themselves to cut off the Russians from their port. By keeping close to the shore line, four of the Russian destroyers reached harbour. The *Ryeshitelni* and *Stereguschi* were detected and blocked. Two Japanese destroyers took on one Russian each. Despite steering problems the *Ryeshitelni* made the safety of harbour; *Stereguschi,* the best and most recent addition to the flotilla, was not so lucky. A 1-pounder shell passed through her flimsy sides and struck a steam pipe between the boiler and engines. An explosion killed most of the engine room staff. The captain tried to keep her on course but, like a clockwork toy, the speed dropped and she wound down as four circling enemy destroyers raked her from stem to stern. The crew stayed at their posts firing their weapons until they in their turn joined the carnage on the deck. Eventually only four Russians remained capable of moving about the ship, and two of these were wounded.

The crew of the *Stereguschi*, now seriously on fire and settling, could see the destroyer *Sasanami* dropping a cutter which made its way towards their stricken vessel. The tattered white and blue Imperial Russian navy flag was hauled down as the prize crew leapt aboard with whoops of joy. The flag was grabbed as a souvenir. The boarding party divided. Stepping over corpses, limbs and entrails, one group made for the captain's cabin in search of documents while the other raised the Rising Sun and then passed a tow to *Sasanami*. It was now daylight and the *Sasanami* was within the range of the fort's guns. A lookout shouted that the Russian cruisers *Bayan* and *Novik* were making their way gingerly out of the mined harbour entrance. 'Full speed ahead,' ordered the captain. The tow line parted and the waterlogged destroyer sank. There was no time for the Japanese to pick up the few survivors as the Russian cruisers had now opened fire and were in close pursuit. Makarov was flying his flag from the *Novik,* but on meeting the entire Japanese fleet moving towards Port Arthur he ordered the cruisers about, passing among the surviving crew of the *Stereguschi* who were left to drown. As the *Novik* returned to harbour, soldiers and sailors stopped work to cheer their hero Makarov. They could not imagine Stark going to the rescue of a ship in trouble. Then they were reminded of the reality of their situation as Japanese shells fell among the forts, fleet and town. It was 14 March, the day the Guards Division landed unopposed at Chinampo on the Korean mainland.

Makarov became exasperated by the poor standard of his fleet's training. Gradually, through his inspirational leadership an improvement developed but he was not universally popular among his subordinate officers, many of whom disliked his driving power. Now the entire fleet could leave the harbour in two to three hours. The fleet deployed to the open sea, new defences were thrown up, and naval gunfire teams were formed to direct the battleships' fire upon the enemy. The fleet was now both better prepared and motivated than at any stage during the war. On 22 March the *Fuji* and *Yashima* had taken station in Pigeon Bay to fire their by now leisurely programme when they were startled to find shells falling around them. The naval gunfire support teams were having an effect and, if one surprise was not enough, the second was positively shocking, for heading towards them was the Russian fleet led by the cruiser *Askold* flying Makarov's flag. The *Fuji* was damaged before the Japanese Second Division's arrival encouraged Makarov to return to harbour. He had made his point. While *Fuji* steamed back to Sasebo for repairs, the Japanese Naval Staff realised that the Russian fleet was growing in stature. The Guards Division was barely ashore in Korea. This new mobility was an unacceptable threat to the Japanese lines of communication and Togo was accordingly directed to make another attempt at sealing the harbour at Port Arthur.

He had already taken this contingency into account. He decided to use those officers who had been on the first operation. The crews were to be different and were selected from a list of 20,000 volunteers. Four old steamers had been requisitioned, displacing between 2,000–3,000 tons; they were larger than before. Command was given to the originator of the scheme, Commander Ryokitsu, on board the *Chiyo*. Each ship was ballasted with cement and stones and incorporated a fail-safe detonating system.

On the evening of 26 March the four tramps steamed at 10 knots through a corridor formed by the mighty ships of the First and Third Divisions. With the roar of many *banzais* in their crews' ears, they were shepherded northwestward by escorting destroyers and torpedo boat destroyers. The moon in its first quarter had set at midnight. The sea was calm and covered in a carpet of mist. Just before 2.30 a.m. the escorts peeled off, leaving the steamers to make their way in single file for the harbour entrance. At 3.30 a.m., with less than two miles to travel, the ships were detected. A gun was fired from the signal station on Electric Hill. Dozens of searchlights were turned on along the length of the mouth of the entrance. Like four marathon runners the steamers made doggedly and slowly for their goal, while all around the crescendos of awakening cannon were doing their utmost to stop them.

Commander Ryokitsu was in the wheelhouse of the leading steamer *Chiyo*. Despite the murderous fire they were making good progress and holding the exact course. Suddenly, in the glare, Ryokitsu saw before him the Russian destroyer *Silny*. Forgetting himself for the moment, he intuitively changed course to ram the *Silny* just as her torpedo tore into *Chiyo*'s side. The steamer's momentum carried her forward before the anchors could securely arrest her. The following ships, blinded by lights, did not see the reason for *Chiyo*'s swerve, and since their orders were to sink alongside her that was what they were going to do. The next steamer came alongside, and although both officers were killed, the detonating charge was blown and the ship settled on the bottom. The third ship came close to the other two and sank just ahead. The fourth was coming at a more pedestrian pace, being ten minutes late. She went too far and her anchor would not hold. She was hit by a torpedo at the same time as the crew detonated the explosives on board. All the while, the two Japanese escort destroyers at the harbour entrance gave covering fire as the steamer crews made their escape. The *Silny* was severely damaged when she took a hit in the boiler room. Seven men were killed and thirteen wounded; more than the Japanese, who lost two officers killed and eleven wounded. The *Silny*, however, had done enough. Port Arthur remained open to the Russian fleet.

On the night of 12 April Makarov was on board the cruiser *Diana*. He was becoming increasingly impatient. His destroyers, which had been sent out on a reconnaissance north of Dalny, had not returned. The ship's lookout, peering through the drizzle, reported activity outside the harbour. The captain, standing by Makarov's side, requested permission to open fire. The Admiral was in a quandary for he knew that the unidentified ships could be his own raw destroyers looking for the harbour entrance. On the other hand, if they were enemy minelayers ... He made a mental note to have the area swept that morning. Consequently no orders were given to investigate or engage the unidentified ships outside the harbour.

Togo had been quick to recognise a pattern in the Russian behaviour for when his ships approached the harbour the Russians would come out and steam up and down, east and west, under the protective cover of the forts. A plan was accordingly formulated for a mining expedition, led by the *Koryu Maru,* to lay mines in the harbour mouth. The fleet was under orders that if the Russians were to follow up subsequently by leaving port, then they were to be engaged to the full. So it was that, although detected, the Japanese were able to complete their planned field of forty-eight mines in the harbour mouth, because the Russians half suspected the activity was their own side's.

As daylight heralded the morning of 13 April, the lookout on board one of the lost Russian destroyers, the *Strashni,* was horrified to discover that the lights which they had closed up on during the night were those of four destroyers of the Japanese Second Destroyer flotilla. The Japanese opened fire from 100 yards. The outcome was never in doubt. The Russians fought valiantly, inflicting damage on two of the Japanese destroyers, but with the majority of the crew dead, and on fire from end to end, the brave *Strashni* began to sink.

Alerted by the firing, the Russian fleet moved southward towards the noise. The cruiser *Bayan* was the first to arrive on the scene, and when she was joined by the *Askold, Diana* and *Novik* the Japanese withdrew. Their orders were to return when the main fleet arrived on the scene. Battleships are slower to get under way but the *Petropavlovsk*, flying Makarov's flag and supported by the *Poltava,* passed over the Japanese mines without mishap. Makarov, remembering the incident of the previous evening, ordered the harbour entrance to be swept for mines. The order was never carried out.

Admiral Dewa observed the Russian fleet as they left harbour and when the battleships *Sevastopol, Pobieda* and *Peresvyet* followed behind the flagship he signalled Togo to spring the trap. Dewa opened fire, gradually drawing the Russians further southward while Togo and his First Division were closing rapidly on the noise of battle. When Makarov saw through the lifting mist the smudge of smoke from Togo's battleship he ordered his fleet about, to return within the range of the guns in the forts.

There were some important and interesting personalities aboard Makarov's flagship that morning. The Imperial House was represented by the Tsar's cousin, the Grand Duke Cyril. The celebrated artist Vasili Verestchagin, one of Russia's greatest painters, had also gone aboard in order to record what was foreseen as an important naval battle. The most poignant was the presence of Captain Crown, late of the *Manjour*. He had been arrested and interrogated in Japan and then expelled. He arrived the previous day from Newchwang and on reporting to Makarov was immediately assigned to the Admiral's staff.

Up in the forts, the gunners witnessed the Japanese closing on the Russians. Makarov signalled for the smaller ships to go inside the harbour, while the larger vessels were to form a line of battle in the roadstead. When the Japanese came within six miles they would be within the effective aimed fire range of the forts. At 9.43 a.m. an explosion under her bows rocked the Russian flagship, a second ripped open a magazine, and a third signified that the boilers had gone. The ship keeled over and went down, bow first, her propellers still turning as they disappeared through flame, steam and smoke beneath the sea. In two minutes she had gone.

When this disaster befell the Russians, the Japanese were 10,000 yards away. The sound of explosions was greeted initially with cheering, until the grim reality dawned on those present. Togo stood quietly on the deck of the *Mikasa* while those around him took off their caps in silence. Togo's report showed that he was not certain which ship had been lost, describing her as 'a battleship of the *Petropavlovsk* type'. She was launched in 1894 and was a modified *Royal Sovereign*. Her sister ships were the *Poltava* and *Sevastopol*. The Russian fleet, now under Prince Ukhtomski, had come within the range of the forts' guns and the engagement was broken off. At 10.15 a.m. the *Pobieda* was rocked by an explosion. The Japanese were now miles away, heading in the opposite direction. The Russians, believing themselves to be the subject of a submarine attack, fired wildly into the sea. When order was restored the fleet entered port led by the battleships. The crippled *Pobieda* brought up the rear, but the absence of the *Petropavlovsk* told its own grim story to those crowding the shore. Six hundred and thirty-five officers and men had gone down with the flagship. Makarov, the fleet's great hope, had disappeared until his body was given up by the sea twelve days later. Vasili Verestchagin and Captain Crown were also lost. More fortunate was the Grand Duke Cyril, standing alongside Makarov on the bridge when the explosion occurred. He was found in the water by a destroyer, badly burnt and suffering from cuts and bruises.

An air of gloom fell upon the Imperial Russian fleet from which it would never recover. The death of Makarov removed at a stroke the growing confidence of the navy, while at home the disaster merely fuelled the revolutionary clamour. The Japanese fleet was anchored off Elliot Island on 14 April when the news of Makarov's death was confirmed. Togo read out the Reuter telegram, after which he ordered his fleet to fly their flags at half mast and observe a day's mourning for an honoured opponent esteemed as a Samurai. In Japan, funeral processions filed through the cold night in honour of a respected adversary.

The death of Makarov signalled the end of a phase in the naval action as attention shifted to land operations. This did not mean that all naval activity came to an end, for on 3 May, Togo launched a further blocking expedition on Port Arthur. Eight steamers, bigger and faster, took part in the ritualistic attack. It was to be the last such effort as it failed in its aims, with greater loss of life. Nevertheless, Togo declared the attack to have been successful, thereby leaving the way clear for the landings of the Second Army. This false-hood therefore put great pressure on Togo to ensure that the Russian fleet could not sail to interfere with planned landings on the peninsula. Port Arthur was as good as blockaded, but the period heralded the beginning of Japanese losses. On 12 May a destroyer was accounted for by a mine at Tal-ienwan. In the same area, *Miyako*, a third-class cruiser, was also lost on 14 May. The worst disaster befell the Japanese the next day. The Tyne-built bat-tleship *Hatsuse* ran into a speculative minefield laid by the *Amur*. Like the *Petropavlovsk* before her, she disappeared within a minute. Striking a second mine, her magazine went up, taking the upper deck high into the air. The battleship *Yashima* closed in to assist but hit a mine in the same field. She sailed hesitantly away from the fortress so that if she should sink, her demise would not be seen by the Russians. She sank in the early evening. (News of the loss of the *Yashima* was not released to the Japanese public and strict cen-sorship was imposed throughout the Japanese fleet.) Two separate collisions that day saw the cruiser *Yoshino* and the gunboat *Oshima* destroyed. The total Japanese disaster on 15 May surpassed that of the loss of the *Petropavlovsk* but Witgeft, Makarov's replacement, made an ineffectual response with the sixteen available destroyers and the opportunity to capitalise on the disas-ter was lost.

The Japanese believed that the *Hatsuse* and *Yashima* had been struck by Russian submarines. The signal was made, 'Look out for submarines', at which point the *Shikishima* began firing into the sea. Submarines were in the process of being acquired and constructed in both countries but were not used. At the time there was little information in the public domain on the use of submarines. They were introduced into a 1900 Greenwich wargame but an air of uncertainty and caution overshadowed their operation. A con-temporary British authority described the submarine as an 'underhand method of attack' and recognised it as being detrimental to a nation depend-ent upon sea trade. A Dutch submarine that featured in a film of 18 July 1904 was purchased by the Japanese. They had been less overt in 1902 when an order was placed for five Holland-design submarines on the American Fore River Company. These thirteen-man, petrol-engined submarines were equipped with one 18-inch torpedo. The boats, built in great secrecy, were sent, dismantled, by rail to Seattle and thence by sea to Yokosuka. They arrived on 12 December 1904, but their assembly was delayed until

March–May 1905; eventual commissioning of the first boat on 1 August 1905 was too late for it to take part in the Russo-Japanese War.

The Russians were further advanced than the Japanese in the development of submersibles. The *Drzewicki* class numbered fifty-two miniature boats, of which the more numerous Type-3 had a crew of four. Employed in the 1877–8 Russo-Turkish War, the boats were designed to fix mines against the hulls of enemy ships. At war's end, as is the wont of governments, further development came to an end. The boats were used in the close defence of defended localities until 1886, when the majority were converted to buoys. An exception was the three-ton submersible *Keta*, a modified *Drzewicki* designed for coastal patrol and fitted with a petrol engine. During the Russo-Japanese War it was beached on the Amur estuary during an abortive attempt to sink a Japanese destroyer.

Four of the six large *Kasatka* class submarines, commissioned in 1904, were sent to Vladivostok during March–May 1905, but too late to take part in the battle around Port Arthur. Interestingly, the Imperial Russian Army was taken with the idea of submarines, and built four Holland boats for their own use. However, in 1904–5 a surprising *naïveté* pervaded both the Russian and Japanese sides as to the use, effect and capabilities of submarines. Instructions given to Lieutenant Steer* of the *Novik* read as follows:

> Seize the submarine by its periscope then smash it by blows
> with a mallet, so as to blind its crew. Better still, wrap a flag or a
> piece of canvas around it; or lastly – and this is probably the
> best way of all – tow the said submarine by its periscope into
> the inner harbour.

* After the war Lieutenant Steer was posted to Vladivostok where he commanded the submarines until 1906. He appeared to be a bright officer and wrote a book on the exploits of the fighting *Novik*. In 1907 he commanded the destroyer *Skory*. His crew mutinied and he was assassinated in his cabin by a petty officer. Port Arthur, or to use its Chinese name, Lushun, is now an important Chinese naval base.

CHAPTER FIVE

YALU

Togo's first attack on Port Arthur, while not being entirely successful, signalled the all-clear for landings in all but the south of Korea. The concurrent success of the naval attack at Chemulpo, however, made the alternative plan of a landing at Pusan thankfully redundant. The initial landing by the Twelfth Division would go in at Chemulpo until the thaw opened up other ports to the north to accommodate following divisions. The Second, Twelfth and Guards Division components of the First Army were all mobilised before the opening of hostilities. The Japanese were aware that they could bring troops to a battlefield faster than the limited Russian railway. In their desire to hit the Russians at the earliest opportunity, a significant body of senior Japanese army officers wanted the Guards Division to follow immediately behind the Twelfth.

There were, among the Japanese General Staff, those officers who had analysed the potential logistic problems of fighting in Korea during the transition from winter to spring. This problem had received constant attention throughout the autumn manoeuvres between 1901 and 1903. Kodama was furious that his fellow generals were not prepared to learn from the experience gained in 1894 and the obvious conclusions arising from successive post-exercise reports. Accordingly, he ordered the Twelfth Division, which landed between 17 and 22 February, to march north to Pyongyang. The Guards Division remained on standby at Hiroshima but advance parties from the Second Division landed with the Twelfth.

Winter weather in this region begins in October and lasts until March. The thaw occurs in March and April, making the roads impassable, but this

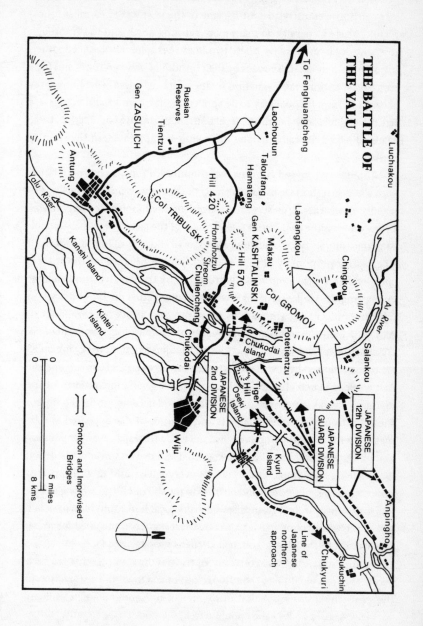

THE BATTLE OF
THE YALU

Liuchiakou

To Fenghuangcheng

Laochoutun

Russian
Reserves

Gen ZASULICH

Tientzu

Taloufang

Hamatang

Laofangkou

Chingkou

Hill 420

Antung

Col TRIBULSKI

Hanluhotzu

Gen KASHTALINSKI

Makau

Col GROMOV

Salankou

Ai River

Yalu River

Kanshi Island

Hill 570

Stream

Chulienchenng

Potetientzu

Chukodai
Island

Kintei
Island

Chukodai

JAPANESE
2nd DIVISION

Tiger
Hill

Oseki
Island

JAPANESE
GUARD
DIVISION

JAPANESE
12th DIVISION

Anpingho

Wiju

Kyuri
Island

Line of
Japanese
northern
approach

Chukyuri

Sukuchin

0   0

5 miles

8 kms

Pontoon and Improvised
Bridges

N

situation does not last long since the hot sun dries out the countryside. By any standards, the countryside at this time of the year was at its most inhospitable. There were but two main roads running north and south through the peninsula's mountains. These two highways were not metalled, differing only from more minor roads by their breadth of between thirty and forty feet. The situation was not helped by the peasants' habit of scraping away the topsoil from the roadway to be applied to their own smallholdings as a fertilised loam. Often below the level of the surrounding countryside, these roads collected the rain, making them almost impassable for the country carts.

A rough and rugged country, bad communications, a poor population with a seasonal shortage of supplies, and the limitations imposed by uncompromising weather, only served to exacerbate the problems of waging war. In few wars has the evidence of the relevance of the factors of military administration – simplicity, co-operation, economy of effort, flexibility and foresight – been so appropriately displayed. The Japanese advance northward was spearheaded by the commissary protected by the cavalry and infantry. Pyongyang, 150 miles north of Seoul, was entered first on 21 February by a transport officer who, with a party of twenty men, drove out the Cossacks. Along the route towards that town four further supply posts were established, enabling the cavalry screen of the Twelfth Division to enter Pyongyang on 23 February, followed by the main body arriving between 25 February and the first week of March. The logisticians had made good preparations for the division's arrival. A palace was requisitioned and became the focal point for the collection of supplies. Blankets and mounds of rice appeared as if by magic. Herds of cattle, observed and noted by the Japanese agents living among the Koreans, were bought, collected and driven towards the depot. Quartermasters beavered away. Outside every village and suburb appeared noticeboards assigning areas and quarters to the still distant advancing troops. Maps, drawings and diagrams showed every local house and road in detail. When the tired troops arrived, their quarters had been prepared for them, fires were lit in the streets, and field kitchens supplied hot food.

While bargaining was going on for the purchase of pigs at a fair rate, coolie convoys would head southward out of the town in the direction of the approaching soldiers. With the exception of gun ammunition, no military package exceeded 75 lbs – the optimum weight for one coolie to carry. Further calculations would extrapolate these loads to so many for a pony, a cart, and so on. Uniformity of size was therefore important, as was the correct labelling of each packet. The coolie army had been instantly recruited and numbered 10,000. They were paid wages well above the market norm and the status of village leaders was recognised by decorating them with stripes of red to show that they held privileged positions in His Imperial Majesty's Japanese Transport Corps.

Refreshed and refurbished, the Twelfth Division had vacated Pyongyang by 18 March, moving on to Anju which had been occupied the previous week by two squadrons of Russian cavalry. The vacuum at Pyongyang could now be filled by the remaining elements of the First Army. Reconnaissance at the mouth of the Taitong River, where the port of Chinampo is located, reported that the ice would be clear in a few days.

Chinampo led directly to Pyongyang and therefore offered the obvious attraction of avoiding the twelve-day march from Seoul. General Kuroki, the commander of the First Army, despatched the advance parties of the Guards and Second Division from Ujina, the port of Hiroshima, reaching Chinampo on 13 March. By 29 March, the whole of the First Army had landed in Korea.

The thaw which permitted the opening of Chinampo brought the anticipated chaos on the roads. Routes repaired by engineers were soon torn to shreds by guns; carriages and carts bogged in the mud of the roadways. In some cases, infantry were making less than five miles a day. The Japanese intelligence knew that there were only an estimated 2,000 enemy cavalry between them and the Yalu. They pondered why it was that they were not being severely interfered with along this long and laborious route. Alexeiev was applying the Tsar's directive literally in so far as there was to be no overt Russian action against the Japanese while they were on Korean soil. The Russians still believed that the option existed for the Japanese to have the Yalu as their objective with no aspirations to advance over the river into Manchuria. Accordingly, Alexeiev's orders were to accept a Japanese landing 'on the whole extent of the western coast of Korea as high as Chemulpo' and to permit their exploitation as far north as the Yalu. There were real logistical difficulties too. The Russians had nowhere near the logistical organisation of the Japanese, being forced to live off the land. Thus they came into immediate conflict with the local population whose resistance to them was being fuelled by a previously unseen form of oriental jingoism. Effective action by Chinese Hunhutze guerrillas and North Korean irregulars upon the Cossacks did much to relegate the conflict by the Japanese and Russians south of the Yalu to little more than minor skirmishes.

Japanese impatience to push on returned. Tokyo wanted the First Army to attack over the Yalu, while the Second Army under General Oku was to land at Nanshan to cut off Port Arthur from the mainland. Observers outside the High Command believed Kuroki's progress against an insignificant enemy to be inexcusably slow. Kuroki wished to dispense with his advance guard and push on with his main body up to the Yalu where he knew Kuropatkin was establishing defences. Only the coastal road could be utilised to move a large body of troops, for to have used interior routes would have put the First Army's advance across a forty-mile front. Kuroki could barely feed his advance guard, so precarious was the supply situation. He ordered a new logistical appreciation and plan to be drawn up by his staff. This confirmed the western route as the only option, with supply depots needing to be placed strategically along the way. Additionally, the port of Rikaho was selected as a new landing and supply base. In order to protect this new facility, the advance guard was moved some four days' march to the north. When it was discovered that this guard, consisting of the bulk of the cavalry of the Guard and Twelfth Division, two regiments, two mountain batteries and a company of engineers, required for its support two-thirds of the army's regular transport, it was quickly thinned out. After reorganisation and regrouping, a general advance was considered feasible on 7 April. The Russians were also experiencing logistical difficulties. The route across Lake Baikal was unavailable for three weeks, which meant their army in Manchuria would have to draw the requisite 25,000 tons of food and fodder from their own stocks and from local resources.

Some days' delay was imposed by storms and heavy floods which had destroyed a number of bridges. By the second week of April the Japanese on the Yalu were in precisely the same position occupied by their forbears in August 1894. Ten years previously the Japanese were on the threshold of a deep and bitter winter whereas now they had the prospect of moving into the region's short summer. Lessons had been learned. By 21 April the army was concentrated and hidden south of Wiju, drawing its supplies from Rikaho, Boto and Chinampo. By now, both armies and navies had been joined by a number of foreign military observers and foreign correspondents, accredited and unaccredited. More were on the way.

The intention of foreign nations to learn lessons from the wars of others was demonstrated by the role of the foreign military observer, a role which became institutionalised during the American Civil War 1861–5 and the Franco–Prussian War 1870–71. The alliances which followed-on from these wars and the perceived impact of technological revolution upon modern warfare were responsible for a quantum leap in interest in the monitoring of the events on both sides of the Russo-Japanese War, on land and at sea. There were as many as one hundred foreign military observers from sixteen countries in Manchuria and Korea.

Britain provided the largest proportion of observers for she recognised that, as the ranking power, she had the most to lose in not keeping abreast with the developments and potential of modern warfare. The Royal Navy's last serious battle had been Trafalgar, 1805, and her army's last conventional war had been the Crimean War, 1853–6. Colonial conflict, as in the Boer War, 1899–1902, provided Britain with no compelling evidence as to how the next continental war would be fought but what it did do was raise worrying questions concerning the performance of her army. The Imperial Japanese Army had scant regard for the British Army, whereas the Imperial Japanese Navy (and Russia) rated the Royal Navy highly. Even though Captain William Packenham became a personal friend of Admiral Togo, he never felt sufficiently confident to test this friendship by going ashore. Geographical factors provided Britain with further reason to be interested in how the Japanese managed the war. It was the naval strategist Corbett who remarked: 'What the North Sea and the English Channel are to ourselves, the Sea of Japan and the Straits of Korea are for the island empire of the Far East.'

Russia had good reason to regard as spies the three military observers she accepted from Britain, among whom was Brigadier W. H-H. Waters. Russia was no more relaxed with the Admiralty's appointee, Captain Eyres, later captured in Manchuria by the Japanese. The two American observers, Lieutenant Commander N. A. McCully and army Captain M. V. Judson, made rendezvous at St Petersburg with the military representatives of nine other countries. Both, however, were excluded from the Tsar's welcoming reception due to continuing displeasure with the conduct of USS *Vicksburg*. After being duly warned that no information was to be transmitted which might be of possible benefit to the Japanese, the observers' train, the Siberian Express, departed on 2 April, arriving at Irkutsk on 12 April, a respectable time for that journey.

Britain used her position as ally of the Japanese to persuade Tokyo to accept thirteen British and Empire observers. In so doing, she also raised the expectations of other foreign powers keen to be well represented on the Japanese side. Under normal circumstances, the discreet Japanese would have politely rejected or substantially reduced the numbers requested for military accreditation but, for Japan, these were not normal circumstances. It was a Japanese war aim to maintain the goodwill of the Great Powers, thereby ensuring not only that none intervened on Russia's behalf but also that they remained amenable to Japan's constant need to raise loans and pay their interest so as to sustain the war.

The Vietnam and Falklands experiences have served to highlight a problem with press relations that is assumed by many to be new – that of finding the acceptable common ground between two sets of irreconcilable rights. Correspondents in the Spanish-American War and the Boer War had established the trend by sending their editors information that was of use to the enemy. In their reports from such battlefields the Japanese attachés advised their government to draw up a suitable contingency plan to deal with the press.

> Men like Archibald Forbes and Dr Russell would not have brought the profession of war correspondent to this pass; but there have been so many less worthy men in the business in recent years that it is done to death. The authorities cannot discriminate or can only do so occasionally.

So wrote the Japanese-accredited Thomas Cowen of the *Daily Chronicle* in 1904. A view from the Russian side was penned by Douglas Story:

> Those of us who take our functions seriously, who realise that war correspondence is as much a profession as that of the soldier or the engineer, resent the intrusion of the callow sensation mongers vomited from a hundred yellow journals.

On 29 February of that year, Japanese paranoia towards the press would be further fuelled by the publication in *The Times* of this despatch from Chemulpo:

> The Japanese disembarkations during the last few days have been confined to supplies, the transport corps, and ponies, of which there are 4,500. The total number of troops landed is 20,000, including the Twelfth Division and part of the Second

Division. Another disembarkation, believed to be on a small
scale, is taking place on the coast immediately south of Haiju,
whence the troops will advance parallel to the Peking road,
thus effecting a gain of five days' march. It is supposed that
8,000 troops, with a few guns, are now advancing beyond
Seoul towards Pyongyang.

From this point, the Japanese exercised stringent control over foreign
and domestic correspondents. The editor of one Japanese newspaper was to
be arrested and tried for passing on information to an enemy. He had reported
a Japanese victory without authority. The Russian press was not similarly
controlled. According to the German Official History, 'The Russian press frequently stabbed out something worth knowing.'

On Saturday 30 April the Russians evacuated all foreign correspondents
to Mukden. They were treated little differently to their colleagues with the
Japanese. According to Douglas Story, 'Correspondents belonged to a species
of which they had had no previous cognisance, and the first to arrive among
them were regarded with distrust and apprehension.' There were advantages,
however, in being with a defending force since despatches could be sent
from, or along, the line of communication. No such advantage exists for the
attacker, whose correspondent is being drawn away from his means. A
solution to this problem was found by Lionel James, the thirty-two-year-
old *Times* correspondent. He chartered a 300-ton steamer, the *Haimun,* and
filled it with the latest radio equipment with which he could communicate
directly to his control station at Weihaiwei. He reported an attack on Port
Arthur as it was happening, thereby achieving a new first in the history
of journalism.

Russia derived much of her intelligence from the London newspapers
which, in turn, were read avidly by the Japanese. The Imperial Russian
Embassy telegraphed information to the Intelligence Headquarters at St
Petersburg where, after analysis, intelligence reports were sent to the front. On
occasions, the Russians played on the Japanese fallibility to observe everything. One St Petersburg newspaper reported that their forces on the Yalu
had the capability of setting the waters afire with burning oil. This report
was transmitted to the Japanese spymaster on the Yalu for verification. It
was, however, the Russians who were to be more severely wrong-footed by the
British press. Theirs was the ultimate sin of believing what they read. Reported
landings at Gensan on the east coast of Korea and in the neighbourhood of

Port Arthur, transport fleets seen off Yingkou and true reports of supply difficulties, led the Russians to assume erroneously that there could be no Japanese action until mid-May. They perpetuated their laissez-faire attitude by not stepping up war preparations; indeed, on 28 April, General Rennenkampf's cavalry division was withdrawn from its position on the Yalu to commence its divisional drills. At the same time, the first phase of errors in deployment occurred when the available force was spread widely over twenty miles of the river bank to guard against every contingency, and the reserve placed on the right flank near Antung.

On 15 February, General Kuropatkin, Minister for War, had presented to the Tsar his plan of campaign for war in the Far East, a war which he personally did not favour. So impressed was the Tsar with this five-point strategy that he appointed General Kuropatkin to command the army in Manchuria. This command did not include the forces at Vladivostok or the Ussuri, while at Port Arthur General Stoessel reported to Kuropatkin and Admiral Alexeiev who remained as Viceroy and Commander-in-Chief of all the Russian forces, both naval and military, in the Far East. Before he left St Petersburg on 12 March, Witte, Kuropatkin's former cabinet colleague, had advised his friend the general, tongue in cheek, to return Alexeiev to the capital under arrest. Many a true word is spoken in jest, but this advice contained an ominous ring of truth.

Kuropatkin's appointment prompted a great wave of public support, for he was a soldier with a good reputation. Honours and favours were lavished upon him. Now aged fifty-six, he had not seen action since Plevna, where he had been Chief-of-Staff to Skobelev. As a military commander, his principal military problem was one of time and space. He estimated that he required six months to achieve a force of 200,000 to give him sufficient superiority to undertake the offensive. His options were first, to assess the limit of the Japanese progress northward in those six months, establishing a strong defence to the north of this perceived limit of the advance. Second, his least favoured option, in the event that the political will did not exist to trade space for time, was to establish a forward defensive line in the south. The line of defence would be protected by a covering force established to gain the necessary time by imposing delay upon the enemy.

Not unexpectedly, Alexeiev refused Kuropatkin permission to abandon any territory on the Manchurian side of the Yalu. The general's reconnaissance of Liaoyang and its environs after his arrival there on 28 March confirmed its suitability both as his headquarters and for the initial forward defence. The Yalu, 120 miles to the south, was to be the line on which the covering force was to be deployed. General Zasulich, the new Eastern Detachment commander, had arrived on 22 April. His orders were specific. The mission given to him by Kuropatkin was 'to retard the enemy in his passage; to determine his strength, dispositions and lines of march; to retreat as slowly as possible into the mountains', there to engage in obstinate resistance. Further directions from Kuropatkin insisted on firmness combined with prudence in opposing the passage, and warned Zasulich to avoid a decisive battle with superior forces.

One philosophy of Clausewitz which the Japanese had learned through their Prussian association was the strategy of bringing superiority to bear at a given point. Japanese intelligence had shown that the Russians could be outnumbered at any point the Japanese chose. The same intelligence indicated that Russia did not have the resources to sustain forward defence. Japan could draw upon her great communications advantage, particularly since Russia's sea power was virtually neutralised. All depended on the quality of the untested Japanese soldier and how he would fare against the military forces of this great European power.

On 15 April Kuropatkin issued a memorandum in which he said

> In the Japanese we shall in any case have very serious opponents, who must be reckoned with according to European standards. It is very important that they should not gain the consciousness of victory in the opening combat when they will be superior in numbers. This would still further raise their spirits.

Kuropatkin's grudging respect was not shared by the majority of his army, who regarded the Japanese as insignificant 'monkeys'. Numbered among those was General Zasulich who believed he could take on and beat the Japanese. For their part, the Japanese army were bracing themselves to emulate the achievements of their naval brothers. They had all been imbued with Kodama's directive of 'absolutely winning the initial battles of the war'. Kuropatkin's view was well known. He knew the psychological value of a Japanese victory, not only for the Japanese but also at home where disturbances and revolutionary zeal were becoming more frequent. He wrote: 'No terrain, no locality, should be regarded by us of sufficient importance to warrant the risk of permitting the Japanese to gain a victory over our advanced troops.' The world's attention was drawn inexorably towards the Yalu River.

The Yalu is a river of many moods and adopts a different configuration according to the season. At the end of April, the winter's ice had gone and while the river was not as swollen as in summer, the icy water of the spring thaw flowed hurriedly to the sea. On the opposite bank from the city of Wiju lay Chuliencheng. The town sat some two miles back from the river, being built on a number of hillocks from which its name, 'nine connected forts', is derived. Between the two settlements is an open stretch of water varying from one to two miles in width. Just below this point, the river divides and the disrupted chain of islands then continues down to Tatungkow and the sea. A mixture of small trees and shrubs grow on the array of islands, providing rare cover in an otherwise open, sandy plain.

There were no bridges between the two banks, the crossing having to be negotiated by sampans and small junks. Japanese sappers were to report to General Kuroki a rare setback to their well-laid and meticulous plans. The river, mud banks and islands had all changed so profoundly since September 1894 as to make their bridging plans worthless. The shortfall in bridging was largely to be overcome by Japanese ingenuity and the availability of abandoned timber in the Russian yards at Yongampo. The early occupation of the Yalu Islands had now become imperative in order to effect a detailed reconnaissance of the right bank.

Flowing from the north and joining the Yalu just above Wiju and Chuliencheng is the Ai River. Slicing through the high ground from Fenghuangcheng it leaves rough steep crags until near the junction with the Yalu. At this point, on the eastern bank, is a prominent feature called Tiger's Head, half a mile in length and 500 feet high. The promontory appears isolated but is connected to the main feature by a low neck. It is ground of tactical significance, since in Russian hands their artillery could prevent the daylight crossing of the Yalu, while in Japanese hands it would be the fulcrum around which their efforts could be turned against the Russians in any direction. Seven miles from Chuliencheng and connected by a road squeezed between mountains and muddy river banks lay the fortified town of Antung. At this point the river accepts vessels of moderate draught and, according to the Russian appreciation, was highly vulnerable to a Japanese landing. The Japanese did nothing to dissuade the Russians from this view. It had been near this point that the Japanese had crossed the river against the Chinese in 1894.

Russian forces on the Yalu consisted of the Third Siberian Army Corps together with General Mischenko's Trans-Baikal Cossack Brigade. At Antung, under Major General Kashtalinski, were deployed 2,580 riflemen, 400 mounted scouts, sixteen field guns and eight machine guns. Also on the right flank but four miles to the north at Tientzu was the reserve consisting of 5,200 riflemen and sixteen guns. At Chuliencheng, under Major General Trusov, were 5,200 riflemen, 240 mounted scouts and sixteen guns. The right flank, stretching from the mouth of the Yalu to Takushan, was allocated to Major General Mischenko, under whose command were 1,100 cavalry, 2,400 riflemen, eight field and six horse artillery guns. To the left flank, from Anpingho to Hsiapuhsiho, forty miles north-east on the Yalu, were allocated merely 1,250 cavalry, 1,000 riflemen and eight mountain guns.

Excluding seven companies in the rear guarding the lines of communication, the combatant strength on the Yalu, distributed over a distance of 170 miles, was 16,000 riflemen, 2,350 cavalry, 640 mounted scouts, forty-eight field guns, eight mountain guns and six horse artillery guns. Over the river, to the south of Wiju, preparing, was a force of 42,500 Japanese.

The Russians had spread themselves out piecemeal along the river. At the base of the hills were the Russian trenches, uncamouflaged and open to full view from the opposite bank. Guns were similarly disposed and clear to see. The sight amazed the military correspondent of *The Times*, who wrote: 'The Russians on the Yalu are thus much exposed, and if they elect to stand here they deserve to suffer for it.' The Russians, by placing themselves behind a broad and unfordable river, had lulled themselves into a false sense of security by failing to understand their inscrutable enemy's propensity towards the indirect approach, surprise and security. They relied on the winning qualities of the stoical Russian peasant in defence.

Japanese intelligence, spies and their own reconnaissance force, sometimes plying the river disguised as fishermen, had gradually put together the Russian order of battle. Records indicate that by 23 April the Japanese knew the layout of the Russian trench line and the details of his defensive formation in the area of Antung. The Japanese estimate of Russian troop strength was exceeded by only 1,000 men and their estimate of guns was only two less than those deployed. While Russian security was criminally lax, that of the Japanese was impeccable.

If Kuroki was to enjoy any success against the Russians it was essential that his enemy should maintain their linear deployment while he concealed both his strength and point-of-crossing prior to the attack. He displayed surprising ingenuity for the time. Reconnaissance from the high, home river bank was forbidden. Screens of trees and dry *kaoliang, a* type of millet that grows to a height of ten to twelve feet, were erected on the left bank of the Yalu where the road would have otherwise been overseen from the opposite bank. Gun and troop movements were thereby conducted in complete secrecy. Trees and bushes were continually being moved to screen some activity or equipment. The Russians failed to notice what had previously not been there. Ian Hamilton, destined to command the allied forces at Gallipoli, was surprised and bemused by this novel approach to warfare. Were he to have been served by energetic, innovative and imaginative subordinate commanders, the Gallipoli story could have been entirely different.

By 25 April, the time had arrived when no further preparations could be made without updating the reconnaissance of the main channels of both the Yalu and Ai. These activities could not be completed as long as Russian detachments held the islands of Kyuri, Oseki and Kintei. That evening, six batteries were moved forward to support an infantry attack. Reconnaissance patrols had located most of the Russian positions and even gunboats and torpedo boats off Antung had drawn fire, both giving away the Russian positions and adding evidence to the threat to the right flank. At 9.45 p.m. two battalions of the Second Division crossed in pontoons to Kintei Island, where they landed unopposed. Immediately the sappers prepared a bridge. At 4 a.m. the next morning a force of 250 soldiers from the Guards Division were engaged when no more than three of their boats had reached Kyuri Island. One hundred and fifty Russians fired into the ranks of the Japanese and twelve fell. The Japanese, reinforced by more boats arriving, pressed home their attack. Warning beacons burned throughout the early morning as the Russians withdrew, having abandoned both Kintei and Kyuri Islands. The loss of the two islands led the Russians to evacuate Tiger Hill, which was occupied by a delighted but surprised Japanese force. The Japanese were now in a position to conduct their river reconnaissance and to cut communications between Zasulich's headquarters and his left flank force.

The engineers determined that ten bridges with an aggregate length of 1,630 yards would be required. One-third of these were made from thin sheet steel prefabricated pontoons weighing less than 100 lbs, thereby being coolie-portable. The remainder were obtained either through local resources or the flourishing supply port at Rikaho. Following a feint attack on Chuliencheng, a bridge made up of native boats placed side by side was set across the Yalu. It was never intended for use. While the Russian gunners worked to distraction to destroy this bridge, the Japanese engineers worked quietly on those bridges required by the plan, one south of Wiju, the remainder to the north. As Russian guns revealed themselves, so they were systematically destroyed. While the construction was under way, a flotilla of six boats appeared off Antung, shelling and machine-gunning the Russian positions. The local commander, convinced that this was the prelude to the main attack, sent to Chuliencheng for reinforcements. These alarms had been continuous over the previous ten days. The Russians were tired and confused.

Kuroki now had all the information he required to formulate his plan of action. His orders required him to advance to Tangshancheng, between Antung and Fenghuangcheng, and dig in until the Second Army had completed disembarkation. Then, both armies were to operate in concert. The master plan required Kuroki to cross the Yalu on 30 April. Following a joint meeting between General Oku Yasukata, Commander of the Second Army, and Admiral Togo on 25 April, both concluded that they could not reach the deadline for a landing on 1 or 2 May. Tokyo ordered Kuroki to delay his attack until dawn on 3 May. Kuroki argued forcibly that all the conditions were favourable and that the plan should not be changed. He was granted his wish.

Kuroki concentrated his attention upon the weak Russian left flank. He needed to find a crossing point over the Yalu and reconnoitre the ground between that river and the Ai. His enemy, not dissimilar from Montcalm at the Plains of Abraham, had dismissed the approach over the Ai and up the heights as not being a possible option. In their view, the crossing of the Ai required boats. It seemed logical, therefore, that until intelligence indicators identified the movement of boats into the region, a threat in this area could not manifest itself. The Japanese found a crossing point which could be covered from the right bank at Sukuchin. Reconnaissance by forward elements of the Twelfth Division confirmed the local Chinese view that troops at light scales and mountain guns could cross the terrain from one river to the other. The configuration of the river and shortage of bridging equipment required two divisions to follow the same route to their forming-up place. Additionally, it meant that the leading division would be isolated for a day. In view of Russian reactions to date, Kuroki decided to take the risk. The Twelfth

Division had further to march and they were allocated the right flank of an army attack from Salankou on the Ai to Chukodai on the Yalu. In the centre were the Guards who were to cross the Yalu via Kyuri and Oseki Islands, taking up positions on Chukodai Island to the north and south of Tiger Hill. The Second Division took up the left flank.

At 10 a.m. on 28 April, General Kuroki issued orders for the attack to take place on 1 May. On the day the order was sent, the exhausted horses and untrained muleteers arrived from Chinampo with the secret Japanese weapon – the 'Corps' artillery, consisting of twenty 4.72-inch howitzers organised into five batteries. Thus had been effected an idea initiated by the Japanese Military Attaché during the Boer War. It had not been previously conceivable to move heavy guns across difficult terrain until it was done first by the Boers and then by Captain Percy Scott. It was he who had placed 4.72-inch naval guns on carriages of his own design for the march on Ladysmith. (Until recently, Scott's feat was commemorated each year at the Royal Tournament, London, in the naval field gun race.) An order was therefore made on Messrs Krupp of Essen by the Japanese ordnance procurement for their own 4.72-inch howitzers. The Russians were to receive a costly jolt. The next night, the guns were moved across the new pontoon bridge to Kintei Island, to be collocated with the Second Division's artillery. Under the cover of darkness they were eased into prepared trenches camouflaged by screens of timber and trees. Connecting trenches simplified command and control and assisted the continual watering that would be required to keep down the dust. Observation posts to the flank and rear were connected to the guns by telephone. All had maps showing the Russian positions annotated to reference points so that fire could be brought down on particular squares. A high proportion of the available ammunition was shrapnel, destined to terrify the Russians. Under orders not to open fire until 1 May, unless a suitable target appeared, the howitzers remained undetected throughout the battle.

Ordered to cross the Yalu on the night of 29 April, the Twelfth Division had moved three batteries into Chukyuri to cover the sappers preparing the bridging. At 11 a.m., under covering fire, elements of the division moved forward to the river and by 2 p.m. a battalion had crossed to the right bank, brushing aside light Russian opposition. When news reached Zasulich, he ordered reinforcements to move to Anpingho. He still regarded the activities of the Twelfth Division as a feint, a view assisted by the appearance of the Yongampo flotilla off Antung on 29 and 30 April. The reinforcement was accordingly delayed, and on 30 April countermanded. Kuropatkin continued his careful and detailed supervision of his subordinate, sending orders and advice with monotonous regularity. His behaviour was considered to be intended to counter the directions being given to Zasulich by Alexeiev, still distrusted by Kuropatkin but nonetheless loyally supported. Among the myriad of information emanating from Liaoyang was the sage advice that Zasulich should watch his centre and left. Additionally, he was instructed to keep active lookout across the whole front, not losing touch with his enemy.

Prompted at last to do something in this area, at 4 p.m. on 29 April, Zasulich despatched a battalion of the Twenty-second East Siberian Rifle Regiment, supported by mounted scouts and two guns, to cross the Ai River and recapture Tiger Hill. The battalion group successfully drove the Japanese picquet from the hill, who moved away in good order to rejoin their division on Kyuri Island. This reverse was one of the few suffered by the Japanese. It did not directly affect Kuroki's plans, causing minor delays to the construction of bridges from Kyuri and Oseki Islands.

The next morning, the Japanese observed the Russians digging in on Tiger Hill. The Guards' divisional artillery, on a hill south of a bridge leading to Kyuri Island and a mile and a half north of Wiju, opened fire. There was no response from the Russian guns. With no option but to press on with the reconnoitring, at 10 a.m. two groups of sappers in boats set out to survey the mainstream opposite Chukodai. Half an hour later, a battery on the high ground to the north-east of Chuliencheng fired upon the Japanese engineers in the river below. Immediately, the six batteries of the Twelfth Division and the 'Corps' 4.72-inch howitzers replied. In sixteen minutes the Russian battery had been neutralised, suffering the loss of five officers and twenty-nine men killed and wounded. Another Russian battery located east of Makau then took up the fire, only to be similarly despatched by the Guards' artillery. The Russians had invited destruction for, unlike the well-hidden and camouflaged Japanese guns, David Fraser of *The Times* reported, 'The spokes of their wheels, the gunners and their every movement being plainly discernible with glasses from the Korean bank.'

Major General Kashtalinski had taken over the Chuliencheng sector from Major General Trusov, who had fallen ill on 28 April. All the indicators and all the advice proffered by his subordinates suggested in the strongest manner that a major attack was imminent. So severely had his artillery and infantry suffered that at 11 p.m. on 30 April he requested from Zasulich permission to withdraw to the hills behind Chuliencheng. Kashtalinski's assessment was strongly supported by Zasulich's Chief-of-Staff, who had been in the thick of the bombardment. Zasulich would not listen. His orders from Alexeiev were clear; he knew he could beat the Japanese. Besides, having just the day previous reported to the Tsar the heroic recapture of Tiger Hill, a withdrawal now would appear strangely incongruous. Kashtalinski was forbidden to withdraw, 'on any pretext whatsoever', although authority was given for troops to retire to take cover from the effects of the artillery bombardment. As a sop, an infantry battalion from Tientzu was moved under his command. Soon Zasulich would hear that the force on Tiger Hill, fearing encirclement, had abandoned the promontory at midday. The feature was seized by the perspiring advance guard of the Guards linking up with the left of the Twelfth Division.

The Twelfth Division was making good progress in three columns towards the Ai River. Last light heralded the movement of the other two divisions so that the whole army, like a swarm of ants sweeping over rivers, across bridges and defiles, made its inexorable progress to predetermined startlines immediately opposite the Russian positions. As the British Official History so aptly said, 'Thus a force of little more than seven battalions and sixteen guns were distributed over a front of some six miles, and was about to bear the whole brunt of the Japanese attack.'

It was a misty night, and rain clouds provided the Japanese with welcome additional security but the less welcome threat of flash floods. An approach march at night culminating in a dawn attack was a new phenomenon of warfare. The silent move of a whole army at night was a classic, and the key to the morning's victory. As Thomas Cowen of the *Daily Chronicle* reported:

> The men had to march, wade, wait their turn at a plank bridge
> or shallow ford, help each other up a slippery bank, pass, in
> single file sometimes, through a willow copse, wait, climb,
> jump, mud-scramble, and march again, for about six hours,
> getting into positions, 'lining out' in front of the long-extend-
> ing Russian trenches. No light was allowed, nor a voice above
> an undertone, for the most part there were no roads to march
> on, but the men had to cross fields, grope in the gloom for
> strange paths, or struggle past obstructions where no path

could be found, using dry water-courses as tracks till they led
into pools, over stubbly cornfields, in and out among tenantless
farm buildings, up country lanes and hillside footpaths, each
officer and NCO peering into the gloom, feeling his way to the
appointed spot, consulting a rough sketch plan and drawing
his men after him.

While the success that morning was due to the skill and determination of
the Japanese forces, that success was none the less aided and abetted by the
ineptitude and incompetence of their enemy.

At 3 a.m. the Russian Twelfth Regiment reported hearing the sound of
wheels on the islands and guns crossing bridges. Zasulich did nothing to
prepare to move his reserve other than to despatch a machine-gun company.
Curiosity began to get the better of him and he moved up to Kashtalinski's
headquarters overlooking the Yalu.

By 5 a.m. the customary fog was being evaporated by the early morning
rising sun. Ironically, the Russian positions, facing eastward, had this rising,
fiery orb in their eyes as they squinted unbelievingly across the valley to
their front. They could discern from opposite Chuliencheng to Salankou, a distance of six miles, three blue-coated infantry divisions waiting in shell scrapes,
ready to pounce. Sermons prepared by regimental priests, whose function it
was to combine piety with patriotism, would go unheard in this sector that
day. Indeed by the end of the day, few of the Russians there would be alive to
hear at all.

The scream of Japanese howitzer shells broke the quiet of the morning,
searching out the Russian artillery. There was no reply. The gunners were
under orders from Kashtalinski not to reveal their positions. The Japanese,
concerned lest the Russians had withdrawn their guns out of range, were
soon to be reassured when a battery in the area of Makau replied. In a few
minutes, these six guns were silenced and in the absence of other artillery
entering the fray, the full weight of the Japanese artillery was directed upon
the shelter trenches of the Russian infantry. In view of the ineffective Russian
artillery, Kuroki amended his plan of using the Twelfth Division to encircle the
enemy positions prior to a second-phase attack by the Guards and Second
Division. At 7 a.m. he ordered a simultaneous advance of all three divisions.

The Japanese rose from their trenches, their blue uniforms conspicuous
against the yellow sand of the plain. Like thousands of lemmings they rushed
to the 200-yard wide waters of the Ai being funnelled by the few crossing

points. The icy, fast-flowing water tugged at them, taking away their breath as it passed their chests. Weighted down by three days' supplies, they were struck by the first Russian volley at 500 yards as the advanced troops were halfway across the river. Although still at extreme range for rifle fire, the weight of shot reaped its harvest among the closely packed ranks of Japanese. Nevertheless, the advance maintained its momentum and soon the river had been crossed in force. The Russian volleys continued to take their toll against the impetuous Japanese advance heading from the river bank up the series of low knolls rising to Chuliencheng. But this was pointless slaughter. There were other ways the Japanese could prove their superiority over the heroically immobile Russians at less cost. The order went up and down the line, 'Take cover and fire at will.'

The Second Division had suffered so severely around Chuliencheng that it had become disorganised. The Twelfth Division was in good order and all three divisions were receiving welcome and essential assistance from their direct support artillery. The gently rising, soft but irregular ground suited the Japanese infantry. As they leapfrogged forward using fire and movement to good effect, they were soon close to the Russian forward positions. As their enemy withdrew to take up positions in the rear, they were hit by the full weight of the Japanese artillery fire. A brave but pointless company counterattack by the Twelfth East Siberian Rifle Regiment was swept aside. By 10 a.m. the main body of the Russian force was in full retreat through Chuliencheng. An attempt was made by the Japanese to block the road to Fenghuangcheng to the north of Chuliencheng, and it took the full weight of the Russians to dislodge them from their withdrawal route. General Kashtalinski was fully aware of the collapse of his right flank, but the situation was still not lost as long as the left flank, under Colonel Gromov, held.

Colonel Gromov was holding the forward slopes overlooking the Ai in the area of Potetientzu. Under his command were two battalions of the Twenty-second Regiment. His mind was already being concentrated by the right of the Guards Division, now over the river and having penetrated his thinly held line. At this juncture, he received news of the approach of the Twelfth Division which had been delayed on a particularly difficult stretch of the river. He rode off to investigate, and found what he estimated to be five or six battalions advancing on his position. He ordered a partial withdrawal which became a general withdrawal when the Japanese turned his flank. He intended to adopt a new position at Chingkou, but the rapid advance of the Japanese forced him to place his force on the saddle between Chingkou and Laofangkou.

The Russians had retired in reasonable order. Other than Gromov's two battalions, and his loss of six guns, the balance of the force was in good condition as it prepared new defences on the Hantuhotzu stream which ran two miles inland, parallel to the Ai River. The force at Antung had been shelled by the Japanese flotilla, but they and the reserve at Tientzu had so far played no part in the battle.

General Kuroki ordered the Guards to occupy the hills above Hamatang, the Second Division to march on Antung, and the Twelfth Division to march south to Taloufang. The Twelfth Division had anticipated its orders and, having swept through Chingkou, was en route to Hamatang, a route which would bring it into conflict with Colonel Gromov. General Kashtalinski had been able to hold the Guard and Second Division on the Hantuhotzu. They had by now advanced ahead of their supporting artillery fire. This pause gave General Zasulich time to withdraw his troops at Antung back to Tientzu. In order to cover this withdrawal, two battalions of the Eleventh East Siberian Regiment and a battery were detached to bolster General Kashtalinski's position on the Hantuhotzu. With them they brought orders that the force was to hold the Japanese advance until the right flank had withdrawn. While the Second and Guards Divisions were held in the centre waiting for their artillery, the Twelfth Division was closing on the hapless Colonel Gromov. Equally unfortunate was General Kashtalinski who, in the absence of evidence to the contrary, believed that all was well with his left flank.

By 12.15 p.m. Colonel Gromov, in the face of extreme odds, decided to withdraw to Liuchiakou. He sent a report to that effect to General Kashtalinski's headquarters. Having despatched his wounded, two guns and four companies, an officer on General Zasulich's staff who arrived on the scene at 1 p.m. ordered him to retreat via Laochoutun. The wounded and four leading companies were recalled and Gromov passed along the line of communication to the rear without further loss. (General Kashtalinski was not to receive Gromov's message until 4 p.m. The colonel was court-martialled for his precipitate withdrawal. Although exonerated, he could not face the ignominy and disgrace. He blew out his brains with his service revolver.)

It had been just before noon that General Kashtalinski had heard from an assistant surgeon that Colonel Gromov had withdrawn from Chingkou with the Twenty-second Regiment in disarray and, further, that the Japanese had occupied Liuchiakou. The scouts he had sent out to reconnoitre returned to confirm the news, reporting that a substantial body of troops was advancing on Laofangkou. Still in doubt, General Kashtalinski rode out to see for himself. He stared into the face of disaster. He ordered an immediate withdrawal from the Hantuhotzu to Tientzu. As his rearguard he selected the Eleventh Company of the Twenty-second Regiment. Orders were sent to the newly arrived reserve, the two battalions of the Eleventh East Siberian Regiment, to occupy the 570 feature to the east of Hamatang. As the going was extremely difficult even for infantry, their accompanying battery of guns was ordered back to withdraw along the axis of the retreat, the Fenghuangcheng road.

Just after 2 p.m. the battery's eight echelon wagons were at the northern mouth of the gorge, some 1,000 yards south-east of Hamatang, when they came under fire. The Fifth Company of the Twenty-fourth Japanese Regiment, the Twelfth Division's advance guard, had reached the rough and rocky north-west slopes of the hills dominating the road. The wagoners forced their horses into a gallop and reached Tientzu without further incident. The following guns were not so fortunate, for the Japanese took deliberate aim at the horses and a number were lost. The battery commander immediately ordered his guns into action to support the Eleventh Regiment, which was guarding the defile through which General Kashtalinski had to pass. The gunners unlimbered the guns as in a drill, swinging the guns around, gouging out arcs in the damp, red shingly soil. Their target was the Fifth Company, now the subject of Russian infantry attacks in an effort to budge the unwelcome enemy before they could be reinforced.

The Russian Twelfth Regiment passed through the valley with great difficulty, but soon the efforts of the Fifth Company blocked the valley so that following units had to make a detour through the rough terrain to the south of Hill 570. While the infantry could make their way over the rough terrain, the guns could not, and they gradually fell back into the valley to support the remnants of the Russian force. The Fifth Company had been reduced to half its strength, and it would only be a matter of time before it would be forced to loosen its hold on the defile, thereby allowing the Russians to escape to safety. In the distance, above the tumult of battle, there came a faint, imperceptible noise gathering intensity like a roll of thunder, to be accompanied by the sound of jingling. Then, suddenly, the noise stopped some way off. After a few minutes a new noise joined the battlefield: crash, bang and swish, as Japanese shrapnel tore into the ranks of the attacking Russians. Three batteries of the Twelfth Division had arrived, and with them had come the leading elements of the Guard and Second Divisions. The time had come for the Russians to extricate themselves as best they could. The battle was lost.

The Eleventh East Siberian Regiment had succumbed to the pressure imposed by the Twelfth Division and was driven from the hills north of Hamatang into the valley. Already, the majority of their twenty-six officers and 900 men had been killed or wounded. The valley, no more than half a mile wide, was quite open, extensively cultivated, with fields extending high up the hillsides. Except for occasional patches of long grass, there was little cover from the hail of fire pouring down from the heights. More Russian blood flowed into the blood-red soil. Quite without warning, the regiment's priest, in full regalia, flowing black beard, mitre, cross in hand, stood up. The surviving Russians in that regiment stood up too, and followed the priest up the valley towards safety. 'God have mercy,' he cried. Still the fire was coming down, and still the Russians were taking casualties. The first of three bullets to hit the holy man pierced his lung. He tottered and fell, his cross spattered by his own blood. His assistants pressed forward, picked him up and, one on either side, resumed the march through the valley. Gradually, the firing petered out. The Japanese troops stood up among the rocks and mix of fir and oak-like trees. Their shouts of acclaim for their honoured, vanquished enemy reverberated around the hills in salute to the bravery which had unfolded below them. (The hero priest of the 11th Siberian Rifles was evacuated to the Red Cross hospital at Mukden, where he made a physical recovery from his wounds. He did not recover from his psychological wounds, becoming mad.)

This magnanimity was not extended to all Russians. The 650 men holding out on Hill 420 south-east of Hamatang were driven towards the Twenty-fourth and Forty-sixth Regiments. Those in the valley continued to fight, cannons pointing in all directions. When a company of Fourth Guards, with bayonets fixed, charged, screaming 'Banzai!', the white flag was sadly and reluctantly raised.

At 5.30 p.m. the sun was setting upon this, the first battle of the war. It was a battle that should never have been. An Oriental army had beaten a European army, and the effect upon Japanese confidence and morale was incalculable. The number of casualties had been light in relation to other wars or battles to come: 2,700 Russians were killed, wounded or taken prisoner, against the Japanese loss of 1,036 killed and wounded. The Russians lost twenty-one of the twenty-four guns engaged in the action, as well as eight machine guns and nineteen wagons laden with ammunition.

The Japanese chose not to pursue the retreating and demoralised Russians. The Russians did not take the opportunity to adopt intermediate positions in the mountains overlooking the road to Fenghuangcheng, or on the Great Wall to the south of that town. They were hell-bent to reach Liaoyang as quickly as possible. The strategically important town of Fenghuangcheng was by-passed and left to be occupied at a leisurely pace by the Japanese on 5 May. By retreating north-west towards Liaoyang instead of south-west towards Port Arthur, they handed to the Japanese the option of landing where they pleased on the Liaotung Peninsula, isolating Port Arthur and dividing the Russian force in Manchuria. While Kuropatkin set about reinforcing Liaoyang on 3 May, Tokyo received Togo's report that Port Arthur had been completely blocked. Baron Oku's Second Army was already embarked, riding off Chinampo. They were ordered to Liaotung, where Oku had commanded the Fifth Division in the Sino-Japanese War. He knew the ground well and what was required.

The defence of the Yalu was strategically sound, but failed in its tactical execution. It is unlikely that any river line can be held against a determined enemy, particularly in the Russian case, where their numbers were in excess of that required for observation but insufficient for defence.

Zasulich allowed himself to become mesmerised by his right flank when the centre of his position, Chuliencheng, was where the reserves should have been. He had to endure the conflicting instructions of both Alexeiev and Kuropatkin and, although he favoured the former's attitude, the turning of his left flank and Gromov's withdrawal in reality left him little option but to fight on the day as he did. He is not free from censure, for he fought on the ground of his own choosing in forward, inadequately prepared positions. There was little he could do regarding his soldiers' relative lack of expertise and training. They invited destruction by their poor fieldcraft, poor marksmanship, and the dated habit of indulging in volley firing.

The battle of the Yalu was not only the decisive battle of this war, but was also a battle which ranks as one of the most important in the annals of warfare. The threat posed by Korea had been removed. Russia demonstrated her inability to go on the offensive, and her inability to match the fighting qualities of the Japanese at sea, and now on land. Russia had severely under-estimated her enemy. The 'monkeys' had seen off her troops in a manner so impressive as to open the previously tied purse strings in London and New York to finance Japan's further progress in the war. The psychological impact on Russia was immense; this disgrace was the beginning of her downfall, it was the beginning of many beginnings. From this point can be traced the inevitability of the end of the old colonialism, an impetus toward the development of world communism and its own attendant form of colonialism, and the euphoria which swept Japan into other wars, and the ultimate thermonuclear response. 'The echoes of the battle will reverberate afar,' wrote the military correspondent of *The Times,* 'and distant is the day when the story will weary in the telling, among the races of the unforgiving East.'

CHAPTER SIX

NANSHAN

Energetic Russian diplomatic pressures were applied in an attempt to persuade the Sultan of Turkey, against whom the Russians had fought in 1877, to release the Russian Black Sea fleet. No less energetic were the ambassadors of other interested countries equally as keen as the Sultan to keep the Russian fleet to the north of the Dardanelles forts. Resigned now to that *fait accompli,* the undisguised examination of the contingencies of redeploying the Baltic fleet went ahead. With the notable exception of the Japanese, many of the leaders of the first-class navies regarded the Russian plan as sheer posturing. Simple examination of the logistically desirable but problematical best case voyage via the Suez Canal suggested that the fleet of twelve warships would take at least sixty-three days, consuming 65,000 tons of coal. All but 15,000 tons would require to be carried by colliers and trans-shipped in the open sea.

This would be an enormous gamble, for the redeployment of the fleet would denude the European naval defences of the Empire at a time when the political situation in Europe and Russia was highly volatile. If, when the European fleet arrived in the Far East, it should find that Port Arthur had fallen and Vladivostok was blockaded the situation for Russia would be catastrophic. Bereft of base and coaling facilities, the fleet would fall easy prey to the Japanese navy and another emphatic nail would be driven into the coffin of Imperial Russia.

Despite her naval losses and the disaster on the Yalu, Russia was still very strong. It could be argued that by encouraging Japan to extend her lines of communication by launching enveloping attacks on to the Kwantung

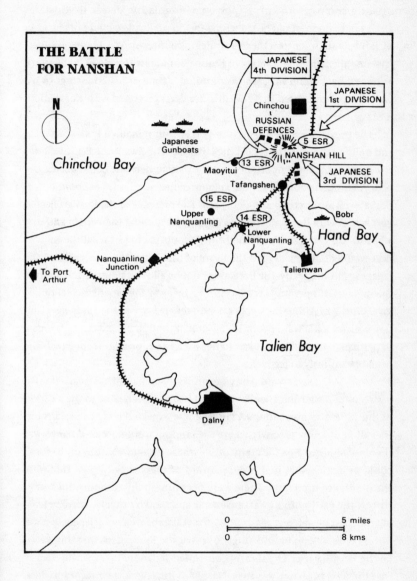

THE BATTLE FOR NANSHAN

N

JAPANESE 4th DIVISION

JAPANESE 1st DIVISION

Chinchou

RUSSIAN DEFENCES

5 ESR

NANSHAN HILL

Japanese Gunboats

Chinchou Bay

13 ESR

Maoyitui

Tafangshen

JAPANESE 3rd DIVISION

15 ESR

Upper Nanquanling

14 ESR

Bobr

Lower Nanquanling

Hand Bay

Nanquanling Junction

To Port Arthur

Talienwan

Talien Bay

Dalny

0   5 miles
0   8 kms

Peninsula and Liaoyang, Russia was recoiling as a spring ready to launch counter-moves with her considerable reserves. Commentators were already drawing comparison with Napoleon's humiliating defeat in Russia in 1812, but to do so would be stretching the point. Russia would not abandon Manchuria in order to achieve a strategic counter-stroke. Many observers had absolute faith in the ability of Kuropatkin to ride the blows, to reinforce as he fell back upon his resources and, at a time of his choosing, to hit back. This presupposed that the ultimate decision rested with Kuropatkin. It did not.

The presence of the Russians in Port Arthur remained both a political and military thorn in the side of the Japanese. The Kwantung Peninsula was of extreme strategic importance to Japan. From here she could ensure the benevolent behaviour of China, guarantee her naval lines of communication as well as the command of the sea. The presence of the Russian fleet at Port Arthur with its repair facilities meant that nothing was certain and that all planning in the area was fraught with doubts as to just what the Far East fleet would do. Discussion of the move of the Baltic fleet concentrated the Japanese mind. Clearly, the fleets must not be allowed to unite and, despite the dangers of opening a second front, it was to the Japanese a labour of love. With Port Arthur back in her hands, the message to the European coalition which took it from her in 1895 would be both loud and clear. To Russia in particular, it would be a blow to her Far Eastern prestige from which she would be unlikely to recover.

On 5 May the Second Army began its disembarkation near Pitzuwo between the Tasha and Lilan Rivers. This had also been close to the location of the 1894 disembarkation. A landing was expected by the Russians but they did not know precisely where the landing would occur. Pitzuwo was the only landing area for many miles where disembarkation on to rocks could be achieved at high tide. Seaward of these rocks at low tide were three miles of mud flats. There were of course many rumours, fuelled in part by the early withdrawal of General Mischenko's cavalry thereby leaving the coast unwatched at a critical time. A bombardment by Japanese naval forces between Kaiping and Yingkou convinced Kuropatkin that this would be the landing site. The tightly controlled Japanese press wrote openly that the next objective was to be Nanshan. In view of their record to date, the Russians tended to believe that it would be anywhere but. The arrival of the eighty transports of the invasion fleet at Pitzuwo was observed by a few Cossacks of the First Verkhne-Udinsk Regiment. The armada was drawn up in three lines from where each vessel was taken in turn to her predetermined anchorage.

Shells from two accompanying cruisers drove off the Cossacks to make their report. A thousand-strong naval landing party waded waist-deep the thousand yards to shore where they raised the Rising Sun on the hill. With the beachhead secured, the troops began to disembark, wading through the thick glutinous mud. The next day, however, a gale blew up and disembarkation had to be suspended. General Oku reassessed the landing site, chosen in peacetime off a chart, and decided to move to a sheltered position a few miles to the west. As the steamers were unloaded they returned independently to Japan. The junks and sampans they had carried to disembark their troops were gathered and lashed together. Planking was laid over the top to make a floating jetty for the unloading of cargo which very soon extended 1,000 yards out to sea. Twelve feet wide, it could cope with a shelving sea bed and the fifteen-feet rise and fall of water.

All this activity was taking place within sixty miles of the enemy's fleet. The Japanese fleet's base had been moved temporarily to the nearby Elliot Island. In order to cover his position, Togo placed sixty destroyers and torpedo boats between Port Arthur and the point of disembarkation. Additional protection was afforded by guarding the eighty miles between Elliot Island and the mainland with a combination of guard ships, booms, nets, dummy mines and patrol boats. The disembarkation was to go on unhindered. A strategically placed regiment could have caused chaos but these resources were deployed elsewhere and the opportunity was missed. What then of the Russian navy; were not the advantages of swift, brave action far beyond the risks?

Admiral Alexeiev had been ordered by the Tsar to leave Port Arthur. On 5 May he left in a special train for the city of Mukden leaving General Stoessel in command of the Kwantung Peninsula, General Smirnov in command of the fortress, and Admiral Witgeft commanding the naval forces. The Japanese landings were known to be taking place. The junior officers awaited their orders, but none came. Commander Semenov, writing in *Rasplata,* was an important barometer of the views of the junior officers:

> Suppressed indignation prevailed throughout the squadron,
> and grew from day to day. As a matter of fact we still had avail-
> able three undamaged battleships, one armoured, three first
> class, and one second class protected cruiser, four gunboats

and over twenty destroyers. With this force we could unquestionably have taken something against the disembarkation
which was taking place only sixty miles from us.

On 6 May the Viceroy signalled Witgeft to the effect that attacks on the enemy's transports would be very 'desirable'. What was implied was clear but there was no order and the weak Witgeft convened a council of war. It was as though no senior naval person was prepared to issue an order on his sole authority. Prior to departing Port Arthur, the Viceroy had instructed the two destroyer flotilla commanders to discuss interference with the landing with Admiral Witgeft. Alexeiev was clearly avoiding the decision to risk the annihilation of the Russian fleet by interfering with the Japanese landings. He preferred to let a subordinate take a decision which he, as Commander-in-Chief of all armed forces in the Far East, was in the best position to make. Witgeft played safe and his committee decision was to do nothing. The council's reasoning was that the fleet was weak and that any damage would affect the navy's role of supporting the Baltic fleet when it arrived. It was felt that a foray by destroyers was doomed and a signal to that effect was despatched to Alexeiev, known in the fleet as the 'Great Edict of Renunciation of the Navy'. The despairing junior officers were now to witness the removal of their heavy-calibre guns to bolster land defences. Perhaps an attack on the Japanese would have been foolhardy but equally, perhaps, in the predictable morning fog something could have been achieved. Makarov might have tried but the blunt Commander Semenov lays the blame clearly at Alexeiev's feet for suppressing initiative and originality thereby killing the navy's offensive spirit.

The Japanese Second Army consisted of three divisions, the First (Tokyo), the Third (Nagoya) and the Fourth (Osaka). General Oku's orders were to seize Dalny for use in future operations. En route he would need to take Nanshan, but a very real risk to his flank was posed by enemy operations from the north. He had already called for reinforcement by the Fifth Division and First Cavalry Brigade but he decided to commence his operation by 15 May without them. The Third and Fourth Divisions were ordered to block the threat from the north while the First Division was ordered to advance south on Chinchou. Japanese intelligence reported that the Second Brigade of the Fourth East Siberian Rifle Division under Major General Nadyein had been reinforced to divisional strength from Port Arthur. This was not correct since the brigade's task was to guarantee the safe passage of a final ambulance train along a route being interfered with by Japanese troops. Nevertheless, General Oku directed the First Division against the brigade. At 12.30 p.m. the two forces met. The Russians fell back to Nanshan under covering fire, losing 150 officers and men killed and wounded while the Japanese lost a similar number. By this action General Oku had achieved a strategic vasectomy for he had now cut the road and rail communications of the Kwantung Peninsula from the north. If he could hold that ground, then the 30,000 Russian troops incarcerated in Port Arthur could not be directed against Japanese activity elsewhere. To achieve that aim, Oku had to seize and hold the feature known as Nanshan.

The Liaotung and Kwantung Peninsulas are connected by an isthmus no more than 4,000 yards wide from the high-water mark. On both sides is a muddy foreshore which at low tide can add collectively a further 4,000 yards of width. To the east lies Talien or Hand Bay and to the west is Chinchou Bay. To the south-west, some thirty-five miles distant, lies Port Arthur. Astride this strategic feature, overlooking road and rail communications, is a group of hills spread from shore to shore and rising to over 300 feet. Whoever controlled these hills controlled the land approach to Port Arthur. The close proximity of the Nanshan feature to the sea meant that the defence and attack would be a joint navy-army operation. Admiral Makarov stopped here en route to Port Arthur and, surveying the scene, advised that heavy guns be mounted on Nanshan with their arcs of fire covering the seaward approaches.

The Russians were determined to hold, for a while at least, the Nanshan feature to bar the Japanese advance on Port Arthur. The position consisted of a group of hills forming a circle one mile in diameter. Viewed from the north, the site resembles a single wall but in fact presents three distinct salients separated by deep ravines, except that the ridges in the centre and east are connected by cols. The position is overlooked four miles to the east by the 2,200-feet Mount Sampson and from the south-west by the heights near Nankuanling. The slopes leading up to Nanshan are bare and glacis-like, affording extensive fields of fire. For the most part, the soil is quite soft and easy to excavate but further up the slopes the camouflaging of earthworks proved to be virtually impossible. The route leading to the lower slopes was across bare but ploughed fields, giving infantry reasonable cover on their way south.

> If a Russian division of 8,000 to 12,000 men, backed up by fifty
> or more siege guns and sixteen quick firing field guns, cannot

> hold 3,000 yards of front, strongly entrenched, and secure on
> the flanks, against the rush of infantry in the open restricted to
> a frontal assault, it is hard to say what position it can expect to
> defend with success.

Thus commented *The Times*' military observer, yet the task of defending Nanshan fell not, as he suspected, on the Fourth East Siberian Rifle Division under Lieutenant General Fock but upon Colonel Tretyakov of the Fifth East Siberian Rifle Regiment. General Fock, a police general, was a product of peace; like so many of his kind who had risen to high rank as trainers, administrators or social smilers, he was unable to make the essential transition to a general at war. He was susceptible to others' ideas. Kuropatkin did not wish a repeat of Zasulich's pointless defence on the Yalu. Herein lay an element of confusion in the aim of this division, for Kuropatkin cautioned Fock against delaying for too long the withdrawal from Nanshan. He did not mean to imply that withdrawal was a necessary part of his strategy and, indeed, General Stoessel advised Fock to hold Nanshan with Tretyakov's regiment and to assume the offensive as soon as the Japanese came near.

Two miles to the rear of the Nanshan feature in the village of Maoyitui was the Thirteenth East Siberian Rifle Regiment and two miles to the rear of them was the Fifteenth East Siberian Regiment. To their south-east, two miles away in the village of Lower Nankuanling, the Fourteenth East Siberian Rifle Regiment was stationed. On the finger of Talienwan was a battery of heavy guns covering north over Hand Bay where the improvised gunship *Bobr* was positioned. She was sealed in and protected by a thick minefield across the mouth of the bay. On Nanshan, therefore, Colonel Tretyakov had eight of his companies in the front line, one and a half companies in local reserve, two companies of the Thirteenth East Siberian Rifle Regiment in general reserve and scouts from the Thirteenth and Fourteenth East Siberian Rifle Regiments. In all, he had approximately 2,700 riflemen. To his north lay the three divisions of the Second Army, the Third Division having been released from its holding position in the north by the arrival of the Fifth Division.

On 19 May the Tenth Japanese Division landed at Takushan. The landing was to further mystify and mislead the Russians but the division's aim was to fill the vacuum between the First and Second Armies and afford flank and rear protection. The Fourth Division, west of the railway, was to the north of the walled city of Chinchou; the First Division in the centre and the Third Division, on the left flank, held the region of Mount Sampson. The total combatant strength of the Second Army was 38,500 of which riflemen numbered between 30,000 and 31,000. The Russians had in the field 17,000 of whom only 3,000 were to be engaged in the forthcoming battle. Colonel Tretyakov had helped fortify the positions on Nanshan during the Boxer Rebellion. They had a garrison at Chinchou but for the defence of Nanshan had prepared positions for a garrison of two battalions and ninety guns. These were now in a state of disrepair.

A plan forwarded in 1903 to repair the fortifications was rejected by the Kwantung Province council on the grounds that 19,000 roubles was too expensive. When war did break out, the plan was hurriedly approved but the cost of hiring additional labour and building the fortifications exceeded 80,000 roubles. The engineers set about improving the existing redoubts and batteries. The ground was still frozen and the earth hard as rock. Five thousand coolies supported the soldiers among whom, in disguise, was Colonel Doi of the Imperial Japanese Army. The eastern side of the feature was well protected by minefields and a double barbed-wire fence over which the Russians had superb fields of fire. The western side was also festooned with barbed wire across the ravines but here the wider foreshore of Chinchou would seriously impede movement. The Russians appeared to believe an attack from this area would be unlikely, as indeed they had neglected to consider the effect of Japanese warships directing enfilade fire from the unmined waters of Chinchou Bay. The southern side had not been neglected for the Russians regarded a landing in their rear as a distinct possibility.

An almost continuous line of shelter trenches ran around the top of the hills like a monk's tonsure with additional rows providing a depth of up to four lines of alternative trenches. The lessons of the Yalu had been well learned. The guns were dug in and connected by telephone. Behind the highest battery was a dynamo which supplied the searchlights that scoured the front at night. But despite all these advantages, the fields of fire and unhindered observation, Colonel Tretyakov was not happy. He recognised that the earthworks pinpointed his positions leaving them vulnerable to reverse and enfilade fire. He fully recognised the weakness of his west flank and its susceptibility to being turned. Command and control were difficult and the prospects for counter-attack and withdrawal were unfavourable. He preferred to sit further south to allow the isthmus to constrict and concentrate the Japanese so that they could be hit at that point. For this plan Tretyakov would have needed at least two divisions, which he recognised as impossible, so he concentrated his efforts on pleading to be reinforced. Fock consistently rejected his pleas, saying finally, 'Less heroism is required to defend this position than to retreat from it.' General Kondratenko, the well-respected commander of the Seventh Division, chipped in at Tretyakov, now being regarded by some as a moaner, that his regiment should defend the position to its last drop of blood. As a sop, however, Tretyakov was given two scout detachments, which were assigned to the outposts.

The sum of the Japanese artillery was 198 field and mountain guns. There were no 4.72-inch howitzers in the Second Army order of battle. The Russians had forty-eight quick-firing field guns among their total of 114 guns. The remainder was a ragbag collection, with the thirteen heaviest guns varying in calibre from 4.2 to 6 inch facing east. Of those on the west coast, only sixteen 3.4-inch guns could fire in the direction of the bay. They would have to contend with a naval flotilla bearing fourteen guns of calibre from 4.7 to 10.2 inches. For the Russians, however, there was the advantage of cover and the disadvantage of having only 150 rounds per gun. The Japanese were obliged to fire their guns from exposed positions to the north of Nanshan.

By the morning of 24 May, Oku was ready to commence his attack. A signal arrived from naval headquarters to the effect that, subject to favourable weather, the gunboats *Akagi, Chokai, Heiyen* and *Tsukushi*, carrying between them fifteen medium calibre guns, three 10-inch and twelve 4.7-inch guns, would be available to shell the Russian positions over the next two days. The main assault was postponed until the morning of 25 May except for long-range shelling and an attack on the walled, fortified town of Chinchou by the Fourth Division. The Russian garrison at Chinchou comprised no more than 400 men and four old artillery pieces. This artillery was quickly neutralised by the Japanese who, in turn, drew fire on to themselves from the Nanshan position. Unseasonal rain came down in torrents and the cold Mongolian wind froze the infantry and engineers of the Fourth Division as they made for the walled city's north gate. This division was from Osaka and, since time immemorial, Osaka soldiers had had a reputation for failing. They were regarded by their comrades as the 'Unlucky Fourth'. It was not bad luck that saw them repulsed that day, just a lack of dash and determination. The same appalling weather prevented the naval vessels from arriving and Oku accordingly postponed the attack on Nanshan until the 26th when he would go with or without the navy. Meanwhile, Colonel Tretyakov, peering out from his bunker into the torrential rain, could see the deluge uncovering the topsoil around his protective minefield, exposing mines and command detonating wires. There was no opportunity to restore the situation.

The rain continued throughout the night of 25–26 May. The Fourth Division made a second attempt on the city's north gate. Their progress was picked out during the frequent flashes of lightning and although they succeeded in laying a mine they were forced away before it could be detonated. Attempts to scale the wall were similarly frustrated and it was a cold, wet, depleted and dejected party which made its way back through the torrential rain to their own lines only to be cut down by their own forward picquets. No progress towards the capture of Nanshan could be made while Chinchou still resisted. Seeing the Fourth Division fail again, the First Division of its own volition sent two battalions against the eastern gate. At 5.20 a.m. the sappers blew in the gate and the infantry swarmed through. The Russians left by the south gate but were mown down by the fire of the Fourth Division, only half of the company managing to reach the trenches on the Nanshan feature.

The attack on Nanshan was scheduled just prior to first light at 4.30 a.m. but, following the rain the countryside lay shrouded in a clammy, heavy mist. After an hour's delay, the artillery began a three-hour exchange. Much of the Japanese artillery effort was concentrated on the protective minefields, a waste since the mines had been exposed by the heavy rain and could therefore either be avoided or have the conducting wire snipped through. The Japanese flotilla entered the battle at 6 a.m. firing from Chinchou Bay. By 7 a.m. the weight of Japanese fire was beginning to tell on the Russians as much as their own logistic problems. This fire fight could be heard by the Third Army's advance guard which had made a difficult landing to the southwest of Pitzuwo. The landing of the main body became delayed due to bad weather. Both the Second and Third Armies had therefore landed near Pitzuwo, a far from ideal place to put armies ashore but the best that was available. Given this predictability it remains an indictment of Russia's military initiative and spirit that these extremely hazardous landings should have been unopposed. Tens of thousands of men and a moribund fleet at Port Arthur might have been usefully employed to disrupt the landings.

Meanwhile the infantry attack had begun. The Fourth Division advanced from Chinchou along the sandy stretches of beach. Observing this threat to the left flank, two batteries were withdrawn from the Nanshan feature to take up better positions to the south-west. Seeing this action, the Japanese flotilla mistakenly believed a retreat was in progress and moved away to the south, intending to impede the withdrawal. The Fourth Division was receiving close support from the Fourth and Thirteenth Artillery Regiments who had done well to neutralise the artillery on Nanshan, but the removal of the naval gunfire was cruelly felt when the two batteries which had moved to the rear tore into the packed ranks of the unfortunate, unlucky Fourth Division. They suffered heavily. The Japanese flotilla was hurriedly recalled by signal but it was not until 10 a.m. that its guns resumed the action. The ships remained until 2 p.m. when the ebbing tide forced their withdrawal. The gunboat *Chokai* had been hit and she carried away her dead captain and a number of wounded. The Japanese attempt at joint army-navy co-operation had been frustrated by weather and tide which were beyond their control but, what was within their control and found wanting was an adequate ship-to-shore communication system.

The problems of advancing three divisions along such a narrow front was being sorely felt by the Japanese. They were not much drawn to the Prussian philosophy of advancing in a solid phalanx. This was known colloquially at the time as 'Algerian Tactics', named after the French frontal attacks which secured their foothold in North Africa. But this war was different, the world had moved on. Nanshan was witnessing trench warfare, barbed wire, minefields, searchlights and flares, machine guns, tethered observation balloons, radios, telephones and railways to deliver soldiers, supplies and *matériel*. This was a new, modern dimension which the French had not faced. Oku, however, preferred the prospects of a three-pronged, simultaneous attack to the perceived attrition attendant upon a phased approach.

At midday the Japanese, believing the Russian will had been eroded by the renewed fire from their flotilla, ordered two battalions forward to seize the advance trenches of the supposedly shell-shocked defenders. The story is taken up by *The Times* correspondent:

> At first the straggling walls of Mauchiaying give them some
> cover, under which they have a moment's breathing space.
> Then the gallant little infantry press on again up the breast of
> the slopes of the Russian position. It is an almost impossible
> task. As yet the defenders are not sufficiently shaken. An ava-
> lanche of concentrated fire from the infantry in the trenches,
> the machine guns in the Russian works, and the quick firing

field artillery supporting the defences strike the Japanese to the
full. They melt away from the glacis like solder before the flame
of a blow pipe. A few who seem to have charmed lives struggle
on till they reach the wire entanglements. It is a vain, if heroic,
effort. Wasted within fifteen minutes, these two battalions cease
to exist except as a trail of mutilated bodies at the foot of the
Russian glacis.

The situation for the Japanese was critical. The First Division was stopped
within 300 yards of the Russian trenches. Two of the three battalions con-
stituting the army reserve were moved forward to enable that ground to be
held. The Third Division was to find itself enfiladed by Russian infantry on the
southern shore of Hand Bay while the gunboat *Bobr* superimposed her fire
on some effective shooting by a battery firing from Tafangshen. To the Third
Division was assigned the last remaining reserve battalion. The Nanshan feature had been charged nine times throughout the day and now, at 6 p.m.,
after fifteen hours, a stalemate had been reached.

Both sides had exhausted most of their artillery ammunition. Although
Tretyakov had now deployed the last of his local reserve to his right flank,
he had successfully held off three Japanese divisions. Behind him, General
Fock had in reserve an under-strength Thirteenth and the entire Fourteenth
and Fifteenth East Siberian Regiments. The two promised companies, which
were not permitted to be placed in the line, had not arrived when Tretyakov
asked for reinforcement from the general reserve. The Russian position was the
stronger of the two but it was this refusal of Fock's to reinforce Tretyakov's
success which led to the ultimate Russian defeat. Fock had allowed himself to
become mesmerised by the perceived threat of a Japanese landing in
Tretyakov's rear. He need not have concerned himself because the Japanese
military approach to the Nanshan battle had been dominated by low-level
tactical rather than operational or military-strategic level thinking.

While the centre and right flank were holding, the constant Japanese
shelling on the Russian left flank was beginning to take effect. The Fifth and
Ninth Companies had lost half their number to artillery fire when they were
driven out by the Japanese Fourth Division advancing along the coast. Wading
through deep water and thick mud, under accurate fire, the unlikely troops
of the Fourth Division's Seventh Brigade pushed on shouting their war song,
'Easy to cross the River of Ai'. The two awaited companies arrived to reinforce Tretyakov at 6 p.m. and most were sent to the threatened left flank

where hand-to-hand fighting had developed waist-deep in water. 'When the Russians finally retreated, the water was literally crimson,' reported the Reuter despatch. The Japanese turned inland and pursued the Russians up the ravines, capturing two redoubts, and drove in the left flank to overlook the Russian line of retreat. Fock, who was now forward on this flank, ordered the companies in his vicinity to withdraw. He did not pass this order to Tretyakov who was still doing his utmost to restore the situation.

As the Japanese right drove up the feature, new impetus was given to their compatriots in the centre and on the left who surged forward in a victorious onslaught. There was some confusion and desperation on the Russian part but in the main the withdrawal, now under Japanese artillery fire, was orderly, making its way back to occupy Tretyakov's next line of prepared defences to the south. Some Russians refused to retreat, holding their ground until overwhelmed by superior numbers. While touring the new defences, checking on positions and arcs of fire, Tretyakov's attention was drawn to the railway station at Tafangshen, the site of his reserve ammunition. It was on fire. He rushed off to investigate but was not as close as some when the dump blew up, killing a major and twenty soldiers. He was enraged to find the station had been destroyed on Fock's orders and his manner was not helped when he discovered for the first time that the three regiments deployed to his immediate south had not been committed. They would have been more than adequate to turn the tide against the exhausted Japanese.

Panic soon overwhelmed the Russians. Men left their positions and fled to the safety of the south; some of the remaining guns careered down the bumpy tracks into the night while shots from the north were followed by shouts of 'Cavalry – Japanese Cavalry'. The Japanese cavalry had in fact been prevented from pursuing the Russians by the broken ground and darkness. The exhausted Japanese bivouacked on the captured hills while the guns remained where they were. This had been an impressive and tenacious victory gained irrespective of loss. While the Japanese rested, Tretyakov had restored some order and following behind his regimental band he pondered what might have been had anything like the available strength been employed. He knew he had fought well, losing only 450 men during the day. What made him bitter was the loss of 650 men during the withdrawal. He was to be further embittered when he met General Stoessel on 30 May.

At 7.20 p.m. the flag of the Rising Sun was raised over Nanshan heights. By 8 p.m. the exhausted Japanese were engaged in bivouacking and feeding.

They had indulged in only opportune bites to eat throughout the long day. Now, as their quartermasters and officers moved among them, gathering and collating the statistics of battle, they ate the cold, stale boiled rice of the previous day, too hungry to re-cook it. The tally of losses on the Japanese side was 739 men killed and 5,459 wounded. Among those killed was Katsusuke, the twenty-six-year-old eldest son of the 1894 victor of Port Arthur, General Nogi. He died of his wounds on 30 May 1904. When the general heard the news, he was about to leave for the front at the head of the Third Army to emulate his earlier victory by retaking Port Arthur. 'There is to be no funeral ceremony, no mourning until the end of this war,' he said, 'when my surviving son and myself will be among the mourners or the mourned.' So saying, he left to join the war in which his surviving son became numbered among the mourned.

That night, the Japanese ammunition crisis was indelibly underlined. They had attacked with a total of 198 rounds per gun divided between limbers, first-line and second-line wagons. At the day's end, the guns had each fired on average a total of 174.5 rounds, thereby using in this one small battle more ammunition than they had used throughout the entire Sino-Japanese War. (At Nanshan the Japanese fired over 34,000 rounds of which ninety per cent were shrapnel, and over 2.2 million rounds of small arms ammunition. The news jolted Tokyo. It was a portent of things to come, an indication of the amount of ammunition required to dislodge an entrenched and well-prepared enemy. The pattern was to escalate to such a degree that by 1917, in preparation for the third battle of Ypres, the British artillery fired in two weeks 4,283,550 shells from guns of calibres ranging from 18-pounders to 15-inch howitzers.) Not until the arrival of two ammunition columns and a supply column on 27 May was it possible to push forward a brigade to occupy Nankuanling Junction and Talienwan.

Dalny, the jewel of Russian Imperial aspirations in the east, sat less than eight miles from Nankuanling Junction. Here lay a very suitable alternative line of defence which many Russians rated as superior to Nanshan, but no attempt was made to hold the line. It was towards Dalny that the disillusioned soldiers of Tretyakov's regiment trudged, leaving behind eighty-two artillery pieces and ten machine guns. They had not even the comfort of a meal for, in his zeal to evacuate, General Fock had ordered their rear echelon and field kitchen back to Port Arthur. The bad news was brought to Dalny at 11 p.m. when a train arrived to announce the fall of Nanshan. Panic was rife. Acting on General Stoessel's orders to evacuate, but not by rail, the mayor gathered together a mixed group of 600 Russian nationals to evacuate southward. They moved off at the speed of the slowest, encouraged onward by the explosions of the half-hearted destruction of the Dalny facilities so lavishly provided at the expense of Port Arthur's defences.

General Stoessel reported officially that it had always been his intention to abandon Nanshan. He dismissed the loss of weapons as not being of great significance since they were 'old pieces taken from the Chinese in 1900'. His real feelings were reserved for the hapless troops of Tretyakov's command. The fury and venom of this vain, unpredictable and arrogant man struck the troops paraded before him on that morning of 30 May. 'You are', he shouted, 'a wretched undisciplined corps of traitors, cowards and blackguards. I will try the lot of you by court martial. How did you dare leave Chinchou? Don't dare to show yourself in Port Arthur, lest by your presence you infect the whole garrison with your cowardice.' Then, with reluctance, the general carried out the Tsar's orders by awarding the Cross of St George to the wounded. The sixty crosses available made little impression on the numbers wounded. Tretyakov was to write in his book, 'These were the sole recipients of rewards for the Nanshan battle, those slightly wounded receiving nothing for their bravery.' There were, however, three subsequent unwounded recipients of the Cross of St George for their bravery at Nanshan. All three were officers and one was General Fock. (Both Stoessel and Fock were to be court martialled, the former for, among other things, embellishing Fock's role in the battle, and the latter for failing to support Tretyakov and other lapses in command.) An officer wrote:

> Many unworthy officers who have done nothing to deserve
> good of their country have been plastered with orders by
> General Stoessel who wished to help them on. In the majority of
> cases these were either officers of high rank who were intimate
> with him, were with him in the China campaign, or were liked
> for family reasons.

On 30 May, the Japanese Third Division entered Dalny unopposed. They found that the town and its resources had suffered severely from the attention of the enterprising Chinese. Much of the stocks of the food supply had been dispersed, but although railway bridges were down, the fabric of a port with its wharves, docks, 290 railway wagons, electricity supply and workshops

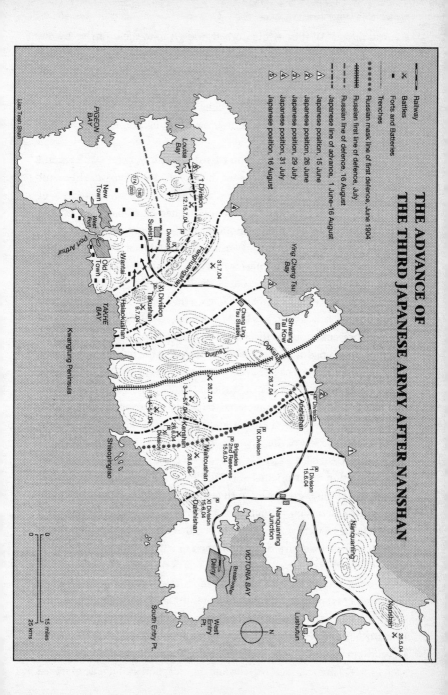

THE ADVANCE OF
THE THIRD JAPANESE ARMY AFTER NANSHAN

Railway
Battles
Forts and Batteries
Trenches
Russian mask line of first defence, June 1904
Russian first line of defence, July
Russian line of defence, 16 August
Japanese line of advance, 1 June–16 August
Japanese position, 15 June
Japanese position, 26 June
Japanese position, 29 July
Japanese position, 31 July
Japanese position, 16 August

was still intact. 'All this,' wrote Corbett, was given to the Japanese 'by the Russian fear of what they might have done and not by what they did'. The task of mining the waters had been well executed by the Russians and it was still to be a few weeks before the impatient Third Army could fully utilise the port for further activities against Port Arthur. The port of Talienwan was allocated to the Second Army as their base for operations northward to Liaoyang.

The Japanese Eleventh Division passed through General Oku's Second Army on the battlefield and was joined there by the First Division. They went forward as General Nogi's Third Army, towards Port Arthur, the capture of which they had been assigned. The Russians had fallen back to a fifteen-mile-long line of defence running from Shiaopingtao on the east coast, about ten miles south-west of Dalny, to Anshishan on the west coast. Anshishan is approximately eighteen miles from Port Arthur. The Russian position masked their first line of defence but its significance was the ground, of vital tactical importance – Waitoushan, 800 feet, and Prominent Peak, 1,000 feet.

Prominent Peak, which was later named Sword Hill or Kenshan by General Nogi, was important to the Russians for the security of Port Arthur (the comings and goings of the fleet could be seen with the naked eye) and similarly important to the Japanese because it overlooked Dalny. The first Japanese attack in the battle of the Passes, launched on 26 June, quickly accounted for the feeble defenders on Waitoushan but faced sterner opposition on Kenshan. The appearance of a Russian naval force off Shiaopingtao, and its disruption of the left of the Japanese line, delayed the eventual taking of that feature. General Stoessel was allegedly incensed and ordered the immediate restoration of the original line. The Russians made no fewer than five determined counter-attacks upon the two observation points. They came very close to success on a number of occasions but, as was a feature of this war, the Japanese were yet again able to find that little bit extra to deny them their victory. Stoessel now ordered his men to fall back the two–four miles to the Green Hills or Taiposhan prepared line of first defence.

General Nogi bided his time, content to hold this new position while reinforcements and *matériel* were brought into Dalny. His staff included the Dalny harbourmaster and a liaison officer from Admiral Togo's staff. By mid-July, the Ninth Division had come under command to join the First and Eleventh. In addition, Nogi commanded two independent reserve brigades, each of 9,000 men, a naval brigade and an independent brigade of mixed artillery which included 15-centimetre howitzers. The number of bayonets available to the Third Army exceeded 60,000.

On 26 July, the Japanese Third Army advanced against the well-prepared Russian Green Hills positions, often dominating precipitous slopes, but the line's weakness lay in its length and the railway to the west offering the Japanese an unmistakable outflanking option. After three days of bitter fighting without the benefit of food, drink or sleep, the Japanese breached the line. The Russians, who had fought extremely well, withdrew, many in junks assembled for such a contingency. The Russians suffered 1,000 casualties but Nogi's losses were similar to those of Oku at Nanshan – he lost over 4,000 killed and wounded. Nogi quickly followed-up the Russian withdrawal, forcing the Russian defenders all too easily from the Fenghuangshan or Wolf Hills position. 'Early on the morning of 31 July,' wrote Tretyakov:

> I learnt that our men on Fenghuangshan had hurriedly retreated into the fortress without offering any serious resistance to the enemy. This was extremely unwelcome news, for now we should have to come into direct touch with the enemy round the fortress itself.

However, Nogi met strong resistance at the Orphan Hills, lying just outside the permanent fortifications of Port Arthur and, with his own men exhausted, the Japanese advance lost momentum and came to a halt.

CHAPTER SEVEN

TELISSU

According to the *Royal Navy Signal Book* of 1744: 'Land officers have no pretence to command at sea. Sea officers have no pretence to command on land.' It was not, however, inter-service rivalry which spawned the disastrous conflicts and disagreements between Admiral Alexeiev and General Kuropatkin. The philosophical differences between Kuropatkin's concept of rear defence as opposed to Alexeiev's forward defence were a direct reflection of each individual's attitude and interest. The anti-war Kuropatkin had no wish to take the offensive until he was ready, that is, until the precarious trans-Siberian railway brought him sufficient men and *matériel* with which to assume the offensive. The interests of Alexeiev and his friends at court were intertwined in the Royal Timber Company and their substantial financial commitment throughout Manchuria. Moreover, Alexeiev was the responsible officer for the territory under his control. It was not something his own sense of prestige and importance could easily surrender. As a sailor, he placed undue value upon Port Arthur as the home port of the Pacific Squadron. Kuropatkin was therefore put in an invidious position. 'He was', according to Waters, 'subject to the Viceroy who interfered disastrously more than once.'

The seed of the problem began in the summer of 1903 when, as Minister for War, Kuropatkin was sent by the Tsar to the Far East to review the situation. True to form, the Tsar had attracted to him an entrepreneur with some experience of the east. His name was Captain Alexander Bezobrazov. He gradually inveigled himself into the Tsar's favour by stories of the economic possibilities in the Far East, particularly through timber. Bezobrazov rose to the rank of Secretary of State immediately prior to his unexpected and premature retirement in Switzerland.

In March 1900 Bezobrazov and the Grand Duke Mikhailovitch established the East Asiatic Company with half the shares owned by Nicholas's Cabinet and the remainder divided among the court and trusted colleagues. Sergius Witte, the Finance Minister, saw the nature of this economic club only too clearly as being provocative to Japan. His intervention persuaded the reluctant Nicholas to wind up Bezobrazov's company. Not one to allow sleeping dogs to lie, Bezobrazov then set in motion plans to bring down the Finance Minister in order to safeguard the permanent establishment of his timber concession through the total annexation of Manchuria. Battle lines were drawn up. The opponents to the scheme, 'the mangy triumvirate', were Witte, Lamsdorf and Kuropatkin. Against them were ranged the heavy guns of the Cabinet as well as the support of the Governor of Kwantung, a relatively unknown admiral named Alexeiev. Bezobrazov was to have his way. Instead of withdrawing from Manchuria as provided for by treaty, Manchuria was reinforced without Kuropatkin being consulted, and the Russian Lumber Company of the Far East was formed with much the same financial interest as its short-lived predecessor.

Kuropatkin's Far East tour was to culminate in a conference at Port Arthur between 1 and 10 July. He was en route there from Japan where he had assessed Japanese attitudes at first hand. He reported to the Tsar his misgivings of the timber concession: 'It is no longer possible to present this enterprise as a purely commercial venture, and in the future it will inevitably preserve a great and alarming political importance.' The meeting at Port Arthur concluded that the timber interests should be entirely commercial and the governor, Alexeiev, was ordered by Kuropatkin to withdraw the Russian forces protecting the enterprise on the Yalu. (Alexeiev did not comply with these orders.) Secondly, to maintain Russia's status and dignity in the area, the meeting decided that the post of Viceroy of the Far East should be established. This latter proposal was one of considerable significance since the Viceroy would control military and political activities and be answerable only to the Tsar. Such a man, by his conduct, advice and interpretation would be the arbiter between peace and war. It was this aspect which attracted Kuropatkin to covet the position. He was becoming increasingly disillusioned in St Petersburg and saw in the Viceroy's appointment the possibility of still keeping Russia at peace but in a more friendly and amenable environment.

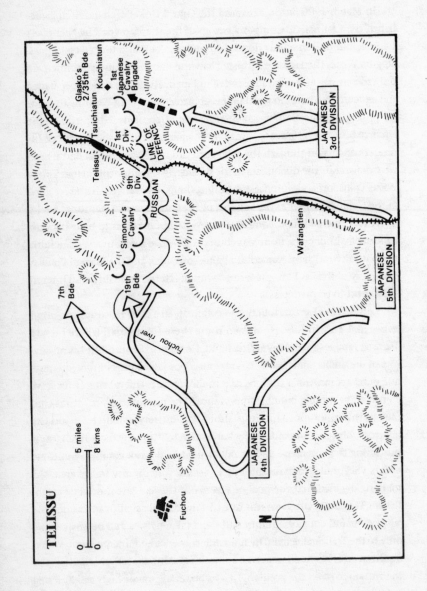

TELISSU

Glasko's 2/35th Bde
Tsuichiatun Kouchiatun
1st Japanese Cavalry Brigade
Telissu
1st Div
9th Div
LINE OF DEFENCE
RUSSIAN
Simonov's Cavalry
19th Bde
7th Bde
Fuchou river
Wafangtien
JAPANESE 3rd DIVISION
JAPANESE 5th DIVISION
JAPANESE 4th DIVISION
Fuchou
N

0   5 miles
0   8 kms

Bezobrazov was sent by the Tsar to accompany Kuropatkin on his Far East visit and to report back secretly in advance any conclusions that the Minister for War might have reached. The agenda had been simple, to find a solution to the Manchurian problem. In his possession Bezobrazov carried a signal indicating the Tsar's agreement to Japan having a free hand in Korea. The signal was never introduced at the meeting. After the conference, those attending went their separate ways. Bezobrazov made his report to the Tsar and on 12 August the Tsar announced the creation of the Viceroyalty and, on Bezobrazov's recommendation, Alexeiev to fill it. The diplomatic and public services were amazed. It was not so much that this was the first occasion a military person had been appointed to a crucial civil office, but rather the view of the quality of the proposed incumbent. On 14 August the dumbfounded Kuropatkin resigned, and two weeks later Witte, who regarded Alexeiev as a buffoon, was removed from power. Bezobrazov had achieved his aim and his associate, Alexeiev, had risen to a position arguably second in importance in Russia only to that of the Tsar. The Russian people were not motivated by such fanatical political and military drive as that which fuelled the Japanese people. To them, it was an unpopular war, fought for the financial benefit of the ruling classes without even the harmonising influence of being contested within the bounds of the homeland. As the weeks gave way to months, with the virtual defeat of the Imperial Russian Navy, after the disasters on the Yalu and at Nanshan, the public feeling against the war and its perpetrators gained momentum. Initially, the ethnic groups of the east, principally Siberians, had been called up to secure the aims of this 'short victorious war'. Now the Europeans in the west, regulars and reservists, were being mobilised and drawn into the vacuum of the Manchurian cauldron. The rumblings of discontent had been fostered by the writing emanating from the navy, the less regional and at grass roots the more truculent of the two services. Supportive cries were to be taken up by peasants and soldiers.

Domestic costs had soared. The economic effects of the military monopoly of the railways were felt in cities and villages alike, particularly since the 1904 harvest had failed. The war became the catalyst to rally and mobilise the grievances of those alien to the Tsar and his regime. Talk of revolution was in the air and now, regularly, a conspiracy of one form or another was uncovered. It had become a matter of considerable political importance for some sign of military success to assuage the gathering destructive forces.

Public opinion had developed as a relatively new force in Russia and this was an emboldened public which viewed retreat as a disgrace and the abandonment of Port Arthur as unacceptable. The national focus was upon Manchuria where it appeared that a force of 45,000 and the navy had been sealed up in Port Arthur while a greater force at Liaoyang had been beset by immobile indifference. The messages from the court and the press in St Petersburg to Alexeiev to do something were loud, clear and persistent.

General Kuropatkin, reactive rather than active, had still not formed a clear impression of enemy dispositions and intentions. The First Japanese Army had forced the Yalu, heading north-west towards Liaoyang. The Second Japanese Army had landed at Pitzuwo, seizing Nanshan and Dalny. The Tenth Division, the nucleus of the as yet unidentified Fourth Japanese Army, was known to have landed at Takushan while a Third Japanese Army was still held back in Japan for the assault on Port Arthur. 'It was incumbent on us, therefore', wrote Kuropatkin, 'to exercise great caution, and to keep our forces as far as possible concentrated, so as to be ready to meet the attack of two or even three armies.' So slow had been his reinforcement through the pedestrian railway system which in early May had risen to three trains a day each achieving less than six miles an hour, that Kuropatkin seriously considered withdrawing completely from Liaoyang to Harbin. The political facts of life, however, required him to go forward. The reasons were summarised in the newspaper *Viedomosti*: 'Out of loyalty to Port Arthur's garrison and to the navy but more important, to deprive Japan of the moral advantage to be gained by the capture of Port Arthur.' But then, it was not generally thought that there was any prospect of Port Arthur being lost. The *Novoe Vremya* expressed the opinion: 'Port Arthur, according to the conviction of the best authorities, is not merely a first class fortress, but the most impregnable of all first class fortresses'.

Witte had despised Alexeiev as not being an army man and the fact that he could not ride a horse appeared the ultimate damnation. It was Alexeiev's Chief-of-Staff, General Jalinski, who translated his chief's dogmatism and inflexibility into a modicum of military logic. Having been given the aim of going forward, he determined for Kuropatkin two courses of action: either to contain the Second Japanese Army and attack the First and Fourth Japanese Armies in the direction of the Yalu, or to take up the offensive against the Second Army to the north of Port Arthur while blocking General Kuroki. As in most good military appreciations of the situation, it was to be the last course that was to be adopted, but not without a howl of justifiable protest from Kuropatkin.

Those to whom the military staff system is foreign will be unaware of what is colloquially known as 'situating the appreciation'. This, simply, is a guise for the illusion of choice. The desired course is contrasted with such glaringly unsuitable options that the initiator's wishes are embraced, yet all the time having given the hint of an array of possibilities. The Yalu course of action was so weak that it was intended to be rejected while pretending that Kuropatkin, as land commander, did have a choice.

In Kuropatkin's view such an attack from the direction of Liaoyang would have left the Russian right flank exposed as well as its rear from a possible landing of the as yet unlocated Third Army. (Russia regarded the landing of the Third Army at Yingkou as probable.) Having allocated troops for flank and rear protection, only sixty or seventy of the ninety-four battalions which constituted the army in mid-May would have been available. The railways did not run towards the Yalu. Therefore, with all local food resources exhausted, supplies entering Liaoyang would need to be transshipped by road. The transport bill for supplies for sixty or seventy battalions was massive; so much so that resources only existed to carry up to a maximum of four days' supplies. This gave the force a two-day radius of action. The Japanese intelligence would doubtless have been aware of this factor. Possessing pack transport and mountain artillery, which the Russians did not, they could have withdrawn in contact until the Russians reached the limit of their advance and then assumed the offensive. Given the superior Japanese mobility and the impending arrival of the rainy season, this course added up to what Kuropatkin described as 'impracticable'.

The Port Arthur option was much more involved and convoluted. The limitations imposed on Kuropatkin by Alexeiev included the employment of a force to block the passes through the Fenshuiling mountain range to the First Japanese Army as well as placing a reserve at Haicheng. Once the troops had been allocated to tasks, the residue was one corps of twenty-four battalions available for operations against Port Arthur. Kuropatkin was to write in his book, *The Russian Army and the Japanese War*:

> In view of the possibility of Kuroki taking the offensive in superior force (after reinforcement by the troops already beginning to land at Takushan) against our cordon, which extended along the Fenshuiling range for more than sixty-six miles, and in view

of the possibility of the Japanese cutting off any detachment
moving on Port Arthur by landing somewhere in its rear, the
despatch of this corps 130 miles to the south could not but be
considered a most risky and difficult operation.

Despite his justifiable pessimism it was clear that only an operation in
the direction of Port Arthur would relieve that city. The danger was that in
allocating the resources to achieve that aim, the signal would be given for
the First Japanese Army to advance and for the Third Japanese Army to land
at some strategically significant point, so, in relieving Port Arthur the prospects
of defeat in detail for Kuropatkin loomed larger than life. He was implacably opposed to this military nonsense and set about having the orders to
advance rescinded.

Cautious and ponderous, Kuropatkin lacked the flair and bravado of a
Wellington or Napoleon but he did share the latter's view of the value of a
fortress. While Napoleon did not regard fortresses as impregnable, he did
see them as a means with which to 'retard, weaken and annoy an enemy'.
It was certainly not Kodama's wish to be diverted from his principal aim of
destroying the Russian forces at Liaoyang. He was to be overruled by the
same pressures that were being brought to bear upon Kuropatkin to save the
fort – prestige. Neither general wished to split his forces and neither was
to be permitted the option. Kodama was to allocate to Nogi, who had seized
Port Arthur in 1894 with one regiment, initially the First and Eleventh Divisions for the task. In the event, he would need four divisions. Despite the
misgivings of the generals, it was sound strategy for Japan to besiege Port
Arthur. On the debit side was the fact that Nogi's army was not available for
the battle at Liaoyang. More important, however, was the influence of the
siege upon the Russians. Kuropatkin was prevented from withdrawing progressively northward along his line of communications and this guaranteed
that he would be brought into early action against his wishes. On 11 May,
Kuropatkin told the chiefs of foreign missions dining with him 'that he had
been opposed to the war, had said so to the Emperor at a council meeting,
had declared it would last one year and a half and cost not less than eighty five
millions sterling; Russia he had said, was not prepared for war'.

Kuropatkin's original intention, having effectively manned and victualled Port Arthur, was to allow it to ride out the storm. He had not counted
upon the effect of General Stoessel upon the Viceroy. Stoessel, a veteran of the
Russo-Turkish War and the Boxer Rebellion, was Governor of Kwantung

province, an area which he had effectively abandoned over a forty-eight-hour period of gross incompetence. He exercised a disturbed and disturbing influence over Port Arthur, an area for which he was not the authorised commander. However, he outranked the pliant but aggrieved commandant, General Smirnov. 'You will remain commandant,' he declared, 'but I shall run the fortress. Whether legal or not, it is my affair. I will answer for that.' He terrorised his soldiers and caused serious divisions between the navy, whom he collectively loathed, and the army. The fortress had been provisioned to sustain twelve battalions for twelve months. With an establishment now of twenty-seven battalions inflated by the refugees from Dalny, it could not hold out for more than six months. A few enterprising sea captains were still beating the Japanese blockade, arriving in Port Arthur with much needed provisions, to be turned back by Stoessel. Only the direct intervention of Smirnov persuaded Stoessel to accept the tinned milk offered by a French sea captain who was ordered never to return. Stoessel was a man imbued by his own sense of self-importance, a hero, a man of destiny, regarded by many as a dangerous lunatic. Kuropatkin ordered him to leave Port Arthur on a blockade-beating destroyer. His refusal was one more charge to be raised at his court martial.

On 23 May, General Jalinski arrived at General Kuropatkin's headquarters situated in a railway carriage at Liaoyang. He had brought with him the Viceroy's Yalu or Port Arthur options. The Viceroy was becoming increasingly agitated by the regular defeatist reports of Stoessel. Stung by the loss of Nanshan the previous day, Kuropatkin departed by special train to Mukden on 27 May to discuss the Viceroy's plans. He arrived at 5 p.m. and, after what the St Petersburg correspondent of the *Echo de Paris* described as 'a violent discussion', left by train at 10 p.m. In describing the relationship between Alexeiev and Kuropatkin, the London *Times* had hit the nail on the head when it reported: 'The point of view of the two men is not the same; the difference is profound, and the effect is likely to be disastrous.'

Both men saw that there was no room for compromise in their diametrically opposed positions. Alexeiev proposed, therefore, to put both cases before the Tsar for adjudication. Each commander filed his own report to St Petersburg. Alexeiev's case had a strong naval bias, pointing out the need to save Port Arthur as a base for the fleet. He drew particular attention to the effect the fall of the fort would have on Russia's morale and prestige in the world. Kuropatkin consistently maintained the view that a move southward would leave his rear and flanks exposed to intervention by the First and Fourth Japanese Armies. He stressed the importance of building up his army's strength at Liaoyang. Port Arthur had no tactical significance, he said, and should therefore defend itself. Lord Salisbury had expressed his agreement with that sentiment in 1898: 'I think Russia has made a great mistake in taking Port Arthur; I do not think it is of any use to her whatever.' When Russia's foremost military strategist, General Dragomirov, was consulted by the advisory councils in St Petersburg, he advised that both the army and the navy should abandon Port Arthur.

The Tsar convened a council of war – an unusual step for the Autocrat of All the Russias. He called for General Sakharov, Minister for War, Admiral Avellan, Minister of Marine, and Plehve, Minister of the Interior. The navy, the aristocratic service and darling of the court, was to have its way. Yet nagging illogicalities existed. Witgeft was being pressed by Alexeiev and the Tsar to take the Far East fleet to Vladivostok, seemingly because they did recognise ships and fortifications to be a contradiction in terms. In addition, an acute shortage of coal had developed at Port Arthur. None the less, Port Arthur was to be held, 'as the Baltic Fleet would not know where to go if Port Arthur were to fall'. A further trump card was the aspect of prestige. The council accordingly advised that General Kuropatkin should be instructed to attempt the relief of Port Arthur. A message reportedly from the Tsar to Kuropatkin informed him reluctantly to acquiesce: 'The time is ripe for the Manchurian army to assume the offensive.' Politically ripe perhaps, but militarily there was no prospect for success, just the inevitability of disaster.

Up until early June, activities away from the Kwantung Peninsula had been notably quiet as both sides strengthened their positions. The most extraordinary aspect of the campaign to date had been the similarities of the Japanese strategy of 1894 and 1904 but, more surprisingly, the reaction of the Russians to that strategy mirroring, in effect, the action of the Chinese before them. They had not learned from the lessons of history. First they permitted their fleet to be neutralised, as had the Chinese. Pyongyang had been occupied in the same manner, as had the Russian defeat on the Yalu been influenced by the same ruses and the same attack across the Ai. The landing at Pitzuwo in 1904 was in almost the same place as the landing which had taken place in 1894, since records of that time annotate the spot as being the only suitable landing area. The Second Army had advanced to Nanshan, fought the Chinese there and had moved on to take what was then a less attractive Dalny, but none the less replete in logistics and *matériel*. From there they seized Port Arthur before turning north to come alongside the First Army waiting above the Yalu for a joint operation to the north, ostensibly towards Mukden.

Now, at the beginning of June 1904, confronting General Kuroki's First Army were Lieutenant General Keller supported by Major General Rennenkampf with 23,000 infantry, 3,600 cavalry and ninety guns. Against General Oku's Second Army was the bulk of the First Siberian Corps under Lieutenant General Stakelberg with a dispersed force of 30,000 infantry, 3,000 cavalry and 100 guns. In the centre, confronting General Nozu's Tenth Japanese Division, was Major General Mischenko's reinforced Cossack Brigade. To the rear, at Liaoyang, and including those regiments at Mukden, was General Kuropatkin with his growing reserve of 36,000 infantry, 6,000 cavalry and 120 guns. The European Thirty-first Division had arrived but en route and still awaited were the remainder of Tenth Army Corps and two cavalry divisions. So complete was the Japanese strategic domination that the Russians, like the Chinese before them, were forced to counter the Japanese options by guarding everything and being weak everywhere. To guard against a threat to Vladivostok was a garrison force of 23,000 troops who could have been well used in the forthcoming push to the south.

Russia's strategic lifeline, the railway, was also hugely manpower intensive. Any threat to the railway was a direct threat to the Russian ability to continue with the war. This fact served to maintain General Kuropatkin in a continuous state of nervous energy; 55,000 men were deployed to defend the line between the Ural Mountains and the Manchurian frontier. Within Manchuria, a force of 25,000 men was assigned to protect the railway. Every bridge had a guard. Japanese agents directed the Hunhutze brigands against targets on the railway. The Chinese division posted in the area to control these outlaws had little effect, and in one month ninety attempts to disrupt the railway had occurred between Mukden and Tiehling.

On his way south, following his testy meeting with Alexeiev, Kuropatkin stopped at Haicheng to visit the headquarters of Lieutenant General Stakelberg, the commander of the First Siberian Corps. He, like the Viceroy and Kuropatkin, had his headquarters in a railway carriage – not a reassuring omen. There he gave verbal orders which at best could not have been more than half-hearted, as can be supposed from the written orders issued to Stakelberg on 7 June:

Your Excellency's Army Corps is detailed with the object of
drawing upon itself the greatest possible number of the
enemy's forces and thereby weakening his army operating in
the Kwantung Peninsula. Your advance, therefore, against the
enemy's covering troops must be rapid and energetic, in the
hope of crushing his advanced detachments should they prove
to be weak in numbers. In the event of your encountering superior strength decisive action will be avoided and in no case will
you allow the whole of your reserves to become engaged until
the conditions are entirely clear. The object of our southerly
movement is the capture of the Chinchou (Nanshan) position,
and thereafter an advance on Port Arthur.

Again, Russian intelligence was shown to be woefully lax. Two days
earlier, on the 5th, General Baron Nogi had arrived north of Port Arthur to
assume command of the Third Japanese Army comprising the First and
Eleventh Divisions. Securely entrenched between Pulantien and Pitzuwo
were the Third, Fourth and Fifth Divisions of General Oku's restructured
Second Army. (The Sixth Division was also a constituent part of the Second
Army but only one battalion had arrived in time to fight at Telissu.) Thus,
in the general area where a few weeks earlier a Russian regiment had held at
bay three Japanese divisions there were now no less than five Japanese divisions upon whom a weakened corps was about to be launched.

Unable to restrain their enthusiasm for the forthcoming offensive towards
Port Arthur, the Russians in St Petersburg had prejudiced security. General
Oku first heard rumours of the proposed advance on 29 May. He was not,
however, in a position to achieve a great deal since demands elsewhere on
shipping and transport meant that he did not have the logistical wherewithal
with which to advance. On 30 May he sent forward the First Cavalry Brigade
commanded by Major General Akiyama to reconnoitre to the north of
Wafangtien in the area of Telissu.

The ultimate aim of the Japanese strategic manoeuvre was to bring
together three armies, in superior numbers, at a given point to confront and
beat the Manchurian army. The Japanese target, therefore, was Liaoyang. The
physical nature of the country made the advance of these armies reasonably
predictable once their presence had been determined. It was, however, the
nature of the country and its climate which imposed real difficulties on both
sides. The advance by the Japanese was barred by two high mountain ranges,

the Hsiungyaoshan and the Fenshuiling. From here, the northern spurs of
these ranges separated the eastern Russian force from their compatriots in
the south-west. Similarly, the Japanese found the prospect of concerted effort
frustrated by the southern spurs descending from peaks in excess of 3,000
feet. To the east, the Japanese First and Fourth Armies had the prospect of
an advance through wooded, precipitous mountains dominated by the
Motien and Fenshui Passes, both in Russian hands. General Oku did not
have such a daunting task. Although the terrain he would have to follow
was not ideally suited to all arms co-operation, it none the less provided a
fifteen-mile strip running north–south between sea and mountains identified in the centre by the Russian army's vertebrae, the railway.

On 30 May, Akiyama's cavalry and a Russian cavalry brigade under Major
General Samsonov converged upon Telissu. For the next few days, while progressively being reinforced, each side tested the other by daily reconnaissance
and skirmishing. This phase witnessed the only evidence during the campaign of the utilisation of cavalry shock action. On this occasion, the Second
Squadron of the Thirteenth Japanese Cavalry Regiment was charged in its
left flank by two squadrons of the Eighth Siberian Cossacks who reportedly
used their lances to good effect. While Japanese casualties were not heavy,
this bruising of Japanese ego was to determine for the Japanese Cavalry
Brigade a position on the right of the line, in the mountains where they
could be employed only in their dismounted role. By 3 June, General Akiyama
had reported the advanced elements of the First Siberian Army Corps at
Telissu. His brigade was then withdrawn. The appearance of mountain artillery
in the field revealed the build-up of Japanese forces to General Samsonov.
(Ten years later would see Samsonov and Rennenkampf as army commanders in General Jalinski's North West Army Group. To all three fell the disgrace
and stigma of the defeat by the Germans at Tannenberg. That conflict of
August 1914 was an extension and final postscript to the Russian stupidity and
disasters evident in 1904–5. Samsonov, depressed by his own abysmal performance which had seen 370,000 men defeated, racked by asthma, and
hiding from the Germans, used his own revolver to end his life.)

On 5 June, General Stakelberg arrived at Telissu, the same day as the
main body of the First Siberian Corps detrained. As he began his personal
four-day reconnaissance he ordered General Samsonov to occupy a fortified
position five miles to the south. Stakelberg's strategy was to leapfrog towards
Port Arthur from one defended position to another. On 6 June, General Oku

received reports of the advance of the Russian cavalry. Since this appeared to be the first move of the force assigned to relieve Port Arthur, Imperial Japanese Headquarters ordered its forces elsewhere to step up active operations in order to weaken Stakelberg's force by threatening his communications.

As early as 2 June the First and Fourth Armies had been put on what might euphemistically be called the 'offensive'. The First Army was not ready to go forward but none the less attacked Russian outposts on the Liaoyang road. The build-up of the Tenth Division at Takushan was by no means complete but General Kawamura, intending to capture Hsiuyen, persuaded General Kuroki to put under his command a Guards brigade group. Japanese misinformation released news of the advance of the reinforced Tenth Division two days before it actually occurred. Hearing of the 'advance' on 5 June, General Mischenko withdrew and informed General Kuropatkin. On 6 June the Japanese advance began and, after attacking Mischenko's cavalry, they occupied their limited objective of Hsiuyen on 8 June. Concurrently, on 7 and 8 June, a torpedo and gunboat squadron bombarded the Kaiping coast, effectively requiring the Ninth East Siberian Rifle Division to be detained there rather than accompany Stakelberg's Corps on his drive to the south.

On 9 June Japanese reconnaissance of the gathering Russians assessed their strength to be in excess of two divisions supported by three or four cavalry regiments. It is probable that General Kuropatkin was unaware of the landing of the Eleventh Japanese Division near Pitzuwo and, in the absence of intelligence to the contrary, assumed the aim of the Second Japanese Army to be to attack Port Arthur. He envisaged Stakelberg's initial contact to be with the Second Army's rearguard in the region of Pulantien. It was a relieved Commander-in-Chief who heard of the digging-in of the Tenth Division at Hsiuyen and the withdrawal of the gunboats. This relief was reflected in his decision to allow the corps commander to concentrate his command at Telissu. Part of the Ninth East Siberian Rifle Division was released and travelled eastward from Kaiping for Telissu with Stakelberg who arrived there at 1 p.m. on 13 June. On entering his headquarters he received a cavalry report that an estimated 20,000 Japanese were moving north from Pulantien. Stakelberg thought the report to be wildly exaggerated and assumed this to be but a reconnaissance in force. He was sufficiently concerned to ask for the balance of the Ninth East Siberian Rifle Division plus the available reserves. Kuropatkin was co-operative and although some troops arrived in time for the battle others merely arrived in time to complicate the corp's retreat.

The cavalry who had sent the news to Stakelberg had comprised three Cossack squadrons and scouts. On the night of 12 June they were despatched to break through the supposed covering force's outposts at Pulantien. That was the day that Oku's supplies had arrived. On 13 June the advance of the Second Army began, the first of the converging strategic movements which were to conclude with the battle of Liaoyang. The Cossacks withdrew at speed to report what they had seen to their sceptical commander. Stakelberg wisely abandoned his offensive and awaited the Japanese attack on his prepared position to the south of Telissu.

By dusk on 13 June the Japanese had reached to within six miles of Wafangtien. On 14 June they advanced on the Russian trenches some fourteen miles away.

The village of Fuchou lies twenty miles as the crow flies from Telissu. It is the largest settlement in the immediate area and nestles in the Fuchou valley. While the river is wide, it is only during very heavy rain that anything more than a shallow thread of water is in evidence on the broad sandy bed. On either side of the river is a wide expanse of flat, alluvial cultivated soil where *kaoliang* and Indian corn grows. Here and there are thick clumps of willow and poplar trees. The low hills on either side of the valley sport copses of stunted oak, wild cherry, plum, pear and some small trees and scrub. There are many Chinese villages and smallholdings in evidence in the valley, tucked away under arboreal shade and enclosed by stone walls. Heading upstream in the direction of Telissu the ground rises steeply to higher hills to a maximum of 1,500 feet. At this point, the river is 150 yards wide and fordable. The railway, running north–south, crosses the river for the first time at Telissu where, joining the road, it passes up a defile beyond Telissu. On either side of the defile rise steep and bare peaks.

General Stakelberg deployed his troops astride the railway to the immediate south of Telissu. To the west of the railway lay the representative brigade of the under-strength Ninth East Siberian Rifle Division and five battalions and two batteries. East of the railway, with the bulk of the force, was the First East Siberian Rifle Division of twelve battalions and four batteries. Lieutenant General Simonov had arrived to command the nineteen cavalry squadrons previously under Samsonov and took up the right of the Russian line. Two regiments of the Ninth East Siberian Rifle Division and a regiment of the Third Siberian Infantry Division were still to arrive by rail. The Japanese had the exact details of the Russian deployment. Oku directed the Third and Fifth

Divisions to a frontal attack, the railway being the divisional boundary, while the Fourth Division was sent on a sweep to come up the Fuchou valley from the west to turn the Russian right. To summarise: in the east, the Russians deployed a division supported by four batteries and the Japanese one division and a cavalry brigade. In the west, the Russians had a brigade with two batteries, and nineteen cavalry squadrons against two Japanese divisions.

The skirmishing on 13 June between the two armies had been of little consequence but already the early summer heat was affecting the troops. Since Nanshan, the Japanese had begun to change from their blue serge to khaki drill uniforms. Ivan had discarded his overcoat and astrakhan cap in favour of a cotton blouse and forage cap. His felt under-boots were replaced by the soft, long, leather boot worn by infantry and cavalry alike. They had perspired pints to prepare their position. While they may have been grateful for the assistance of the impressed coolie force with the digging, there was nothing subtle about it. Top soil clearly delineated the line of defence on the forward slopes which was closely followed by insignificant strands of barbed wire. The line of defences ran for eight and a half miles. The rough shelter trenches were approximately nine inches deep with fifteen inches of parapet. Riflemen crouched shoulder to shoulder without overhead cover to await an enemy whose favour of shrapnel should by now have been indelibly imprinted in the minds of the Russian military hierarchy. Below them the valley afforded the attacker good covered approaches and provided the Russians with poor fields of fire. To the south, a screen of higher hills hid the approach of the Japanese whose movement and shelter in the ravines and valleys frustrated the efforts of the Russian artillery.

This was to be a battle won and lost by artillery. When on 13 June Stakelberg saw the deployment of his artillery, he remonstrated with the gunners that they should fire from covered positions. Gunners are not noticeably receptive to being told how to use their guns. The more senior officers insisted that guns could be fired only at stationary targets from covered positions. The junior gunner officers complained of this folly to their superiors, yet they were rebuffed and orders were issued for direct laying. The new Russian quick-firing gun appeared in this battle for the first time but its effect was largely wasted for want of time for crew training. In fact the Russians had only had these guns for four months and, as one observer commented: 'in many, if not most, cases, had not carried out any practice with them; the supply of ammunition was no doubt a factor'.

On the morning of 14 June the three Japanese divisions advanced. The Third and Fifth Divisions kept contact as they moved on either side of the railway embankment while the Fourth Division moved off to the north-west in preparation for its left hook on the Russian right of the line. The Sixth Division had begun to land and was ordered to send its advance elements forward in order to reinforce Oku's reserve which on the day of the main battle comprised only two battalions. The Japanese move had been rapid and had caught the Russians by surprise for they had not had time to lay telephone lines, needing to rely throughout the battle on runners. Gradually the Russian screens were swept before the Japanese advance until at 2 p.m. the first Russian gun opened up on the Japanese from the centre of their position. The Japanese replied, using only the guns of the Third Division, teasing out the Russian artillery so that by 3 p.m., with the artillery duel at its peak, they knew the position of every Russian artillery piece. During this period, a reassessment of the Russian strength was put at just under three divisions. Oku knew that the Russians were being reinforced through the railway which prompted him to attack without delay. The Russian strength was 27,000 rifles, 2,500 sabres and ninety-eight guns. Reinforcements arriving the next day, the 15th, increased these totals by 3,000 rifles and two guns. The Japanese strength totalled 36,000 rifles, 2,000 sabres and 216 guns.

Concurrent with the artillery duel, a probing attack was launched by the Thirty-fourth Japanese Regiment on the left of the Russian line. The First and Second East Siberian Regiments consolidated to see off the Japanese attack but not without heavy casualties to the Second Regiment. By midday, the Fourth Division had arrived at its start line on the left bank of the Fuchou River. Having picqueted the high ground across the river it settled down for the night. The GOC of the Japanese Fourth Division, Lieutenant General Baron Ogawa, reflected upon his orders which arrived at 5 a.m. on 15 June from Oku:

> As no danger is to be anticipated from the direction of the
> valley of the Fuchou river, you will detach a force of at least one
> brigade of infantry which will attack the enemy's right flank and
> help the advance of the other divisions.

Ogawa had cleared the town of Fuchou of its outposts. The Russians had been unable to use their heliograph to warn Stakelberg of this threat due to the seasonal fog.

The relationship between Stakelberg and Samsonov was not good, prin-cipally because Stakelberg had no confidence in the ability of Samsonov's predominantly Cossack cavalry. During the course of a tour of the future battlefield, a British observer pointed out its vulnerability to being turned on its right flank. Stakelberg replied: 'I have a (cavalry) squadron or so near Fuchou, but, if three Japanese squadrons advance, mine will retire without finding out the Japanese strength.'

During the night of 14 June, Samsonov's cavalry had detected the Japan-ese advance on Stakelberg's right flank and the first note to that effect was sent to Stakelberg's Chief-of-Staff. The British observer who had earlier been in the company of Stakelberg happened to be present when the note arrived. The Chief-of-Staff told him that it was a report from Samsonov telling of Japanese moves against the Russian right flank. 'I remarked', wrote the observer, 'that his Chief had mentioned the possibility to me and would be glad to hear the news. My companion replied that Samsonov's cavalry was useless, and that he did not intend to worry Stakelberg about the message.' The turning of the right flank at Telissu proved to be the deciding factor in the Russian defeat.

Oku established his headquarters at Wafangtien where he had arrived at 3.30 p.m. By 11 p.m. he had decided to launch his main attack of two divisions upon the Russian left and centre up the line of the railway at dawn on the 15th. While the Russian attention was concentrated on their left, the Fifth Division supported by elements of the Fourth would turn their right flank.

Stakelberg was unaware of the fact that a Japanese division was sitting to the west of the railway, poised to attack. The main activity had been the probing attack on his left by the Third Division which had led him to believe that this was where the main force was located. He ordered Major General Glasko, commanding his reserve brigade of infantry, to move from the centre to the already heavily weighted left flank. Glasko arrived at 6 p.m. and placed himself under the orders of Major General Gerngross, commanding the First Division. Three-quarters of the Russian force was in the east, there was no reserve available to assist in the west until the anticipated reinforcements arrived by rail that night. Stakelberg, like Oku, had determined to execute a dawn attack on the 15th by means of a counter-stroke.

A counter-stroke, unlike a counter-attack, is aimed generally at the destruc-tion of enemy forces rather than the seizure of terrain. The enemy advance is blocked by a strong defensive line while the enemy is hit by a formation from the flank, like a hammer hitting an object held in the grip of the jaws of a vice. It is the crème de la crème of the tactical art because it is a most difficult manoeuvre to achieve. History underlines that successful counter-strokes have rarely been premeditated but have depended on opportunism, the flair and élan of the commanding general and, frequently, the arrival of fresh troops on the field. Some of the factors upon which success depends are training, communications, co-operation, security, surprise and timing. The crucial importance of surprise and timing tend to indicate that a counter-stroke is unlikely to succeed against a quality enemy when it exists as a formal element of a larger operational plan.

General Stakelberg did not issue an operational order for the counter-stroke but sent the various commanders separate memoranda. One did not know what the other was to do. The memoranda established that the operation was to begin between 1 and 2 a.m. on 15 June, but in any event before daybreak. The exact timing was left to the mutual agreement of Gerngross and Glasko who had under their command for this operation sixteen battalions, or half the available infantry.

During the night, while orders were being passed down the chain of command, troops on either side did not achieve much sleep. The Russians in their trenches peered into the darkness, the gathering mist in the valley before them rising to erase the silhouette of the hills beyond the ravine. The opportunity for a hot samovar brew, the much-favoured puff on the papyrus that passed as a cigarette, was reserved for those with the baggage train. For those in the trenches it was black bread, brought up by CQMSs at dusk, and water, as much to dampen throats drying from nervous tension as to slake their thirst. The noise of Japanese preparations drifted across to them as the opposing guns were being dug into covered positions. The adrenalin was flowing along the Russian line that night. At 2 a.m. shots were fired from the Russian position into the night to be joined by a nervous fusillade along the whole line. The Japanese had begun to close on the Russians from midnight. Once the officers had restored order, the night passed quietly until daybreak at 4 a.m. revealed the field of battle, blanketed by the morning mist.

General Gerngross had decided to launch the counter-stroke at 4 a.m. He informed General Stakelberg of his decision and awaited his commander's approval. Since he did not request approval, none was forthcoming and he did nothing. Glasko had sent a runner to Gerngross for his orders but, having failed to obtain any, turned to Stakelberg who refused to intervene. By now it was 6.40 a.m. and Glasko, after discussing the situation with his staff, decided to take the matter into his own hands and attack. At this moment, orders arrived from Gerngross confirming the attack which he had already set in motion with a promise of support. As the troops set off to attack, an orderly arrived with new orders for Glasko from Stakelberg:

> If the Japanese advance with superior force against our centre
> or in any other direction, the Corps will fall back slowly to
> Wauchialing. In this case, Major General Glasko will hold the
> line Kouchiatun–Tsuichiatun as long as possible, in order to give
> the troops falling back by Telissu time to traverse the defile
> north of Tsuichiatun. Should the Japanese retire, the troops will
> halt, and await further order.

Seldom can a commander about to launch a confident attack have been so deflated by orders which indicated that his superior officer was anticipating not a glorious victory but the by now routine defeat.

There had been no reference to his attack and the highly confused Glasko called back his troops and occupied the Kouchiatun–Tsuichiatun line. Meanwhile, Gerngross, not having been privy to Glasko's orders and therefore still dependent upon his support, moved to attack after 7 a.m. Gerngross's force of three infantry regiments advanced over a front of 1,500 yards in three echelons. Although this deployment meant only a third of the force was able to bring fire to bear at any one time, it did achieve a shock effect upon the Third Japanese Division now confined to their shelter trenches. General Glasko was again ordered forward and, despite poor Russian artillery support, the situation on the Japanese right was becoming serious.

Hearing this news, General Ueda, commanding the Fifth Division, determined that resolute action was required. His guns had crossed the river at 7 a.m. and immediately Simonov's cavalry was attacked. Believing he was required to fight only a delaying action, the cavalry commander withdrew his force to the north-west, thereby exposing the right flank of the Russian infantry. The success of the Fifth Division was reinforced by the arrival of the Fourth Japanese Division who combined to flow around the thinly held western Russian outposts, gradually eroding the defences until they were overwhelmed. The Japanese guns were always well forward. They effectively harassed any attempt to reinforce and turned their attention upon their enemy's gun teams so that thirteen guns could not be evacuated.

At 11 a.m. Stakelberg received a disturbing message which had originated from his cavalry at 6 a.m. to the effect that a strong force of Japanese was advancing from the south-west on Telissu. At that moment, Stakelberg had a reserve of two battalions and a further two detraining at Telissu station. Stakelberg could not be faulted for his bravery. Immaculate in his white uniform, he personally gathered his four battalions and launched into the forward elements threatening his right flank. It was too late, the enemy was too strong. Having had two horses shot from under him, Stakelberg issued orders to retreat at 11.30 a.m.

The courage being displayed to the west of the railway line was also matched in the east. The Russians had improved their firepower by bringing three infantry regiments into line. The winning influence of the Japanese artillery was nullified largely by the nature of the ground and the divisional commander's ability to reinforce along the whole of his line. So furious was the confrontation that at one point, where the lines converged, the opponents having run out of ammunition hurled rocks at one another. General Oku sent half his reserve to assist – one battalion.

Glasko's advance had been delayed by difficulties experienced in moving his supporting artillery over the difficult terrain. His orders were to advance against the Japanese right flank and to support Gerngross's First East Siberian Rifle Division. For much of that morning, General Gerngross's attention had been held by the developing threat to the west of the railway. Gradually, as his own right became exposed his artillery was eliminated. His right flank regiment was subjected to the heavy enfilade rifle and artillery fire of the Fifth Division and suffered heavy casualties. Glasko had failed to arrive and Gerngross, on his own initiative, at midday ordered his division to withdraw. This order coincided with Glasko's delayed advance which fell upon the First Japanese Cavalry Brigade to the right of the Third Division. The force was well supported by the Russian gunners but the withdrawal of Gerngross made its position untenable and it too withdrew.

With the prospect of the first reinforcements due just after 2 p.m., Oku released his last reserve battalion to join the Third Division as they pressed home their advantage. Four batteries were passed through the railway gap at 2 p.m. to take position on the feature known as Lungwangmiao situated astride the former Russian line of defence. Here they found thirteen abandoned Russian guns. Below them, heading north up the Telissu defile, were the four regiments of the First East Siberian Rifle Division. Loaded with shrapnel, these guns took terrible revenge. In the east and the west, a contraction of the Russian lines towards the centre had begun.

Stakelberg personally directed the withdrawal from the west but it was in the defile at Telissu that he risked losing the bulk of his corps. The rearguard of the Ninth East Siberian Rifle Division gallantly held the heights west of the Telissu railway station so that the wounded might be evacuated. At 2 p.m. the insistent whistling of a steam locomotive announced the arrival at the sidings one and a half miles from the station of the two remaining battalions of the Ninth East Siberian Infantry Regiment from Kaiping. Shells exploded around them as they detrained, formed ranks and were ordered hurriedly to deal with a threatened Japanese encirclement aimed at cutting the railway two miles to their rear. The Transport Corps had blocked the route at Panlashan and exit through the defile to the north was impossible. The First East Siberian Division, continuing to be cut down by the relentless Japanese artillery, spilled over into the mountains in the east where for a number of days they would be hunted, killed or captured. By 3 p.m. disaster stared Stakelberg in the face.

Then occurred a torrential rainstorm. Visibility fell to almost zero and the condition of the roads following the heavy Russian usage precluded a pursuit of troops already tired and short of ammunition. Covered by his cavalry, Stakelberg withdrew to Kaiping.

A study of the battle is replete with reasons for the Russian disaster. Their soldiers, as stoically brave as ever, had fought as gallantly as before. Those wounded interviewed by a correspondent of the *Russkoe Slovo* in the hospital at Liaoyang did not mention any suspicion that their methods were outdated or their generals increasingly fallible and suspect. 'Their only grievance was that our inferiority in artillery had made the day go against them.'

It is strange that Stakelberg should have selected this salient, divided as it was by the Fuchou River. His best prospect of success would appear to have been to concentrate on one bank of the river. Then, he might have avoided being turned on both flanks and exposed to fire from all directions. The failure to inform Stakelberg of the build-up of Japanese forces on his right flank proved to be a fatal error of judgement. One observer played down the effective Japanese gunnery by saying, 'In the position taken up by General Stakelberg round shot or Greek fire would have been almost as damaging.'

The Russian attempt to relieve Port Arthur had been nipped in the bud. Telissu was an important battle for it was the first to be fought virtually in the open. The Russian strength had been less than the Japanese but, given their choice of ground and being on the defensive, they should have had more than enough to see off the Japanese. The Japanese losses, killed, wounded and missing were 1,137 while the Russian losses were over three times that figure. Japanese confidence and their feeling of invincibility continued to gain momentum. The most prophetic comment on this battle is appropriately left to General Hamilton, the Indian Army's senior observer and Churchill's future protégé at Gallipoli, who said of Kuropatkin: 'When a gross palpable blunder in elementary strategy is made by a general of repute, it should not be necessary nowadays to seek for the statesman who is usually quite apparent.'

St Petersburg digested the bad news with dismay, yet government and people were becoming immune to the shock emanating from disasters both at home and abroad. Despite his best intentions Kuropatkin's strategy reverted to the defensive.

In the *Revue Militaire Générale,* General Langlois identified certain principles of war which had been emphasised in this conflict. One was the superiority of the offensive over the defensive. Writing in 1924, General Sir Horace Smith-Dorrien, who had based much of his training on the lessons arising from this war, said:

> Were I asked what particular principle stood out beyond others
> as proved to the hilt in that war, I should say it was the marked
> advantage of the offensive. The force taking the offensive
> makes its own plans and follows them, whereas the one on the
> defensive is in a chronic state of anxiety and has to conform to
> the movement of the adversary. Kuropatkin lived in a fog.

Hamley's *Operations of War* was very precise on this point: 'Victory can only be won by striking.' It is relevant to note, however, that the strategist Clausewitz described defence as the stronger form of war. Kuropatkin's situation underlined Clausewitz's defensive dictum with a precise template. Here was a general with the time and space with which to defend, to build up his strength prior to launching an offensive against a weakening enemy. It was becoming clearer that the ultimate philosophical test would occur at Liaoyang.

CHAPTER EIGHT

THE ADVANCE ON LIAOYANG

With the exception of a cavalry detachment sent to Wanchialing on 17 June, after the battle of Telissu, the Japanese Second Army rested for four days upon the field of battle. During this period, the remainder of the Sixth Division arrived to come under Oku's command. There was no rest for the defeated soldiers of Stakelberg. Russian intelligence, grossly overestimating the strength of the Fourth Army, saw in the posturing of the Tenth Japanese Division a threat to Kaiping. Orders to occupy that town were passed to Stakelberg who resumed his march northward from Wanchialing during the evening of 16 June. This move caused much discomfort to the tired and dispirited soldiers whose traditional sense of humour and stoicism were frayed and ragged. Matters were not helped by a group of Cossacks loosing off some rounds into the late evening, causing Stakelberg and the division with which he was travelling to deploy until daybreak. Protecting the movement was a rearguard commanded by Major General Samsonov who had resumed command from the sick Lieutenant General Simonov. By 20 June, the First Siberian Army Corps was in position in the area of Kaiping.

A constant criticism of military observers across the whole international spectrum referred to the apparent Japanese inability to follow up and pursue. They appeared imbued with the habit, once having secured their immediate objective, of then resting on their laurels. It is true that the Japanese were short of cavalry and the ground did not always lend itself to their proper use. Although the Russians would be withdrawing, they were rarely completely beaten. Their rearguards had the capability to maul severely light mounted follow-up forces. Pursuits need fresh troops and supplies. The

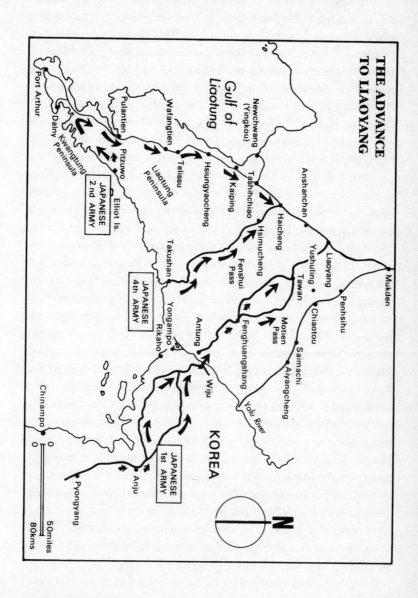

THE ADVANCE TO LIAOYANG

Port Arthur

Dalny

Kwangtung Peninsula

Pulantien

Pitzuwo

JAPANESE 2nd ARMY

Elliot Is.

Wafangtien

Liaotung Peninsula

Telissu

Hsiungyaocheng

Kaiping

Tashihchiao

Gulf of Liaotung

Newchwang (Yingkou)

Anshanchan

Haicheng

Hsimucheng

Fenshui Pass

Takushan

JAPANESE 4th ARMY

Yongampo

Rikaho

Antung

Fenghuangshang

Motien Pass

Tawan

Yushuling

Liaoyang

Chiaotou

Penhsihu

Mukden

Aiyangcheng

Saimachi

Yalu River

Wiju

Chinampo

KOREA

JAPANESE 1st ARMY

Anju

Pyongyang

0   0
50miles
80kms

N

Japanese victories were frequently snatched only after the commitment of the last man from their reserves and the exhaustion of their combat supplies.

As in all fields of human endeavour, however, problems are easy to identify; it is their solutions which win prizes. None the less, this laissez-faire attitude was seen elsewhere in the preparation of the Japanese communications. Prior to the war, the Russians had done very little to improve the roadways and this inaction was also reflected in the Japanese who had no concept of preventative maintenance. They had the resources, they had the labour and they had the need, but herein lay, for an otherwise superbly prepared force, a curious blind spot. They learned from their mistakes, for inaction and tardiness in following-up were not faults in evidence in 1941.

Supply difficulties were being experienced by all four of the Japanese armies. Oku was dependent upon supplies reaching him from the central ordnance depot at Pulantien. The joint effects of the danger of war and the impending monsoon caused many of the carters upon whom the Japanese depended to refuse to move outside the immediate area of their own homesteads. In General Kuroki's area a light, manual railway had been built connecting Antung with Fenghuangcheng, thereby relieving much of the logistic worry. Although the Russians had abandoned large numbers of railway wagons on the Dalny railway, they had the good sense to remove all the engines. Japanese and Russian rolling stock did not share a compatible gauge but, showing much foresight, the Japanese had bought suitable engines from America. However, a foray by the Vladivostok Naval Squadron on 15 June intercepted the two steamers carrying the engines and consigned them to the bottom of the sea to join the siege artillery awaited by Nogi's Third Army. Notwithstanding these problems, it was essential that all three of the armies advancing on Liaoyang should do so in concert, to exert a constant pressure all along the Russian line so that no one army could be engaged decisively in isolation. In order to gain access into the Liao valley, the Japanese were obliged to attack and win control of the passes of Fenshuiling, Taling and Motienling. All fell between 26–30 June.

General Count Keller had assumed command of the Russian Eastern Force from Zasulich after the Yalu debacle. His force of some 25,000 was holding the Motien Pass and lying astride the Antung to Liaoyang road. Keller, a brave and intelligent man, had spent his apprenticeship with Kuropatkin under Skobelev. He remained a loyal and personal friend of Kuropatkin over whom he wielded considerable influence. Keller observed the similarities of the Japanese strategy unfolding before him with that which had occurred in the Sino-Japanese War. He forecast that the three Japanese armies would converge at Haicheng as they had done ten years previously. Kuropatkin concurred and set about building a strong force at Haicheng with a view to stopping the advance of either the Second or Fourth Armies, or both.

Kuropatkin now began confusing and disruptive troop movements as he endeavoured to plug either the real or imaginary gaps in his line. A brigade of the Thirty-fifth Infantry Division was taken from Stakelberg to hold a position at Tashihchiao although it did not take part in the impending battle. Keller, whose position at Motienling had been weakened already by the demands of Telissu, found his originality of thought rewarded by orders to send two regiments to Haicheng. Believing that Kuroki's First Army, still at Fenghuangcheng, would strike westward, Kuropatkin ordered Keller to march against Fenghuangcheng with a view to making the Japanese nervous for their right flank and lines of communication. (A detachment was located forty-five miles to the north-east at Aiyangcheng and a Guards brigade was still in support of the Fourth Army.) With a similar aim in mind, General Rennenkampf at Saimachi was ordered to direct his 5,000 cavalry against Kuroki's detachment at Aiyangcheng.

Keller formed up all the troops he could muster, seven and a half battalions, and advanced against Kuroki's army. In thirty-six hours, his force had covered forty miles. Now exhausted and extremely nervous, they were within ten miles of Fenghuangcheng. Not one single Japanese had they met. Keller ordered his troops to retire and they arrived back at the passes on 18 June with orders to hold the left flank. The cynical observation of General Kashtalinski, reported by von Tettau, a German observer with the Russians, was that all the move had achieved was the ruination of 8,000 pairs of boots – an item in short supply. On 19 June, the Japanese heard news of Rennenkampf's intended action against Aiyangcheng. The Japanese reinforced their detachment from Fenghuangcheng in order to maintain superiority. Rennenkampf attacked on 22 June but was driven off by the weight of fire. In not attacking these two weaker forces, Kuroki displayed remarkable tactical restraint. He had no wish to divulge his true strength, preferring that the attention be held by the railway, thereby affording him, when he was ready, an uncomplicated advance on Motienling.

Orders to prepare to move were received by the Fourth and First Armies on 19 and 22 June. General Kawamura decided to attack Fenshuiling, held by an entrenched Russian brigade, on 27 June, the day he personally anticipated the Second Army arriving at Kaiping. Envisaging the Russian preoccupation with Fenshuiling, Kuroki decided to attack Motienling on 30 June.

The Japanese, of course, had experience of Motienling, 'Heaven Reaching Pass', in 1894. They did not share the following negative tactical assessment by a correspondent:

> The position is a forest-clad mountain about one thousand feet
> above the river and valley, and traversed by a steep and wind
> ing path. The mountain is crowded with angles and 'dead'
> ground, on which large bodies of men could lie in perfect
> security. The slopes are steep and there is no field of fire. The
> Russians, therefore, had formed a correct estimate of the
> tactical features of the Pass, and had not wasted their energies
> on any defensive works.

Demonstrating remarkable co-operation, both armies advised General Oku of their intentions, but by 21 June Oku's advance up the railway had run out of steam at Hsiungyaocheng for want of supplies. Here he was to remain until 6 July while the logisticians grappled with their supply problem.

The cart convoys from Pulantien to Telissu were made more efficient and the powerless railway wagons were organised into trains of up to forty wagons, each wagon pushed by a coolie platoon of sixteen men. Although the situation improved, the logisticians were merely holding their own with the rail link and were quite incapable of building up a reserve. An option to use the sea lane south of Port Arthur, the straits of Peichihli, and land supplies near Hsiungyaocheng was abandoned due to the events of 23 June.

For a number of weeks the timid Admiral Witgeft had been under pressure from Alexeiev, and ultimately the Tsar, to sail his fleet out of Port Arthur to join the Vladivostok squadron. Order, counter-order, disorder were the rule of the day covering a three-week period. The closest the fleet came to its proposed departure was on 20 June when, with a full head of steam, it looked forward to departing the claustrophobic confines of Port Arthur. That they did not was not of the navy's making but due to an over-zealous editor of Bezobrazov's *Novoe Krai*. He published a special edition announcing the fleet's departure that day. Although the copies were recalled, Witgeft had no option but to postpone his departure yet again. The fires in the boilers were allowed to die down, increasing the navy's exasperation, mistrust and doubts as to their own abilities. Certainly among the middle-ranking officers, the Japanese were held in grudging respect through their attitude and determination. Commander Semenov's diary continued as a good barometer of what the more junior officers were thinking: 'Why, the Japanese were often better informed than we officers, who were reduced to guessing.'

After more postponements, with euphoric anticipation, the fleet left harbour, beginning at 4 a.m. on 23 June. Having passed through the minefield, they formed up in a marshalling anchorage which transpired to be a Japanese minefield. Semenov's estimation of the Japanese intelligence was confirmed in his own mind when he discovered that the fleet's secret anchorage had been mined. The ultimate occurred to convince him of Japanese infallibility when the fleets met at 6 p.m. Among the funnels and superstructures the formal lines of the *Chinyen* stood out. She was an old battleship captured from the Chinese in 1894. Under normal circumstances she was confined to policing the Straits of Korea. Her appearance now led the Russians to believe that they had the whole Japanese fleet to contend with.

The Russians afforded the Japanese too much credit. Togo had despatched a strong force of eight cruisers to the Sea of Japan to deal with the Vladivostok squadron which had sunk the Japanese steamers on 15 June. While the *Chinyen*'s appearance worried the Russians, the appearance of the repaired *Tsarevitch* and *Retvisan* in the Russian fleet horrified Togo. On this occasion Japanese intelligence failed, for Togo had not expected to see these two battleships which gave the Russians a six to four advantage. None the less, the overall size of the Japanese fleet, totalling fifty-three ships against Witgeft's eighteen, was more than sufficient to make the Russian admiral pause for thought while his ships went to battle stations. By dusk, the opposing fleets were sailing parallel courses eight miles apart. The evening promised to be bright and moonlit. This was the time when big ships' effectiveness decreased in direct proportion to the increased effectiveness of the torpedo boat destroyers, of which Togo had many. Cautiously, Togo steered his flagship towards the Russian line. Witgeft's nerve failed and he ordered his fleet to starboard, to return the twenty three miles to Port Arthur and a low tide. 'I decided to return,' he explained, 'esteeming that these tactics would occasion less loss.' The *Mikasa* was brought back on course as the Russians turned away, Togo allowing his torpedo boat destroyers and the minefields to work their own attrition on the Russian fleet. He could not risk his remaining battleships. This latter fact emphasised the bankruptcy of Russian maritime strategy. How much more sensible to engage the Japanese head-on, thereby wreaking unacceptable attrition, if not destruction, upon an irreplaceable resource, rather than to sit bottled-up in a besieged fortress to await the attention of the army's heavy artillery. Keeping the Pacific fleet in being in order to be joined by the Baltic fleet depended upon far too many assumptions.

The Russian fleet was remarkably unscathed while it sat waiting for the rising tide to allow them to enter port. Only the *Sevastopol* was damaged on a mine and no vessels were hit by gunfire or torpedoes. Five Japanese ships were slightly damaged by fire from the forts. Togo had secured his aim without risking his battleships. On the other hand, Russian officers and sailors had sunk to the depths of despair and desolation. Many now believed that they and their fleet were doomed.

The ability of the Russian fleet to leave harbour in strength was a salutary lesson for the Japanese. It was this event which made the provision of escorts for supply ships crossing in front of Port Arthur impossible. Instead, the logisticians put their point of entry at Talienwan from where supplies were carried by cart across the isthmus and loaded on to some seventy hired junks plying between Chinchou Bay, Hsiungyao and points north. In this way, Oku's supply situation was gradually to improve.

On 24 June, Imperial Japanese headquarters issued a strange order:

> The fact has been proved that the Russian fleet is able to issue
> from the harbour of Port Arthur. The transport of provisions
> which will be required by the combined Manchurian Armies
> after their arrival at Liaoyang is therefore rendered uncertain,
> and it is not advisable for the Second Army to advance further
> north than Kaiping for the present. The battle of Liaoyang,
> which it was anticipated would be fought before the rainy
> season, will now be postponed till after it. Arrange your
> operations accordingly.

The headquarters must have known that the Second Army would not be ready to move for a fortnight. It is inconceivable too that the army would have been permitted to advance to Kaiping while the prospect of the Fourth and First Armies being blocked at the passes of Fenshuiling and Motienling still existed. To do so would have invited the destruction of the unsupported Second Army by a concentrated Russian force. Military reverses do not assist the soliciting of international funds to pursue the war and Japan was not given to the taking of unnecessary risks.

The actions of the Japanese army commanders lends credence to a view that the order was aimed not for their consumption but for the Russians. Certainly, they did not alter their own plans put in motion to secure the passes by 4–5 July. They uncharacteristically ignored the order. Kawamura's main body began its advance on Liaoyang on 25 June, having made contact on the left with a detachment from the Second Army. The next day, General Kuroki's main body headed north towards the pass of Motienling.

The sensitivity afforded to the Russian maritime capability to move out of Port Arthur was also uncharacteristic. Troop and supply movements remained unaltered and Marshal Oyama, the Japanese land commander, was routed past the fort as he sailed for Kaiping on 6 July. It was known that a duty Russian destroyer made regular runs to Yingkou; and it was by this means that Kuropatkin had intended to relieve Port Arthur of the disobedient General Stoessel. The implied nervousness of the Japanese may have been aimed at giving the Russians the confidence to come out to do battle.

Perhaps Russia had intercepted or received the Japanese orders. Had not Witgeft been so utterly unenterprising and reluctant to obey the orders of both Alexeiev and the Tsar, the Far East fleet might well have been encouraged into battle. On land, the Japanese strategy was aimed at securing the mountain passes before Oku closed with the Russians. The supposedly fake Japanese orders implied the contrary; rather an approach on Haicheng as they had done in 1894. The effect they desired was achieved, for Kuropatkin released his hold on Motienling by covering the approach of Oku's army. On 26 June Count Keller had forfeited a further regiment in favour of Haicheng where Kuropatkin had arrived on that very day. The strength of Russian units in the town's vicinity was forty-one battalions and eighteen cavalry squadrons.

On 26 June, formal land action was taken against Port Arthur which saw the Japanese overwhelm the outposts and close up to the Russian line. (The story of the siege from this point to its conclusion is contained in Chapters 10 and 11.) Meanwhile, the Fourth Army was en route for the pass at Fenshuiling from where the road descends to Haicheng and Tashihchiao lying astride the railway. The pass is guarded to the north with high pine-clad mountains with precipitous slopes. To the south lie less daunting hills over which there are tracks running parallel to the main approach. On the pass the Russians had deployed three infantry regiments, three batteries and a Cossack regiment. To the west lay General Mischenko with his Cossack brigade supported by an infantry regiment. During the night 25–26 June a balanced Japanese force moved along an unguarded path to work round the rear of the Russian right flank. They took with them Maxim machine guns and mountain artillery. Another group, having discarded the regulation boot in favour of Japanese straw sandals, scaled the northern face undetected and moved around the Russian left flank. These detachments took all day of 26 June to take up their positions while the force allocated to the frontal attack kept up a steady bombardment to hold the Russians' attention.

The battle proper began at 5.15 a.m. on 27 June with an artillery duel. The Russians had camouflaged their guns in the trees and their range cards related to distinguishable features below them in the valley. The frontal attack floundered but by 7 a.m. the encirclement preparations paid off for the Russians found they were virtually surrounded and being fired upon from almost every hilltop. Gunners and horses were taking casualties so, by 8 a.m., the Russian guns were forced to move. The cessation of artillery fire became the signal for the frontal attack to pick itself up again and with accurate supporting artillery fire it overwhelmed the Russian position. By 10 a.m. the Russians were in retreat towards Hsimucheng encouraged by murderous volleys from the heights just vacated. This withdrawal placed Mischenko's left in danger and, having been prevented from making a counter-attack, he withdrew at 7 p.m. Casualties on both sides were nevertheless relatively light.

The Japanese capture of Motienling on 30 June was possibly the war's greatest coup, but yet leaves the question unanswered as to why the positions were abandoned. The roads up through the passes are very poor and their condition had not been helped by the deluges of rain over a four-week period. The logistical support of troops was difficult but since these features were the key to the door of the Liao plain it would not have seemed impossible to make provision for the necessary contingencies. The fact is that Motienling should have been virtually impregnable; some observers likened it to Thermopylae. Yet the otherwise sound Count Keller abandoned the position with hardly a shot being fired. Even a small number of Ivan Leonidas could have inflicted delay and casualties among the Japanese. Keller's strength was estimated at eleven battalions. What was in Keller's mind will not be known since he was killed in an attempt to retake the pass. Kuropatkin's unanalytical statement merely said: 'Our cavalry and infantry, while retiring under pressure of the Japanese, ascertained that the attack on each of the three passes was made by a superior force.'

Perhaps Keller rued the day that he drew Kuropatkin's attention to Haicheng, for ever since that time regiments had been continually withdrawn from him and moved throughout the theatre. The Ninth East Siberian Rifle Regiment, which had a key role in the defence of Motienling, was extracted from the passes four days before their fall in order to reinforce Haicheng. This was a period of great indecision and a period when the morale of the Russians took a tumble as they were marched from pillar to post to guard against the threat of the day. An account of the movements of the Twelfth East Siberian Rifle Regiment over a two-week period is extracted from the British Official History:

> This regiment had been ordered to Anshanchan on 15 June,
> but on reaching that place had been at once sent back to
> Count Keller. On the 26th it received orders to move to Tawan;
> but while on the march it received another order to retrace its
> steps and, at 1 a.m. on the 27th, reached the camp at Chiner-
> htun which it had left the previous morning. There it was met
> by an order from General Kuropatkin directing it to march at
> once to Haicheng. Leaving camp again at 4 a.m. on the 27th, it
> reached Haicheng on the 28th only to find it was to move next
> day to Liaoyang, this time by rail. Arriving there on the 30th,
> orders were again received to rejoin Count Keller.

The second of the three lessons elucidated from the Manchurian War and underlined by General Langlois had been the influence and maintenance of morale.

Early rains from 27 June to 5 July provided a foretaste of what was to come. Movement along the roads became impossible as carts became bogged and the civilian carters fled to the security of their homes. Infantrymen, preferring not to wear both boots and the clinging mud, marched barefoot from place to place. Sickness increased, and it was not unusual for those suffering from dysentery to fall exhausted in the roadway to be swept away in nullahs and drowned by the frequent floods of water. For the Japanese, their logistics had failed again. Kuroki's First Army was put on half rations while his Twelfth Division, having consumed its emergency rations, was ordered to withdraw the twelve miles back to Saimachi. If the rain had persisted for a further forty-eight hours, Kuroki would have been obliged to retire his force back to Fenghuangcheng.

As the rains came to a temporary end, both sides were in need of intelligence as to opponents' strengths and intentions. The withdrawing Russians learned the obvious lesson that they were unable to solicit information from the locals for the latter's fear of reprisals from the advancing Japanese. They needed to know whether the Japanese were aiming for their left flank or intending to cut westward to the railway. On 4 July a reconnaissance in force was launched against Motienling by three battalions. It was not well co-ordinated and was repulsed without difficulty. Japanese intelligence was not up to its usual standard either since it credited Keller with a strength of two divisions.

Sun Tzu, the Chinese strategist, wrote in *The Art of War* in 500 BC:

> Raising a host of a hundred thousand men and marching them great distances entails heavy loss on the people and a drain on the resources of the State. The daily expenditure will amount to a thousand ounces of silver. There will be commotion at home and abroad, and men will drop down exhausted on the roadways. As many as seven hundred thousand families will be impeded in their labour. Hostile armies may face each other for years, striving for victory which is decided in a single day. This being so, to remain in ignorance of the enemy's condition simply because one begrudges the outlay of a hundred ounces of silver in honours and emoluments, is the height of inhumanity. One who acts thus is no leader of men, no present help to his sovereign, no master of victory. Thus, what enables the wise sovereign and the good general to strike and conquer, and achieve things beyond the reach of ordinary men is foreknowledge.

The Japanese derived their 'foreknowledge' through a number of sources. Very often the Chinaman in the field was co-opted to report what he had seen. The Russians' selection of reverse slope positions prior to the forthcoming battle of Tashihchiao was not primarily to protect the infantry from the effects of direct fire but to keep the strength of the force secret from what Douglas Story described as the ubiquitous 'peasant parasites in pigtails'.

The Russians' disadvantage was not that they stood out like sore thumbs in this environment, for many of their soldiers from the eastern regions could pass equally well as Chinese or Japanese. Among Russian baggage captured by the Japanese in front of Port Arthur was a suit of Chinese clothes. 'Sometimes they would send out scouts dressed as Chinese natives to spy out our advance lines.' Their handicap, once they had gleaned information of the Japanese, was in the transmission of that intelligence back to their own side. Happy to take messages about the countryside for the victors, the Chinese would not collaborate with those they perceived as about to be vanquished.

The Japanese had observed in human nature what the Russians had not: the danger inherent in the frequently automatic assumption that a person filling a lowly job or one not requiring a great deal of intelligence is in himself unintelligent and incapable of harming security. There are many examples of the Japanese using this failing to good effect, as surely as it is being used elsewhere to good effect today. The sole hairdresser in Newchwang was an unprepossessing Japanese who cut the hair of the Russian officers of the garrison. He was a captain in the Imperial Japanese Army. Nothing succeeds like success, for much the same was to be revealed in December 1941 in Hong Kong. There, the Japanese hairdresser who had been in the Colony for seven years and cut the hair of the Governor, Commander British Forces and Police Chief, presented himself to his captives in the uniform of a commander in the Imperial Japanese Navy. Thus the Japanese demonstrated much empathy with Sun Tzu's thoughts and views of the honourable activity of spying and its necessary preparation. The Japanese had, the Russians had not, and therein lay the reason for much of the latter's misfortune.

It was now evident to the Japanese that the co-ordination of the move and attack on Liaoyang and the siege of Port Arthur could best be commanded not from Tokyo but from a field headquarters. Some reshuffling of the military leadership, taking full account of tribal sensitivities, saw the appointment of Marshal Oyama as Commander-in-Chief of the Japanese forces in Manchuria and General Kodama, the 'Kitchener of Japan', as his Chief-of-Staff. They left Tokyo by rail for the port of Ujina, passing through fields of jubilant peasants sending them to war with the greatest encouragement. Their object was to collocate with General Oku's headquarters at Kaiping which, on the date of their sailing – 6 July – was still firmly in Russian hands.

The 6 July had been the Imperial Japanese headquarters' original date for the advance of the three armies. On this day, now properly provisioned,

General Oku led his four divisions northward. By midday 7 July the divisions halted five miles to the south of Kaiping having experienced little opposition on the way. Japanese reconnaissance and local information indicated that Kaiping was held by Stakelberg's First Siberian Corps while to the north, at Tashihchiao, was Lieutenant General Zarubaiev's Fourth Siberian Corps, still in the process of being reinforced.

Rising directly above the city of Kaiping is a semicircle of hills which dominate the flat, open ground to the south. On the hills and the area thereabout was stationed a force of 20,000. The Japanese avoided being caught in the open country by a night advance which had brought their guns to a position at 5.30 a.m. on 9 July from where they could engage Kaiping. Fearing envelopment, Stakelberg conducted that phase of war at which he was most adept, the withdrawal. This was achieved, 'in good time and with perfect regularity'. The Second Japanese Army dug in on the hills to the north of the town where they were to remain until 22 July. During this period, the new supply system using road, rail and sea means was able to establish a sufficient reserve of supplies to maintain Oku's army for twenty days.

Alexeiev, who had adopted a low profile after Telissu, now sought further offensive action. In his view, Kuropatkin should be able to block the Second and Fourth Armies and take the offensive against the First Army, forcing it back to Korea. Kuropatkin dallied; he wanted to await the arrival of further reinforcements, particularly Seventeenth Corps, before doing anything. He had formed an opinion that the strength of the Japanese forces was twice what it actually was while, surprisingly, Alexeiev and Jalinski held a much more accurate perception of their true strength. Kuropatkin was not opposed to the offensive, but he did not favour the Viceroy's idea of engaging only the First Army; he wanted a general offensive across the whole front. A general offensive could not be initiated until after the rains in mid-August and, in Kuropatkin's estimation, would require a reinforcement of a further four corps. No general offensive could therefore occur during the month of August.

Alexeiev persisted. Kuropatkin should do something. Against his better judgement, Kuropatkin ordered Keller to conduct a partial offensive against Motienling with the Eastern Force. The Southern Force was ordered to withdraw if attacked. The proposition, therefore, envisaged Keller's Eastern Force of forty battalions attacking Kuroki's First Army of almost eighty battalions while the securely dug-in Russian Southern Force of ninety-seven battalions should give ground if attacked by the combined ninety battalions of the Second and Fourth Japanese Army. Langlois's third and final lesson was that unity of effort is essential to success and he stressed that half-measures lead only to failure.

Kuropatkin as much acquiesced with Keller's desire to attack Motienling as obeyed his superior's wishes. Reinforced by the Ninth Division Keller advanced in three columns up the roads of the Lan Valley where the Second Japanese Division held the passes. 'Taking into consideration the considerable increase of the Eastern Force, I ordered Count Keller to take the offensive, so as to again get possession of the passes,' wrote Kuropatkin. 'He did so, but although he had forty battalions under his command, he advanced with only twenty-four.'

The Russians advanced during the night 16–17 July upon the Japanese positions which were all connected by telephone so that the alarm was easily raised. At 8 a.m. the main force of Russians, attempting a frontal assault in the open, was cut down by the Japanese artillery. Their own artillery did not come into support until 2.10 p.m. when the infantry had effectively withdrawn. The efforts of the two smaller columns were equally fruitless. Keller had kept one-quarter of his force in reserve. General Hamilton witnessed this action and observed that the Russians still utilised section volley fire, that they had little idea of the use and value of cover and that their officers took undue risks. Their ability and skill at withdrawal received favourable comment: 'It is passing strange that soldiers so steady and formidable in retreat should be so sticky in the attack.'

After withdrawing, Keller dug his force into a position near Tawan, astride the Fenghuangcheng–Liaoyang road. Encouraged by the failure of this force, Kuroki sent his Twelfth Division against the town of Chiaotou, a springboard for a possible attack on the Russian lines of communication at Mukden. The Russian strength here was a brigade group of Tenth Corps. Having been subjected to attacks on 18–19 July, with its right flank turned, it gave way and fell back along the road to Liaoyang. Rennenkampf's cavalry was posted twenty-five miles to the east of Chiaotou although Rennenkampf, shot through the thigh on 13 July, had been superseded by General Liubavin. Again, the Cossack cavalry demonstrated its reserve and ineffectiveness by not coming to the infantry brigade's assistance. They were territorial soldiers led by romantic, aristocratic European officers whose general lack of intelligence was veiled by a disarming smile and oozing charm. They did not see themselves as

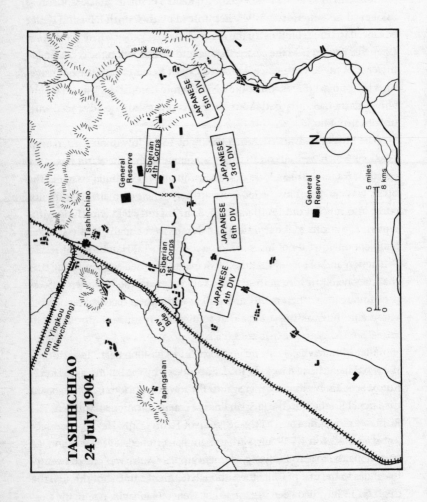

TASHIHCHIAO
24 July 1904

Tungia River

JAPANESE
5th DIV

Siberian
4th Corps

General
Reserve

JAPANESE
3rd DIV

N

General
Reserve

JAPANESE
6th DIV

Tashihchiao

Siberian
1st Corps

JAPANESE
4th DIV

5 miles

8 kms

from Yingkou
(Newchwang)

Cav
Bde

Tapingshan

risk-takers but rather as reconnaissance troops; saw their task to provide information, not to indulge in low, beastly fighting. Rarely have such large numbers been sustained in the field at such great cost to so little effect.

The result of the loss of Chiaotou was to bring the Twelfth Japanese Division into line with the remainder of the First Army. The railway line between Liaoyang and Mukden was now threatened via the approach from Penshihu where a Russian garrison was posted. The Tenth Corps was ordered to regain Chiaotou while Keller was instructed to hold firm at Tawan.

The conflict between Alexeiev and Kuropatkin rumbled on. The different strategic philosophies of both men were represented to the Tsar who supported Kuropatkin's yet told Alexeiev, 'I do not wish to sway your decisions which are your prerogative as Commander-in-Chief.' Alexeiev had gained his naval command experience during five years spent aboard the cruiser *Kornilov*. Now, there was insufficient naval activity upon which to direct his energy which came in fits and starts. He was not prepared to allow Kuropatkin his way. With the relative improvement in weather permitting an increase in the rate of reinforcement, he planned the formation of two armies with himself as the supreme commander and Kuropatkin as one of the army commanders. He saw nothing untoward in his desire to command the entire field army; after all, had not Kuropatkin in 1900 made him an army corps commander during the Boxer Rebellion? His vague and only peripheral experience of land warfare deterred neither his zeal nor aspirations.

At a meeting on 20 July at Mukden, Alexeiev gave Kuropatkin his outline plan to reinforce the Eastern Force which, under Kuropatkin's immediate command was to engage that army which most threatened their position – Kuroki's. Unconvinced but obedient, Kuropatkin returned to Liaoyang where he publicly announced his intention to resume the offensive. Orders were despatched to the Tenth and Seventeenth Corps placing them under command of the Eastern Force. While Kuropatkin was en route to take over direct command, the Second Japanese Army resumed its northward movement, in effect consigning the Eastern Force's plans to the waste-paper basket.

Oku's army advanced on 23 July having been delayed for twenty-four hours by heavy rain. His intelligence had told him that an enemy force of almost four divisions had prepared defensive lines some ten miles long to the south of the town of Tashihchiao. The town was of strategic importance as it sat upon the railway junction of the main line and a secondary line leading to the old treaty port of Yingkou (Newchwang). The seizure of both the railway junction and the port would greatly ease the Japanese logistic worries. It was obvious that the Russians would offer stout defence.

Oku was uncharacteristically cautious as he moved northward. With the First and Fourth Armies still in the mountains, he approached to contact in extended line along a front of twelve miles with his cavalry brigade screening his left flank. On his right flank was the Fifth Division, then the Third, Sixth and Fourth Divisions on the extreme left. That evening the divisions halted five miles to the south of Russian entrenchments while the staff collated the information gleaned that day from the reconnaissance.

Kuropatkin had personally selected the Tashihchiao position and ordered that it should be fortified. Stakelberg's First Siberian Army Corps had fallen back to conform with Lieutenant General Zarubaiev's Fourth Siberian Army Corps. Zarubaiev was the overall commander under orders to withdraw on Haicheng if pressed by the enemy. Clearly Kuropatkin intended this to be but a holding engagement prior to the foreseen battle at Haicheng, a battle which was not to materialise.

The right flank was occupied by Stakelberg's corps with Zarubaiev on the left. Stakelberg's right of line rested on the railway with his flank protected by General Kossagovski's cavalry brigade. (Kossagovski had assumed command of Samsonov's brigade.) Zarubaiev's left was on the Tungta River watched by General Mischenko's cavalry. A general reserve of ten battalions and sixteen guns lay to the left of centre in two separate groups. There was, however, a distinct difference between the ground on the Russian left and that on the right. The left was hilly and broken by ravines. The fall of Fenshuiling had made this flank vulnerable to subsequent advances of the Fourth Japanese Army. The right was on low flat ground, the 'going' of which had been greatly impaired by the recent rains. The abundant *kaoliang* had been cleared to the south of the position to a distance of 1,500 yards to provide good fields of fire. A number of isolated hillocks presented the Russians with a series of strategically placed observation posts, like fire towers watching for danger in the forest of millet below.

Oku had moved his forces along the plain to the north of Kaiping. On either side of the road – to the left to the sea, and to the right to the lower mountain slopes – lay the swaying carpet of green, glossy *kaoliang*. Villages scattered generously throughout the plain served to imprint on the *kaoliang* a disrupted pattern. Although not fully grown, the millet at six feet afforded the advancing Japanese some cover from view. The Japanese approach was not seriously interfered with, although the Fourth Division on the left flank paused to repulse an annoying foray of cavalry, while the Fifth Division on the right found it difficult to keep abreast due to the more difficult hilly terrain.

The intelligence picture put together by the Japanese gave them cause for concern if not alarm. Their preference for turning one or both flanks posed serious threats to their advanced position. An attempt to turn the Russian flanks on this ground would have exposed their communications to a counter-move. Oku decided to risk nothing. He issued orders for the Fifth, Third and Sixth Divisions to launch a frontal attack on 24 July, aware also that the movements of the Fourth Army would prey on the Russian minds. Oku's Fourth Division was held back on the left flank to support the flank most likely to be subjected to a counter-stroke or counter-attack. It would 'take up a position near Wutaishan and will hold it in strength as a protection for the left flank of the army. No advance will be made therefrom until it is observed that the general attack elsewhere is succeeding.' A cavalry brigade screen was established on the far left of the Fourth Division while a reaction force of two infantry regiments which served also as Oku's only reserve was held under his own personal command.

In the debriefing held by the Russian staff after the war, Zarubaiev stated that he was confronted by both the Second and Fourth Japanese Armies. Herein may well have lain a degree of defensive reflection, for contemporary evidence indicates that the Russians had identified a force somewhat in excess of three divisions moving up to Tashihchiao. The locations occupied by the Fourth and Sixth Divisions were each correctly identified as being in divisional strength, while a blurring of the troops of the Third and Fifth Divisions in the hills led the Russians to believe this to be one division with the reserves to their rear. General Mischenko had worried Zarubaiev by a premature report of the move of the Tenth Japanese Division. In fact the division moved the next day against the Second Siberian Army Corps of General Zasulich. A courier brought the news to Zarubaiev at 2 p.m. during the battle, the timing of which coincided with a query from Stakelberg as to whether or not the time was right to withdraw.

General Oku's own account of the Russian defences indicated that this was to be no Telissu: 'The defences were perfect from a standpoint of field tactics. The enemy's artillery had skilfully utilised the nature of the ground, and taken positions so well covered that it was difficult to ascertain the exact location of his guns.' The ground lent itself better to concealment than at

Nanshan and Telissu but still the infantry trenches were easily identified. That the same cannot be said of the artillery is due to Stakelberg. His Commander Artillery had prepared his initial gun positions in the open until ordered by the corps commander to move the guns and employ indirect means. The vacant gun emplacements were to be heavily engaged by the Japanese gunners. Only one battery in the corps was to be badly hit and that was when a change of positions made the muzzle flashes visible to the enemy. The Fourth Siberian Corps had not been at Telissu and in consequence its artillery suffered heavily as a result.

The early half light of Sunday 24 July revealed to the Russian outposts not only the peasants fanning out from their clustered mud buildings into the fields of millet, but something more formidable: three Japanese divisions advancing in line. The Fourth Division had stood fast as ordered. There had not been any preparatory fire, the first Japanese guns coming into action at 5.30 a.m. By this time, the Russian Fourth Siberian Army Corps had safely advanced from a resting position on the reverse slopes to occupy their trenches. The initial action on the left flank was confined mostly to a duel between the gunners. In the centre, the Sixth Division's attack was so half-hearted that Stakelberg kept his force on the reverse slope without bothering to occupy the trenches.

It had passed midday and the hot Manchurian sun beat down on the waiting Russians, protected from the sun's effects only by their unsuitable forage caps. Red Cross orderlies moved along the lines to tend those afflicted by sunstroke and to remove those who had died. Stakelberg, dressed all in white, looked calm and cool, yet he was nervous. At 1 p.m. he despatched an aide to Zarubaiev suggesting that they should withdraw. He said that in his judgement he was about to receive the main attack and to put his troops forward in their trenches would only invite heavy casualties. He reminded Zarubaiev that this was not part of Kuropatkin's plan of campaign. The aide arrived at Zarubaiev's headquarters at the time Zasulich's news of the move of the Fourth Army was received. It should be remembered that the Russians believed the Japanese Fourth Army to be considerably larger than it actually was. Disturbed though the Commander of the Fourth Russian Corps was, he was not sufficiently disturbed as to agree to a daylight withdrawal with the temperature soaring above 100 degrees F. He sent a message back to Stakelberg that he would consider withdrawing at nightfall.

There was little cause for Stakelberg's pessimism. At 2 p.m. twelve of the thirteen Japanese batteries opposing his corps were assigned counter battery tasks against two Russian batteries beyond the hill line and camouflaged among the millet. At 3 p.m. a reinforcement Russian battery was to join them and they combined to keep both Japanese infantry and guns at bay until nightfall. Japanese impatience and lack of range forced upon them the relocation of their guns. In consequence, they suffered losses to both crews and horse teams. Future engagements would see fewer attempts at manoeuvre, and guns, once in position, often remained there until nightfall. Overall, however, the First Siberian Corps was not pressed and with artillery assets to spare, placed three batteries in support of the Fourth Siberian Corps.

Meanwhile, at 10.30 a.m. the Fourth Japanese Division had moved up into line. Shrugging off further interference from the Russian cavalry, the division came up upon the left of the moribund Sixth Division. At 1 p.m. General Kossagovski had made a weak attack upon the Japanese left. Coming under fire of the Japanese First Cavalry Brigade his cavalry and supporting guns turned about and headed for the security of the north. Kossagovski claimed that the ground was too boggy to employ cavalry but he had served to attract Oku's attention to the threat to his left. At 8 p.m., acting on information that the Russians were preparing to counter-attack his left flank, Oku released one of the two regiments in his reserve to fill the gap between the Fourth and Sixth Divisions. (The movement seen by Oku's spies was the preparation for the withdrawal.)

Action towards the Russian left flank was much more dangerous and hectic. The Third and Fifth Divisions combined their attention that morning against the weak point of the Russian line, the centre. Showing unusual co-operation the divisions of the Fourth Corps cobbled together a force of fifty-six guns of which thirty-two were the new quick firers. The seventy-two guns of the twelve batteries supporting the two Japanese divisions could not compete with the Russian rate of fire and in addition were outranged.

Before noon, Zarubaiev issued instructions for the move which Oku most feared; a counter-attack. General Shileiko, posted on the extreme left of the Russian line, was ordered to move against the flank of the by now wallowing Fifth Japanese Division. He was instructed to confer with the cavalry commander Mischenko and the commander of the general reserve. Mischenko agreed to place cavalry under Shileiko's command but the approach to the general reserve for two battalions was refused on the grounds that no orders had been received. The spectre of poor command and control had again raised its ugly head. Shileiko's pathfinder battalion, performing the concurrent initial reconnaissance, was torn to shreds in a crossfire of artillery and rifles, while a portion of Mischenko's cavalry paraded on the periphery to no effect before withdrawing. The opportunity to threaten the Japanese had been lost.

Meanwhile, at 2 p.m. Oku invited the commanders of his right flank divisions to press on with the attack, with or without their artillery. At 3.30 p.m. the Japanese advance resumed under cover of indifferent artillery fire support. Their forward troops shuddered under the weight of the Russian volleys and, like ice before a fire, the assault evaporated leaving a residue of dead and dying. Checked again, the Fifth Division passed the baton to their left and relied upon their artillery to fight the battle on their front until nightfall. The reinforced Third Division moved forward and made some progress until the Russians were also reinforced. A much-respected Japanese battalion was launched to seize a key Russian feature but a charge and counter-attack sent it tumbling to the valley below. Action in the Third Division's sector continued sporadically but the heat and exhaustion had taken its toll elsewhere along the line where the opposing infantry had succumbed to inactivity.

Stakelberg's Commander Artillery had much cause for satisfaction. The sound tactical employment of his guns had ensured that the attack of the Second Army had come to a grinding halt. Not one Russian major unit had been dislodged from the main position. In reserve the Russians still had six battalions while the Japanese had but one regiment. The gunner brigadier looked at his watch. It was 5.30 p.m. and he felt tired. Already the sun was sinking into the Gulf of Liaotung whose shores were a mere ten miles to his right. He peered into the distance trying to discern the reason for the quiet when suddenly the peace was disturbed by the crash of Japanese guns. They had moved to their left and found the location of the artillery command post. An exploding shrapnel shell shredded his arm to pieces.

The Commander Fifth Japanese Division, not best pleased by his division's performance, requested and received Oku's permission to launch a night attack. The rising of the moon at 10 p.m. appeared to signal the division to pick itself up, descend its feature, cross the valley and climb the slopes still littered with its own dead. With screams of 'banzai', and against very light opposition, they surged through three lines of defences. Gradually their progress was taken up along the whole line as the other divisions moved forward.

By early afternoon of 25 July the Russian position was in Japanese hands. The Russians had gone, leaving only a rearguard. Yet another brilliant withdrawal had been conducted because, according to the Russian Chief-of-Staff, General Sakharov, the officer commanding did not deem it possible to accept battle the next morning while defending a position with a front of ten miles. There are varied accounts of the numbers of casualties suffered by both sides. Those published by the Japanese and as reported by the Official British History appear suspect. A consensus of views suggests that both sides lost a thousand men, killed, wounded or missing.

The Viceroy had not been impressed by the success of the withdrawal and sent off a signal of complaint to the Tsar. He stated that there had been no reason to retreat. He pointed out that the threat of the Fourth Army was adequately covered by Zasulich's corps and there were untouched reserves at Haicheng. Kuropatkin supported Zarubaiev's decision to withdraw and stressed that the loss of Yingkou, which fell on 25 July, and the centre of communications at Tashihchiao had strategic benefits in so far as his front was reduced by twenty miles.

The two Russian corps withdrew to Haicheng. Oku remained at Tashihchiao until 1 August when he marched again northwards with three divisions, the Fifth Division having been detached on 28 July to the Fourth Army.

The withdrawal of the two Russian corps had left General Zasulich in an exposed position at Hsimucheng. Some precautionary measures were taken by ordering the retreating corps to leave rearguards in order to protect Zasulich's flank from interference by the Second Japanese Army. In addition, while the Fifth Japanese Division was being transferred to Nozu, Mischenko's cavalry joined Zasulich to bring the Second Siberian Corps and a brigade of Tenth Corps to total thirty-three battalions, thirty-one squadrons and eighty artillery pieces. (The regiments of Tenth European Corps each had four battalions. There were two regiments to a brigade and two brigades to a division.) The Russian orders required them to reconnoitre to determine whether the Japanese were moving to the north-west. The nub, however, was to offer strong resistance to the Japanese but to withdraw on Haicheng rather than suffer a severe defeat.

Nozu's Fourth Army consisted of the Fifth and Tenth Divisions and, reflecting the infusion of territorials in the theatre, the Tenth Kobi (Reserve) Brigade. The orders given to Nozu were that he should attack the Russians when the opportunity was presented. Suitably reinforced, he located his force three miles from the prepared Russian positions at Hsimucheng. At 2 a.m. on 30 July, the Tenth Division and reserve brigade moved forward against the Russian position while the Fifth Division moved off to the left intending to cut the enemy's line of retreat.

The Russian defensive position straddled the Haicheng road as it came through the mountain passes. Because it had been adjusted to reflect the southern advance of the Japanese, and because the rocky and mountainous ground had not been easy to prepare, the position left much to be desired. The brunt of the main Japanese attack on 31 July fell upon the right of the Russian position. Mischenko's cavalry and the Fourth Siberian Corps' rearguard withdrew but the remainder of Zasulich's force, with great bravery, held its ground regularly counter-attacking against superior numbers. The Fifth Japanese Division, moving up to the Russians' right, joined a detachment of the Japanese Third Division sent by Oku. Although still holding his position, at 11 p.m. Zasulich received an order from Kuropatkin to withdraw to Haicheng. The door to Haicheng was therefore pushed wide open for the Fourth Japanese Army and it allowed their unhindered junction with the forces of Oku's Second Army.

The battle at Hsimucheng on 31 July, which had cost the Russians 1,550 and the Japanese 836 casualties, coincided with two engagements between the First Japanese Army and the Russian Eastern Corps. The Russian mobilisation to regain the strategic town of Chiaotou had begun on 24 July from a start line on the Lan River. Here had been assembled the Russian Ten Corps, less one brigade, under General Sluchevski while the Mukden road was guarded by General Liubavin's cavalry. Much was expected of the Ten Corps from Europe, for a general view among the Russians was that the Japanese would be no match for European soldiers. Kuropatkin's initial inspection of the corps on 23 July gave less grounds for optimism. Discovering they had no pack animals, the limitations imposed on their ability to take the offensive or operate in hills were obvious. General Kuropatkin had moved forward to command this force but, hampered by the lack of information regarding the enemy, Kuropatkin procrastinated and wasted four valuable days.

On receiving news of the withdrawal from Tashihchiao, Kuropatkin returned to Liaoyang but not before imposing upon Sluchevski the same strategy for an advance intended to have been used by Stakelberg at Telissu. The Tenth Corps, divided into an advance guard, main body and left and right flank guards, caterpillared forward against the isolated Japanese right flank occupied by the Twelfth Division. The cautious advance recommenced on 29 July progressing from one entrenched position to another so that at any one time there was a rear, intermediate, main and advanced position. Sluchevski had been expressly forbidden to follow up the withdrawal of the Japanese outposts until the enemy's previous position had been entrenched. His disposition reflected the need, while advancing, to beat off a Japanese attack, fight a main defensive battle and to secure his flanks from the threat of envelopment. On 30 July, the requirement to change artillery groupings and the promise of reinforcement of a brigade from Seventeenth Corps saw the advance come to a complete halt while the diggings grew deeper.

Fifteen miles distant but separated by virtually impassable mountain ranges lay Count Keller's two divisions. He was dug in behind the Lan River in the area of Tawan and Yangtzuling, three miles to the south. His orders were to remain firm while Sluchevski advanced. Thus on 30 July General Liubavin's cavalry, General Sluchevski and Keller's corps were immobile. On that day, Kuroki had determined with Oyama's blessing to resume the offensive with a pre-emptive strike at 3 a.m. on 31 July. To meet this attack the three Russian generals, who collectively outnumbered Kuroki, acted independently. In a well co-ordinated attack, the Japanese fell upon a Russian defence divided and lacking in control and cohesion.

The Japanese dispositions saw the Twelfth Division at Chiaotou opposite Sluchevski separated from the Second Division by the same distance that separated Sluchevski from Keller. The Second Division was guarding Motienling while to their left was posted the Guards Division. The prospect of two distinct and separate battles was guaranteed.

On the early morning of 31 July, four battalions of the Japanese Second Division moved off along a goat track to join a brigade group of the Twelfth Division assigned to attack the Russian brigade holding a key pass at Pienling, two miles to the south of Yushuling. While the Russian brigade was isolated, it held a good strategic position; it had not taken the precaution of digging in, neither were its guns able to support the chosen position. The brigade of the Twelfth Division was sufficient to remove the ill-prepared Russian brigade which was unfortunate to be intercepted in a defile by the reinforcements moving up from the Second Division. According to the British Official History, Part 11:

> In places the path was so narrow that the Russians could not
> move more than four abreast, and so steep were the hill sides,
> that they were quite unable to deploy for attack, or to make
> any effective reply to the Japanese fire. In this short space the
> losses suffered amounted to five or six hundred killed and
> wounded.

Complete disaster was prevented by the unlikely arrival of a Terek-Kuban cavalry regiment who dismounted and held the Japanese temporarily at bay with rifle and machine-gun fire.

Meanwhile, a Japanese advance on Sluchevski's left flank on the Yushuling during the night caught the Russians by surprise. A vigorous battle ensued during which the Twelfth Division made some gains. The momentum was lost and the summer's heat caused a pause between midday and 3 p.m. after which a straightforward fire fight developed. At sunset the Japanese right flank found themselves in the same position they had held at 9 a.m. Rations were called up together with a re-supply of ammunition while the soldiers settled down for a night's sleep prior to resuming their attack in the morning.

During the afternoon's lull, Sluchevski received a telegram from Kuropatkin with news of Keller's battle some fifteen miles away. The news was not good, neither was Kuropatkin's decision not to send to Ten Corps the promised reinforcement brigade from Seventeenth Corps. The Ten Corps had suffered 2,000 casualties and committed its reserves, yet the essential reinforcement was denied by Kuropatkin because, 'the direction of the main effort of the Japanese had not yet been disclosed'. At 6.30 p.m. Sluchevski's cavalry flank guard gave a mistaken report that Japanese artillery and infantry were turning his left flank, an area which should have been secured by Liubavin's cavalry. Other than initiating two feeble threats against the Japanese, Liubavin's cavalry did not commit itself to the fight. When a premature report of Keller's retreat arrived, Sluchevski decided to withdraw over the Lan River under cover of darkness.

The road through the Motien Pass ran up into another pass en route to Anping and Liaoyang. Yangtzuling, thirteen miles north-east of Tawan, blocked the further move of Kuroki's army. Not surprisingly, it was the centre of Count Keller's position. The heights above the roads and watercourses were occupied by the Russians, forming a rough semicircle around Yangtzuling. There was some dead ground which favoured the attacker and the rough, rugged terrain afforded the prospect of only passive defence, preventing any possibility of counter-moves. However, ahead of the dead ground was the open valley of the Lan River and other minor valleys dominated by Russian guns. (Only thirty-two of the sixty-eight available artillery pieces were deployed and took part in the action.) The villages in the valleys were occupied by the defenders yet they had neglected to fortify the stone houses as indeed they had neglected to remove the *kaoliang* to improve their fields of fire. None the less, this was a strong Russian position with one division up and one in reserve.

Kuroki's plan was to hold the Russian front with the depleted Second Division and turn their right with the Guards Division. The attackers moved up into their positions in the moonlight of 30 July. The preliminary bombardment commenced at 6 a.m., being progressively joined by other guns once they had taken up fire positions in the difficult terrain. The Russians were effective in snuffing out much of the Japanese artillery effort. At 9 a.m. the Guards infantry advance began. At 3.30 p.m. it had stopped, having achieved nothing but casualties. Kuroki bolstered the under-strength Second Division with the right flank of the Guards Division, threw in all but two battalions of his entire divisional reserve and ordered the force forward. The Russians launched a brave but unsuccessful local counter-attack. The Japanese followed up and the Second Division succeeded where the Guards had failed. As they advanced, the Russians withdrew from an almost impregnable advanced position which was occupied by the mystified Japanese at 5.30 p.m. Elsewhere, the Japanese began to bivouac for the night, intending to resume hostilities in the morning. That night the Russians withdrew. The Russian casualties had been less than the Japanese, a mere 400, and a whole division was in the rear in reserve. The reason for this debacle stems from an event which occurred at 2 p.m. that afternoon.

The immaculate General Count Keller had been much in evidence throughout the day. He was a loved, respected and compassionate leader, given to encouraging and cajoling his men. His white beard belied his fifty-five years but his starched white tunic set him apart from the perspiring gun team that he was encouraging. The Japanese were becoming noticeably successful in identifying and going after the Russian leadership in the field. They exploded a shrapnel shell next to Keller. It tossed him aside, killing him instantly and leaving thirty-seven wounds on his body. This blow to his troops was no less severe than the loss of Makarov to Port Arthur.

General Kashtalinski replaced Keller and decided to draw on his reserves to maintain the equilibrium. The decision was referred to Kuropatkin who objected on the by now predictable grounds that 'the main effort of the Japanese had not been disclosed'. Given the withdrawal at Hsimucheng and Yushuling, Kashtalinski reconsidered his situation and made what Kuropatkin described as 'his too hasty decision to withdraw' that night.

Other than the localised slaughter at Pienling, the Russians had not suffered a severe setback but were not to be prevented from once more demonstrating their unnecessary proficiency at the withdrawal. On 1 August the Japanese First Army moved twelve miles closer to Liaoyang but made no further effort to follow up their success. Not one of Kuropatkin's formations had been spared defeat. As *The Times* correspondent observed, 'There is such a thing as the tradition of defeat, and unenviable is the army that creates it.' The Commander of the European Seventeenth Corps, General Baron Bildering, was appointed Commander, the Eastern Front. He took under command, in addition to his own corps, the redesignated Eastern Force, now the Third Siberian Army Corps and the Tenth Corps. The two opposing armies spent the next three weeks facing each other separated by only a six-mile strip of mountains.

On 3 August Haicheng, which had promised so much, was entered against light opposition. Although the Russians had spent much time, effort and money in fortifying the surrounding area, the expected battle of Haicheng did not take place. The Russians failed in the attempt to destroy their supplies which fell into grateful Japanese hands to whom, too, the intact railway bridge was a welcome bonus.

It was here at Haicheng that the Second and Fourth Japanese Armies met amidst much rejoicing. The retreat from Tashihchiao had indeed reduced Kuropatkin's front by twenty miles but, significantly, it had served to reduce the Japanese front from 140 to forty-five miles. The main body of Japan's enemy had now placed itself on the railway at Anshanchan, twenty-two miles to the north-east of Haicheng and twenty miles west of Liaoyang. The three Japanese armies paused to restock, restore and reinforce prior to the resumption of their unfettered aim of bringing the Russian Army in Manchuria to battle at Liaoyang.

CHAPTER NINE

LIAOYANG

Any acquaintance of Kuropatkin's meeting him in Liaoyang on 26 July for the first time in six months would not have recognised him. The troika drawn by three black horses, led by an escort of Cossacks and followed by a pristine staff, hurtled through the crowded streets of Liaoyang. Seemingly weighed down by the recent defeats which had necessitated his return from the Eastern Front, he sat huddled in the carriage, grey, gaunt, aged, looking ahead, not seeing the salutes being offered to his right and left. Here was a former minister used to political chicanery, a military man endowed with distinguished war experience, cultured and imaginative. That the Japanese were but a few miles from the city's gates was more attributable to his failure as a general than to any other single reason. His caution, acquiescence, inability to bear responsibility, lack of determination to execute his own plans, and the gradual erosion of his confidence being replaced by an awesome respect for his enemy, were the nails in the military coffin of his career. His reasons cabled to the Tsar for the non-event at Haicheng and the withdrawal towards Liaoyang were an indictment as much of himself as of his officers, soldiers and the whole *raison d'être* of the war. These were:

> The Japanese superiority in numbers. They were accustomed to hills and hot weather; they were younger, carried lighter loads, and had numerous mountain artillery and pack transport. Their energetic and intelligent leadership. The extraordinary patriotism and military spirit of their troops; and the lack of such a spirit on our side (caused by general ignorance of what we were fighting for).

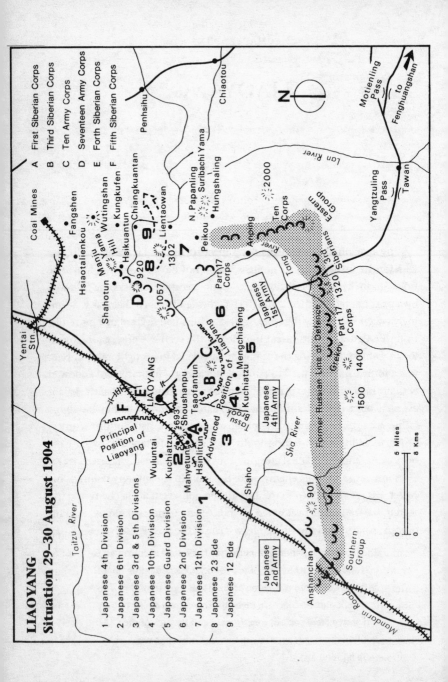

LIAOYANG
Situation 29–30 August 1904

A First Siberian Corps
B Third Siberian Corps
C Ten Army Corps
D Seventeen Army Corps
E Forth Siberian Corps
F Fifth Siberian Corps

1 Japanese 4th Division
2 Japanese 6th Division
3 Japanese 3rd & 5th Divisions
4 Japanese 10th Division
5 Japanese Guard Division
6 Japanese 2nd Division
7 Japanese 12th Division
8 Japanese 23 Bde
9 Japanese 12 Bde

Japanese 1st Army
Japanese 4th Army
Japanese 2nd Army

Principal Position of Liaoyang
Advanced Position of Kuchiatzu

Former Russian Line of Defence
Eastern Group
Southern Group

Coal Mines
Yentai Stn.
Fangshen
Hsiaotalienkou
Shahotun Manju Yama Wutingshan
Hill Kungkufen
Hsikuantun
Chiangkuantan
Lientaowan
Fenhsihu
N. Papanling
Suribachi Yama
Hungshaling
Peikou
Part 17 Corps
Anping
Ten Corps
Chiaotou
to Fenghuangshan
Motienling Pass
Yangtzuling Pass
Tawan
Lan River
Tang River
3rd Siberian Corps
Part 17 Corps
Grekov 1400
1500
901
Anshanchan
Shaho
Mandarin Road
Sha River
Taitzu River
Wuluntai
Kuchiatzu
Mahyetung
Hsinlitun
Shoushanpu
Tsaofantun
Tassu Brook
Liaoyang
Mengchiafeng
Kuchiatzu
693
920
1057
1302
2000
1320

Liaoyang was a city of 60,000 permanent inhabitants. After Harbin, it was the second city of Manchuria and the Russian military capital in the south. The railway ran generally north–south crossing the east–west flow of the Taitzu River north of the city. Within the right angle forming the south-east quadrant lay the square-shaped city approximately two miles by two miles with walls twenty feet thick and forty feet high. The walled city had not been fortified but three lines of defences fanned out from the city, over-flowing the confines of the south-east quadrant to its north and west. The furthest elliptical line of defence was forty miles long, containing within its boundary what Kuropatkin was to describe as his 'zone of manoeuvre'.

The road-railway running south from Harbin remained the Russians' sole line of communications while their Japanese enemy had the benefit of two. Liaoyang was an important road junction. The old Mandarin road ran up from the west coast of the Liaotung Peninsula and Port Arthur while another led through the passes into Korea. On each of these roads was poised one of the two wings of the Japanese army. The Taitzu River is a tributary of the Liao flowing east to west into the sea. To its south it has three important tributaries: the Lan and Tang Rivers to the east of Liaoyang and the Sha River to the south. In the dry season the Taitzu was a lethargic, meandering and polluted ribbon of water varying in width from twenty to 200 yards with a depth not exceeding much more than three feet. Consequently it was not a barrier to military operations and provided plenty of fording sites. Now, in mid-August 1904, after days of torrential rain, the moody, angry river was a raging torrent running fast, wide and deep, confining crossing to the seven bridges.

The battlefield of Liaoyang was a place of marked contrast. To the west of the Mandarin road lies the flat, open plain of the Liao Valley. Its very fertility was represented by the close-growing and abundant *kaoliang,* now over nine feet high. The growth of this crop was a factor overlooked by the Russians in March when they set out their defensive positions. To the east of the Mandarin road, the fingers of the spurs rise to join up into difficult, mountainous country. In patches are clumps of low scrub but the higher ranges are for the most part bare. In the valleys are the predictable farms with terracing seemingly making a half-hearted attempt to provide a ladder up the steep slopes.

The heart of the city of Liaoyang was the railway station positioned just outside the north-west wall. It was a hive of activity bringing soldiers, supplies and *matériel* to war. In close proximity to the station were the headquarters and administrative buildings requisitioned from the Chinese. Despite the threat of the impending battle, the Russians endeavoured to allow life to follow its normal course. This was no easy matter because the daily deluges which had begun on 7 August had confined most activity to indoors. Outside, the streets were a quagmire and the summer heat and rains conspired to inject their own lethargy. The Russians sought solace in their vodka and the ladies of pleasure, both seemingly in plentiful supply. Kuropatkin, who epitomised the moral qualities of a puritan, acquiesced in this debauchery. He permitted his Chief-of-Staff to afford more attention to his girlfriend than to the burgeoning staff work, taking on the additional load himself. Only on one occasion did this placid façade crack. The persistent drunkenness of the Grand Duke Boris rankled with Kuropatkin and, after respectful warnings had been ignored, the duke was sent packing.

Kuropatkin blamed the abandonment of Haicheng on the demoralisation of the Eastern Group following their defeat on 31 July, and on the need to reduce the gap between the two groups. Liaoyang was therefore a suitable position from which to fight what Kuropatkin described as a 'decisive battle'. Defeat for the Russians here, however, would threaten their communications through China, deprive them of the resources of the Liao plain, upon which their interior economy depended, as well as put the fate of Port Arthur beyond doubt. However, the Russian Official History is quite clear that Kuropatkin's aim in withdrawing to Liaoyang was to buy time to reinforce and, if that aim failed, to continue his retreat to Mukden. His declaration of intent to fight a 'decisive battle' was at this early stage a possible ploy to pacify the Viceroy.

Both Russian leaders met at Liaoyang on 3 August. Both recognised the dangers inherent in a Japanese turning movement over the Taitzu and the threat thereby imposed on Mukden. Alexeiev was persistent in his demand that an offensive against the First Japanese Army should not be delayed. Kuropatkin patiently pointed out to his superior the military facts of life. The morale of the Eastern Group had been badly affected by their defeat; there were insufficient officers; that their strength should be seen both qualitatively as well as quantitatively – there were far too many untrained second-category reservists in the ranks; and the shortage of transport and mountain artillery was a constant problem. Kuropatkin refused to go forward and Alexeiev departed with what he believed was a compromise in that Kuropatkin would not retire but would fight at Liaoyang.

Liaoyang was protected by three lines of defences. The innermost, known as the 'principal position of Liaoyang', had seen preparations for defence as early as March 1904. This line ran close to the city being anchored across the river on the northern bank. In the line were eight forts where 130 old-pattern guns had been dug in. Flank protection, obstacles, ditches and overhead cover provided an impressive line of defence. That the position had been fully reconnoitred and mapped by Chinese working under the orders of Lieutenant Colonel Isauma operating out of Liaoyang was not its sole disadvantage. The position was overlooked from the high ground six miles to the south-east. If the high ground fell into enemy hands, the whole of the city and the railway station would fall within the range of observed Japanese fire. It was not until 23 August that the Russians responded to this blinding glimpse of the obvious and allowed themselves to be drawn forward. They prepared an 'advanced position' along an approximate radius of seven miles from the city centre. The line ran from Manju Yama in the north-east to, with some minor exceptions, the 693 feature overlooking the railway. The position currently occupied by the Russians was some fifteen miles south and east of this line. It was described as the Anshanchan–Anping position. Not as strong as the main position, entrenchment had started in March, but it still provided a substantial if extended obstacle to a Japanese advance.

The Russian staff perceived two basic courses of action as being open to the Japanese. First, to turn a flank and second, to throw a frontal attack against the successive lines of defence. For the Japanese to turn a flank would necessitate the crossing of the river, leaving that portion of the force vulnerable to the activities of the substantial Russian reserves. The frontal attack would progressively exhaust the Japanese, setting them up for the classic counter-stroke.

The coming battle would be the first occasion that both armies would fight under the direct command of their respective leaders. An unusual feature was that the ground was of each general's choosing. The Japanese army was a well-oiled machine with high morale, confident, well practised and undefeated. These were the qualities required by Kuropatkin in order to co-ordinate a mobile defence. These were exactly the qualities absent in his army. So far, Kuropatkin had been able to dismiss his reverses as planned withdrawals or as not having been of significance. It is true that the Japanese victories had not been decisive, as their enemy had always slipped away having conducted one brilliant withdrawal after another. Liaoyang would be a final test of wills where the excuses would run out.

The Russians were divided into three groups, the Southern Group, Eastern Group and the reserves. General Zarubaiev's Southern Group consisted of the First, Fourth and Second Siberian Corps entrenched at Anshanchan. Five to ten miles to the south of this position were the advanced guards with the army reserve culled from all three corps and located three miles to the north of Anshanchan. There was a twelve-and-a-half-mile gap between the two groups. This area was screened by eleven cavalry squadrons and six guns under General Mischenko's command. The recently arrived cavalry general, Baron Bildering, commanded the Eastern Group of the Third Siberian and Tenth European Corps. They were deployed in a semicircle between the Tang and Taitzu. On the other side of the Taitzu, covering the left flank of the army, was a brigade from Seventeenth Corps. A bridge connected this detachment with the main body. The reserve at Liaoyang was under Kuropatkin's command and consisted of thirty battalions drawn from the Second Siberians and Seventeenth Corps. At Mukden was the recently arrived Fifth Siberian Corps from which eight battalions were ordered to the Taitzu River to guard the left flank. Also arriving at Mukden were the advanced elements of the First European Corps. The remainder of the army was frittered away on other duties providing garrisons, detachments and guards. Particular care had been taken to guard and protect the flanks and the railway. While most of the detachments were posted in the east, the threat to the railway from the west had not been neglected.

The possibility that China might enter the war on Japan's side provided Kuropatkin with additional food for thought. This was not sound Japanese strategy, for Chinese intervention would have drawn first France and then Britain into the turmoil with an aim of ceasing the hostilities. Such a move would not have been in Japan's interest and she satisfied herself by teasing Russia with the prospect through rumours emanating from her widely deployed espionage network. Most plausible was a report that General Ma's 30,000-strong Chinese army was massing on the western borders of Manchuria. Another rumour had a Japanese army landing at Yingkou and yet another had the Hunhutzes about to declare a formal alliance with the Japanese.

Kuropatkin's state of mind was not helped by the usual poor intelligence and the divided counsels of his generals. A key factor in Kuropatkin's defensive attitude at Liaoyang was that he believed he was significantly out-numbered. While the armies were massive by the standards of the day and surpassed in size only once previously in 1870 at Sedan, the numeric advantage rested with the Russians. Under Kuropatkin's command were 158,000 men while Oyama had 125,000. Notwithstanding the relatively poorer quality of the Russians, their self-inflicted dispersion and the higher proportion of Japanese infantry, the mathematics would still not appear to have favoured Oyama's prospect as the attacker.

The situation at Port Arthur was carefully monitored by Oyama. News of Nogi's desperate and unsuccessful attacks on 7–9 August and 19–24 August indicated that no reinforcements would come from that direction. For reasons unknown, the Seventh and Eighth Japanese Divisions were held back in Japan. With no prospect of reinforcement and further delays likely to play into the hands of the Russians, Oyama determined to retain the initiative.

He knew exactly the Russian strengths and dispositions and knew that each day they were growing stronger. He was ill at ease with his force separated by a twenty-five-mile gap and saw tactical benefit in joining forces at Liaoyang before the improving weather goaded his enemy into action. The Japanese First Army was much closer to Liaoyang than the Second and Fourth Armies. He had no intention of presenting either of these vulnerable wings to be engaged separately by the Russians before he could concentrate. Confirmation of Nogi's failure at Port Arthur was received on 24 August, the day after Oyama ordered the advance on Liaoyang to be resumed. Oyama would not wait for Port Arthur to fall or for the wet season to end.

Kuropatkin laid much of the blame for his poor intelligence on his cavalry, 'old men on little horses'. They had failed in that one function which they did regard as theirs; the provision of information. Too often it was inaccurate and exaggerated. The Russian cavalry was three times larger than that of the Japanese. Their lack of determination in breaking through hostile screens and their disdain for approaching enemy infantry resulted in a Cavalry Corps being formed under the direct orders of Kuropatkin. So short were the Russians of intelligence that rewards were offered for prisoners of war (100 roubles for a private and 300 roubles for an officer).

Each extra day in August was a bonus to the Russians in Liaoyang. The Viceroy, who controlled the distribution of troops, permitted the Fifth Siberians assigned to Vladivostok to be diverted to reinforce Liaoyang. Time was needed too in order to complete the preparation of the 'advanced position'.

Kuropatkin's plan was to hold the line Anshanchan–Anping with a strong covering force of three corps. Until 24 August their function had been simply to observe and then to fall back on the hastily prepared 'advanced position'. The theory was that by reducing his front, he was able to find a reserve of two corps which could be manoeuvred in superior numbers against any Japanese foray. His plan did not excite the Viceroy, General Bildering, the commander of the Eastern Group, nor General Sluchevski, Commander of the Tenth Corps. General Bildering had become exceedingly sensitive about fighting in front of an unfordable river and recommended that the whole force should be withdrawn to Liaoyang without fighting. Sluchevski recommended a new defensive position between Mukden and Liaoyang. Kuropatkin records the situation in his memoirs:

> These officers reiterated the same opinions still more forcibly
> early in August, when the difficulty of moving their troops
> towards Liaoyang became greatly increased by the heavy rains.
> The Viceroy, who was much perturbed about the fate of Port
> Arthur, by the news of the unfortunate result of the naval oper-
> ations on August 10 [see page 210], and whose fears were
> increased by Stoessel's highly alarmist reports, was at the same
> time urging me (August 15) to assist the fortress and make an
> advance of some sort – though it were only a demonstration –
> towards Haicheng.

As if to appear more sinned against than sinning, Kuropatkin confided his quandary to the Tsar. While it is believed that the Viceroy was ordered to stop interfering, the signal in response to Kuropatkin had a sting in the tail. The Tsar told him that as commanding general he was in the best position to decide what had to be done. Similarly, it was made clear where the responsibility would lie if the army were to be defeated.

As early as 7 August, Kuropatkin had informed Bildering that a 'decisive battle' would be fought on the Anshanchan–Anping position. By 9 August, however, he was informing the GOC the Third Siberians, General Ivanov, that the position was to be occupied by rearguards only and that serious conflict was not to be entered into. Realising that their orders were diametrically opposed, the corps commanders sought clarification. Ross reports what Kuropatkin said: 'They were to avoid a desperate struggle and simultaneously to hold their positions and gain time, but to retreat to the main defences at Liaoyang if seriously attacked, without permitting themselves to be demoralised or disorganised.'

The corps commanders went away to plan the probability of the retreat of their corps from their defended positions before a shot had been fired. It was little wonder that Ivan was becoming discouraged by his leadership. Then, on 23 August, Kuropatkin changed his mind. The 'decisive battle' on the Anshanchan–Anping position was back in vogue. Referring to the arrival of the Fifth Siberians and the impending arrival of the First European Corps, Kuropatkin wrote to Sluchevski, the Commander Tenth Corps:

> Under these circumstances, I do not think we need confine ourselves to fighting rearguard actions in the positions occupied by the Tenth and Third Siberian Army Corps and by the troops on the southern front. I am resolved to fight in those positions with all the forces apportioned to their defence, to beat the enemy back and to assume the offensive should a favourable opportunity present itself.

Kuropatkin's change of heart could not have been entirely due to the improving reserves situation. Reinforcement was, after all, proceeding in accordance with an established plan but was still, according to reports, insufficient to counter Japanese superiority. Other favourable factors had to be in train for Kuropatkin to take further risks with his troops' morale. The Russian General Staff conferences furnish two reasons: the three weeks' inactivity of the Japanese, and a report from spies that the Japanese intended to remain on the defensive. The reason for giving credence to these reports was the critical situation at Port Arthur. A Chinese spy working for the Russians and also a correspondent attached to General Oku's headquarters reported to Russian Intelligence that three to four Japanese divisions had been withdrawn from the Second Japanese Army and despatched to Port Arthur. According to the spies, they would be replaced in due course from Japan and would land at Yingkou. The reports concluded that the Japanese feared a Russian advance on Haicheng. None of this, of course, was true but was in all probability further evidence of Japanese misinformation.

More reassuring news was fed to the Russians. A further Japanese division had been 'moved' from Haicheng to Port Arthur. According to a variety of sources Oku's army had been reduced to 30–40,000 men while Telissu had seen a massive accumulation of cholera-afflicted troops. Everything possible appears to have been done to encourage Kuropatkin to capitulate to what the Japanese knew to be the Viceroy's wishes to leave the forward entrenchments for an offensive towards Haicheng. If the Japanese really were concentrating their efforts against Port Arthur and merely defending in decreasing numbers in front of Liaoyang, then Kuropatkin could have been tempted to abandon his predetermined defensive strategy. Herein lies a curiosity, for although he told Sluchevski to be prepared to assume the offensive should a favourable opportunity occur, no such orders were passed to the Army Group Commanders, Bildering and Zarubaiev. Bildering's own orders for the Tenth and Third Siberian Army Corps were that they should defend obstinately but, rather than be overwhelmed, should withdraw to prepared positions. General Kuropatkin issued confirmation of these intentions on 24 August. The situation at the outer defences had therefore changed from that of observing to offering a stout defence. Such a disposition was probably the best that the Japanese could have hoped for. Oyama's force was divided, off-balance and not in strongly defended positions. As Field Commander, it is unlikely that he would have welcomed the forward movement of the Russian Manchurian Army, but he would not have been displeased by their holding of the relatively weaker and extended Anshanchan–Anping line.

The courses open to the Japanese were broadly similar to those assessed by the Russians. The first course saw the Fourth Army being strengthened at the expense of the First and, in conjunction with the Second Army, endeavouring to smash through the Russian right, the Fourth Army hitting the front and the Second Army the flank. This course was rejected due to the vulnerability of the First Army to subsequent Russian action. The second course was to strengthen the First Army and go for the Russian left. This course was discarded because it would have weakened the Second and Fourth Armies astride the lines of communication and, in addition, would have involved crossing an unpredictable river. The Japanese toyed with a third course of using a strengthened Fourth Army to punch a hole through the Russian front, but the strength of the Russian reserves made this the least likely choice. Finally, it was decided to pursue the simple expedient of continuing the advance, exerting pressure across the whole line until the combined force could initiate a converging attack. Oyama would decide to go left, centre or right at the appropriate time at Liaoyang and not before.

From his headquarters at Haicheng, Oyama issued his orders aimed at driving the Russians from their forward position into their main position by

28 August. To the First Army was assigned the mission of forcing the west bank of the Tang on 26 August and joining up with the Fourth Army. The Fourth Army was to move northwards to within two to three miles of the Russian main defences with a view to attacking these positions on 29 August. The Second Army was to take up a position on the Sha River with a view to operating in concert with the Fourth Army on 29 August.

The general advance of the First Army was ordered for 26 August although the Guards Division moved three days earlier in order to reach its start line. Their mission was to attack the Russian right lying astride the main road. The major attack was to be conducted by the Second and half of the Twelfth Division against Ten Corps' position shielding Anping. The remainder of Twelfth Division, reinforced by part of the Kobi brigade, was to attack the Russian left. This main attack was scheduled for the night 25–26 August. The ground over which the Japanese advanced was atrocious. They encountered much difficulty in moving their mountain guns, invariably settling for indifferent positions on indifferent roads and providing, therefore, indifferent support. The Russians did not suffer this disadvantage. They had found the time to manoeuvre their guns into good indirect fire positions. The guns of the Third Siberians fought particularly well while those of Ten Corps maintained their poor reputation. They were never able to compensate for the time lost in training on the recently acquired quick-firing guns.

General Mischenko, who was previously guarding the gap between the two Russian groups, had been withdrawn. His troops were allegedly exhausted and were brought back into reserve to form Kuropatkin's promised Cavalry Corps. The gap was currently filled by weak, all-arms detachments. The advance of the Guards Division now threatened the Third Siberians while the Tenth Division of the Fourth Army was moving north-eastward into the gap, threatening to turn the Russians' inner flanks. So inflated was Kuropatkin's assessment of enemy strengths that he believed the Guards Division to be equivalent to three divisions. The Russians indulged themselves in a flurry of reinforcement. Kuropatkin ordered Seventeenth Corps to stand-to at their rendezvous point while Ivanov, GOC Third Siberians, called forward one of Seventeenth Corps' divisions, the Thirty-fifth, without seeking Bildering's permission. To assist the Third Siberians to withhold the perceived threat from the right, Ten Corps was ordered to attack eastward on 26 August. Reserves were therefore committed in a southerly direction before the Russians had been attacked. A report from General Liubavin on 25 August that there was no likelihood of the Japanese crossing the Taitzu focused both Kuropatkin's and Bildering's attention on the right of the Third Siberians and the gap in the line. Ten Corps was now exposed to the combined attacks of the Second and Twelfth Japanese Divisions.

Over the period 24–25 August, the Guards Division drove-in the Third Siberians' outposts. During the night of 25 August the inevitability of a Japanese attack was self-evident and Ten Corps' own attack was called off.

At 6.10 a.m. the Japanese artillery in support of the Guards Division opened up on the Third Siberians' position, a precipitous ridge rising 1,000 feet above the river valley. The Russians took up the duel from excellent fire positions and, continuing until 4 p.m., removed the Japanese artillery threat from that quarter. They proceeded, unchallenged, to hit the Japanese until 8 p.m.

The attack on Third Siberians' right by the Guards Division was severely hampered by the aimed fire of the Russian infantry and the very effective artillery fire. Nevertheless, they continued forward without artillery support of their own and threatened to break through into the gap between the two Army Groups. Meanwhile, Colonel Martinov of the Zaraisk Regiment, part of the Thirty-fifth Division supported by a cavalry squadron and battery of guns, heard the sound of firing while still five miles off. He had been pushed forward to reinforce the front but, without orders, he turned off the main road towards where the noise of fighting was loudest. En route, Martinov came against the Russian right held by General Grekov and a number of cavalry squadrons. Grekov gave Martinov an outline of the situation and he moved to put in a counter-attack. No offer of assistance was forthcoming from the cavalry who, despite the critical situation in front of them, sat idle all day. Martinov moved unseen up a valley, appearing on the left of the advancing Japanese line. Three battalions were immediately launched into the Japanese flank to such good effect that General Asada's brigade was forced to withdraw. The attacker became the attacked and sent an urgent message for reinforcement.

The Guards' divisional commander, seeing the entrenched heights occupied by the Third Siberian Corps, had very early on assessed the need for reserves. At 8 a.m. he applied to Kuroki for assistance and was promised the whole of the army reserve. Unfortunately, the latter was making a forced march from Fenghuangcheng and was likely to be exhausted by the time it reached the Guards Division at 6 p.m. Then what use was this reserve, comprising just the Twenty-ninth Kobi Regiment? Kuroki had gone into battle with his entire army reserve, consisting of a territorial regiment, not even on the battlefield.

In order to save Asada's brigade, his divisional commander ordered a three-battalion attack against the centre of the Third Siberian Corps. This move was never anything more serious than a diversion. Again, the superiority of the Russian gunnery was to tell, for the Japanese infantry was not to get within 1,000 yards of the Russian trenches. By 4 p.m., with their own artillery snuffed out and having completely failed, the Japanese withdrew under the cover of a violent storm. The Guards Division had that day lost 1,000 men killed and wounded.

The Tang River, running north of Anping to its junction with the Taitzu, flows through the strategic Hungsha Pass. Four miles to the north-east of Anping is a saddle known as the Hungshaling. The feature is 1,900 feet high and dominates the Tang Valley. Upon this feature sat the Tambov Regiment, part of the Ninth Infantry Division. The divisional commander had placed nine battalions in the front line, each responsible for approximately a mile of front, while in his divisional reserve were seven battalions. Only two field batteries and four mountain guns had been placed in position. The Ninth Division was about to receive Kuroki's main central thrust of the Japanese Second Division supported by the Twelfth Division's Twelfth Brigade. To General Kigoshi's Twenty-third Brigade was assigned the difficult task of seizing the Hungshaling, the key to the Hungsha Pass.

The Hungshaling is a steep and rocky ridge, the northern end of which covers the Taitzu River while the southern end overlooks the Tang River flowing through the Hungsha Pass. The lower slopes are covered with trees and scrub but the last thirty–forty yards are steep and open. The Tambov Regiment and six field guns were posted on the narrow twenty-yard-wide ridge. Against this position Kuroki held little hope of success, but although apparently strong, the Hungshaling had its weaknesses. The overall observation was good but immediately to the front of the ridge was a carpet of dead ground which could not be covered by the rifle fire of the defenders. The gun positions were limited. To counter an advance within a one and a half mile radius required the guns to be brought forward to compensate for the steep fall of the ground, thereby skylining the gunners. In addition, the rise of the ground to the left and right of the guns severely limited their arcs of fire.

Ten Corps had adopted a forward position some two miles in advance of their prepared battle positions. This initial position dominated the Lan Valley and was a good springboard for offensive action. It was not a good defensive position since it could not be adequately supported by artillery and had too much dead ground to its front. The corps held a line seventeen miles long, manned by fourteen battalions with four battalions in depth and two in reserve. The Second and Twelfth Japanese Divisions attacked the Tenth Corps position on the night 25–26 August. The Second Division advanced in two columns attacking the right of Ten Corps. By 8 a.m. the attack petered out having made no progress. Anticipating a counter-stroke, the divisional commander called for reinforcement. There was none. The Twelfth Division which had advanced in five columns had met with more success when two columns penetrated the Russian line. The Russians withdrew to their battle positions to the rear but, in so doing, exposed the left flank and the Hungshaling.

The key to the centre was a 2,000-feet-high advanced feature which had resisted the Japanese attacks. As long as the Russians retained possession of this mountain, the Japanese could not advance. The danger was, however, that if the Tambov Regiment failed to hold the left flank the whole position would become unhinged, necessitating a Russian withdrawal across the Tang.

At 8.30 p.m. on 25 August the Twenty-third Japanese Brigade began its approach against Hungshaling. As they left One Tree Pass, three miles east of Peikou, the two batteries of mountain guns peeled off and emplacements were prepared. Just after 1 a.m. two battalions joined up on a prominent spur known as Suribachi Yama, while to their north-west a regiment with two mountain guns had established itself on the North Papanling. The progress to this stage had met with little resistance. Now the Japanese were exposed and every effort by isolated parties to cross the open ground was defeated by the combined effect of the rifle and artillery fire from the heights above them. These pointless Japanese heroics were stopped until daylight made it possible for them to resume with artillery support.

At dawn the struggle began in earnest. The Japanese guns at One Tree Pass were moved forward, thereby subjecting the Tambov Regiment to their fire as well as to rifle fire from the north and north-east. The Russian commander called forward three companies from his reserve as a spirited counter-attack was launched with the bayonet against the breathless Japanese struggling to gain the hill. For two hours the battle ebbed and flowed. The Russians received the news that the Ninth Division on their right had withdrawn. Their reserve was down to half a company while the Japanese had none. The Russians resorted to the rudimentary but effective method of rolling rocks on the sheltering Japanese, killing and maiming many. By midday both sides were exhausted and, as if signalled by a bell in a boxing bout, the round ended.

General Sluchevski, the Tenth Corps Commander, watched the progress at Hungshaling with much alarm. Four times he appealed for reinforcements. Bildering believed his reports to be exaggerated and refused to release the Third Division being held back in the event that the Taitzu was crossed; he remained mesmerised by the threat to the gap and the apparent corroboration provided by Ivanov's extravagant estimate of the number of enemy confronting him. Sluchevski therefore cobbled together a local reserve of four companies and during the lull sent them forward to the Hungshaling.

At 3.30 p.m. the crash of Japanese guns signalled the resumption of hostilities and the final round of the struggle for Hungshaling. An attack from the south made no progress and was extinguished by the heavy rain that began at 4 p.m. A concurrent attack from the north in regimental strength was much more successful. The Japanese swept past the abandoned battery on the col which had inflicted such heavy loss upon them. The battery commander had been wounded at 2 p.m., adding to the unit's fifty per cent casualty list. Although the guns were lost, their sights and breech blocks had been removed. Still the Tambov Regiment had clung to the south of the feature but now, with their CO wounded and 500 of their 2,500 strength dead or wounded, the regiment withdrew at 6 p.m. through Peikou under cover of the heavy rain.

Military men quite frequently suffer a form of tunnel vision in terms of their own boundaries. It is a recognised form of military myopia that looks at cause and effect in terms of the reassurance of an individual's brigade, division or corps boundaries. Many budding military tacticians are guilty of fighting in tubes, failing to comprehend the effects imposed by a neighbour, perhaps not so clever, not so well equipped, not so well motivated, who on giving up the unequal struggle imposes upon the smug next-door formation the equal effects of his own defeat. There was nothing complacent about Ten Corps, but the defeat of the Tambov Regiment at the hands of the Twelfth Japanese Division negated completely the success of the Third Siberians and was to decide the fate of the day.

While the Tambovs were withdrawing, Sluchevski sent the last regiment of his corps reserve to Peikou and again appealed to Bildering for help. At 8 p.m. Bildering gave way and agreed to place two regiments under Tenth Corps' command but, as was so often the case, it was too late. When Kuropatkin heard on the telephone of the fall of Peikou he ordered its recapture that night, for in Japanese hands the whole line of the Russian retreat was threatened.

The heavy rain continued into the evening. Reports came through that the Tang River was rising, that the ford would soon be impassable and that bridges might be lost. The only possible crossing point for Ten Corps was a bridge three miles north of Anping that was now dominated by forward Japanese elements at Peikou. The partial withdrawal of Ten Corps had also threatened the position of the Third Siberians. That evening, Kuropatkin reverted to his original plan of drawing the Japanese astride the Taitzu River and attacking one part through the bridgehead. He therefore ordered the whole army to withdraw to the advanced position.

The situation facing the Southern Group had been nowhere near as desperate as that facing the Eastern Group. The ground between Haicheng and Liaoyang is ideally suited for rearguard actions since the spurs running westward off the main feature provide a series of stop lines, many of which had been fortified. Bearing in mind the fact that the Japanese approach was confined to the road and railway, Zarubaiev had a series of options as to when and where he would accept battle. His mission had been to offer resistance but to withdraw once the enemy formed up for a major attack. The 26 August had been a quiet day on this front, the fighting having been confined to the withdrawal of the Russian advanced guards. At 6 a.m. on 27 August, the Southern Group began to withdraw, two hours after receiving Kuropatkin's orders.

The Japanese reconnaissance did not discover the retreat of the Eastern Group until 8.30 a.m. on 27 August. The Russians had conducted a difficult and dangerous withdrawal under cover of the continuing heavy rain and fog. The condition of the roads deteriorated but the weary and dispirited Eastern Group arrived at their 'advanced positions' without further conflict on 28 August. The troops of the Southern Group were not to be so fortunate.

The Southern Group had made a good break-clean assisted by the same wet and misty weather. Oku was not to hear of the Russian retreat until 8 a.m. and it was not until 2.30 p.m. that the report was verified. The weather and the state of the roads sapped the energies of the withdrawing Russians. General Stakelberg, commanding the First Siberian Corps, asked of General

Zarubaiev, Commander of the Southern Group, that his soldiers might be permitted to rest on 28 August. Zarubaiev agreed and ordered all rearguards to stand fast. For some reason, the Second Siberian Corps under General Zasulich did not comply and continued to retreat under some pressure from an advancing Japanese division. This move exposed the left flank of the stationary Fourth Siberian Corps holding a central position. They could not retreat because the road northward was already blocked. The Third and Fifth Japanese Divisions moved in on the tame Russian Corps which Zarubaiev did his best to protect. An order was sent after the retreating Zasulich to halt. He did not. The order was repeated. Kuropatkin then entered the fray and ordered Zasulich to cover the withdrawal of the corps he had abandoned and, 'if it were necessary to do so to cover the retreat of those Corps, to fight to the last man and perish'. Gradually the tired Russians were taken into the advanced lines. The withdrawal was fraught to the end, but professionally conducted against the nimble Japanese. The command of the First Siberian Corps rearguard was complicated when a shell removed the head of the commander and the shoulder of his principal staff officer.

The state of the road brought no solace to the tail-enders. Many supplies and much *matériel* were abandoned, as was a battery which was quite literally buried in the road. Teams of twenty-four horses were harnessed to a single gun but were unable to move it. The whole battery was abandoned to the enemy when the exhausted gunners began to take casualties from the rifle fire of the advancing Japanese.

So ended the first round of the battle for Liaoyang, the first conflict on the outer line of defence. It had been for the Russians a confused and confusing affair. Again, the Russian soldiers had shown great fortitude and bravery. The Third Siberians and Ten Corps had not been defeated in this battle but they were placed in such a position that they had to withdraw, accepting the stigma of defeat and a further blow to their morale. Bildering received a letter from Kuropatkin when he arrived in the advanced position. 'Unfortunately', he wrote, 'all this could have been foreseen'. That in itself was an indictment. Why had he then put forward two army groups to expend their energies in an extended position if he saw the inevitability of withdrawal? Strategically placed delaying parties could have won him some time in which to improve his advanced position. At this point, the only Russian troops in the theatre not to have been defeated by the Japanese were the Fifth Siberian Army Corps, and they had not yet entered the conflict.

The contraction of his line of defence resulting from the withdrawal to the advanced position had enabled Kuropatkin to place his Seventeenth Army Corps on the north bank of the river. He remained extremely concerned lest a turning movement against his left flank should cut his road and rail communications, thereby making his position in Liaoyang untenable. He had good reason, for a bend in the river at Manju Yama lay only eight miles from the north-easterly line of the railway. Two distinct features guarded that approach and the roads from the east, Hills 1057 and 920, the latter being known as the Hsikuantan feature.

The main defences to the south of the river were of mixed quality. Shoushan Hill was key terrain which overlooked both the railway and the Mandarin road. It had therefore been well prepared. Shoushan Hill was also known as Hill 693 or Cairn Hill due to the large stone pinnacle which shared the peak with an artillery observation post. To its west, providing flank protection, was Samsonov's cavalry, eventually replaced by Mischenko's. The hill was to the right of the First Siberian Army Corps' position which extended along the curved line of hills to Hsinlitun.

The railway ran close to the west side of Shoushan Hill, its twelve-foot-high embankment strengthening an already strong position. The Russians had emulated the Boer habit of defending the base of a feature and the villages of Mahyetun and Kuchiatzu had been turned into fortified positions or strongpoints. A whole machine-gun company occupied Kuchiatzu. Artillery was set back in tiers in depressions in the ground and was controlled from the peak which afforded excellent observation to the south and west. From this position, and from a tethered observation balloon above Liaoyang, virtually every Japanese artillery piece could be identified in the fields of *kaoliang* below.

The Japanese had brought up their medium guns and some heavy Krupp guns captured at Nanshan, but the terrible state of the roads confined the majority of these assets to the general line of the railway. Most of the forward Russian trenches were therefore protected from the effects of medium artillery fire. A further Russian bonus was that the Japanese consistently shielded their field guns from the superior range of the Russian field artillery at the expense of their infantry. The depth of the series of lines of trenches afforded further strength to the position. These ran from below the crest of the hill downhill in tiers. The trenches were stoutly made of sandbags and stone with splinter-proof interconnecting covered ways. Three to four hundred yards forward of the advanced trenches and covered by aimed fire was a broad, high barbed-wire fence. Wide gaps were left in this obstacle as if to channel the enemy into preferred killing zones, but it is more probable that time had not allowed its proper completion. The slopes were also strewn with mines.

The Russians had cleared fields of fire some 1,000 yards from the lowest trenches. The millet had been broken down to a height of three feet and then interwoven to form an effective barrier. The limitations placed on the use of mounted cavalry was accepted by both sides since the *kaoliang* inhibited their conventional use. None the less the terrain to the west of Shoushan Hill provided the possibility of counter-moves by infantry. Behind the curve of the six-mile-long feature, reserves could be marshalled out of sight and there were many covered lines for withdrawal. Additionally, a light railway had been laid to deliver artillery ammunition to the centre of the arc held by the First Siberian Army Corps.

A three-mile gap existed between the First and Third Siberian Army Corps. This was the valley of the Tassu Brook. When the initial reconnaissance was conducted in March, the *kaoliang* had not been in evidence. Consequently, it had been decided to dominate this gap by firepower, both direct and indirect. There was not now time to cut the *kaoliang* which provided an assailant with an excellent covered approach into the heart of the Russian position and Liaoyang. On 28 August an *ad hoc* detachment approximating to a brigade had been drawn together to hold an area already identified by the Japanese spies as a weak point.

The defences to the east of the Tassu Brook, held by the Third Siberian Army Corps with Tenth Army Corps on their left, were not so well prepared. Along this front, the *kaoliang* was less pronounced. Where it did exist, it had been cut little more than 500 yards from the forward trenches. To complicate matters, the presence of numerous rocky ravines provided an assailant with covered approaches to within a few hundred yards of the Russian positions. The Russians were still digging throughout the night of 29 August and when the Japanese attacked the next morning their defences had not been properly completed. Nevertheless, the positions occupied by the Russians were immensely strong. In reserve, Kuropatkin held under his command the Second, Fourth and bulk of the Fifth Siberian Corps.

The centre of Oyama's order of battle had been delayed by the seasonal rain. While he awaited their arrival to complete the thirty-mile-long Japanese line, his reconnaissance parties were putting the time to good effect by finalising their details of the Russian positions. The Russians had not wasted their time either, spending it on ground orientation for the recently withdrawn troops and improvements to their positions. For both commanders and their armies this was to be the lull before the storm, for in the unnatural quiet before the impending battle was the undoubted realisation that for both sides the battle of Liaoyang was to be their ultimate test.

As darkness fell, Oyama issued his orders to attack. He placed the Second Army's Fourth Division under his own direct command but their principal task was to protect the left flank. He assigned to the remainder of that army the task of occupying the area from the Shoushanpu position to Hsinlitun, overlooking the Tassu Brook. On the right of the Second Army was the Fourth Army allocated the area from Hsinlitun to Tsaofantun. The progress of the advance was to be regulated by the First Guards Brigade. The remainder of the Guards Division, assisted by the Third Brigade and a Kobi regiment, was to attack the line of hills running north-east of Mengchiafeng. To the Twelfth Division, supported by the Fifteenth Brigade and the Second Division's artillery, fell the task of crossing the Taitzu River to turn the Russian left flank.

Discounting the reserves, the relative strengths of the opponents saw three Japanese divisions about to attack the First Siberian Corps west of the Tassu Brook. To the east of the brook were posted the Tenth Division, Tenth Kobi Brigade, the Guards Division and Third Brigade to be opposed by the Third Siberian Corps and Tenth Corps. Assuming a successful crossing of the Taitzu, the Second and Twelfth Divisions would encounter the Seventeenth Corps. An unknown quantity was the likely effect and impact of Umezawa's brigade based on Chiaotou. Kuropatkin therefore substantially outnumbered the Japanese in the east and although he was weaker in the west, his troops held impressive positions supported by strong reserves. The question being asked by the military observers was whether the tactic of offensive-defence would work for the Russians.

Kuropatkin's concept of operations was commendably simple. He intended to absorb the initial blow at the advanced position, execute one of his well-practised withdrawals to the main position, redeploy the forces made available due to this contraction to the north of the river in order to launch a massive counter-stroke against that portion of the Japanese army which had crossed. This tactic is one of a number of possible variations and is the one that a weaker force might be expected to implement to defeat the stronger. Such a tactic was employed by Wellington. For it to succeed, surprise is of the essence, to so mesmerise the opposition while a superior force is concentrated as to blitz the detached force from a flank.

A further variation on this theme is to establish a portion of the force to absorb the efforts of the entire opposition until the stage is reached that the attacker is exhausted and vulnerable to the counter-stroke. An examination of offensive-defence battles fought in this manner reveals that the vast majority were won where the defender had a greater strength than the attacker. At Liaoyang, the statistics favoured Kuropatkin but his dispositions were such that less than half of his troops would meet the Japanese attack. The balance was almost equally divided between the General Reserve and troops on flank and detachment duties.

Oyama had no clear indication of Kuropatkin's plan. He remained, in that respect, reactive throughout. It is reasonable to believe that he would have been au fait with the doctrine of that German strategic guru of the new Japanese army, von Moltke. In the solution to his fiftieth problem, von Moltke wrote:

> According to my opinion, owing to improvements in firearms, the tactical defensive has gained a great advantage over the tactical offensive. It appears to me more favourable if the offensive is only assumed after repulsing several attacks of the enemy.

It is perhaps for this reason that Oyama kept the Fourth Division under his operational control to meet possible Russian counter-moves and why he was to display great reluctance to release the division back to under command Second Army.

The role of the reserves was most important at Liaoyang. While the Japanese, as usual, involved themselves with total commitment and held reserves of no great significance, this was not in accordance with Kuropatkin's perception. He had predictably over-assessed the Japanese strength. He believed that they would hold back substantial reserves in order to effect a *coup de grâce*. Kuropatkin determined that he would only trigger his massive counter-stroke once the entire Japanese force was committed. He would await an indication of the 'direction of the principal effort' before launching his 'decisive blow'. A straw poll held among the many military observers would still have found a majority favouring Kuropatkin's position. Brigadier W. H-H. Waters, a British observer attached to Stakelberg's First Siberian Corps, made this sage and enlightened comment:

> It was interesting to hear the arguments of those who derided the idea of Kuroki venturing to assail the Russian communications, for they omitted one essential point: they based their reasoning on the false assumption that the Russian army could at any time be moved without difficulty in any direction.

The morning of 30 August brought an inauspicious beginning to the Japanese fortunes of war. At daybreak, the commander of the attack's regulating brigade, General Asada, was informed that the Tenth Division on his left was preparing to advance. The First Guards Brigade artillery was therefore ordered at 6 a.m. to commence preparatory fire. The reaction from the Russians was as effective as it was massive. The British attaché with the Guards Division was to report 'a regular canopy of bursting shrapnel hung over the Weichiakou valley all day'. Asada dallied, hoping for the artillery fire to abate, but it did not. Just before midday he ordered forward his Second Regiment. By this time Ivanov, the Third Corps commander, had placed all his reserves in the line having reconstituted a corps reserve from attachments rushed over from Tenth Corps. The Second Regiment was not to reach to within 1,000 yards of the Russian lines and suffered seventy-one killed and 325 wounded. By last light the First Guards Brigade had not progressed forward of its morning start line.

To the right of the First Guards Brigade was the Second Guards Brigade. Some skirmishing occurred in the early morning but the commander of the Second Brigade otherwise waited for the First Brigade to move. At 11.30 a.m. the impatient brigade commander decided to act on his own account and sent forward into the attack a regiment supported by a Kobi battalion. This attack was aimed at the 1,030-feet feature to the front of the arc formed by the deployment of the Third and Tenth Corps. The ground here was held by the Eleventh East Siberian Regiment and the Thirty-sixth (Orel) Regiment. Just after noon, the Russian position was reinforced by three battalions to confront the Japanese, now 1,000 yards from the Russian lines. At this point, the attackers were met by heavy fire and were forced to advance in company rushes of 100 yards. The Fourth Guards Regiment on the right, seeing this progress, joined the advance supported by unusually effective Japanese artillery fire. Four batteries concentrated upon the guns and forward trenches, some of which were vacated by the defenders. Little by little, using fire and movement, the Japanese line made its irregular progress forward, successively occupying the vacant Russian trenches. At this critical juncture four new Russian battalions arrived on the scene, but the positive action of a battery commander saved the day. He saw the infantry situation crumbling before him and brought his battery around from the rear of Hill 1030 and over open sights poured shrapnel at 400 yards into the advancing Japanese ranks.

While the Russians were winkling the residue of the Japanese out of their forward trenches, the Commander of the Guards Division was reading an ominous signal which had arrived at 3.30 p.m. from his cavalry. It read, 'The Tenth Division and left wing of our division have been heavily engaged since the morning and a large column of the enemy is threatening the Fourth Army.' For the remainder of daylight the infantry in contact sustained a heavy fire fight but at last light the remaining Japanese guns ceased firing. The Commander Second Brigade advised the divisional commander that he would be unable to defeat an enemy counter-attack from his forward position. With great reluctance, the divisional commander ordered the brigade back to the morning's start line. The troops were unused to reverses and were exceedingly dejected, particularly in view of the fact that five companies of the reserve had remained uncommitted. The question they pondered was what had happened to the Second Division's Third Brigade on their right? The Japanese were indeed experiencing a disproportionate degree of 'friction' that day. A mix-up had occurred with the orders. While it was intended that the Second Division's Third Brigade should support the Guards, confirmatory orders were not forthcoming until 7.30 p.m. In the meantime, an officer on Kuroki's staff, of his own volition had arrived at the headquarters of the spectating brigade to suggest they should do something to ease the lot of those being slaughtered on their left flank. The brigade was preparing to comply with orders to rejoin the Second Division but, on being acquainted with the situation, agreed to attack. It was too late. By the time the brigade was ready to move, darkness fell. The Russians had been fortunate for the left flank of Ten Corps had been spared any attack, thereby allowing reserves to be moved to bolster the left. That the Japanese were outnumbered was unfortunate; that they were unable to co-operate proved disastrous. The situation reports accumulating at Oyama's headquarters in Shaho village provided him with clear evidence that the Russians were not withdrawing to Mukden and that he had a fight on his hands.

This truth was confirmed by the experience of the Tenth Japanese Division. At 5 a.m. the division, supported by two Kobi regiments, advanced on the heights to the south and west of Tsaofantun. Just south of the main Third Corps position was an isolated battalion position on a hill north of the village of Kuchiatzu. (Not to be confused with a village of the same name in the vicinity of Hill 693.) The third battalion of the Twenty-third East Siberian Regiment bore the full brunt of the right of the Japanese attack which was supported by six batteries of artillery. The Russians left their trenches and charged to meet the advancing Japanese with their bayonets. This phenomenon was noted elsewhere on the battlefield by a British Captain, J. B. (James) Jardine, attached to the Second Division:

> Whenever one side charged, the other side always charged to meet them. To a listener the effect was extraordinary. A hot musketry fight might be in progress, when suddenly the Russians would sound the charge. Instantly all firing would cease on either side, the Japanese cheering wildly in answer to the drums and bugles of the enemy. The Russians cheer 'Hoorah!', the Japanese, on such desperate occasions, cheer 'Wa-a-a!' The impression given by these cheers, mingling with the rattle of the drums and the clangour of the bugles, was more melancholy than martial, sounding like a prolonged wail of grief ascending from the troubled earth up into the dark heavens.

This was an appropriate requiem for the Russians who, having given up their protection, were overwhelmed by a superior Japanese force. In twenty minutes, the battalion lost all its officers and non-commissioned officers as well as 304 out of a total of 502 soldiers. Again, a Russian battery came forward into the open and at a range of 600 yards provided the necessary covering fire for the remnant of the shattered battalion to extract themselves. (This battery suffered heavy losses and for the last two hours was only able to fire one gun.) Here, the advance of the Japanese right column was held while reinforcements were brought up into the Russian main position.

The overall Japanese plan to unhinge the Tassu Brook position was for the Fourth Army's Fifth Division to turn the inner flank of the First Corps position while their Tenth Division was to turn the inner flank of the Third

Corps. This latter role had been given to the left column now moving northward into the jaws of the valley. Ivanov had reinforced his right strongly to meet this assault. When the Japanese reached to within comfortable artillery range they were struck by four batteries from the flank and one from the front. So severely were they hit that they were required to be reinforced that morning by two regular battalions and two Kobi companies. This gave the group added momentum and carried them forward to within 500 yards of the Russian positions. At this point, the *kaoliang* had been cut down and the lack of cover prevented any further progress. All the while, the Russian reserves were being sent forward. Ivanov had used three battalions of his reserve in this area and Kuropatkin ordered forward a regiment from the Second Corps. At the same time, the artillery assets were strengthened and ready to halt the resumed Japanese attack at 3 p.m. Gradually the Japanese were turned and a Russian advance recovered those villages lost earlier in the day. At the same time, the reinforcements from the Second Corps arrived to alter the balance in the east of the area to Russia's advantage. The Japanese were rolled back, even from the hill wrested from the battalion of the Twenty-third East Siberian Regiment. The whole line held by the Third and Tenth Corps had therefore stood its ground and the Japanese withdrew after a severe and unusual tactical reversal.

Kuropatkin's astute perception of the likelihood of a Japanese turning movement, even to correctly identifying the crossing point, led to a requirement to have a reserve of fresh cavalry. Orders were issued for Mischenko's weary cavalry to replace Samsonov's on the Russian right flank with Samsonov's cavalry passing into reserve. What followed was an example of how a relief in place should not be conducted. Samsonov withdrew without relief. When Mischenko arrived on the right flank on 30 August he was horrified to discover that the First Japanese Cavalry Brigade had taken up position in the village of Wuluntai. The Japanese guns were already engaged in shelling Hill 693 and Mahyetun. For the Japanese in this sector, therefore, the beginning appeared more promising than the concurrent activities in the Third and Tenth Corps areas.

While the First Cavalry Brigade covered the left flank the Second Army advanced along the railway. On the right was the Third Division, the Sixth in the centre and the Fourth under Oyama's command on the left. The Fifth Division from the Fourth Army was ordered to support the right of the Second Army. At 6 a.m. that division's artillery opened fire. The infantry advanced in two columns with the Third Division advancing in tandem. The combined force wheeled to their right opening a gap between the left of the Third Division and the right of the Sixth.

Stakelberg of the First Siberian Army Corps made an early bid for reinforcements. (Stakelberg and the late General Keller were rated the best Russian commanders by the Japanese.) Having committed a regiment from his corps reserve he asked Kuropatkin for a division. Kuropatkin believed that the Japanese could not be strong everywhere and declined to provide assistance, that is until the situation in the Third Corps area had been stabilised. To that end, Stakelberg was instructed to assist the Third Corps and that if both positions were to become untenable, they should withdraw to the inner defences.

As the attacks on the troops holding the opening to the Tassu Brook gained strength, Stakelberg sent a further urgent request for reinforcement. At the same time he released two battalions from the corps reserve to the hard-pressed divisional commander, with the warning that Kondratovich must now find his own salvation with what he had. Noting that the anticipated attack on the right flank had not developed, Stakelberg repositioned one of his batteries to take the advancing Japanese divisions in the flank. The fire of this battery tilted the balance in Russia's favour and despite energetic reinforcement by Oku, the situation to the west of the Tassu Brook was stabilised. It was at about this time that news of a further Japanese repulse at Port Arthur spread through the trenches giving the defenders added heart.

The Japanese Sixth Division's attack on the Russian right had not developed because it literally bogged down in the low ground, turned into a swamp by the heavy rain which fell throughout the day. Although the Japanese approach march had begun at 6 a.m. it was not until 11 a.m. that the line was complete and ready for the assault. The slow progress of the Japanese was monitored both from Hill 693 and from the observation balloon. At 12.45 p.m. Stakelberg requested more reserves, but already two battalions from the Fifth East Siberian Division, a Regiment from Fourth Siberian Corps and one and a half batteries were en route to his location. They would not arrive until after the initial assault on Hill 693.

Stakelberg continued to plug the gaps in his line and send forth reserves until his corps reserve was reduced to four battalions. By 2 p.m. the first of the reserves sent by Kuropatkin arrived. The accompanying message informed the corps commander that this reserve was not to be used 'without particular necessity or until your own corps reserves have been exhausted'. The commander of the reserve was additionally informed that he was not to make his reserves available to Stakelberg until he had satisfied himself that the First Siberian Army Corps had no corps reserves left. Kuropatkin sent further reinforcements to Mischenko and a mixed force of fifteen battalions drawn from divers corps to assist the turning movement developing to the north of Hill 693. This move was uncoordinated, had no nominated commander, no precise orders and arrived in a haphazard manner. Four of these battalions were prompted by the local commander to attack a village and eject the Japanese, but otherwise the force satisfied itself just by extending the Russian line, opting not to attack the Japanese.

The Japanese Sixth Division had been held to the west of the railway. Very little of their bogged divisional artillery was available to support the infantry, most of the support being provided by the guns of the Fourth Division at the limits of its range. At 1.40 p.m. a brigade attack was ordered against the village of Kuchiatzu. The *kaoliang* cover ended 1,000 yards from the objective where the brigade was met first by heavy artillery fire and then by the full weight of a company of machine guns. The Russians reportedly felt great admiration for the Japanese as through their sights they watched these little men in khaki being bowled over as they pressed fearlessly on in the open towards the Russian lines. The Japanese artillery, straining to find the extra yards of range, took a heavy toll on their own men, leaving the bemused Russian peasant to believe this to be a ploy to encourage the Japanese to greater things. Reuters described the scene of rows and rows of Japanese infantry approaching the trenches, being mown down, filling the trenches with their bodies and new waves passing on over the bodies of the dead. An inkling of the psychological effect of modern war was becoming apparent: 'an officer went mad from the sheer horror of the thing'.

By 4.40 p.m. Stakelberg was able to report that he had not lost a foot of ground. Oku had just finished reading a signal from Oyama telling him that the Tenth Division was in trouble and that it was urgent that the Second Army should clear the Shoushan feature of the enemy and come to the aid of the Tenth Division. Four battalions were released from the Fourth Division to assist on the left of the Sixth Division. They attacked and held a village but were driven out by a Russian counter-attack. Mischenko's cavalry was ineffectual. The General requested infantry support to assist in clearing the enemy-held villages. Two battalions arrived at 6 p.m. but the cavalry commander believed this to be too late and withdrew northward to safety.

As darkness fell, the Russians had good reason to be pleased with themselves. They had had the best day of the campaign and messages of victory were already being flashed to St Petersburg. Kuropatkin's main concern was to recover his reserves, of which twenty-two battalions and fifty-six guns had been despatched to satisfy demands from the front. Stakelberg had raised his chief's ire by using four reserve battalions before his own corps had been fully committed. Those same four battalions and six others were to cause an exchange of vitriolic signals indicating that the Commander-in-Chief was beginning to feel the strain. When a number of orders to Stakelberg and to the troops concerned had not been complied with, a final signal was sent which included:

> Do not lose sight of the fact that each battalion which you fail
> to return to me may exercise influence on the success of the
> operations which have been confided to me; and that, con-
> versely, your retention without justification or authorisation of
> more than ten battalions, will render you morally responsible
> for defeat, if such should occur.

Stakelberg did not reply to the signal but immediately returned the ten battalions to the Fourth Siberian Army Corps.

That night, an air of acute depression pervaded the Japanese headquarters. This was particularly evident at Oku's Second Army headquarters. Throughout the night, numerous attacks were launched against Hill 693 and Mahyetun but, other than one temporary local success they were all repulsed with heavy loss. A further seventy-two heavy guns were ordered forward during darkness, bringing the total facing Stakelberg's corps to 306. Oku's adjutant recounts the atmosphere:

> That night the General's office was quiet though it was lit. He
> called no one. The roar of cannon reverberating from the skies
> over the battlefront, and the sound of raindrops, were louder
> than the night before. Again this night many young heroes
> would breathe their last in a foreign land bathed in mud.

To demonstrate that only success succeeds, three major generals were demoted for their doctrinaire approach to tactics and the resultant heavy loss of life. One of the relegated generals was the father of Japan's Second World War military leader, Tojo Hideki.

If any of Japan's generals were to succeed where all the others had failed, then that man was that positive, dynamic achiever, General Kuroki. He commanded a superb army superbly served by an excellent staff:

> If however, I admire the commander of our dashing First Army
> for accepting a crushing responsibility, not only without tremor
> but with a smile, I admire the General Staff just as much though
> in quite another way, for the eager and positive loyalty with
> which they labour untiringly to impress all outsiders with the
> idea that Kuroki thinks of everything for himself whilst his assis-
> tants are merely the blind and passive instruments of his
> authority.

This harmony between commander and staff reflected in the results of their soldiers was highlighted by Hamilton as his lesson of this war. He continues:

> To change our characters so that you and I may become less
> jealous and egotistical, and more loyal and disinterested
> towards our own brother officers. This is the greatest lesson of
> the war.

While his staff was engaged in the early planning for the Second and Twelfth Divisions to cross the Taitzu, Kuroki and two of his aides stood on a hill looking toward Liaoyang. They believed they saw Russian troops retreating from the river in the direction of the city. A massive exodus of trains was also observed but, had a closer examination been possible, these would have been revealed as ambulance trains. Kuroki's impression of a general retreat was corroborated at midday by a messenger from the Guards Division. Bold action was required and Kuroki, out of contact with Oyama, issued orders at 1 p.m. on his own initiative for the army to execute the river crossing at 11 p.m. that night.

Kuroki's misapprehension led him to decide to put two divisions on the wrong side of an unpredictable obstacle, crossing at a point identified by the enemy to be the target upon which the entire Russian tactical plan was intended to revolve and destroy. So unbounded was his confidence that he recognised the key role his Third Brigade had in supporting the Guards and he agreed to them remaining under command of the Guards Division. His confidence was to be seen in his troops moving down towards their assembly areas. But for their air of determination they could have been mistaken for a rabble as they marched out of step, shouting, singing and smoking. They gave the impression of an intoxicated bunch of farmers off to a clay-pigeon shoot. They were indeed intoxicated, not by liquor but rather by their own conviction of invincibility. At midnight, the soldiers began to move unopposed across the Taitzu River some fifteen miles to the east of Liaoyang. The shingle bottom was firm and the water approximately three feet deep. *The Times* described Kuroki's depleted First Army as 'a force manifestly incapable of carrying through its task with the desirable vigour and completeness should the enemy display the slightest knowledge of war'.

In his report to the Tsar on 30 August, Kuropatkin confided that he thought that part of Kuroki's army had not been engaged and that it was to be anticipated that they were being held back in order to cross the Taitzu. The Russians believed that they had accounted for the presence of approximately five and a half Japanese divisions out of their total perceived strength of thirteen divisions. It is not difficult to envisage, therefore, the possibilities conjured in Kuropatkin's mind as to the strength of the force assigned to the expected turning movement across the river.

Russian dragoons watched the Japanese cross the Taitzu and establish their bridgehead. A message was sent to Kuropatkin at 6 a.m. but the telephones proved troublesome and he was not to hear the news until 11 a.m. on 31 August. Within half an hour, Seventeenth Corps was ordered to site a brigade on the Hsikuantun feature and to push a covering force out towards the east. General Orlov's reserve brigade was ordered to follow down the railway spur to take up a position at the Yentai Mines. Meanwhile, at the river, reports of rafts and then a bridge percolated back to Russian headquarters. The Japanese had received their orders at 11 p.m. the previous night. The Guards Division and the Third Brigade were to remain detached to the Fourth Army. The intermediate objective of Fifteenth Brigade was the small hill of Manju Yama and the village of Hsikuantun with the ultimate objective being Hill 920. The Twelfth Division's mission was to intercept the communications between Liaoyang and Mukden.

The Russians lost an important opportunity when they failed to strike against the predicted Japanese river crossing. However, the Russian headquarters had received persistent reports of the crossing of the river from the 28 August onwards. Liubavin's cavalry screen withdrew in the face of the Japanese, leaving the infantry to make a belated report to Kuropatkin. The

Russian Commander-in-Chief had, in any event, decided to await definite confirmation from General Bildering before taking action.

The morning of 31 August witnessed the resumption of hostilities in the eastern sector. It was to prove, however, a confused and half-hearted affair confined essentially to artillery duelling. A mix-up in Japanese command arrangements resulted in the Tenth and most of the Third Corps being barely engaged. As Vasiliev looked out from his position on the left of Ten Corps' line he saw further movement towards the site of the river crossing. It was apparent that he was not to be attacked and he proposed to Kuropatkin that he should be allowed to launch an attack against Kuroki's weakly protected line of communication. It transpired that only four understrength Japanese infantry companies were assigned to rear area security duties. At 8.30 a.m., in anticipation of approval, a battalion was sent a mile and a half forward of the main position to secure a prominent ridge, a springboard for future action. Vasiliev was not to be rewarded for his initiative. Kuropatkin would not tolerate any extension of the line in this sector and, further, told Vasiliev that if he was so lightly engaged, he should send back all his surplus troops to strengthen the General Reserve.

The battle in the west was entirely different. Oku's army, assisted by Nozu's Fifth Division, resumed the slogging battle against the First Siberian Army Corps. The additional heavy guns had arrived by rail the previous night. To support the morning's attack, therefore, Oku had arranged in a semicircle 234 field guns and twelve heavy batteries. At 4.30 a.m. the Japanese fire mission began. Shrapnel ricocheted on and around the cairn. The single telephone wire from the artillery observation post could not cope with the traffic to the Russian guns in the rear. A secondary and dangerous back-up communication system employed soldiers lying on their stomachs passing messages hand to hand down the human chain to waiting messengers to the lee of the feature. Despite the weight of fire falling on and around the hill, the infantry were not severely affected as their trenches were strong and deep.

At 3 a.m. four regiments of the Third Division and one from the Fifth attacked towards Hsinlitun. They were unable to penetrate the wire obstacle and the ditch beyond. They withdrew but remained pinned down by the combined effects of rifle and artillery fire. On the other side of the ridge, a battalion had succeeded in overcoming the wire obstacles but was thwarted by the minefield.

The Japanese Thirty-fourth Regiment advanced up the hill immediately to the south of Hill 693. They were impeded by the *kaoliang* and the thick sticky mud which made the normally nimble infantry slow and ponderous as they advanced up the steep slopes. The Japanese persistence paid off when two Russian companies in the lower trenches were overwhelmed. The Japanese moved forward but there were less of them now. Their heroic efforts were rewarded when they captured the inner trenches encircling the top of the hill. The Japanese artillery, unaware of their infantry's success, shelled their own men. The Russian artillery engaged them from the three other sides supporting a series of counter-attacks. By now many of the Japanese infantry had run out of ammunition. When this was discovered, the Russian infantryman showed that he had become battle-hardened as he moved forward with enthusiasm to allow his bayonet to do its grisly work. At 8 a.m. the remnants of the Japanese regiment made a fighting withdrawal to the bottom of the hill while all the time the Russian artillery and rifle fire of the reserves took their toll. The regiment's total casualties were 487 killed and 632 wounded including all the officers. The Third East Siberian Rifle Regiment which had faced the Japanese lost thirty-five per cent of its officers and twenty-eight per cent of its men. *The Times* correspondent recalled: 'When we viewed the position, Russians and Japanese were lying intermingled waist-deep in the ditch, while from parapet to entanglement, perhaps 150 yards, the thick trail of prostrate khaki told a tale that no pen can describe.'

A second attack was planned by Oku supported by all his artillery assets. This new assault had some success but was never able to be decisive against the continual appearance of fresh Russian reserves. A similar dramatic struggle was taking place for Shoushan Hill. A surprise attack on the defended villages of Mahyetun and Kuchiatzu had failed and the machine guns had again reaped a terrible harvest among the Japanese infantry. On the extreme Russian right things were quieter but no less significant.

Oyama remained wary of a counter-attack against his left flank and had not further committed the Fourth Division. His entire line of communications was dependent upon the left flank being held. It was of considerable strategic importance. At 4 p.m. the Commander-in-Chief was finally swayed to place the fresh division under Oku's command to give new impetus to an attack on Stakelberg's right. The posturing of Mischenko's cavalry, however, was misinterpreted as the feared counter-attack and the Fourth Division was diverted to meet it. By the time the truth was discovered, it was dark and too late.

By nightfall, 31 August, the Russian line had not only held again but had inflicted 3,000 casualties on the Japanese. The First Siberian Corps was exhausted and unable to conduct counter-moves. Their corps reserve had been reduced to eight companies but the Army Reserve was almost intact and the other corps quite fresh. Kuroki's activities, however, continued to worry Kuropatkin who at midday had sent to his corps commanders a contingency plan known as 'Disposition No. 3 for the Manchurian Army'. This plan required a retreat into the main defences at Liaoyang while a massive General Reserve was to be launched against Kuroki's force, now estimated to be between 65–70,000 men. At 7.30 p.m. the corps commanders were ordered to implement Disposition No. 3. As Kuropatkin explained to St Petersburg:

> My general reserve was no longer strong enough to ensure a counterstroke in a southerly direction being successful. A withdrawal into the main position shortened the length of line to be defended, making it possible to concentrate a considerable portion of the army north of the Taitzu. There was undoubtedly a danger of Kuroki cutting our communications, and the most pressing duty of the army seemed to be to guard them.

By this crucial order, Kuropatkin passed to his enemy, the more tired and more demoralised of the two armies, a massive psychological victory. He transferred to his own winning team the very inflictions which had beset the Japanese by forcing upon them another dispiriting withdrawal. His poor intelligence in affording to the Japanese greater strength than they possessed contributed to the problem, as did his blind and inflexible pursuit of the offensive-defence. The 31 August plan required offensive action, not preoccupation with the husbandry of massive reserves. All three of the corps in contact had preserved to a greater or lesser degree their own corps reserves. Two cavalry divisions and thirty-four battalions within the Army Reserve and various out-stations were still intact. At midnight the Third Japanese Division launched another attack against the First Siberian Army Corps. By 1 a.m. the Japanese had discovered that their enemy had conducted another brilliant withdrawal. By 3 a.m. the Japanese stood on the heights which had caused them so much loss and frustration. As they looked out towards Liaoyang in the early light of dawn, the orders were passed for the guns to be brought forward.

The first of September was the anniversary of the battle of Sedan, the critical and humiliating defeat of the French following the Prussian invasion of France in 1870. Oyama was aware of the significance of the date, prompted no doubt by Major General Meckel, student of von Moltke and inspiration of the new Japanese army. (As a young officer Kuropatkin had been present at Sedan as a Russian observer.) The Japanese commander was keen to execute his own 'Sedan of the East'. Meckel made frequent reports to the German General Staff with a view to fine-tuning existing contingency plans. Among these was the Schlieffen Plan formulated in 1877 for the next invasion of France. Of the senior German officers, only Meckel had confidence in the Japanese ability to win at Liaoyang. There is a common though unsubstantiated belief that when the Liaoyang model of combat was superimposed upon the map of Europe, Berlin recognised that the need to find room for the right-flanking movement would involve the violation of Belgian territory. Such a belief may be crediting German strategists with a degree of strategic competence not evident in 1904–5. This period was the time when the custodianship of the Schlieffen Plan passed to Moltke the Younger. He amended Schlieffen's plan considerably but paid scant attention to the modern lessons to be learned from Manchuria. The antecedents of the 1914 attack on France are not to be found in Manchuria but in the Battle of Cannae, 2 August, 216 BC.

Oyama's belief that he was dealing with the remnant of a routed army was brought back to earth by reconnaissance showing two fresh corps, the Second and the Fourth, holding the inner defences. The efforts of his Fourth Army, the freshest of the troops available to effect a pursuit, were frustrated by heavy artillery fire. For the remainder of the troops south of the river, the day was spent in recuperation, administration and logistics in preparation for the resumption of battle. The First, Third and Tenth Russian Corps were being extracted from the battle to form the General Reserve, the sledge-hammer planned to crack the nut presented by Kuroki. The all-important counter-stroke would not be ready, however, until 3 September.

To the north of the river, Kuroki had been joined by Umezawa's reserve brigade and was occupying a six-mile line – longer than his small force would normally have been expected to hold. That morning, he had received orders from Oyama not to commit his force until the situation became clearer. The day before, Kuroki had seen the fires from the grain being burned in Liaoyang and noted the disappearance of the observation balloon which had floated over the city. Reports of the unabated flow of rail traffic northward and the news of the Russian withdrawal confirmed in the mind of this irrepressible commander the view that the situation was indeed now clear. A general retreat appeared to be in progress and Kuroki set about the deployment of his army to intercept the railway line.

The Seventeenth Siberian Army Corps was divided into three groups. On the right the Third Division held Hill 1057, the left was held by Lieutenant General Dobrjinski's Thirty-fifth Division on the 920 or Hsikuantan Feature, with the corps reserve immediately to the rear of the left flank in the village of Shahotun under Major General Glasko. The left of the corps was in a position to present the greatest obstruction to Kuroki's plan. Their total strength at this point on the Russian left was thirty-eight battalions, fifty-four squadrons and 150 guns. Kuroki's force comprised twenty battalions, three squadrons and seventy-two guns. To his west and east were substantial numbers of enemy. To their north-west at the Yentai Coal Mines were Samsonov's cavalry and a reserve brigade commanded by Major General Orlov.

At 4 a.m. Kuroki crossed the river by bridge at Chiangkuantun and climbed Swallow Hill to gain a panoramic view of the future battlefield. Six miles to the west he could see the Hsikuantun feature rising 300 feet above the river. From the north-east of this hill ran a relatively insignificant spur. Kuroki fixed his gaze on this seventy-five-foot-high knoll, 400 yards long and only a few yards wide. Of all the terrain in Liaoyang this apologetic little hill, barely visible above the *kaoliang,* was the tactical key to the battlefield; it was the Russian vital ground. Vital ground is that terrain the possession of which by an enemy will seriously interfere with the successful defence of the position. Kuroki had to take this hill in order to pass through to the railway. In addition, possession of the knoll would inhibit the movement of Russian troops from Liaoyang to the north and east. The Russians had to hold the hill to frustrate the Japanese plans. They named the place *'ssopka',* but it is more commonly known by the Japanese translation of 'rice cake hill' – Manju Yama.

At 7 a.m. the Twelfth Division advanced and seized the line Kungkufen–Wutingshan, the latter village without opposition. A battalion of the Third Brigade had crossed the river but the remainder awaited the construction of a second bridge. The Second Division's Fifteenth Brigade, commanded by Major General Okasaki, came up on the left of the Twelfth Division and joined in the preparation of shelter trenches. To Okasaki's brigade was assigned the mission of seizing the Hsikuantun feature and Manju Yama while the Twelfth Division was to push on and cut the railway.

At 8.30 a.m. an artillery duel began. The Japanese were unable to seek out the Russian guns and sought consolation by bombarding the infantry on Manju Yama. The Russians were false crested and engaged the ridge beyond the Japanese guns. At 9.30 a.m. Fifteenth Brigade should have crossed its start line but Okasaki delayed the attack in order to have the support of Twelfth Division. The commander of that division had been agitated by reports of troops manoeuvring to his north. Orlov's brigade was identified in a defensive position and the divisional commander advised Okasaki that with this threat to his right flank, the brigade would have to go alone. The Twelfth Division did put its artillery in support of the guns of the Second Division which were in direct support of Fifteenth Brigade.

Early that morning, Kuroki grasped a glimpse of what was now obvious. It was evident that the Russians were not retreating and it was clear that Kuroki was in danger. He did not shrink from his duties and took a leaf out of the Prussian book. Umezawa was ordered to the Yentai Mines to deal with the Orlov manifestation and a Kobi regiment was called forward as reserve. The Third Brigade was instructed to move to the north of the river and the Twelfth Division was required to hold the right flank with one brigade and send the Twenty-third Brigade in co-operation with the Fifteenth against Manju Yama.

The remaining two hours of daylight witnessed a heavy fire fight between the Japanese and the Russians on Manju Yama. So strongly was the knoll fortified that Okasaki decided that the feature could not be taken in daylight. The Russian commander had come to the same conclusion and thirty minutes of preparatory artillery fire beginning at 7.20 p.m. proved him to be correct. The Japanese infantry disgorging from the close *kaoliang* unnerved one battalion but they were temporarily rallied. By 10.30 p.m. the Japanese had occupied the north of the hill. Meanwhile, a Japanese thrust towards Hsikuantun resulted in the evacuation of the position by the Russian regiment holding the ground. They withdrew back into the reserve position without informing the troops on the left and right. Similarly, some of the artillery, under the same vague Seventeenth Corps orders to reconnoitre the enemy but 'without recourse to fighting', also fell back. The vacuum was filled by the Japanese who had now taken the south of the feature and were feverishly digging in to prepare for the guaranteed onslaught. The counter-attack came through the thick *kaoliang* but was repulsed. Moonlight brought a concentration of fire down upon the Russians wedged between the Japanese. At 1.30 a.m. a second counter-attack was launched. It failed and the Russian commander, short of ammunition and without prospect of replenishment through the thick millet, fell back at 4 a.m. leaving his dead and wounded thickly strewn over his former position.

The loss of Manju Yama exposed the flank of Hill 920 and in addition, the room for manoeuvre for the three Russian corps had been severely restricted. In Japanese hands, Manju Yama provided the element of a shield to protect further river crossings. Kuroki again appears to have formed an impression that the Russians were in retreat and his orders for 2 September reflected that view. Umezawa was to continue his approach to the Yentai Mines, sweeping Liubavin's cavalry before him, and the Twelfth Division was to pursue the enemy to the south of the Yentai Mines–Mukden railway junction. The Second Division was to seize Hill 920 and the Guards were to cross the river and take Hill 1057.

The Russian plans were embodied in 'Disposition No. 4 for the Manchurian Army'. The execution of this plan was entirely dependent upon Seventeenth Corps holding the Hsikuantun position. It was evident that Kuropatkin had not heard of the fall of Manju Yama. Bildering had been less than frank when he reported that 'a hill' to the north-east of Hsikuantun had been captured but he promised to recapture the position with his reserves once he had reorganised. According to the Russian plan, Seventeenth Corps was to be the pivot around which the First Siberian Corps, Ten Corps and Orlov's brigade would rotate to fall upon the Japanese. The Third Siberian Corps, less six battalions required at Liaoyang, was to cross the river and wait in reserve at Chanhsitun three miles to the north of Hill 1057.

When the loss of Manju Yama became known, the deploying First Siberian Army Corps was ordered to attack the Japanese between Seventeenth Corps and Orlov's detachment. Orlov was to advance against the Japanese right flank and rear.

Orlov commanded the Fifty-fourth Infantry Division of the Fifth Siberian Army Corps. Of that division, a reinforced brigade was *in situ* comprising reservists from Europe who had only recently detrained after their gruelling journey. It had been practice in Russia to retain reservists of the first category at home to guard against possible trouble on the Austrian and German borders. Orlov had under his command soldiers of the second category, those who had been out of uniform for many years. First-category soldiers received only two weeks training a year and those in the second none at all. These were elderly, cautious men of doubtful military value.

Reservists are only as good as their level of training, leadership and spirit will allow. Wise commanders take note of a reserve unit's strengths and weaknesses and employ them in the most suitable environment, rather as forces for courses. A comparison drawn between Orlov's and Umezawa's reserve brigade is an interesting exercise. It provides a cautionary example to those who examine military balances in purely numerical terms. Orlov's detachment had surprising responsibility forced upon it, particularly in view of the fact that their commander had been reprimanded during the Boxer Rebellion for displaying too much initiative. Their requirement was for a simple, attainable mission with good, clear orders. It would have been sensible for Orlov to have held the Yentai Mines and possibly for a reinforced Samsonov to have taken the former's role.

Orlov's detachment included the cavalry of Samsonov and Orbeliani and came under Bildering's command. Bildering's initial orders to Orlov were issued at 7 p.m. on 1 September. He was required to co-operate with Seventeenth Corps. This he acknowledged, planning to attack the Japanese right if that corps were to be attacked. He requested, if the Japanese attacked him, that Seventeenth Corps should attack their left. At 2 a.m. on 2 September, Orlov was informed that Seventeenth Corps would attack at dawn and that he should co-operate. Orders for the advance of the detachment were issued. Two hours later, a signal from the Quartermaster General arrived: 'Your principal task is to keep in touch with Bildering, and if he is not attacked to act in the manner which has been indicated. If however he is attacked at Hsikuantun you will move to his support by the shortest route.' Orlov did not understand this message for he had not received Disposition No. 4. He cancelled his advance and sent a copy of the QMG's signal to Bildering asking him for clarification. A reply was not forthcoming, for his messenger had become lost in the *kaoliang*.

Rather than do nothing, Orlov took up a position to the south of the Yentai Mines with Samsonov on his left and Orbeliani on his right. At 6 a.m. his guns opened fire on the Japanese at Wutingshan. At 7 a.m. a message from Thirty-fifth Division told of the fight for Manju Yama but said the outcome was by no means clear. Orlov was able to see the Japanese in possession of Manju Yama and the left of Bildering's corps committed. He decided to

General Kuropatkin, Commander-in-Chief Russian Land Forces (from *Cassell's History of the Russo-Japanese War*)

Admiral Alexeiev, Viceroy of the Far East (*Cassell*)

Vice-Admiral Makaroff (from E. K. Nojine, *The Truth About Port Arthur*)

Colonel, later Lieutenant-General, Tretyakov (from N. A. Tretyakov, *My Experiences at Nan-shan and Port Arthur with the Fifth East Siberian Rifles*)

Admiral Rozhdestvenski (*Cassell*)

BELOW Field-Marshal Oyama with behind him, in his shadow, the real commander of the Japanese forces in Manchuria, General Kodama, the 'Kitchener of Japan' (*Arnold*)

General Baron Kuroki
(*Cassell*)

BELOW The Yalu battlefield
seen from Tiger Hill. In the
foreground is the River Ai,
in the centre left the town
of Chuliencheng with the
forward defences clearly
visible. In the distance is
the Yalu, with its pattern
of islands (*Cassell*)

Attachés and observers with a grandstand view of the Yalu battle. They failed to learn the lessons which, in hindsight, pointed to the nature of the Great War (from *Collier's Weekly*, 'Russo-Japanese War, A Photographic and Descriptive Review')

ABOVE The Russians demonstrated the tactical prowess of a bygone era. They learnt the hard way that bunched ranks without overhead protection invited the shrapnel attacks with which the Japanese were happy to oblige (*Bulla*)

OPPOSITE TOP The Russians, seen here moving up to their start line for a frontal attack on the Japanese positions, were execrable in their conduct of this phase of war (*Cassell*)

OPPOSITE CENTRE The Russians were much more accomplished in the execution of the withdrawal, thanks largely to the Imperial Japanese Army's frequent inability to follow up (*Cassell*)

OPPOSITE BOTTOM Cossacks assembling for an attack. Neither side used their cavalry to good effect. They failed to find a useful role in this, the first truly modern war (*Cassell*)

A portent of what was to come – a Russian trench on the Eastern Front (*Nojine*). Compare this to the Japanese winter trenchworks near Mukden, right (*Cassell*)

Japanese field surgical team patching up the wounded prior to evacuation and more comprehensive surgery (*Cassell*)

BELOW The Japanese 11-inch guns were an essential force multiplier in breaking down the Russian defences (*Underwood*)

TOP 203 Metre Hill where the last reserves are seen assembling in the rear (*Nojine*)

ABOVE Japanese sapping outside Port Arthur (*Cassell*)

The strength of the Russian defences at Port Arthur took the Japanese by surprise. This is Fort Chikuan. The Japanese hurled themselves at such defences with amazing bravery, dying by the thousand in the surrounding ditches and obstacles (*HMSO, Crown Copyright*)

BELOW Japanese casualties in the ditches around Port Arthur (*Underwood*)

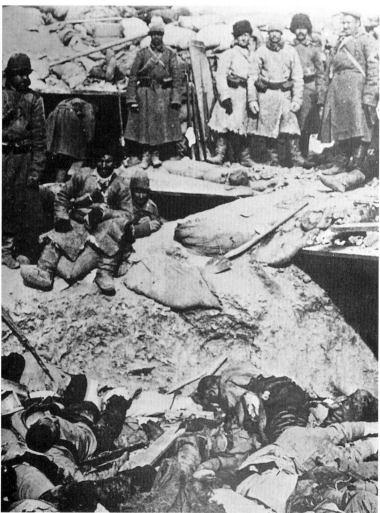

TOP Admiral Togo made three unsuccessful attempts to bottle up the Russian Fleet inside Port Arthur harbour. Steamers sunk in the attempt are seen here from Golden Hill (*Arnold*)

RIGHT Togo had a superb fleet. This is the ill-fated Tyne-built battleship *Hatsuse* (*Imperial War Museum*)

BELOW Port Arthur's East Basin and dry dock under Japanese bombardment (*MoD UK*)

TOP Sunk and damaged Russian ships after the fall of Port Arthur. From left to right *Peresvyet, Poltava, Retvizan, Pobieda, Pallada (MoD UK)*

ABOVE The development of submarines and submersibles was in its infancy. This is believed to be the beached three-ton Russian submersible *Keta (MoD UK)*

RIGHT A group photograph taken after the fall of Port Arthur with Generals Nogi and Stoessel in the centre. The implications of this battle would lead to Nogi's suicide and the court martial and sentence of death passed on the Russian hero of the moment, Stoessel (*Kyodo PS*)

TOP & ABOVE The Japanese indulged in novel logistic plans. These coolie-portable galvanised metal boxes when made into pontoons were built into bridges such as that over the Taitzu, near Liaoyang (*Cassell*)

TOP The Japanese suffered horrendous casualties in and around Liaoyang. Here bodies are collected in the *kaoliang* as a preliminary to cremation (*Underwood*)

ABOVE By the time the Russian army had withdrawn back to Liaoyang they fought their guns to good effect (*Collier's*)

LEFT Japanese 11-inch ammunition point (*Underwood*)

LEFT Captain Nikolas L. Klado, Admiral Rozhdestvenski's *bête noire* (*Cassell*)

RIGHT Captain William C. Pakenham RN, British observer assigned to the Imperial Japanese Navy, friend and confidant of Admiral Togo

BELOW Admiral Togo's flagship *Mikasa*

TOP Admiral Togo aboard *Mikasa* ten minutes before the beginning of the battle of Tsushima (*Capt. G. A. French CBE*)

ABOVE After the Battle of Tsushima Admiral Rozhdestvenski made his escape aboard the destroyer *Bedovi*. Intercepted by two Japanese destroyers, the *Bedovi* was towed to the Japanese port of Sasebo (*MoD UK*)

LEFT The captured Russian battleship *Orel* showing signs of wear and tear (*MoD UK*)

The peacemakers on board the *Mayflower* at Portsmouth, New Hampshire. On the left Sergius Witte, centre President Roosevelt, second right Baron Komura (*Underwood*)

advance. Leaving Samsonov's cavalry, two battalions and eight guns to defend the Yentai Mines, he moved forward. His concept of operations was to block the Japanese at Wutingshan, at the same time easing the bulk of his force through to Manju Yama.

Orbeliani's cavalry led the advance forward while the guns were left to move down into the *kaoliang* to find fire positions to cover the advance of the infantry. The cavalry screen found Wutingshan heavily defended and, like a curtain on a stage, exited to the left and right exposing the hapless infantry. The accompanying guns had become lost in the *kaoliang* while those left on the Yentai position were soon neutralised by the Japanese.

For the 'townies' the entering of the tall, humid, dark depths of the millet forests where unseen creatures slithered away from under their boots was in itself a daunting experience. Light percolated through as they made their noisy way southward. Drenched in sweat they paused frequently to catch their breath while their inexperienced officers endeavoured to relate their compasses to the indifferent maps and features which they could not see. Their problems had only just begun, for Kuroki's response to his belief that a Russian retreat had resumed was to order northward the crack Twelfth Brigade from Wutingshan. Both brigades advanced at the same time and were on a collision course in the depths of the *kaoliang* forest.

Soon the advance guards met, the Japanese falling with enthusiasm upon the reservists. Faced with no artillery support and the evaporation of many of his soldiers into the depths and safety of the millet, Orlov was forced to call forward four of his five reserve battalions. By 1 p.m. Orlov was in a hopeless position. His main body was being subjected to effective, professional attrition while his left flank was about to be turned. Amidst all this mayhem and slaughter there came a messenger from headquarters telling him of the reverse suffered by Seventeenth Corps and that he was to 'act with caution'. At 1.10 p.m. he replied: 'As I am unable to effect a junction with either the First Siberian or Seventeenth Corps, I am falling back on Yentai Station.' On this occasion, the Japanese did not neglect to pursue their by now terrified opponents in what developed into a panic-stricken rout.

Stakelberg's weary First Siberian Corps was advancing in two columns and the forward elements had arrived at Hsiaotalienkou. Here they met Orlov's rabble on their flight westward. The corps endeavoured to stabilise the position and rally the reservists by sending forward a regimental-sized attack towards Fangshen. Orlov was sent for and was brought in front of the very tired and unwell Stakelberg. He was told his fortune in a very heated dialogue which concluded with Orlov being ordered to remount and lead his one remaining battalion back into the *kaoliang* forest towards the Japanese guns. Obedient to the last, Orlov, supported by the brigade commander and the remaining battalion, advanced. The Japanese waited until the group was within a few yards range before opening fire. The battalion was destroyed, the brigade commander killed and Orlov hit five times in the head and stomach. The remainder of the unfortunate brigade arrived in dribs and drabs back at the Yentai Mines to be met by the horrified Eighty-sixth Infantry Regiment which had just detrained from Europe.

The situation around the city of Liaoyang was not giving the Russians undue cause for concern. A major attempt to take their flank had been blocked. The worst danger came from the accumulating effects of the Japanese artillery fire. The heavy guns had been dragged up Shoushan Hill and fired on the western defences from the former Russian positions. *The Times* correspondent recorded:

> The civilised world had never seen anything to compare with
> the final preparations for the advance of the Japanese infantry.
> The massed and scattered batteries took the line of Russian
> resistance in sections. The 250 guns opened first on the Russian
> settlement. Great columns of dust and smoke rose up from
> amidst the grey stone buildings. Then suddenly out of this
> whirlwind of bursting shell shot up great tongues of lurid flame.
> The very rocks of Shoushan quivered with the blasts of ever
> recurrent discharges. The air shrieked with the rush of high
> velocity projectiles.

The railway station, heavily utilised to evacuate wounded and non-combatants, was a prime target. There were reports of shells falling among the wounded on the platform, of would-be passengers fleeing, abandoning their baggage to be pillaged by the coolies, and enterprising Cossacks availing themselves of gratuitous champagne from the wrecked restaurant. The British Lord Brooke was in the city at this time and he witnessed 'shells burst over the post office, the Red Cross tents, the station garden, the hospital, and also in the park under the ancient pagoda, where a crowd of people who had been refreshing themselves at a restaurant there, headed by the restaurant keepers, fled helter skelter'.

The German observer, von Tettau, climbed the small hillock to the north of the gap between Hills 1057 and 920. News of the Orlov debacle had not yet been received but elsewhere the lot of the Russians appeared to be most promising. This astute German tactician had gone forward to watch the perceived Russian counter-move. He was perplexed, however, to discover that two and a half army corps merely watched and waited. He could not fathom the reason for the hesitation.

The situation facing the First Siberian Army Corps, while not grave, was not entirely rosy. The need to rescue Orlov's command had taken them further to the north than they would have wished and the regiment sent forward to assist Orlov returned having been severely mauled. Nevertheless, the Japanese advance had been blocked and Kuropatkin ordered Stakelberg not to continue his advance. At the Mines, Samsonov was being attacked by Umezawa's brigade which, having seen off Liubavin's cavalry, had moved westward in compliance with orders. Liubavin discovered the true strength of Umezawa's force and resumed his attack from the north. Umezawa stopped his attack against Samsonov, turning his attention northward towards Liubavin. Kuroki's determination to assume the offensive whatever the cost had turned a threat to his right flank into a threat to the Russian left, thereby paralysing the possibility of the counter-stroke upon which the Russian tactical plan depended.

Having spent the night in a railway carriage, Kuropatkin left Liaoyang at 6 a.m. for the eastern side of the battlefield. En route he passed the deploying troops of the Third and Tenth Corps. At 10.30 a.m. his army headquarters occupied the same hillock as that used earlier by von Tettau. No sooner had he arrived than three conflicting and contradictory signals were handed to him. From these he was able to deduce that all was not well at Manju Yama. One of the signals, from Bildering, reassuringly stressed that he was about to regain Manju Yama and Hsikuantun. Kuropatkin sought clarification and halted the Tenth Corps in his immediate area to be used as a possible reserve. A message was sent to General Zarubaiev at Liaoyang to make a 'demonstration' because 'it is necessary that I gain two days'. Zarubaiev conducted his demonstration at the cost of 1,200 Russian casualties but all Japanese assaults elsewhere had been repulsed.

The task of recapturing Manju Yama fell to General Dobrjinski's Thirty-fifth Division reinforced by one brigade from Tenth Corps. At 8 a.m. twelve batteries, later to be fifteen, opened fire on the Japanese trenches. The infantry, however, had already been withdrawn with orders to occupy their positions once the Russian infantry attack began. Bildering replied to Kuropatkin's demand for information by responding that 'generally speaking' he was about to attack. Of Dobrjinski's own ten battalions only six and a half deployed through the dense *kaoliang* to the start line while a further thirty-seven waited in reserve. There then occurred a change of mind. The attack was postponed until the evening but the information was not passed to seven companies who attacked unsupported and in consequence were defeated with heavy loss.

It was at 3.30 p.m. that Kuropatkin received definite news of Orlov's defeat at the hands of 'two divisions'. (It was in fact at the hands of the Twelfth Japanese Regiment, who lost 180 men. Orlov lost 1,450.) Stakelberg was ordered to take the remnants of Orlov's force under his command but not to advance further until reinforced by the Third Corps. Although this threat to the Russian communications to Mukden added a new dimension, the original plan outlined in Disposition No. 4 was still to be adhered to. At 3.45 p.m. the remainder of Tenth Corps was sent to Shahotun to reinforce Seventeenth Corps while the Third Corps was kept in reserve to reinforce either the First or Tenth Corps.

The Commander Tenth Corps, General Sluchevski, was placed in command of all troops assigned to attack Manju Yama including Bildering's Thirty-fifth Division. Sluchevski did not know the ground and since he was junior to Bildering he placed himself under the latter's command, thereby reducing the number of commanders planning to attack Manju Yama from four to three. Sluchevski moved forward to reconnoitre but the attack had already begun. No specific orders had been given for the attack, there was no co-ordinated fire plan and no attempt at co-operation between Dobrjinski and Vasiliev whose division from Tenth Corps had arrived that morning.

Meanwhile, Samsonov had abandoned the Yentai Mines. Although severely wounded, Orlov had endeavoured to gather the remnants of his brigade at Post 8, midway along the railway spur. A body of men arriving from the east mistook those already assembled there for Japanese and immediately opened fire. All around the post the cry 'Japanese, Japanese' was heard. Stakelberg, whose humour had not been best pleased by the performance of this brigade, had his echelon transport located nearby. It was blasted by shrapnel and the crazed and wounded horses dispersed all over the plain, taking with them the First Corps' wagons. Infantrymen fired at anything that moved, including one another. Orlov, who was heard to say 'I am finished', was evacuated back to Russia where he recovered from his wounds but not his disgrace.

Stakelberg intended to attack the enemy at moonrise. He sought the assistance of General Mischenko's cavalry but the General, who had been within two miles of the Orlov disaster without assisting, maintained his consistency, declined and withdrew. How right Kuropatkin was to record in his memoirs, 'Until cavalry is educated to feel that it should fight as obstinately as infantry, the money expended on our mounted arm is wasted.'

There were three elements to the attack on Manju Yama. Ekk's brigade on the right comprised seven battalions drawn from the First European and Fifth Siberian Corps. General Vasiliev held the central position with thirteen battalions from Tenth Corps. On the left were six battalions of Seventeenth Corps under Colonel Istomin. A reserve of nine battalions from Tenth Corps was held ready at Shahotun. Still doggedly holding Manju Yama was Fifteenth Brigade reinforced by one regiment.

The preparatory fire by 152 guns had begun at 2.15 p.m. and continued until 7 p.m. but artillery ammunition was becoming in short supply. Ekk's brigade occupied the evacuated village of Hsikuantun at 6 p.m., but their efforts to storm the southern slopes were hurled back. The main attack began as darkness fell at 7 p.m., but seemingly without Ekk's support. The moon had not risen and the darkness was total. During the advance through the *kaoliang* many of the Russians became disorientated. Some Russians fell upon their own comrades, shooting and bayoneting. A large proportion did make its way to the twenty-yard-wide peak where they hurled grenades into the Japanese trenches. They were to have no success and were forced to withdraw at 8.30 p.m.

Later the Russians returned with a supply of magnesium flares. These were taken forward under the cover of darkness and thrown towards the Japanese trenches. They were connected by fuse and on being ignited revealed the full extent of the Japanese position. A heavy volley of Russian fire from 100–300 yards raked the Japanese lines. The defenders, ducking and dodging desperately, 'hurled rocks at the magnesium balls in order to extinguish them. When this failed, a lone infantryman left his trench and, amidst the murderous fire, put out the magnesium flares with the butt of his rifle. He returned uninjured to his trench.'

By 9 p.m. the position in the darkness had become hopelessly confused with troops of both armies intermingled. Bugle calls rolled up from Shahotun while Russian soldiers sang the national anthem to identify themselves. In Hsikuantun, two battalions of the same regiment were engaged in a bayonet fight and were only separated by their band striking up the regimental march. General Okasaki was at a loss to understand the true situation. He ordered his bugler to sound 'ceasefire'. As the Japanese side fell quiet, the Russian position was easily identified by the flashes from their rifles. Some Russian reservists took the bugle call to be the 'withdraw' and required no great persuasion to do so. Okasaki was therefore able to distribute his limited reserves to best effect to meet the next Russian onslaught. Assault after assault fell upon the Japanese until at 11 p.m. they were partially driven down the eastern slopes. Bildering made a premature report to Kuropatkin that the 'pivot' was back in Russian hands.

Nothing was further from the truth. The Russian attack was beaten back leaving three regimental commanders and 300 of their soldiers dead on the ground. Reinforcements were called for and five battalions resumed the assault supported by two of Vasiliev's battalions. The Japanese observed the silhouettes of these last two battalions snaking towards them across the skyline. Rather than await their attack, the Japanese seized the initiative, leapt from their trenches and drove the surprised Russians back to Shahotun. This was the final night attack on Manju Yama. Fifteenth Brigade had held their ground amid much privation. They had endured the heat without food and water and demonstrated to the Russians a principle of the offensive-defence. Later, on 5 September, when the Japanese medical and burial teams had long completed their work with the 1,039 casualties, Hamilton stood atop Manju Yama:

> All along the crest were Japanese trenches. No corpses; only many stains and shapes of clotted blood which even the thunderstorm had not been able to wash away. But when I stepped forward and viewed the western declivity my heart for a moment stood still with horror. Never have I seen such a scene. Such a mad jumble of arms and accoutrements mingled with the bodies of those who so lately bore them, arrested, cut short in the fury of their assault, and now, for all their terrible, menacing attitudes so very, very quiet. How silent, how ghastly; how lonely seemed this charnel house where I, a solitary European, beheld rank upon rank of brave Russians mown down by the embattled ranks of Asia.

Reassured by Bildering's erroneous report that Manju Yama was back in Russian hands, at midnight Kuropatkin set his staff to fine tune the existing plans. Orlov's defeat would mean that the First Corps would need to secure the left flank, but they were reportedly in good heart and about to attack. The news from Liaoyang was good and still in reserve were part of Tenth Corps and the whole of the Third Siberians. The efforts of the Guards Division to cross the Taitzu to reinforce Kuroki were easily frustrated from the defended position around Hill 1057.

At 3 a.m. on 3 September the first of a series of ominous messages arrived at Russian Army Headquarters. General Zarubaiev reported a deterioration at Liaoyang. He had, he said, been subjected to attack by both day and night. His reserves had been reduced to three battalions and he asked leave to bring the garrison from the northern bank over the river. He drew attention to the overall shortage of ammunition being experienced throughout the theatre.

While Kuropatkin was still contemplating the situation and reasoning that he would not achieve his two days' grace without fast remedial action, a further messenger arrived. The Commander-in-Chief read the despatch from General Stakelberg:

> I report that my situation is serious, and that, in consequence
> of the severe losses suffered by my regiments during the last
> five days, I not only cannot without serious reinforcements
> assume the offensive, but cannot even accept battle. I have
> therefore resolved to retreat this night on Liulinkou, where
> I will await fresh orders.

Further messages arrived. One collated the details of the severity of Orlov's defeat while another from Liubavin's cavalry screen placed him within twenty miles of Mukden. Then came a message from Bildering. It said that the Russians had again been forced from Manju Yama and that in the morning Bildering would be obliged to withdraw and thus be unable to hold 'the pivot of the offensive movement'. The time was 4 a.m. and the tired, dispirited Kuropatkin sitting at his field desk picked up a red pencil. Across Bildering's signal he wrote in prominent letters: 'Very unfortunate. But since Stakelberg also has retreated, I must decide to retreat on Mukden and beyond. Concentrate there, reorganise and advance.' The action which had turned the Russian intentions upside down was Kuroki's threat to the lines of communication. Kuropatkin wrote: 'My communications with Mukden being threatened by considerable Japanese forces, I am retiring my army to that place, as its first duty is to protect those communications.'

It is not proposed to document the details of the forty-mile retreat to Mukden which began on 3 September and was not completed until 10 September. It followed the pattern of those previous, methodical and professional withdrawals, with the Japanese for the most part unable to follow up.

> The Mandarin Road, broad as it is and further widened by driving over the fields on each side, was almost blocked. Gradually the baggage and trains of all those army corps to which the roads east of the railway had been allotted converged upon this one route. Frequently vehicles could be seen standing side by side in five or six ranks waiting with a patience peculiar to the Russians for their turn to move on ... But the strange feature pervading the whole scene was the quiet. Russian arms, equipment, harness and wagons make very little noise even on hard ground. But the principal cause of the quietness is that the Russian is at all times quiet and patient, used to unordered methods and accustomed to find his way about amidst confusion.

A report in *The Times*, seeking to identify lessons to be learned from the Russian defeat, spoke of its 'raw material' being:

> embedded in a slough of antiquated barbarous superstition. When war came, modern war with its imperative demand for independence, initiative and intelligence, these qualities were missing. The Russian soldier, when sober and not brutalised by slaughter, is a great, strong, kind superstitious child; as good a fellow as ever stepped, but always a child. Given an educated and highly trained corps of officers of a good class, capable of instructing, caring for and leading him with judgement and skill, the Russian soldier would go far.

At Liaoyang, the Russian infantry had been the prince of the battlefield conceding pride of place to the king, their artillery. As had so often been the case, the gunners achieved the compromise which accepted a reversal instead of defeat in detail. The cavalry had once again failed to play a significant role.

The novelty of co-ordinating the operations of the Japanese army as a single entity for the first time revealed problems in command, control and communications. With the exception of the inept performance of the Guards Division towards the end of the battle, the Japanese army was balanced, fit and dynamic. An examination of the conduct of Umezawa's Reserve Brigade demonstrates the all-pervading quality of the Japanese army.

The brigade had performed as a ubiquitous, military tornado, scouring through the Russian positions flanking the lines of communication. On 1 September it had marched fifteen miles along rudimentary tracks to attack Liubavin's detachment then, on 2 September, it marched twenty miles to attack Samsonov at the Yentai Mines where its strength was reported as two divisions. When Liubavin realised the true strength of Umezawa's command he made a tentative approach on 3 September but was forced back over ten miles. That accomplished, Umezawa wheeled his brigade about and marched back the necessary eighteen miles to resume his attack on Samsonov on the railway. The many reports of this brigade appearing at different places alongside the Russian line of communication, and the exaggerated estimates of its strength, contributed in no small way to the confusion and alarm generated in Kuropatkin's mind.

The trend in sixteenth-, seventeenth- and, to a somewhat lesser degree, eighteenth-century battles had been for the period of actual conflict to be of short duration. Approaches and manoeuvring took time, but engagement lasted rarely more than a day. The battle of Liaoyang had spanned 23 August to 5 September 1904. Some Japanese formations had launched four to five major attacks in thirty-six hours. All the while, the heat, humidity, strain and pressures of battle were sapping, taking their toll, underlining a new phenomenon, the psychological factor. Armies were slow to take note of stress elements in the new modern battlefield. Four decades later, General Patton slapped a psychological casualty, unaware that he was himself a victim of those same pressures and stresses. This irrationality was seen in Stakelberg's pointless destruction of Orlov's remaining battalion.

Russian Army Orders theoretically allowed formation commanders freedom to assume the offensive and to exercise power delegated by the Commander-in-Chief. In practice, this decision-making process was rarely exercised at the appropriate level, generally being referred back to Kuropatkin. Improved communications proved to be a double-edged weapon. The commander was required to maintain contact with Tsar, War Minister, Viceroy, Liaoyang, Port Arthur, and dispersed detachments as well as the full breadth of the thirty-mile-wide battlefield. That he was able to lead a company into attack at the Yentai Mines is not the best example of the behaviour of one who pursued the principle of the centralised command of eight corps. When he put down his red pencil having made the decision to retreat, was his brain capable of rational analysis? What of his reserves? Sedgwick wrote at the time: 'The human factor is of all importance, and undoubtedly strategy as well as tactics have been affected by the exhaustion consequent on the strain of long battles.' One Russian officer's account for failure at Liaoyang had resonance of experience to be re-learned in ten years' time: 'Our soldiers were falling with fatigue and exhaustion; their nerves failed to perform their duties; we were compelled to take into account this psychological factor.' So, whereas battle fatigue had been adduced as one reason for Russia's failure, *The Times* correspondent identified a further serious failure – inadequate levels of intelligence.

> The Russians have been beaten – to put it with brutal frankness
> – because their army though good, is not good enough to fight
> Japanese – patriotism, valour, constancy are all fine qualities,
> and the Russians yield to none in their possession; but all are
> wasted in modern war if not united with intelligence (intelli-
> gence that is associated with education) – and here Russia fails
> – (Kuropatkin) found, as every Russian general must find, that
> his officers were not capable of carrying on an offensive cam-
> paign in rough ground from want of intelligence and fieldcraft.

Had Kuropatkin possessed aggressive cavalry, keen to fight the enemy as well as for reliable information, his decision, tired as he was, might well have been different. Kuroki's unopposed river crossing had been a military crime. As a military manoeuvre, it cried out for the shock action of an all-arms cavalry – heavy response. The situation was not as bleak as it appeared to Kuropatkin. The Japanese were not as strong as reports suggested. The Third Siberians were an untapped reserve who, with the support of the balance of Tenth Corps and First Siberians, had little to lose by going forward against an exhausted and depleted Japanese First Army. Napoleon's view on untapped reserves is well known: 'To be repulsed when one has 12,000 men in reserve who have not fired a shot, is to put up with an insult.' (To his brother Joseph, King of Spain, after Vittoria.)

It is easy to conjecture from the comfort of an armchair but some points are unarguably valid. The Japanese victory was due as much to Kuroki's offensive spirit as to the Japanese Fifteenth Brigade's spirit in defence. Kuropatkin did formulate a sound tactical plan but it failed in its execution because he neglected to secure and hold the ground vital to its success. As ever, the Japanese were keen to press forward and the Russians, never averse to the withdrawal. That Kuropatkin decided to withdraw did not appear to him to have been a defeat. This had been no Sedan. The statistics were apparently on his side. The Japanese lost 5,537 men killed and 18,063 wounded. The losses to the Russians were 3,611 killed and missing and 14,301 wounded. Kuropatkin's attempts to claim a victory were rebuffed by Sakharov, the Minister for War:

> According to generally accepted terminologies the side which attains its object, at whatever cost, has won a victory; while the side which fails to do so has suffered a defeat. At Liaoyang our army fought steadfastly with the obvious purpose of repelling the enemy on the Liaoyang position ... which had been strongly defended for the purpose, and where the whole army was concentrated. In the event, we did not achieve the object aimed at, were compelled by force of arms to relinquish it. Consequently we suffered a defeat.

Liaoyang had been an indecisive battle, indecisive in so far as the Russian army of 200,000 had slipped away to fight another day. Tokyo's celebrations were muted by the news of the horrendous casualties they had suffered, by the fact that the Imperial Russian fleet was still in being and about to be reinforced, and that Port Arthur still resisted their most determined efforts. The conclusion to Part Four of the Official British History, however, puts the victory of the outnumbered Japanese at Liaoyang in its true perspective:

> The importance of this battle can hardly be exaggerated. By their victory the Japanese triumphantly vindicated their strategy and extricated themselves from a position which at one time threatened to prove extremely dangerous. Moreover, the knowledge that they had emerged victorious from a bitter trial of strength gave them that supreme confidence in their own invincibility which is the greatest asset of a soldier. Lastly, a reverse following, as it would have upon the failure of the first general assault upon Port Arthur, must have been disastrous for

Japan. It is not, therefore, without reason that the twelve days
from 23 August to 3 September have been called the most
crucial period in the history of the War.

The Tsar sent Kuropatkin a conciliatory message following the news of the retreat from Liaoyang: 'From your reports of the fighting at Liaoyang I appreciate that it was impossible for you to have held that position longer without risk of being completely cut off from your communications.' He had obviously not forgotten his warning as to the outcome if the army were to be defeated, for on 6 September he decided to form a Second Manchurian Army based on the Sixth Siberian Corps. The Commander-in-Chief of both armies was to be the Viceroy, Admiral Alexeiev.

Much has been made of the 50,000 men in Port Arthur unavailable to Kuropatkin at Liaoyang, but so, similarly, was General Nogi's 60,000, later 120,000-strong Third Army unavailable to Marshal Oyama. The Russians could have been effectively employed away from Port Arthur in the early stages of the campaign, before the Japanese had arrived in Manchuria in strength but, ultimately, Port Arthur's defences would have been pointless without adequate personnel to man the fortifications. These points should be borne in mind as we move on to the siege of Port Arthur. The theory was sound but it failed in practice due to Stoessel's premature surrender of the fortress. In so doing, the entire Russian garrison was denied to Kuropatkin, while over 100,000 Japanese were freed to continue battle in the north.

CHAPTER TEN

A LAUGH TO SCORN

Hamilton's profile of General Nogi is characteristic of his then pro-Japanese sentiments although he was sufficiently astute to recognise that future Japanese aspirations would put them on a collision course with Britain and her interests:

> He is, I feel sure, a man of great nobility of character, endowed with a philosophic heroism which penetrates through the mild dignity of his manners and appearance. He seems utterly simple and unspoiled by success. Although the date of his birth places him amongst the warriors of the old school, yet he has never spared time or labour in his efforts to keep himself abreast of the times. He has read a very large proportion of modern standard military works. If I were a Japanese, I would venerate Nogi.

Togo and Nogi were equally venerated as the heroes of the war but Nogi probably did not deserve Hamilton's rosy, fawning profile. True, he was utterly simple, he was also a veteran, but in order fully to understand the siege of Port Arthur it is necessary to delve into the background of this different and complex general and his role in a different and complex battle.

Notification of Nogi's appointment to command the Third Army after almost three years in retirement came as a surprise to the Japanese military hierarchy. It was not just his age but what he had become – a married misogynist, living a simple, lonely life writing poetry and praising the Emperor Meiji. He had cut his family out of his life as though they had not existed. Privately, he maintained a deep and residual love for his wife and two sons but he chose to adopt a stern, uncompromising façade which kept any apparent weakness such as a protestation of love well below the surface. He had become disorientated, was depressive and unstable.

The original source of Nogi's misfortune was the tribal wars in 1877. During the course of a particularly bloody engagement, his regiment's colour had been lost. Nogi was convinced that *hara kiri* was the only suitable means of atonement. He was dissuaded only by the personal intervention of the Emperor. From this point can be traced the development of a fierce loyalty between soldier and Emperor, a loyalty that was reciprocated; it was a bond which lasted until the Emperor's death, and was to end for Nogi in tragic circumstances.

The zenith of Nogi's military career was the part he played in the capture in one day in 1894 of Port Arthur at the cost of only sixteen of his soldiers. During the 1894–5 war which the Chinese call *Jiawu*, the fortress had been defended by 10,000 Chinese behind permanent but not sophisticated defences bristling with 330 cannon. The Japanese had 100 guns and attacked from the north-west just twenty-nine days after their landing at Pitzuwo.

There then followed the sinecure of the governorship of Formosa, the title of baron and retirement. The subsequent political manoeuvring which was to deprive Japan of his victory engendered in the man a smouldering rage. While age may have sapped his confidence, there was no diminution of the old, tribal fanaticism. This fanaticism, the ease of the first victory and disdain for his enemy blurred his judgement. He was to neglect that most elementary of military dicta: time spent on reconnaissance is seldom wasted. He was an old soldier of an old school, set in his ways.

There were no doubts, however, as to his claim to have been a sensitive, charismatic and highly effective commander. The Reuters correspondent with the Third Army wrote:

> Whatever may be said about the manner in which his enemy was underestimated, or about the astounding lack of information regarding the strength of the position to be taken, and the numbers and spirit of its defenders, it is a fact that General Nogi commanded his army always, in the best possible meaning of the phrase. He possessed the confidence and affection of his officers, and he was universally loved and respected by his men. It was partly this that made his soldiers fight as they did, and I

think it was the consciousness that such was the case that made
his burden of responsibility such a heavy one to carry.

The optimism and requirement that Nogi would do it again, quickly and easily, received stimulation from three quite separate sources. First, reports of the Baltic fleet nearing the completion of its fitting-out in Kronstadt sent bells of alarm ringing through Togo's navy. While he had a surfeit of smaller ships which the Japanese yards could duplicate, they could not provide replacements for the *Hatsuse* and *Yashima*. If both Russian fleets were to unite, the Japanese navy could well be destroyed and the position of the land forces in Korea and Manchuria would therefore become untenable. Second, the losses suffered by the Japanese army had prompted the realisation that reserve duty would need to be extended. Oyama wanted the Third Army to join him on the road to Liaoyang, not to procrastinate in front of a fortress which he considered irrelevant. The final catalyst was Japanese public opinion encouraged by their partisan press. The capture of Port Arthur was to do with the settling of scores and that oriental attitude understood by the word 'face'.

Nogi's motivation was therefore both internal and external. He had landed at Dalny on 6 June 1904, made a pilgrimage to his son's grave at Nanshan, wrote a poem and then organised his army for the so-called Battle of the Passes. This battle saw the Japanese at the very perimeter of the Russian defences; defences which provided few possibilities of turning a flank. The Russian line was continuous. The differences between this front and the one of the next decade running from Switzerland to the sea was that the garrison of Port Arthur was surrounded by the Japanese on land and at sea.

It must have been a matter of lingering regret that as Minister of War, Kuropatkin had stopped the development of the defences of Port Arthur's outer perimeter. The money saved was spent on Dalny where the Japanese Maintenance Area was now luxuriating. This meant that the three Russian lines of defence varied in strength, Maginot-style fortresses alongside basic ditches. General Kondratenko, a popular engineer, had done much to resolve the basic weakness of the Port Arthur position. He arranged his obstacles and arcs of fire so that the Japanese would need to attack through a position of great depth, mutually supportive and capable of all-round defence.

The army of Nippon placed great store in the ability of artillery and the guns of the fleet. They were to rue the earlier loss of their eighteen 11-inch siege guns at sea. The sinking of *Hitachi Maru* and *Izami Maru* by the

Vladivostok squadron, taking their cargo of guns to the bottom, was to have a profound effect on Japanese tactics. The concrete in some of the forts was over four feet thick and would require howitzers of a calibre comparable to the lost guns to neutralise the defences. Indeed Vauban, the seventeenth-century fortress engineer, had written: 'A fortress must be breached before it is assailed.' The Japanese, however, were surprisingly complacent. While it was clear that they regretted the loss of their siege guns, Nogi maintained faith in what he had, plus the available naval guns. Since the threat of an attack on Japan appeared to have evaporated, orders for the removal of sixteen 11-inch howitzers from the homeland had been approved. This would all take time, however; something that Nogi did not have.

The Japanese assumed that the application of pure firepower to a given point would reduce both the obstacle and the will of the defenders to defend. That same misappreciation was apparent in 1914. They were about to fail too in understanding that Port Arthur required a different kind of animal to the greyhounds of the Liao plain. They would need to dust off the old field engineering manuals and update them for this and for the benefit of future conflict. The greyhounds were about to be slaughtered, obliging those who followed to adopt a different function, that of the mole.

Port Arthur had three lines of defence. The old town was surrounded on the landward side by a great ditch. Four thousand yards from the town centre was the old Chinese Wall, not in itself a significant obstacle but strengthened by new forts and reinforcement of the old. Finally there was the series of fortified hills to the north-west and north-east, the battles for which have already been described. Very little within this defence line was irrelevant, much was key terrain, but the development of the effect and range of modern weapons placed great importance on the outer line remaining secure. The identity of the vital ground was simplified by the unusual yet compelling factor of the presence of the Imperial Russian fleet. The whole of the town and harbour were overlooked from 203 Metre Hill. If this hill were to be lost then so also would be the fleet. In May, Stoessel had recalled guns being mounted permanently on Hill 203 on the grounds that a field battery could achieve the same results with greater flexibility. When all was over, Nogi was to say:

> The experiences gained during the siege show that a town or harbour cannot be protected by a ring of works concentrated in its immediate vicinity. It can only be saved from destruction by outlying forts twelve kilometres distant from the vitals they

are meant to cover. To have forts eight kilometres out is,
nowadays, no use. As for a fortified harbour or town without
any outlying works whatsoever, I would merely call that an
expensive shell trap.

The beginning of this new chapter, however, was 7 August 1904. In Harbin,
the Viceroy was penning a further determined signal to the reluctant Admiral
Witgeft: 'I again reiterate my inflexible determination that you are to take
the Squadron out of Port Arthur.' On that bright summer's day in Port Arthur,
while the devout were still at prayers, events occurred to reinforce the Viceroy's
views that Witgeft had to leave Port Arthur. On that day the first shells fired by
the Japanese Third Army landed in the old town, along the quays and among
the fleet; one 4.7-inch shell wounded Witgeft in the leg.

After a few traumas among the depressed and despondent fleet and
encouraged by an insistent message, this time from the Tsar, Witgeft decided
to take his fleet to the relative safety of Vladivostok on 10 August. In the
intervening days, sailors and naval guns were withdrawn from the land
defences and four new captains assumed their first commands. Ten 6-inch
and twelve 12-pounder guns and crews were left behind in key fortifications.
That this was not to be a significant loss was confirmed by the British Captain
Pakenham's subsequent observation that Askold's and Novik's 6-inch guns
were 'ineffective peashooters'. Still, they would have been preferable to the
wooden gun mounted on Sevastopol in lieu of one left in the repair shops.

Witgeft accepted his orders, literally and pessimistically. Among his
squadron were the old, lumbering Poltava and Sevastopol. The Peresvyet and the
Retvizan had been damaged by shellfire, the latter carrying 400 tons of water
which had entered through a hole below the waterline. A subordinate admiral's suggestion that these slow ships should make a concurrent, diversionary
attack on Dalny to allow the faster ships to make the break was declined.
'My orders', said Witgeft, 'are to go to Vladivostok with the whole Squadron,
and that I shall do.'

At 4.21 a.m. the Novik led the six battleships, three protected cruisers and
eight destroyers out towards the minefield. Of the major ships, only the mine-
damaged Bayan remained. Witgeft bade his well-wishers goodbye on the
Admiral's steps before joining the flagship Tsarevitch. His final words to the
group were: 'Gentlemen, we shall meet in the next world.' As he took his leave,
the dawn crackle and boom of rifle and gunfire from the eastern sector reverberated around the harbour. The farewell party watched the great fleet's

ponderous passage through the narrows and out to the open sea. They could have been excused for reflecting that, with the fleet's departure, much of the military justification for either defending or attacking Port Arthur had evaporated.

The fleet passed through the minefield successfully. At this point, the *Ryeshitelni* turned away and made for the port of Chefoo bearing despatches of Witgeft's intentions. His final signal to the Tsar concluded:

> I, personally, and a conference of Flag Officers and Captains, after taking into consideration all the local conditions, were adverse to this sortie which, in our opinion, cannot meet with success, and will hasten the capitulation of Port Arthur, which I have reported time after time to the Viceroy.

The 10 August, the day of the battle of the Yellow Sea, was fine but hazy, the sea was calm and there was a light southerly breeze. Patrolling the sea off Round Island to the south of Port Arthur was the Japanese main battlefleet headed by Togo's *Mikasa* leading *Asahi, Fuji, Shikishima, Kasuga* and *Nisshin*. To the east and west of the port were three Japanese divisions of eleven cruisers. Included in the Japanese order of battle were seventeen destroyers and twenty-nine torpedo boat destroyers.

Almost immediately, the Russian fleet displayed the unwelcome effects of a fleet cooped up in port. The *Tsarevitch* made painfully slow progress while the engineers on board struggled to solve her mechanical problem. No sooner was that resolved than she signalled that she was not under control and stopped. Then, just as both opposing fleets came into sight at a distance of twelve miles, *Pobieda* signalled that she too was not under control and the fleet was forced to heave-to for a longer period. It is of interest that the Russians were still in ignorance of *Yashima's* sinking for subsequent reports identified her as being present.

Just before 12.30 p.m. the Japanese opened fire at 8,000 yards on the by now slowly accelerating Russian fleet. Togo showed the same reluctance to risk his battleships in a duel with a fleet of similar overall strength. His efforts to pass ahead of his opponents, to 'cross the T', were frustrated by the manoeuvring of the Russian fleet, apparently dodging imaginary minefields. By 1 p.m. both fleets were on opposite courses at a range of 10,000 yards and the Russians were making for Vladivostok. The engagements between the battleships were by no means one-sided. The *Mikasa* was hit time and time again while the Japanese suffered from faulty ammunition and worn guns.

Togo was in a quandary. Given current positions and progress, the Russians would escape. He could use the superior speed of his battleships to close the gap, but to do so would put them at what he considered to be unacceptable risk. He decided to evolve tactics which employed gunnery, movement and speed to shepherd the Russian fleet back into Port Arthur. It was a simple plan but difficult to achieve. When his cruisers were let loose upon the Russian cruisers, the Russian battleships forced the Japanese, damaged, back into line.

In the oppressively hot mid-afternoon, the exhausted gun crews paused while the Japanese made every effort to close the distance. At 4 p.m. the *Poltava* began to labour and the rest of the fleet conformed to her slower speed. *Mikasa* sped on, to be almost stopped dead by a salvo of 12-inch shells from the *Poltava* bringing up the rear of the Russian line. Many were killed. As a reward for her impertinence, the guns of most of the Japanese fleet turned on *Poltava* but she continued to fight back. *Peresvyet* was dismasted but further hits were recorded on *Mikasa, Shikishima* and the *Asahi* on which Pakenham was a captivated spectator. *Nisshin* had suffered heavily early in the afternoon and now, with just thirty minutes of daylight remaining, it appeared as though the Russians had outwitted Togo to score an important tactical victory.

Then, at 5.45 p.m. occurred one of those critical events that changes completely the fortune of a battle. Again, luck was on the side of the Japanese. Two 12-inch shells simultaneously struck the Russian flagship, *Tsarevitch*. One brought down the foremast but the second hit the top edge of the starboard side of the conning tower where Witgeft was standing. All that remained of him that was recognisable was part of a leg. His staff and everyone inside were blown to pieces. 'The steel roof of the tower was driven against the man at the wheel, and he was killed and jammed flat against the post with the helm hard over,' wrote Richmond Smith. 'The roof of the conning tower had to be cut away before the corpse could be cut away and the steering gear liberated.' More 12-inch shells fell on the battleship now describing an involuntary circle, narrowly avoiding a collision with *Sevastopol* and *Peresvyet*. They, in turn, had to take emergency action to avoid the *Retvizan* which was endeavouring to follow *Tsarevitch*. The battleships were in complete confusion. Semenov wrote in his diary: 'Their firing was so wild that some of their projectiles fell very close to the cruisers.'

The signal, 'Admiral transfers command', was hoisted above the now stationary flagship. Prince Ukhtomski, who had led the precipitate withdrawal after Makarov's death, hoisted the signal from *Peresvyet's* bridge, 'follow me'. The *Peresvyet* had lost two masts earlier and only those ships nearby could read the unheroic prince's intentions as he made a north-westerly course back towards Port Arthur. The *Novik* was determined to carry out her orders to reach Vladivostok. Those on board held little respect for the prince, believing that he owed his position to connections rather than ability. Steer wrote that 'Prince Ukhtomski had always been considered a second rate man'.

Meanwhile the Japanese closed in on the Russian fleet. The *Retvizan* attempted to ram the *Mikasa* in an effort to draw the fire away from *Tsarevitch*. Darkness now prevented the battleships from following-up and Togo sent in his destroyers. They proved remarkably ineffectual. The *Pallada* was struck by a torpedo as she was about to enter harbour but the fact was that no major ship on either side had been sunk. The morning of 11 August revealed to the cynical and critical Port Arthur land forces five battleships, one cruiser and three destroyers in varying degrees of damage and disarray. The navy's maritime function had ended. Their sailors, guns and ammunition were again destined to supplement the land defences. They had plumbed the depths of humiliation. 'Everywhere on shore, in the streets, in the restaurants, there was nothing but abuse and curses for the naval officers, from the highest to the lowest,' recorded the Russian pressman, Nojine.

The fate of the dispersed fleet was, in the main, more humiliating. *Tsarevitch* had been hit by fifteen 12-inch shells. Her peppered funnels drained her fuel reserve so that there was no prospect of her reaching Vladivostok. (When the funnels of coal-burning ships were holed, the amount of coal required to propel the ship increased in proportion to the damage. *Tsarevitch* burnt 480 tons of coal in twenty-four hours.) Escorted by three destroyers, she made for the German port of Kiaochou where all four were interned for the duration of the war. *Diana* took on coal at Kiaochou and then sailed for Saigon where she was disarmed on 10 September. The officers and crew, among whom was Semenov, returned to Russia for further assignment.

Askold and a damaged destroyer made the port of Shanghai. The normal twenty-four hours' grace expired before any substantial progress with repairs had been made. Japanese ships were sent to the port to observe the rules of neutrality in the same manner as had occurred with Crown's *Manjour*. Both Russian captains, seeing the hopelessness of their situation, disarmed.

Ryeshitelni, which had borne Witgeft's last prophetic message to Chefoo for the Tsar, was located there by the Japanese on 11 August. Despite Chinese and other international objections, a Japanese boarding party took possession of the Russian ship. She was renamed the *Akatsuki* and joined the Japanese order of battle.

Only the *Novik* was to fight again. She was hunted by the *Tsushima* and *Chitose* and found in the harbour at Korsakov on the island of Sakhalin. *Novik* came out at the best speed her boilers would allow, planning to escape southward through La Perouse Strait. The Japanese 6-inch guns trumped *Novik*'s 4.7-inch guns and, severely damaged, she returned to port. Deriving some satisfaction from damaging the *Tsushima,* the crew of the *Novik* scuttled the gallant little ship. Next morning, the two Japanese cruisers entered port and poured shell into *Novik* until she was a total wreck.

The unreasonable disaster which had befallen Russian naval fortunes did not end there. The Vladivostok squadron was under orders to support the efforts of the Port Arthur fleet to reach their new home port. On 13 August *Rossiya, Gromoboi* and *Rurik* set out to assist the Port Arthur fleet. The next day they were intercepted by four cruisers led by the until then out of favour Admiral Kamimura. In the ensuing battle *Rurik* was sunk and *Rossiya* and *Gromoboi* limped back to port badly damaged.

The traditional military strength of the Russian soldier is generally considered to be as a determined and brave defender. Their reputation as experts in field engineering and fortifications, the heirs of Todleben, was reflected in the large number of their manuals being translated into other languages. In order to capitalise on these military virtues they required a brave, determined and charismatic leader. Instead, they were managed by a convoluted joint service committee.

The problem had been exacerbated by the withdrawal of Lieutenant General Stoessel's entire Siberian Corps from the Kwantung Peninsula into the fortress of Port Arthur, commanded by Lieutenant General Smirnov. Aware that there was neither need nor room for two competing lieutenant generals, Kuropatkin on 3 July ordered the senior of the two, Stoessel, to leave by a fast destroyer, command of the fortress remaining therefore in the hands of Smirnov. As has been recorded, the order was suppressed by the despised Stoessel, 'Mad Mullah', who assumed overall command of Port Arthur by right of seniority. A glimpse of the man's modesty was reflected in a signal to Kuropatkin to justify his position in Port Arthur: 'I consider my presence here essential for the good of the Fatherland and our troops.' (Kuropatkin was pre-empted from removing this stubborn incompetent by the Tsar's award to Stoessel of the Order of St George, Third Class, and appointment as one of his ADCs. Ever the diplomat, Kuropatkin did not need to think twice of the implications of sacking the Tsar's hero.) The competent Smirnov, Stoessel said, 'may be all right in his way but he is a professor, not a fighting general'.

It is of interest that of Stoessel's two divisional commanders, his loyal lieutenant, Fock, remained aligned while the popular and competent Kondratenko saw greater affinity with Smirnov. The chain of command, therefore, had Stoessel commanding Smirnov (still the fortress commander) with, under Smirnov, Kondratenko the GOC Land Forces. Major General Byeli commanded all the artillery, including Stoessel's corps except when they were in the field, but reported to Smirnov. To this divided and confusing army chain of command was added the representative of the Imperial Russian navy, anathema to Stoessel as the chairman of the committee. The open hostility between army and navy was fostered as much by Stoessel's cheap, public jibes at Witgeft's procrastination as by the army's perception of the cowering 'fleet in being' and the navy's view that the initial blow to their fortunes was due to the unpreparedness of the fortress defences.

The shelling of Port Arthur, which had begun on 7 August by a pair of land-based 4.7-inch guns, carried on intermittently each day until 19 August. This new threat to the public sent them scurrying to build bomb shelters adjoining their houses. This practice had previously been expressly forbidden by Stoessel who now not only succumbed to the need but was to be a frequent occupant of his own protected hidey-hole. The Japanese fleet too kept up its bombardment, while in the hills to the north-east the army prepared to mop up the two outlying features of the 600-feet-high Takushan and the smaller Hsiaokushan, Big Orphan and Little Orphan Hills.

These hills were not well defended, having a garrison of only three battalions and supporting fire from the eastern forts, but they were steep mutually supporting promontories with only the southern slopes providing easy access to their peaks. To their front ran the Ta River, dammed by the Russians to provide a stronger obstacle. From the Japanese positions to the hills was a half-mile of absolutely open ground. In Japanese hands, the Orphan Hills would complete the Japanese line to the sea, providing a geographic and strategic anchor, but the benefits to be accrued from the taking of the Orphan Hills also had a downside, as explained by one of Nogi's divisional commanders.

> The Great and Little Orphans may be likened to the meat
> between the ribs of a chicken, which is hard to get and yet we
> are reluctant to throw it away. As long as these hills are left in
> the enemy's hands, we are sure to be overlooked and shot from
> them, even though after we have taken them ourselves, we
> cannot help becoming a target for the enemy.

At 7.30 p.m. on 7 August the Japanese infantry attacked from the north-east and north-west. From 4.30 p.m. their artillery had been engaging the two hills and now it was believed to be opportune for the advance to begin. The rain and darkness prevented close support by the artillery and many soldiers were drowned in the Ta before the dam was breached. No further progress could be made that night, and the soldiers rested at the bottom of the hills to await daylight.

At dawn on 8 August, the supporting gunfire began and the Japanese infantry again moved forward, initially without success. At midday, a Russian flotilla led by the *Novik* provided sound reason for the avoidance of a Japanese attack up the easier southern slopes. The Russian naval guns firing from Takhe Bay outranged the Japanese field artillery and their minefields kept the Japanese fleet temporarily at a distance, but 3-inch howitzers, detached to the east coast hills, soon made their presence felt. The flotilla withdrew, thus allowing the infantry to resume its attack. The weight then swung in favour of the Japanese, their shrapnel falling among the brave Russian gun crews, who slumped dead around and over their damaged pieces. Gradually the Russians were forced from their trenches to make their withdrawal down the reverse slope in the gathering darkness of the evening.

The gaining of these two isolated features cost the Japanese 1,280 killed and wounded. Their army expressed in no uncertain terms their dismay at the ease with which the Russians obtained naval support. Stung by these criticisms, the Japanese naval brigade brought up four 12-pounder guns to ensure that there would be no recurrence. On 11 August these guns opened fire on some approaching small Russian ships and from that point this quarter received no further opposing naval harassment. The Russian field artillery sustained heavy fire against the lost hills but the Russians realised that this was a waste of ammunition and the Japanese were left in possession. The Russian guns lost in the battle were to remain on Big Orphan and Little Orphan Hills, surrounded by the skeletons of their crews, until the end of the siege.

At noon on 13 August a balloon rose above the Wolf Hills. It provided

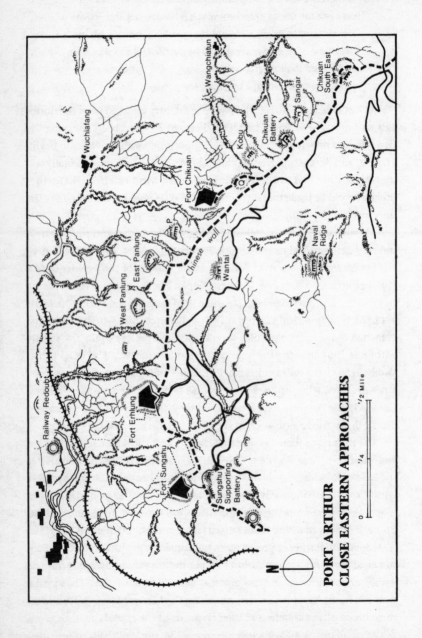

PORT ARTHUR
CLOSE EASTERN APPROACHES

Wuchiatang

Wangchiatun

Sangar

Chikuan
South East

Chikuan
Battery

Kobu

Fort Chikuan

P

Chinese wall

Naval
Ridge

East Panlung

Wantai

West Panlung

Railway Redoubt

Fort Erhlung

Fort Sungshu

Sungshu
Supporting
Battery

N

0   ¼   ½ Mile

the Russian guns with an irresistible target but after thirty minutes it quickly descended. According to Chinese spies, the photo reconnaissance had been conducted under the specific orders of Nogi who was allegedly surprised at the opposition emanating from unlikely places. 'We had no balloons in the fortress,' wrote Nojine, 'nor had we pigeons or wireless telegraphy.' Not that he was impressed with the co-ordination of gunfire within the fortress either. 'Owing to its construction, the officer commanding a section of the fortress artillery not only was unable to issue simultaneous orders to all the batteries under him, but could not even get through quickly to any one of them.'

The reconnaissance revealed nothing to dissuade Nogi from his frontal assault aimed at the heart of the Russian eastern position, the heights of Wantai. He deployed his First Division on the right, Ninth Division in the centre and Eleventh Division on his left. From Wantai, a ravine led directly into the heart of the city. Having made the breach it was assumed that the flanking forts would also fall, leaving the way clear to seize the town. Richmond Smith wrote:

> Looking back, it seemed almost incredible that such a blind confidence should have existed. It was well known among the Japanese officers that Port Arthur was regarded as one of the strongest fortress positions in the world. Knowing this, and being still further impressed with what I had just seen of the position, I ventured to hint at the possibility of failure. That was quite impossible, I was told, everything was progressing satisfactorily. They might lose ten thousand men in the assault, but they would not fail to take the place.

What Richmond Smith could not have seen was something this author noted almost one hundred years later. We have to remember that the value of Port Arthur to the Russians was the port facility and the Russian Pacific fleet. The soldiers were there to protect those assets. Wantai was at the heart of the Russian eastern, permanent, defended position and was Nogi's principal objective. Yet, standing between two Russian naval guns which are still there, and looking towards the harbour, the observer is unprepared for what he sees. From Wantai, the view of the harbour is obscured by an intervening feature, Mount Baiyu. The view of the harbour from 203 Metre Hill to the west is virtually uninterrupted, a point which has important strategic significance. The fact that Port Arthur was never subjected to a preliminary siege is undoubtedly due to General Nogi's conviction that he would repeat his success of 1894. David James, the *Daily Telegraph*'s special war correspondent with the Third Army, insisted that for the price of a division of infantry, the Third Army believed they would take Port Arthur in three days. Indeed, so certain was Nogi 'that the foreign war correspondents ... were unearthed and allowed to see the close of the drama'. Nogi was quite prepared to write off a whole division in order to be free to have a hand in annihilating Kuropatkin's army at Liaoyang. The significance of these factors only became apparent after the failure of Nogi's initial plan to take Port Arthur.

In a feint designed to create a diversion, to create the illusion that the Japanese were slavishly following the successful formula of 1894, and to protect the right flank of the frontal assault in the west, the First Division was ordered to seize 180 Metre Hill as a preliminary to an assault upon the strongly fortified 203 Metre Hill. Beyond the latter point were the New Town and the harbour. It was also hoped by the Japanese that this preliminary operation in the west would draw away troops from Wantai. At 9 p.m. on 13 August a general advance in the west began.

The position of the hills dominated by 203 Metre Hill was within the area of responsibility of the distinguished Tretyakov who was under command of the respected General Kondratenko. Here the Fifth and Thirteenth East Siberians had been reinforced by two companies of sailors. There was a limit to what even Tretyakov could achieve given the lack of preparedness:

> I was very much afraid that the Japanese would take advantage
> of their superiority in numbers, make a night attack, and cap-
> ture our weak trenches, the more so, as we had prepared
> practically no obstacles, not having had time to do so. We had
> only succeeded in putting up wire entanglements across the
> front of the trenches on height 426 and Headquarter Hill.

The Russians suffered severely from errors in placing their artillery on the crests of hills, lessons already learned by their colleagues elsewhere in Manchuria. With their enemy's field artillery neutralised, the Japanese crept inexorably forward but lost hundreds festooned dead and dying on the wire entanglements. It was not the Japanese infantry that forced the Russians out of their shallow, unprepared trenches on the advanced hills but their skilfully hidden artillery. Now the Japanese guns turned their attention on 174 Metre Hill. Streams of Russian wounded were brought down the hill, passing the reserves going upward to take their place. Tired and shocked, the defenders had already shown an inclination to quit the unequal struggle, only to be rallied by the inspirational leadership of their junior officers.

At midday on 20 August a messenger arrived in front of Tretyakov and Kondratenko who had been joined by a group of visitors accompanied by General Fock. The note was from the subaltern in command on Hill 174. It advised that officers and men were again beginning to waver and it was imperative that the one company in reserve should be despatched. Fock overheard the discussion between Tretyakov and Kondratenko and intervened due to what he described as their 'inexperience'. Fock's interference prevented the company going forward and even Kondratenko was conciliatory: 'We will wait a little longer.' Tretyakov knew his men and knew that the reserve would not have been called for had it not been required. He was to complain that, 'Colonel Irman, my immediate superior did not give me any support'. Tretyakov looked up towards the hill, covered in smoke and surrounded by noise. 'I noticed three riflemen running away from the hill, and three men without rifles behind them. I drew General Kondratenko's attention to them, and he evidently realised his mistake, for he said to me, "Ah! Now it is too late!"'

The trickle turned into a deluge. 'A disorderly retreat is always started by one man, and in most cases this man is physically weak … What an enormous influence one man, whether officer or private, can have on the issue of a battle.' Off galloped Tretyakov, Irman and Kondratenko to try to stem the unstoppable tide while fifty of Tretyakov's Fifth Siberians who had not run stood atop the hill firing into the Japanese until they toppled one by one like targets in a fairground. The Russian counter-attack failed and on 21 August the Japanese had also taken the north-east knoll of Namako Yama or 180 Metre Hill. The price the Japanese had had to pay was 1,700 men while the Russians lost 1,100 killed and wounded.

Meanwhile, by 14 August, in response to the deteriorating situation in Port Arthur, the foreign observers had come to a collective decision to leave the fortress. The only available escape route was by native junk across the Gulf of Chihli to Chefoo. In the early stages of the war the junks had run the gauntlet between patrolling Japanese destroyers to bring small quantities of food to the garrison. But of late the number being intercepted and sunk had risen so high that the benefit barely outweighed the risk. One of the first to escape was the American Lieutenant-Commander McCully. He negotiated his embarkation at Pigeon Bay on the 14th, arriving at Shanhaikwan on the 16th. Others followed the American's example but the French and German observers, Commander de Cuverville and Lieutenant von Guilgenheim, were less fortunate. An argument arose between observers and crew and, as a consequence, both officers were murdered and their bodies thrown overboard.

Back in Port Arthur on 16 August the military council was convened to consider the Japanese summons to surrender. Five days earlier, the besiegers had sent the Russians a copy of a message from the Emperor to Nogi under the flag of truce. The offer had been delayed due to the operations in the west so that they 'may be kept free from the disastrous effects of fire and sword as much as possible'. Nogi was ordered to permit all non-combatants to take their leave of the fortress. The offer was rejected by the Russians who believed that the welcome reduction of the feeding dependency would by no means compensate for the intelligence coup which the Japanese so desperately needed. The summons now before them read:

> Although the Russians have given signal proof of their gallantry,
> still Port Arthur must inevitably fall. Therefore, in order to prevent
> useless sacrifice of life, and to avoid the danger of violence and
> pillage by Japanese troops which may have to fight their way
> into town, His Imperial Majesty the Emperor of Japan suggests
> the opening of negotiations for the surrender of the fortress.

Stoessel regarded the summons as a piece of insolence and proposed that no answer be given. Smirnov insisted that military etiquette demanded a response. Childishly Stoessel retorted, 'Well, if an answer must go, let us send a blank piece of paper or else merely write a joke on it.' Exasperated, Smirnov patiently wrote out a response which both he and Stoessel signed: 'The honour and dignity of Russia do not allow of overtures of any sort being made for a surrender.' The message was delivered on 17 August. The British Official History observed:

> At the time of the parley the distance between the combatants
> was nowhere more than a mile, and yet, during the four and a
> half months which were to elapse before the Japanese should
> succeed in breaking down the Russian defence, the combined
> losses were to exceed a hundred thousand men.

On the morning of 19 August the whole array of artillery available to the besiegers began a programmed softening-up of the eastern defences from Fort Sungshu to Chikuan Battery. Many of the defence's guns were to be neutralised during the course of the day including the two 6-inch naval guns of the Wantai Battery. Also included in the fire plan was the Waterworks Redoubt to the north of the railway. The salient formed by this location would threaten the main attack and a battalion was ordered to seize the position. Wantai was the main objective from where it was intended to drive a wedge through the fortifications before cutting back to take forts Sungshu and Erhlung from the rear. This would then provide the platform from which to seize the town.

Lulled into a false sense of optimism by the ease with which the advanced trenches had been taken prior to 19 August, a company got up and rushed forward towards Waterworks Redoubt. All but thirty of the 108 fell. The next day the Russians counter-attacked. The withdrawing Japanese were caught in the open by the field artillery and their bodies remained where they fell until September when the redoubt was captured.

Simultaneously with the attack on the Waterworks Redoubt the Japanese Ninth and Eleventh Divisions moved forward during the night 19–20 August for the frontal assault. In Tokyo, reporters camped outside the War Ministry so as to be able to relay the news of another quick, stunning victory. In the towns and cities of Japan, flags and bunting had been prepared in anticipation of the celebration of this, the most important of victories. The wide and steep-sided gullies running up from the flat, encircling valley floor, pointed the way forward, up to and between the forts. The infantry moved quietly onward, any noise being drowned by the relentless, torrential rain.

More than usual effort was required by the Russian infantry to compensate for the shortcomings of their engineers. They were to display innovation, imagination and improvisation not only in their own fieldcraft but also in basic field engineering. Planks were cut down and nails driven through so that the upturned spikes would impale the feet of the Japanese soldiers through their straw *tabi*. They used telegraph wire to compensate for the shortage of barbed wire; anything to trip an ankle, to break the momentum of the attack. Pickets were in short supply too and the use of timber was not an entirely satisfactory solution since little purchase could be achieved in the rocky ground. Some wire obstacles were connected to the mains power supply. Japanese Intelligence was aware of this latter development but was uncertain whether the voltage was sufficiently high to kill or whether it was simply a low-voltage warning device. It was with the former contingency in mind that wire cutters had been fitted with bamboo handle extensions so as to conduct the electricity. Those who were the first to use the modified cutters were killed instantly. Some of them had 'their limbs split like brushes of bamboo'.

The requirement for night vision had been well considered. There was an abundance of magnesium flares or starshells, and searchlights had been erected at strategic junctures. The starshells were particularly useful because they were less susceptible to counter-fire than the searchlights. 'They were like great electric lamps hanging in the air,' wrote Lieutenant Tadayoshi Sakurai, 'making the whole place as light as day, so that even the movement of an ant could be easily detected.' The Russians had a ten to one superiority in machine guns. These were used in conjunction with the searchlights to switch from target to target at predetermined ranges. The unfortunate enemy was engaged by the machine guns located forward of the lights.

Gradually the Japanese forward movement was disrupted by the combined effects of artillery, machine guns and the appalling weather. Whole companies, their night vision lost to the flares and searchlights, blundered about, coming into machine-gun arcs or torn asunder by shrapnel. In time, the gullies began to pile up with the bodies of the dead and dying. The warm, moist weather accelerated the process of decomposition, making the lot of those waiting for the breaching of the wire obstacles almost unbearable. Cohesion had gone out of the attack as reliance now passed to junior leadership and opportunism.

The morning of 21 August heralded a fine, bright autumn day. Smoke rose from the East Panlung Battery, accumulating in the still air. To the front of East Panlung Fort were the bodies of the attackers, some hung on the wire, others in grotesque positions on the ground. Occasionally, as if by magic, a khaki bundle would pick itself up from the ground and hurl itself back into the watercourse where the Rising Sun was flying. On the left flank, soldiers of the Eleventh Division attempted in twos and threes to leapfrog from one watercourse to another. Invariably they did not succeed, adding to the tally of the machine guns of the East Panlung Fort. Despite the best efforts of their artillery, the Japanese were unable to move forward of the watercourses in daylight.

The Ninth Division had been reinforced by a reserve brigade but still appeared to be making little progress. Eventually their persistence was to be rewarded when a small section knocked out the machine gun at East

Panlung and occupied the trench around the battery. Since the Russians still held the battery, this tenuous Japanese position could be fired upon from there and also from West Panlung. There was insufficient space to absorb many attackers within this shadow of the Russian weapons. Reinforcements crept forward in twos and threes to replace those killed. Russian artillery endeavoured to tease out their unwelcome visitors. Riflemen from the battery had to stand forward of the position to fire on the huddled group but they in turn received the full attention of the Japanese artillery's shrapnel.

Just before midday, one of the Japanese officers stood up carrying the national flag and, accompanied by two or three riflemen, ran towards the Russian parapet. All were shot or bayoneted as they attempted to plant the flag. Shortly afterwards, a group of Russians crawling along the parapet took the surprised Japanese in the flank. They fled towards the watercourses but were rallied and returned to dispose of the Russian counter-attack group.

The Russians began to suffer severely from the effects of the withering artillery fire. Reinforcements were rushed forward. At 4 p.m. a party of sailors joined the defenders at East Panlung but they were unable to counter-attack the Japanese toehold beyond the parapet. A stalemate had been reached for neither could the Japanese cross the parapet without being cut down by the interlocking fire of the flanking forts. One unexpected bonus concerned Fock's continued refusal to comply with Smirnov's order to send reserves forward. His summary dismissal by Smirnov provided much satisfaction to officers and soldiers alike.

The impasse was resolved by a Japanese company commander who, with another company, found himself in a watercourse between East and West Panlung Forts. He observed how all the attention was being concentrated on the eastern fort, while the unassailed western fort was able to give supporting fire to the brother in the east. The infantry swarmed up the north-east slopes towards West Panlung suffering few casualties. The temporarily surprised Japanese artillery was not slow in bringing down supportive fire while the delay in the Russians absorbing what had transpired permitted the Japanese to secure their lodgement. West Panlung Fort was ablaze and by 6 p.m. the Russians had been ejected, although the Japanese were prevented from occupying the interior due to the inferno and the weight of fire coming from the direction of the Chinese Wall.

Now that the supporting fire from West Panlung had been suppressed, two battalions of the Seventh Regiment charged into East Panlung. A reserve regiment from Osaka which was ordered to support the regulars failed in its duty and was to suffer humiliation from its own kind. The soldiers of the Seventh Regiment were determined enough and wrested the fort from the Russians. Of the regiment's strength of 1,800 men, only 200 were present at roll call that evening.

The next step was to seize Wantai. The plan envisaged the right brigade of the Eleventh Division and the left brigade of the Ninth Division using the captured Panlung forts as springboards, attacking during the early morning of 24 August. The infantry assigned to East Panlung moved up through the same gully used the previous day by the Ninth Division and two reserve regiments. 'The dead and wounded were piled one upon another in nooks and corners, some groaning with pain, some crying for help, and some perfectly quiet, breathing no longer,' wrote Tadayoshi Sakurai. The advancing infantry endeavoured not to step upon the dead and dying. Near the top of the gully the infantry came under heavy machine-gun fire. While they took cover they could hear the sound of six field guns being brought up the gully in their direction. The decision was taken to withdraw. The would-be attackers accordingly withdrew down the gully of the dead and dying, only to discover that the horse artillery had run many of them over with their gun carriages. 'Those who had been breathing faintly had breathed their last under the iron wheels those who had already died were cut to pieces. Shattered bones, torn flesh, flowing blood, were mingled with broken swords and split rifles.' Now reorientated and reinforced, the Japanese turned around, making their way once again towards Wantai.

It was an inky dark, moonless night. As the attack got under way, the searchlights picked out the attackers while the Japanese artillery endeavoured to pick out the searchlights. The operators feigned a hit by turning the lights off and when the attention of the artillery shifted would turn them on again. Both Japanese brigades suffered heavily as they climbed over the Chinese Wall and up the slopes. The disadvantage of a split command became apparent while the Ninth Division's brigade awaited the arrival of the Eleventh Division's brigade. Casualties were mounting during the awful wait. Then a messenger arrived to say that the brigade had run out of ammunition and replenishment would take hours. At that very moment the quartermaster's staff and soldiers were collecting clips of ammunition from among their dead.

Deciding that action was preferable to inaction, two companies volunteered to go forward to capture the battery position on Wantai. After some local success the two companies were cut up by machine guns and forced to withdraw having come to within 500 yards of their objective. Just before dawn, the refurbished brigade arrived and attacked, only to suffer the same fate as those before them. Then the remainder of the earlier brigade joined the fray, uniting in a combined but depleted two-brigade attack just before dawn. With the coming of the early morning light came the prospect of artillery support. Four hundred Japanese guns barked out their fire with a creeping barrage. 'It looked as if there was not a single foot of ground which had not its own particular shell, and the whole ridge was enveloped in a thick cloud of smoke and dust from the explosions,' reported Richmond Smith. The optimistic but decimated Japanese brigades crouching in their shelter trenches prepared to move up for the *coup de grâce*. Their first movement brought a hail of shrapnel and machine-gun fire from the Russian defences. A costly lesson of the war had been learned by the Japanese the hard way. The following night, the reluctant infantry was withdrawn to the Panlung forts, leaving their dead strewn in hundreds over the hillside. Here the bodies would decay, their skulls rolling downhill to collect on the level ground to observe one another through eyeless sockets.

The press corps accredited to the Third Army was regarded with some suspicion. They were tolerated as a necessary evil but their continuing presence was guaranteed only by agreement that not one word would be sent to their editors until after Port Arthur had fallen. This had been a wise precaution, for if what these men had seen had been revealed to the world, then the purse strings in the international money markets would have been tightly drawn.

As the statistics of the failed first assault were gathered they passed through the various headquarters gaining momentum until the butcher's bill was placed upon Nogi's desk. He had lost 18,000 men. A full division was 15,000 men so already Nogi had lost his sacrificial division, with little to show for the sacrifice. Since the attack on the Orphan Hills and the loss of 9,000 men between 1–24 August due to sickness, Nogi's casualty list totalled 30,000 men. Under normal circumstances it was one thing for a general to decide to forfeit a division but quite another for those within the equivalent of that division to allow themselves to be forfeited. There are two sets of reasons why the Japanese so willingly flung themselves in front of Russian machine guns – the general and the specific. The general reasons will be drawn together at the conclusion of the book but there are at least three reasons to account for Japanese fanaticism before the defences of Port Arthur. They are revenge related: revenge for the humiliating loss of Port Arthur in 1895, revenge for comrades killed 1894–5, and revenge for their own comrades killed since the Third Army landed.

Nogi's gains had been two forts of doubtful value. They were completely dominated by Wantai, which in Chinese means the 'Watcher's Tower'. A gun emplacement a mere 500 yards to the south was able to pour fire into the Japanese forts. Each fort was held in company strength and suffered a hundred casualties a day. This period emphasised the need to dig to survive. Gradually the Japanese improved their positions and there was a corresponding fall in the number of their casualties. The Russians were busy too with their preparations. Wantai was strengthened and a trench was dug along the base of the Chinese Wall so that troops could move about unseen. All around the perspiring soldiers were strips of cloth, blowing in the wind. These had been dipped in carbolic acid to neutralise, in part, the effects of the nausea arising from the smell of the thousands of decaying Japanese corpses still unburied on the slopes leading up towards Wantai.

On the night 27–28 August the Russians made an ill-conceived and fruitless attempt to regain West Panlung. From that point, events slackened while the Japanese reflected upon their situation. It is arguable whether it had been an error to split the total land forces into an eastern and western group. It is unarguable, having made the decision, that it was an error for the First Division's efforts to be allowed to peter out at the very time the major attack in the east was launched. The division of resources was seen also in the Wantai attack where two brigades from different divisions had separate objectives. That they did not know the ground was apparent when one of the brigade commanders, not unused to that valuable principle of war called surprise, was astonished to survey his objective in the dark. The fort he was required to seize had a moat thirty feet wide and twenty-five feet deep. It was made of masonry and was heavily fortified.

CHAPTER ELEVEN

THE SIEGE AND FALL OF PORT ARTHUR

Nogi needed a new tactic. Those clamouring for quick results would have to wait while Nogi prepared to lay siege to Port Arthur. Marshal Oyama decided to attack Kuropatkin at Liaoyang without delay. The heroism of the Russian soldier had shown that Port Arthur would see more heavy fighting and more heavy loss. For the Japanese, there was at least some consolation in the fact that they could make good their horrendous losses. While the promised 15,000 reinforcements were awaited, Major General Teshima was appointed to command the siege artillery while the engineers, now at the top of the reinforcement list, were grouped under a chief engineer. No role was foreseen for the cavalry reserves who were sent north to join the army in Manchuria. One significant development was the arrival on 14 September of the first battery of 11-inch howitzers, replacing those lost on the *Hitachi Maru*. The barrel weighed sixteen tons and mountings, set in concrete, a further twenty. The shells – described as *portmanteaux* by the Russians and *saké cases* by the Japanese – weighed 500 lbs and had a range of 7,700 yards.

The private soldier in the British Royal Engineers and some Commonwealth armies holds the rank of sapper. (The existence of sappers *(fossatores)* can be traced as far back as the English-Welsh war of 1287.) This name is derived from an earlier historical title of Sappers and Miners. The duty of the sapper was literally to build saps, deep trenches with thick overhead cover providing approaches to or under fixed fortifications. The day of the sapper and miner had been resurrected to play an important role in the unfolding Port Arthur drama.

The first sapping of the campaign was conducted against the Waterworks

Redoubt, also known as the Erhlung Lunette or Railway Redoubt. The Japanese soon found that this business of digging and burrowing was not to their liking. 'It was too slow for him, and it was taxing his tenacity and fortitude to a much higher degree than the most desperate attacks in the open,' reported Norregard. 'They did not like it, and they did not understand it, and the majority of their officers shared their feelings.' The sap was begun from the Russian advanced trench line captured on 19 August and took a generally southern course towards the redoubt. Six hundred and fifty yards of trench-work were required, tons of earth being scooped out and removed along the excavated tunnel. This first siege exercise exhausted the supply of sandbags. Urgent local purchase contracts were placed in Dalny to produce more, although the product, in floral calico, gave rise to ribald comment at the front.

In front of the Panlungs, two thousand yards of trenchwork had been dug to connect these defended localities with the Ninth Division's headquarters. The Russians had been active against the creeping defences, accounting in September for the equivalent of a battalion a week among the Panlung garrison and sappers. The Japanese may not have enjoyed their obligatory mining and sapping but that is not to imply that they were not good at it. David James witnessed these first efforts:

> Broad enough to take in the wheels of a field gun-carriage, and
> sufficiently lofty to allow of upright walking, the levelled floors
> were perfect for marching. At the turnings of every parallel
> there were short branch trenches run out, with sanitary pits;
> and the entire length of trenches were at all times a perfect
> object-lesson in cleanliness, being plentifully sprinkled with
> chloride of lime and kept in naval cleanliness.

What he was describing here in 1904 would find resonance ten years later on the Western Front. Between them, Nogi's three divisions dug between four to five miles of direct parallel during September. The ground was of soft shale to the north of the hill defences but rock was more abundant once the line of the hills was encountered.

After nineteen days' preparation under sporadic fire, the attack was ready to be resumed on 19 September. General Nogi's plan was to make a feint attack against the eastern defences while attacking the Railway/Waterworks Redoubt (Erhlung Lunette), the Sueshi Lunette and launching more substantial, deliberate attacks upon 180 and 203 Metre Hills. At 5 p.m. two scouts advanced from the closest parallel to the Waterworks Redoubt, a distance of approximately eighty yards. Their heads and bodies were protected by steel shields as they zigzagged forward looking for mines. One was hit immediately by a 1-inch shell which blew both the shield and man apart. The second man fared no better, collapsing in front of the redoubt. At 5.40 p.m. the storming party leapt from the forward trenches and at a steady trot made for their objective. The initial attack was stopped and forced to retire. As night fell, the attack was resumed and by 2 a.m. the Russians were obliged to withdraw. The Japanese had lost 500 men but had secured a new platform from which to begin sapping towards Fort Erhlung and, in addition, had destroyed the forts' water supply. The Japanese lost a further 500 men in taking the apparently inconspicuous Sueshi Lunettes on 20 September.

Some of the credit for the Japanese success is attributable to Stoessel. On 31 August he issued an order imposing severe restrictions on the individual actions of independent commanders:

> On the night of 29th and 30th a sortie and an attack on No. 2 redoubt was again made by the scouts and sailors. The former dashed into the trenches, but the sailors did not do all that was expected of them [rarely would Stoessel miss an opportunity to denigrate the navy], so the attack was unsuccessful and the loss of life wasted. No more such attacks are to be made without my personal sanction on each occasion.

For that reason, forays to interfere with the sapping were rarely made. Later, at the Temple Redoubt, an exasperated, brave young officer led such an attack without authority, with dire results. In an order of 9 September, Stoessel deprecated the officer's 'pointless gallant acts'. The order went on:

> This officer is deprived of his appointment for taking his company out without permission and for losing five men killed and nineteen wounded to no purpose; he will not be recommended for any rewards, and will be transferred to the Twenty-seventh East Siberian Rifle Regiment for duty. Colonel Semenov, commanding the Twenty-sixth East Siberian Rifle Regiment, will be good enough to look to the internal discipline of his regiment.

While the Ninth Division was occupied with the Waterworks Redoubt and the Sueshi Lunettes, the First Division had the concurrent task of attacking the Temple Redoubt, 180 Metre Hill (Akasaka Yama) and 203 Metre Hill. In addition to their own direct support artillery, the following artillery assets were placed in support: five naval 12-pounders, two 4.7-inch guns, twelve 4.7-inch field howitzers, twelve 3.5-inch mortars, sixty field guns and eight 4-pounder Hotchkiss guns. From their insubstantial supply of machine guns, twenty-four were allotted to various infantry units.

180 Metre Hill is a dominant, long, narrow hill with steep sides. It was occupied by six Russian companies who held shallow trenches encircling the crest. On the northern peak were two 6-inch guns manned by sailors. The ground was very rocky and little impression had been made in getting through to any depth. There was a shortage of reserves and one of the companies on the feature, Seven Company of the Twenty-eighth Regiment, had performed poorly on 174 Metre Hill on 20 August. 'I had no other unit to send up, and I thought that it would be anxious to redeem its reputation,' explained Tretyakov. The first Japanese breakthrough had already occurred on 17 September when the Japanese attacked, seizing the trenches without a shot being fired. The men had been having their dinner. They were Seven Company of the Twenty-eighth Regiment. The company was ordered back to capture its abandoned trench but 'proved unequal to the task'.

The bombardment of the hill began at 2 p.m. on 19 September and resumed on 20 September assisted by gunboats firing from Louisa Bay. The Russians had lost heavily to the massive weight of artillery fire and by late afternoon on the 20th few of their officers were alive. At 4 p.m. a simultaneous two-battalion attack led the leaderless soldiers to believe they were surrounded. Tretyakov watched helplessly:

> Our gunners failed to locate the enemy's batteries, and thus remained impotent witnesses of the slaughter of our companies. Just then I saw the top of the right flank of Namako Yama covered with grey smoke and the men there rushing headlong down the hill. After the men on the right flank [they were Seven Company of the Twenty-eighth Regiment] had run, the others from the battery and the enemy appeared simultaneously on the crest.

Soldiers were sent off to intercept the flight of the infantry and to get them to re-form on Akasaka Yama. The Japanese had won an important observation post; so much so that the balloon unit was packed and sent north. They found over 130 Russian dead in the trenches and they themselves lost 450 killed or wounded. Also on 20 September the Temple Redoubt fell to a determined Japanese attack.

On 18 September, General Baron Kodama visited the despondent Nogi for the first time. They talked of tactics and the need to push on with the sapping. Nogi's attention was drawn for the first time to the tactical significance of 203 Metre Hill. On 20 September a three-pronged attack was launched against the hill, bypassing the intervening Akasaka Yama. The Japanese were forced back on two sides but gained a foothold in the south-west corner. Here, the Japanese entered a Russian bombproof which was strengthened with the arrival of two machine guns. They held out for two days despite the heroic efforts of the Russians to winkle them out. Tretyakov feared that if the enemy remained and was reinforced the hill would fall, bringing attendant doom upon the fleet.

The Japanese infantry swept relentlessly up the hill supported by their artillery. The Russian machine guns scythed through the ranks while the attackers on the granite slopes built parapets out of their dead and wounded. From this point, they kept up a steady rifle fire, launching occasional attacks which were stopped while the dead were rolled backwards down the hill to join the parapet. Great boulders were launched from the hilltop to break down the lifeless human wall. When the living endeavoured to dodge the rocks, they were picked off by the sharpshooters in the trenches.

Smirnov had gone forward and pondered where the Japanese were holding their reserves. If they were to take advantage of the sudden loosening of the stalemate they had to be nearby, in dead ground or in a ravine. At 1 p.m. on 22 September the reserves, comprising two regiments, were located in a ravine to the south-west of the hill. Smirnov ordered a section of quickfirers to be brought to the lip of the ravine through the *kaoliang* while all the other available guns were laid on the exit points. The section of the Russian guns opened rapid fire at point-blank range on the waiting infantry. They scattered in panic, to be despatched by a furious hail of shrapnel. Few survived.

That night a series of hand-made mines was hurled into the Japanese-held bombproof. Many of the occupants were blown to pieces. The dazed survivors, with their protection gone, fled downhill but were caught on the wire and shot or bayoneted. Two further attacks were launched against the hill but were successfully repulsed. In their follow-up the Russians occupied the vacated Japanese advanced lines. The Japanese, bitterly disappointed, decided to bide their time. 203 Metre Hill was well protected and impervious to most artillery effects up to 6-pounders. They had lost 2,500 men, half of them to the Russian artillery and, for the time being, they had had enough. It had become expedient for the Japanese artillery to destroy the strong Russian defences on 203 Metre Hill.

Life in Port Arthur that September was adapting to its new, dangerous circumstances. The military committee led by Smirnov attempted to generate an optimistic air of confidence. Stoessel never attended these meetings but would frequently change the committee's agreed plans. Moreover, he had reinstated protégé Fock, who remained in low profile, criticising and circulating damaging reports. Stoessel's vilification of the navy continued unabated. For the most part these attacks were unwarranted, for the sailors in the land defences, properly led, equipped and motivated, fought as well as the soldiers. Admiral Prince Ukhtomski was passed over by the promotion of the popular Captain Wiren to admiral to command the fleet. His notification of promotion included an order to take the remnant of the fleet to Vladivostok. He formed a committee, discussed the matter and demurred. The bombardment of the port and ships, which had paused during 9–16 September due to ammunition shortages, resumed. The ships, playing cat and mouse, manoeuvred where possible to avoid the incoming missiles. Most of the smaller calibre guns and most of the crews were now firmly ensconced in the hills surrounding the town.

The reporter Nojine provides a glimpse of life in the port at the time. Stoessel did not trust the man on account of his personal friendship with Smirnov. 'You correspondents are liars', he was told. 'The one who pays most gets the truth.' Perhaps the consul at Chefoo had informed Stoessel that Nojine had endeavoured to smuggle a signal to friends for the Tsar's express information: 'Arthur is enabled to hold out only by the efforts of Smirnov and his excellent assistant Kondratenko. When I give you details your hair will stand on end. Tell the Tsar this for it is absolutely necessary that Stoessel should be removed.' Nojine wrote the news column for the *Novoe Krai*. He complained that the system of dual censorship deprived his reports of interest and accuracy. Stoessel's response was to close down the newspaper for a month.

It did not require a newspaper to spread the depressing news of

Kuropatkin's defeat at Liaoyang nor that the troubled Baltic fleet had been forced to return to Libau. The soldiers persevered. Their access to vodka was reduced in order to resolve the problem of drunkenness. This restriction did not apply to their officers who flaunted their privilege – among them was Stoessel. Food was not yet a problem. Entrepreneurs still managed to evade the Japanese blockade, although most were caught and sent to Dalny where their supplies added to Japanese reserves. Many of the cargoes, while welcome, were comprised of wheat, grain or rice while the real shortages were of butter, milk, eggs, fish and meat. To his credit, Stoessel had applied maximum price levels to these commodities. Horseflesh was plentiful and while at first not popular, any horse killed by gunfire would be speedily butchered and would disappear into battalion kitchens. Rock fish, fresh-water pond fish and birds were eagerly sought-after supplements to the monotonous diet. The Tsar's decision to count each month the soldiers spent in Port Arthur as equivalent to one year's service was popular – almost as popular as the hot bath. Shortage of fuel and the fear that the Japanese, now in possession of the waterworks, would poison the water, led the Russians to cease drawing from the supply. Dependence upon wells led to a decline in baths, hot or cold.

The Russian hand grenade had proved to be very effective against the close-packed Japanese ranks. Three factories in town were in full production. Other ammunition was giving cause for concern. Prematures were responsible for killing and maiming appreciable numbers of Russians. A large proportion of shells failed to explode while a shortage of time fuses restricted the use of shrapnel to only the most special of targets. There was a consciousness too that the stocks were dwindling. A system existed for collecting dud Japanese ordnance which, when re-processed and re-fused, was returned whence it came.

Sickness was not yet a major problem for the Russians although scurvy was beginning to appear and dysentery was making its indiscriminate call. Strangely, it was a matter of considerable worry for the supposedly fastidious Japanese. The number of sick in July was 5,000, in August 10,000 and then back to 5,000 in September. Most of these 20,000 cases were suffering from beri-beri. It is believed that the epidemic was caused by eating the rice which, unprotected, had fermented in the heat and damp. Of the remainder, the sickness was attributable to typhoid and dysentery. The cause of these diseases was not in doubt. Streams ran through the numerous gullies in which the Japanese had concealed themselves. Their sense of hygiene was medieval, a reflection of their home life, and in consequence every source of water was polluted. Brigadier Waters wrote that the Russians were no better, having 'always been accustomed to what we should term the utter lack of sanitary arrangements'. There were flies by the million and the field hospitals were often as not close to kitchens and horse lines. Stretchers congealed with blood were propped up outside the tents and bandages were bloodstained and dirty. Sakurai wrote how large armies of flies attacked the wretched patients, worms would grow in the mouth and nose and some of them could not drive the vermin away because their arms were useless. Summer was, of course, the worst, emphasising Japan's unpreparedness for the large number of casualties.

The neglect of hygiene appeared not to apply so consistently to the individual. It was a habit of the Japanese on waking to pop a toothbrush in the mouth and scrub away. They were meticulously clean, particularly prior to a battle. The unit lines would have a series of large earthenware pots sunk in the ground under which a fire was lit. The soldier bathed himself thoroughly, just his head appearing over the top of the pot. Then he would put on clean clothes to be ready for the morning's battle. His identity papers were tucked away in his uniform for, should he be killed, it was usual for his Adam's apple to be removed and returned to his family. Sakurai's book tells of one incident where he was struck by a Russian soldier's carefulness in observing the rules of hygiene and not drinking unboiled water. The Japanese surgeon said that the Russian, shot through the chest, had less than an hour to live. Breathing with difficulty and blood running from his mouth, he asked the interpreter for a drink of water. A glass of spring water was brought to him immediately but he would not entertain it. 'There is boiled water in my bottle; give me that.'

The rumours of the arrival of the 11-inch or 28-centimetre howitzers preceded them and the Russians offered rewards for details of their location. This war is replete with examples of events which turned the tide in favour of the Japanese. These happenings were frequently accidental but there was no accident in the arrival of these massive guns. After the howitzers' arrival at Dalny from Sasebo there followed a major logistical exercise moving them to their permanent, prepared, indirect fire positions in the east. A small railway was laid to move the 500-lb shells from the ammunition park to the guns. So well concealed and protected were the guns that they were used continuously and never put out of action. By 1 October, the crews had been trained and Nogi and Kodama stood on a hillside to watch the effects. The target was Fort Chikuan, which took a hundred shells. At first the concrete walls resisted, but eventually one burst through, killing the defenders nearby. Many of the shells did not explode, but such was their velocity that they were to cause massive damage, particularly to the houses in the town and the ships in the harbour.

The naval gunfire observer on Namako Yama did not have an unimpeded view of the harbour, yet he was able to predict reasonably well where the ships were. During 4–7 October, the battleships *Pobieda, Retvisan, Peresvyet* and *Poltava* and three smaller warships were struck repeatedly. The error in sending the observation balloon off to the north was now regretted. The Russians were able to utilise the nooks and crannies of the harbour to hide the capital ships from the less than ideal observation post on Namako Yama. A ruse to put the hospital ship *Mongolia* in the line of fire caused a protest to be lodged through the French Ambassador in Tokyo and also caused a massive hole in the *Mongolia*. The Japanese were very pleased with the performance of the new 11-inch howitzers. On 15 October two more batteries of six guns arrived. Four were emplaced ominously within a mile of 203 Metre Hill. 'This was serious news for us,' remarked Tretyakov. 'One could feel that 203 Metre Hill was practically safe against six inch projectiles, but eleven inch were a very different matter.' His solution was 'to delve deeper into the rock'. Elsewhere, men were less philosophical, the telling effects of the big guns escalating the impression of the certainty of inevitable doom. 'The wearing, trying uncertainty, the want of confidence, and the constant, unavoidable danger began to tell,' wrote Nojine. 'The younger men lost their nerve, and suicides commenced.'

The leisurely, random bombardment of the town and facilities continued throughout October, gaining in intensity as additional heavy siege guns joined the order of battle. The artillery inventory now comprised 180 field and mountain guns and 240 siege guns. There was nothing leisurely or random, however, about the fire missions aimed at the ships; they were intense and very specific. On 8 October the *Pallada* escorted by two destroyers was ordered to Vladivostok. That evening *Pallada* returned to Port Arthur severely damaged. One destroyer had been sunk and the other captured. On the land front, the three Japanese divisions had gone to ground. Sapping and mining had begun on the north and north-east front. The First Division's objective was Fort Sungshu, the Ninth Division's Fort Erhlung and Eleventh Division's Fort Chikuan. There was an urgency in the mission due to a belief that Nogi wished to present his hero Emperor with Port Arthur on his birthday, the same day as the Tsar's accession, 3 November. Throughout the month of October the Japanese launched opportune attacks from the forward saps upon the Russians' lower fortifications.

Prior to 26 October the area around the three forts had seen bombardments, attacks and counter-attacks as the now fully reinforced Japanese divisions manoeuvred into striking positions. The sapping and mining had made commendable progress despite the rocky terrain. The Japanese approach had come closest to Fort Chikuan where a tunnel was being driven through the rock towards the walls and was within fifty yards of the moat. The noise of the chiselling was first heard on 23 October. Elsewhere, the thankless task of sapping continued, zigzagging tunnels sneaking forward to a parallel, then to zigzag again forward to another parallel. Because the rock was so close to the surface the Japanese could frequently dig no deeper than two feet and in consequence the saps were often prominently above the ground with sandbag walls. Despite orders to the contrary, the Russians made occasional sorties to destroy the works but Stoessel's limitations effectively constrained the Russians mostly to engaging the creeping saps from a distance. Out of these realities sprang some innovative and rapid research and development on both sides.

The advanced sap in front of Fort Erhlung was still 300 yards from the forward Russian trenches when a hail of grenades scattered the diggers. A reconnaissance revealed the Russians to be employing wooden trench mortars. The Japanese, not averse to copying anyone's original idea, put their own workshops to business to produce something similar though better. In a matter of weeks almost every trench line in the front was to have its own Japanese wooden mortar allegedly capable of firing out to between 250 and 400 yards. In the interim period, the sap heads were protected by springy wire trampolines so that when a grenade hit the wire, it bounced off harmlessly.

For the Japanese a major source of difficulty proved to be the wire entanglements. Much local experimentation had gone into solving the problem, such as new cutters or new ploys. One routine was for the pioneers to feign death and, when the Russians were no longer concentrating on the area, to snip through the wire. This was unsatisfactory, for the Russians responded by ensuring that anything near the wire was quite dead. Another Japanese project to protect their pioneers was an improvement to the body armour which had failed at the Waterworks Redoubt. A new steel plate armour was developed, weighing 40 lbs. Small-arms fire could not penetrate it but the velocity of the round knocked the twentieth-century knights off their feet. The modification which solved this problem was to fasten two poles to the pioneer's waist. These were dragged behind and served to prop him up when struck. Further experiments with bamboo poles to lay smoke screens or to explode under the wire were variations of the Bangalore torpedo. Now torpedoes may be assumed to be weapons of the sea, but not at Port Arthur where it appears that anything was possible. Sailors had mounted torpedo tubes along the walls of Fort Chikuan. Cynics were quietened when a torpedo with a 70-lb warhead was launched with devastating effect against the Japanese sap head.

The entry in the Russian chief engineer's diary of 26 October read as follows:

> At 4 a.m. we suddenly heard the Japs working from the left gallery in front of Chikuan, and the thud of their tools seemed much nearer and more distinct. When I listened to it about 9 a.m. it seemed as if they were at work almost five feet to the left and a little above. The calculations for a camouflet to destroy their gallery worked to a charge of about three hundred and twenty pounds of powder and I at once gave orders for a chamber to be dug out and all the necessary material for tamping it to be got ready.

A camouflet is a mine designed to destroy an underground chamber without cratering the surface. For the defenders it was a question of who was going to be ready to explode their mine first. It was not until 27 October that the Russian device was ready. Smirnov insisted that he should detonate the camouflet and at great personal risk pressed the button. 'Above the caponier* rose a cloud of dust and smoke, out of which projected planks, stones and bodies. We had succeeded, and the garrison breathed again.' In truth, Nojine's comment was not entirely accurate for the Russian detonation had 'succeeded' in providing the Japanese with a way into the fortress.

---

* A defensive position sunk four feet into the bank of a moat with a visible area of observation approximately two feet above ground level. There were strong timber supports and substantial overhead cover.

On 26 October the Japanese barrage opened, 'not rapid but plodding', building in intensity throughout the day, principally directed upon Forts Erhlung and Sungshu. Supported by particularly good artillery fire, the Japanese seized the forward trenches. Over the next two days there were no infantry attacks but a relentless fire poured into the forts and they began to sustain serious damage. On the night of 28 October two Russian counter-attacks in front of Erhlung and Sungshu endeavoured to force the Japanese out of the forward trenches. One failed and one succeeded, although the Japanese withdrawal in front of Sungshu was unbeknown to the naval attacking force. The Japanese reoccupied their trenches at 2 p.m. on 29 October when the three-day cannonade ceased, leaving many Russian guns disabled and defences destroyed.

Preparations for the second general assault were made ready while a diversion occurred on 29 October in Pigeon Bay. After a slow start, the bombardment reached a crescendo from 12.30 to 1 p.m. when all along the line the Japanese rose out of their trenches into the attack. The distance between the two forces averaged between fifty and one hundred yards. The Japanese had to cross rising, open ground but this time they had not the advantage of surprise. The greatcoated Russians had waited patiently throughout the morning, dodging shot and shell. It was a fine and bright day although the north-westerly breeze bore the chill which presaged evening frost. Every available Russian gun had been laid on the parallels at the end of the saps. The smooth bores were loaded with canister. Machine guns were fixed to fire across the obvious line of Japanese advance. Lanyards were ready to be pulled as soon as any movement was noted in the Japanese line. When the movement came, the infantry rose as one out of their parallels, bayonets forward, throwing themselves onward across the eastern front. 'It was magnificent,' wrote James, 'and it was war'. When it came, the fire was murderous. 'The reports merged into one continuous roar and, seen intermittently through the dust raised by the bullets, the stormers looked like men struggling in rough water. So complete had the Russian preparations been that many Japanese had fallen in the act of climbing out of the trenches,' records the British History.

A simultaneous attack had been imperative, for isolated or uncoordinated attacks would only enable the mutually supporting fire of the forts to frustrate the Japanese plans. The Russians had now broken down the Japanese concerted assault and it developed exactly as the Japanese intended that it should not. Against Chikuan Battery the assailants had only to cross forty yards of ground. At the apex of their advance were the regimental colours but in five minutes, when the machine guns and shrapnel fire had abated, the assailants were dead or wounded while a few lucky survivors had withdrawn, to trigger the resumption of the bombardment. The adjoining defence, Kobu, was taken but it was not as important as 'Q' which dominated the approaches to Fort Chikuan from Port Arthur. Many men fell as they crossed the open ground forward of the parapet. One man stood up with a rudimentary flame-thrower and set fire to the shoulder of the defence but to no great effect. Unable to progress, the Japanese withdrew during the night.

At Fort Chikuan, scene of the early tunnelling, the Japanese had been very close to the defences. Although their assault did not have sufficient numbers, a few brave men reached the parapet where they were shot from 'P'. Their bodies remained on the parapet for a month until buried by the explosion of a mine. 'P' lay 200 yards to the west of the fort. It dominated the forward defences of Fort Chikuan and one further advantage was that to its west lay the Japanese-held East Panlung Fort. The battle here see-sawed backwards and forwards until darkness appeared to signal a Japanese defeat. The Commander Sixth Brigade, Major General Ichinohe, put himself at the head of the designated attacking regiment and by his inspirational leadership seized 'P', renamed the next day Fort Ichinohe.

The attack on Fort Erhlung was a disaster. Having struggled through the fire and obstacles to reach the moat, the Japanese found that their scaling ladders were about twenty feet too short. When the press asked the staff what the purpose of the ladders had been, they discovered that it was not wise to press the subject in conversation. The assault on Sungshu met with the same problem. The point of departure of the First Division's attack on Fort Sungshu was the trench line captured on 26 October. The fort was rocked by two explosions during the afternoon. No progress was made during daylight but, in the absence of a counter-attack, the Japanese were able to close up to the fort during the night. Elsewhere, the fighting died away as both armies were exhausted. Nevertheless, the Russians worked hard to repair their damaged parapets which by the morning of 31 October were almost as good as new.

The possession of 'P' and Kobu by the Japanese threatened Fort Chikuan from the flanks. The Russians determined to make one further effort to seize the fort. The storming party was seen off after desperate hand-to-hand fighting, and that concluded six days of almost continuous battle, a battle in which the Japanese lost 124 officers and 3,611 men. The impetuous Japanese had continued in the use of field tactics against a powerfully strong citadel. Their fanaticism, in continually pressing forward at grave risk to life and limb, left an unspoken message for the future. Sakurai writes of the occasion in battle when fire support becomes inadequate and 'our only and last resource was to shoot off human beings, to attack with bullets of human flesh'. They all knew the value of the Third Army to Oyama, of the proximity of the Emperor's birthday, and wished to play their part for the common good but, if they persisted with their flawed tactics, there would be no Third Army.

Nogi was despondent and his army disappointed and demoralised. Again, the severe attrition within the ranks was evident at roll call. The men who should have filled the gaps were sprawled over the hills in front of the Russian forts. 'For days after, one had only to look at the slopes of East Chikuan Hill, covered with the Japanese dead, and the pathetic sight of two regimental flags still flying far up the slopes, to realise that the second tragedy in front of Port Arthur had occurred,' noted Reuter's correspondent. There was no good news to tell the Emperor on his birthday but when the Japanese fired the 101-gun salute in his honour, each round fell on Port Arthur and Erhlung Fort.

News of this, the second defeat, inflamed popular opinion. The Japanese equivalent of *The Times* demanded that 100,000 men should be sent to Port Arthur. Tolerance of Nogi was waning both among the public and the military. Only by the Emperor's personal intervention was the sacking of Nogi prevented. None the less, the impatience elsewhere in the army was evident. Oyama found the continuing unavailability of the Third Army intolerable. He again sent his deputy Kodama to Port Arthur, this time to insist that the emphasis of attack was to be moved away from the heavily defended forts and concentrated on 203 Metre Hill. He was instructed that if Nogi was found to be anything other than completely co-operative he was to be replaced by Kodama. Nogi attempted one further general assault against the eastern defences.

The Japanese had dedicated much of November to field engineering, sapping, mining and filling-in the moats of Forts Erhlung and Sungshu. Elements of the newly arrived Seventh (Hokkaido) Division were included in the attack on 26–27 November. Again the Japanese were soundly defeated, losing over 4,000 men. The butcher's bill may have been larger. James reports there having been 208 officers and 5,933 wounded men in hospital on the night of the 27th, 'but the dead were not then computed'.

It had been a hideous event, more vicious than the two previous attacks, and had ebbed and flowed over the contested ground. General Kondratenko took the precaution of putting sharpshooters to the rear of the forward defended localities. Early in this, the third general assault, when two or three Russians attempted to retire, they were instantly shot. The message passed along the line which held fast. Attention now shifted to 203 Metre Hill where the Japanese were destined to lose 8,000 killed and wounded and the Russians approximately 3,000. Rarely had the world seen such a concentration of slaughter over such a small area. Some commentators hazarded a guess that the destruction seen on 203 Metre Hill would never be repeated. Unfortunately, at another time, in another place, they would be proved wrong.

A cold, intensifying, winter wind of change, blowing off the land mass, began to impose its presence upon events. For the Japanese, who had entered this conflict with 65,000 men* there had been the debilitating effect of sickness. Now the cold weather had killed off the flies, and improvements in their sanitation and diet saw the pendulum of adversity swing towards the Russian side. The Russians had begun the Port Arthur campaign with 43,000 men. The casualties were irreplaceable, and the effects of an indifferent diet and shortage of medicine were reflected in the rampant, vile diseases of scurvy and dysentery. The hospitals were full and manpower in short supply. The reserves were almost entirely comprised of sailors, with soldiers holding the trenches.

In the field the ground was rock-hard, with sapping and the construction of trenches made extremely difficult. The Japanese had adopted an unofficial new form of dress. Their lightweight khaki uniforms were being worn over the blue winterweights, not only for the additional warmth but also to make the wearer less conspicuous over the by now whitening terrain. The frost and snow did not augur well for the wounded, for those left injured on the slopes froze to death during the lengthening nights.

In the summer, Nogi had sat and worked under the acacia tree in front of his two-roomed cottage. Here he would talk to the press corps and direct the battle. Sitting there, sharing the occasional bottle of champagne with the

---

* The reinforcement of a division, additional units (particularly engineers) and individual reinforcements had now brought the Japanese strength to over 100,000.

correspondents, the white-bearded general had reminded one of them of General Ulysses S. Grant. The cold now obliged him to work inside and heightened his reclusion. Rarely would he journey to the front line, seemingly not wishing to witness the results of his decisions. He led a lonely existence, pacing his room, always dressed in uniform, day and night.

The able Kondratenko guessed that the Russians had witnessed the last general assault on the forts for the time being. He guessed correctly that the next objective would be 203 Metre Hill. He took a calculated gamble by thinning out his fortress troops and with the reserve thereby created he was in a position to counter the perceived attack from the west. This had been a shrewd but understandable move, for 203 Metre Hill not only overlooked the harbour but also the interiors of Forts Erhlung and Sungshu.

In fact, 203 Metre Hill was a misnomer. The feature comprised two peaks connected by a sharp ridge. The lower peak of the two was 203 metres while the higher was 210 metres. To the Japanese it was known as Royushan. The peaks were 140 yards apart with, in the dip, the wreckage of four 6-inch guns destroyed some time before. It was a bare feature with hardly sufficient topsoil to support a sparse covering of grass. The Russian trenches had been hewn out of the rock, the builders protected by sandbag walls five feet high and four feet thick. Finding the soil with which to fill the sandbags had been a major problem in this rocky terrain. The Japanese sap, moving out from Ridge 590, had made good progress until it ran up against 203 Metre Hill.

On top of 203 Metre Hill was a strong command post built of timber, steel rails and earth and surrounded by a strong trenchwork. Just below, circling the 600-feet contour, was the main line of defence. The trenchwork was strongest where it faced the Japanese, being deep, having good overhead cover, and strengthened with one-inch steel plate and timber. Its disadvantage was that the lower slopes lay in dead ground and a second but incomplete trenchwork lay a hundred feet below in order to combat that problem. There were some apologetic wire entanglements which had not been greatly developed due to problems in hammering the posts into the ground. A few strategic rifle pits had been prepared but were abandoned when Namako Yama fell. Akasaka Yama remained in Russian hands and had also benefited from recent, urgent preparations. Its northern slope was an almost impossible climb and the gap to 203 Metre Hill was strewn with mines. An important factor in the ensuing battle was that both hills were to a significant degree self-supportive. The exception was the south-west of 203 Metre Hill because this area could not be covered from Akasaka Yama.

Nogi was determined to seize the hill quickly and at whatever cost. Akasaka Yama had to be attacked concurrently in order to negate the possibility of supporting fire. The First Division, reinforced by a Kobi regiment, was detailed for the attack. At 8.30 a.m. on 28 November, backed up by massive firepower, the Japanese advanced from their trenches in a three-pronged attack. The 11-inch howitzers alone poured on an average day one thousand 500-lb shells on to 203 Metre Hill and Akasaka Yama. Two battalions attacked the southern peak, one battalion the northern peak, and three companies Akasaka Yama. The southern peak force used dead ground to good effect and had reached the south-west corner of the hill. Here they became exposed to the shrapnel of the Russian artillery firing from Pigeon Bay. Unable to go forward and systematically being raked and destroyed by shrapnel, at midday the Japanese wavered. They were rallied by their officers and advanced. The scything effect of well-sited machine guns now added to the attrition being caused by the artillery. Only a handful survived but they would not voluntarily retire. At 7 p.m. a Russian counter-attack forced them back to their point of departure. The attack on the northern peak had fared no better. At Akasaka Yama a small lodgement had been made where the Japanese had thrown up a stone shelter some forty yards from the Russian lines. Subsequent attacks that night saw no improvement in the Akasaka Yama area but a small foothold had been secured on the south-west flank of 203 Metre Hill.

Dawn on the morning of the 29 November revealed the slopes strewn with Japanese dead from the base of the hills to the front of the Russian trenches. The Russians had worked energetically throughout the night to repair their position but their efforts were nullified by the bombardment that resumed at daylight. The artillery fire fell on the hills all day as a preliminary to a further optimistic attack on 203 Metre Hill that night. The attack failed and in thirty-six hours the Japanese First Division had become an exhausted, spent force.

Faced with this problem, Nogi issued orders for the First Division to be relieved by the Seventh (Hokkaido) Division. It was while this change was being effected that a staff officer informed Nogi that his favourite son Yasukori, aged twenty-four, had been shot dead. Nogi responded with some facile questions as to whether his son had completed his duty, but the tears welling up in the old general's eyes told the real story. He saw in the death of his son a compensator for his own guilt feeling for the thousands of deaths already incurred in the Third Army. 'I often wonder how I could apologise to His Majesty and to the people for having killed so many of my men.' On being asked what was to happen to his son's body, Nogi said, 'Turn it into ashes.' There is a small memorial stone at the foot of the northern slope of 203 Metre Hill marking the spot where he died.

The Russian force on 203 Metre Hill was a mix of soldiers and sailors. The effects of the heavy artillery ripping through the trenchworks and the tension created by awaiting attacks day and night was taking its toll. The conditions on the hill were horrific. The defenders were obliged to shelter upon and among frozen layers of human debris – dismembered bodies and 'a pulp of mutilated humanity'. Understandably there were among the defenders some who were affected by these dreadful circumstances, with a disinclination to remain in a place where they themselves in time would be added to the pile of torn and mutilated human remains. More than once the sailors initiated a flight to the rear to be met by the brave Tretyakov, arms outstretched, sword in hand, as if ushering back a stampeding herd of crazed ponies. The ploy worked, and with a few careful blows with the flat of the sword across the heads of those in flight the situation was restored. Tretyakov had been given a supply of St George's Crosses, which he awarded on the spot for brave acts. Napoleon had said, 'It is with baubles that men are led.' Tretyakov concurred. 'This method of prompt reward made a deep impression on everyone.'

The hill was gradually and increasingly sponging up reserves to the degree that soon the reserves' reserve would be committed. With a front stretching eighteen miles it was a very risky matter to place the bulk of the force's reserve in one place, particularly since demonstrations were still in progress against the eastern defences. At this point, 9,000 unemployed men of the town were pressed into service. The civilians in the town guard were sent for employment in the hospitals while the medical orderlies they replaced took up arms to join the non-combatants of headquarters and administrative companies in the trenches on 203 Metre Hill.

After a vicious bombardment, the Japanese launched a further attack by the Seventh Division at 2.30 p.m. on 30 November. These brave little mountain men had passed in front of their colours vowing to take the hill or not return. When they came into view of the Russians on the northern slopes the fire was so intense that they had to pause while their own artillery suppressed the Russian efforts. Onward they moved to the Russian trenches, but they wavered and fell back having suffered severely. They re-formed in the dead ground only to be shattered by the shrapnel from the Russian guns firing from Pigeon Bay. The order was passed to withdraw and, of those two battalions, only a handful returned.

A constant stream of two-wheeled hand-carts interspersed between the lines of reserves took food and ammunition up to the defenders on the hill. Grenades were particularly useful in the close-quarter fighting and the three factories in the town were hard pressed to cope with the demand. One day over 7,000 were thrown. On the morning of 30 November a small party of Japanese had succeeded in gaining a foothold on the left flank where they had implanted their flag. Tretyakov records, 'The sight of this flag always filled our men with fury. I knew this, and, pointing to it, shouted to the reserve: "Go and take it down, my lads!" and like one man, our sailors rushed into the work.' Twice more the flag and a small party were to appear on the hill and twice flag and party were removed.

These latter events were to cause consternation at both the Russian and Japanese headquarters. Fock's credibility among the fighting soldiers had plummeted further when he issued a strange, unnecessary, defeatist memorandum at the very time that the ground forces were doing their utmost to stem the Japanese tide. He compared the situation facing those in the fortress to a man with a gangrenous limb. 'In the same way that he must sooner or later succumb, so too must a fortress fall. No commandant should waste his men in an attempt to recapture a position yielded to the enemy.' This was a view shared by Stoessel as they met in an emergency council meeting to discuss the situation on 203 Metre Hill. 'It's absurd to try to hold out there longer,' said Fock. 'We must think of the men. It's all the same: sooner or later we shall have to abandon it. We must not waste men; we shall want them later.' Only the strongest objection by Smirnov prevented a decision to abandon the hill there and then.

That evening Kodama was informed that 203 Metre Hill was at last in Japanese hands. Pleased, he went to bed. Over breakfast he was advised that the hill was in fact still in Russian hands. He leapt to his feet in a fury, hurled his breakfast plate to the ground and went to seek out Nogi. He had retained his letter of authority to replace Nogi but while on the way he reasoned that such a move would dishonour the Third Army and herald Nogi's undoubted suicide. By the time the confrontation between the generals occurred, much of the steam had evaporated. Kodama insisted that he would give the orders on this front, to which Nogi readily agreed.

By now, the Japanese sensed that a direct assault was not going to succeed and that the best solution was to reduce the Russian defences to rubble with the heavy artillery. The loss of the *Saiyen* on 30 November meant that no naval assets were going to be risked in providing naval gunfire support to the infantry's attacks but there was no overall shortage of Japanese artillery. Occasionally the weight of fire paused to permit isolated attacks. On 1 December a Japanese attack gained the southern slope but it was swept away by a counter-attack. Elsewhere, hand-to-hand fighting was in progress, bayoneting and grenade-throwing, while the Russians clung to their ruined trenches surrounded by the debris of their own dead and dying. When attacks withdrew, the artillery barrage resumed. Tretyakov wrote:

> A non-combatant detachment, under a quartermaster, came up to make good our losses of the preceding day. The men were placed in the trenches allotted to the reserves, and the officer stood looking at the road, and the piles of dead lying on it. I suggested to him that he should sit in the trench or stand close up under the almost perpendicular bank of the road. But the young fellow said he was not afraid of such missiles, pointing with his hand to an eleven inch shell which was hurtling away after having ricocheted off the ground; but just at that moment there was a terrific roar, and he was hidden in the black smoke from a large shell that had burst just where he stood. When the smoke had cleared away, he was no longer there.

The assaults had petered out by 2 December and the Japanese used the next three days to improve their sapping and attacking positions. There was to be no relief for the tired, hungry and blasted Russians on the hill. By Nojine's account:

> The fourth day was but a repetition of the preceding three. Shells of all sizes, from eleven inch to small quick firers, rained upon the place. All cover, or anything that looked as if it might afford shelter, had long ago been turned into heaps of stones, iron, beams, rubbish and mangled bodies. During the night

shelters of sorts had been scraped up, only to be swept away by
the first breath of iron which accompanied the morning light.

Tretyakov, already wounded once, was wounded again, this time more severely and he was evacuated from the hill for surgery. Few officers were left on the hill; they were either killed or wounded by what the soldiers described as the 'portmanteaux', the 11-inch shells.

On 5 December, the Japanese saps had approached significantly closer to 203 Metre Hill and Akasaka Yama. At 1.30 p.m. the forward Japanese lines resounded to the clicks of bayonets being fixed. At 1.45 p.m. the covering fire lifted. Major General Saito led the Fourteenth Brigade up the preferred western slopes of 203 Metre Hill at the same time as a regiment attacked Akasaka Yama. While the attack was moving forward, shrapnel and high explosives swept the top of the hill, killing those who had lost the protection of their trenches and preventing reinforcements moving on to the position.

The Japanese climbed the hill suffering few casualties. When they gained the western peak only three Russians were found still alive amidst the rubble. The attackers charged across the gap between what were by now the almost imperceptible twin peaks and met little resistance. Suddenly and surprisingly, on 5 December, the Japanese were in possession of the hill. Much the same had occurred at Akasaka Yama. Their success was due to the weight of artillery which for days had so obliterated the defences that few could have survived. Two counter-attacks were launched by the Russians but these failed and the order was passed to withdraw.

The correspondents with the Japanese Third Army were permitted to visit the hill. These seasoned reporters were sickened by what they saw, for nowhere was it possible to move without treading on some fragment of a human body. Ashmead Bartlett recalls: 'There have probably never been so many dead crowded into so small a space since the French stormed the great redoubt at Borodino.' James wrote of his impression:

> The sight of those trenches heaped up with arms and legs and
> dismembered bodies all mixed together and then frozen into
> compact masses, the expressions on the faces of the scattered
> heads of decapitated bodies, the stupendous magnitude of the
> concentrated horror, impressed itself indelibly into the utmost
> recesses of my unaccustomed brain.

For the man of Nippon it was a matter of importance to him, if and when his body was dismembered by some mighty explosion, that the separate legs, arms or torso should be recognised as *his* legs, arms and torso. Towards the end of the siege, red and white rags bearing the man's name were fastened to his limbs and his name was also written on his clothing.

Two weeks later General Hamilton visited 203 Metre Hill and wrote of his experience in an unusually emotive manner:

> First the hill had been sliced into numberless deep gashes, and
> then these trenches and their dividing walls had been smashed
> and pounded and crushed into a shapeless jumble of stones;
> rock splinters and fragments of shells cemented liberally with
> human flesh and blood. A man's head sticking up out of the
> earth, or a leg or an arm or a piece of a man's body lying across
> my path are sights which custom has enabled me to face with-
> out blanching. But here the corpses do not so much appear to
> be escaping from the ground as to be the ground itself. Every-
> where there are bodies, or portions of bodies, flattened out and
> stamped into the surface of the earth as if they formed part of
> it, and several times in the ascent I was on the point of putting
> my foot on what seemed to be dust when I recognised by the
> indistinct outline that it was a human form stretched and
> twisted and rent to gigantic size by the force of some frightful
> explosion.

The Russians had no more than 1,500 men at any one time on 203 Metre Hill yet the fact that they lost over 3,000 is an indication of the size of the constant transfusion of reserves. For those moving towards the sound of guns came the prospect of confronting the spreading burial grounds behind the hill. Atop the numerous mounds were makeshift crosses at varying angles while in piles, awaiting burial, were the dead of yesterday. For those passing by, going forward, was the reality that their return would be no further than this point.

The Japanese casualties here numbered over 8,000 of which a high pro-
portion were killed or were the wounded who died on the icy slopes. When the fresh Seventh Division moved forward, they met on the roads the hundreds of casualties of the First Division. For them too had been this daunting prospect of looking up towards the hill they were expected to take, strewn

with the bodies of their comrades who had failed in the attempt. At the end of the battle, both the First and Seventh Divisions had virtually ceased to be effective fighting formations.

The Official Japanese Operational Report of 3 December said of 203 Metre Hill:

> This eminence commands the entire view of the west and east harbours of Port Arthur, and the Russian warships are not in a position to escape from the fire of our artillery. It may be thought that much time will be needed to mount heavy guns on the height, but, as a matter of fact, it is needless to bring our large guns there, for, with an observatory and signal station, an accurate fire can be sent from any direction.

No sooner had 203 Metre Hill fallen than the Naval Gunfire Support Team established its 'observatory' on the peak. It is alleged that in the gun-lines, special armour-piercing 500-lb shells were loaded into the 11-inch howitzers and the ships in the harbour were accordingly engaged. By last light on 5 December, one 11-inch shell had hit *Poltava,* blowing up her magazine, and *Retvizan* and *Pobieda* had been seriously damaged. The Imperial Japanese Navy had no concept of the efficacy of indirect fire, believing that the damage would be limited and superficial. Once the morning mist of 6 December had cleared, the Naval Gunfire Fire Support Officer guided 280 11-inch rounds upon the Russian ships. All the ships in the western basin suffered multiple hits. The process was repeated on the 7th, concluding with the sinking of the battleship *Retvizan*. For two more days the artillery fire continued, at the conclusion of which the battleships *Pobieda* and *Palada* rested at different angles on the bottom, the *Peresvyet* was wrecked and the *Bayan* was on fire. The only capital ship not accounted for was the battleship *Sevastopol* which, while struck five times by 11-inch shells, was still seaworthy and therefore still represented a threat to the Japanese. The Japanese navy was of course dumbfounded, not so much by the extent of the damage caused but by the reality that the Russian navy's Pacific Squadron had been destroyed by the Imperial Japanese Army.

Following so soon after losing the nine-day defence of 203 Metre Hill, the piecemeal destruction of their navy had a profoundly depressing influence upon the military and non-combatants of Port Arthur. Nojine had seen it all:

> The enemy's siege batteries set to work to destroy the
> Squadron, which perished under the eyes of the whole fortress,
> and the sailors holding the land positions watched, helpless and
> with sad hearts, as their ships were struck, and one after
> another our great giants went to the bottom.

The strategic factors of remoteness and isolation had come into play to contribute to the destruction of Russia's Pacific fleet. What might have been achieved by determined leadership intent upon taking the battle to the Japanese rather than allowing the ships to become the immobile targets of the Japanese can only be speculated upon. For the Russians, the death of Admiral Makarov had been one of the war's major catastrophies.

The centre of interest was the battleship *Sevastopol*, for only after her destruction would the threat to the Japanese fleet be erased. The Japanese fleet was in urgent need of replenishment and repair prior to meeting the Baltic fleet which was now on its way.

The plight of the *Sevastopol* was not very dissimilar to that of the *Graf Spee*. Despite the secondary armament being ashore, the Russians fought their surviving battleship with great courage to retain some last vestige of dignity. Equally, the Japanese navy felt the need to re-establish their name following the expensive and heroic victories on land. Admiral Togo received a precise order from Tokyo that *Sevastopol* was not to be permitted the glory of an escape. Captain von Essen, formerly captain of the *Novik*, placed *Sevastopol* in the roadstead at the southern end of Tiger's Tail behind a hill which shielded her from view from 203 Metre Hill. She was protected by an anti-torpedo boom and a small, hurrying, anxious destroyer flotilla. Wave after wave of Japanese destroyers sped in to release no fewer than 124 torpedoes in six successive attacks upon the luckless target. For three weeks von Essen survived, sinking two and damaging six Japanese destroyers. Out to sea with the waiting fleet the *Takasago* struck a mine and sank. The odds, however, were stacked against *Sevastopol*. During the night of 2 January, the day Port Arthur capitulated, the crippled battleship, manned by a skeleton crew and under tow of a tug, made for the open sea. In thirty fathoms of water, the seacocks were opened and she sank. Von Essen had ordered that the compartments on one side of the *Sevastopol* be left open and those on the other side closed with a view to her lying on her side after sinking, thus preventing the possibility of her being raised. After the Kingston valves had been opened, 'The battleship keeled over to starboard and commenced to sink,' said von Essen. 'I then went on board the *Silach* and waited for *Sevastopol* to go down, which she did stern foremost. She was ten to fifteen minutes in sinking.'

The destroyers were despatched from the port but they were only to join the increasing list of ships captured or interned. The remaining battleships were firmly held in the mud of Port Arthur harbour. Inside the harbour, the *Peresvyet, Pobieda* and *Poltava* were burning. Togo and Nogi stood together on top of 203 Metre Hill and the Admiral was satisfied that his fleet could now return to Sasebo to prepare for the next round. The correspondents were free to release the news of the destruction of the Russian Pacific fleet. Tokyo went wild with joy. In Port Arthur, Fock was heard to say with relief, 'Thank God that's the end.' As to land operations at Port Arthur, it is necessary to go back to the second week in December.

In Port Arthur, life continued in the same despairing manner. Shells fell unabated upon the town. Ten thousand soldiers were sick. The crowded hospital at Tiger's Tail was hit to add to the squalor, death and confusion. Stoessel, who had opened communications with Nogi, complained bitterly of this inhumane act but Nogi replied: 'What I beg to make special mention of is the fact that owing to your persevering and gallant resistance the number of our stray shots is unavoidably increased; and I therefore sincerely regret that our shots may possibly strike unexpected points.' The culprit had been the smokeless powder used early in the investment to screen the guns' positions. The barrels had now become severely worn to the degree that the Japanese were obliged to revert to the less wearing black smoke powder.

Defeatism was engendered by the dawning realisation that Kuropatkin was not about to raise the siege. The destruction of the fleet implied that the fortress was no longer important, for the Baltic fleet, if and when it arrived, would sail directly to Vladivostok. Surprisingly this pessimistic view was held by only a minority, yet significantly it included Stoessel, his Chief-of-Staff, and the odious Fock. Stoessel had been very slightly wounded and was unable to attend the council of war held on 8 December. He was a nervous man, fully aware that the consensus of opinion ran contrary to his own and that he risked being replaced by an officer coup. The Smirnov and Kondratenko lobby, however, remained loyal to their system and argued that, with at least a month's reserves of food and ammunition it was their duty to continue the fight. 'I cannot allow any discussion with regard to a capitulation before the middle of January at the earliest,' said Smirnov. 'At home they are just preparing to celebrate the jubilee of Sevastopol. Our fathers held out for eleven months! We shall not have completed eleven months till January 8, and only then will the son be worthy of the father.' The majority was firmly of the opinion to persevere and the disconcerted Fock and Stoessel's Chief-of-Staff left the meeting to convey the news. 'As to the surrender of the fortress, I shall know when that should take place, and I will not permit a street massacre,' declared Stoessel.

As if to make a point to the cowering Russian fleet, on 12 December the British steamer *King Arthur* beat the blockade to land 800 tons of cargo, mainly flour but including some hams, sausages and vegetables. Inflation was now rampant and those latter delicacies would have been beyond the reach of the average person. There were still 3,500 horses in the fortress and Smirnov had increased the ration of horsemeat to the sick to half a pound while others received a quarter of a pound a day. Over and above the horsemeat, the combatant soldier's diet consisted of half a pound of biscuit and an eighth of a pint of vodka, hardly sufficient to hold at bay the ravages of scurvy or to keep sentries from falling asleep at their posts.

Mid-December was bitterly cold. On the parapets of the three main forts only the sentries were visible. Those not required for duty were either asleep or trying to keep warm. The wind was icy and except for the bare rock in the lee of the slopes the ground was covered by a carpet of snow. Of the Japanese there was no sign but plenty of sound as they burrowed and mined towards the casements of the great fortresses. This and the trials with gas warfare – the Japanese had set fire to arsenic – brought General Kondratenko to Fort Chikuan (Cock's Comb) on the evening of 15 December. The General was visibly depressed, but perked up to pin the Cross of St George on a gallant NCO. He did not eat his supper and appeared contemplative all evening. At 9 p.m. came the noise of the fifth 11-inch shell since he arrived. It entered through the already weakened wall, killing Kondratenko and six other senior officers. News of Kondratenko's death stunned the defenders, heightening their sense of despair. The general had represented the fighting spirit of the good Russian officers. The impact of his death upon the soldiery was similar to that of the death of Makarov upon the navy.

At 10 p.m. Smirnov's telephone rang and he heard of Kondratenko's death. He was bitterly upset, not just for the loss of a friend but for the loss of an important arbiter between himself and Stoessel. An hour later his briefing officer arrived. 'We must go to Stoessel at once,' declared Smirnov. 'Fock is next in seniority to Kondratenko, and Stoessel will certainly try to give him the vacant appointment. This must at all costs be prevented.' At Stoessel's house they were informed that the general was not to be disturbed, while at Fock's house they were told he had a temperature and could not see anyone.

The next morning Smirnov was surprised to meet a healthy and ebullient Fock. Again he missed Stoessel who was away promulgating Order Number 921. Eventually the two men met and Smirnov outlined his intention to command the eastern front personally while Fock was to be assigned in the west. 'I have already appointed General Fock in place of Kondratenko,' replied Stoessel, raising his voice. 'The order [Order Number 921] is published. You should know by now, General, that I never alter my orders. I never' – shouting – 'alter my orders!' On assuming his appointment, Fock's first directive was to halve the strength of the forts and their supporting flanks.

On 18 December the Japanese fired their 2,000-kilogram mine under Fort Chikuan, which fell that night. On 28 December the mines under Fort Erhlung (Two Dragons Play with Water) were detonated and the fort fell that evening. At 6 p.m. the next day a further meeting of the council of war was convened to discuss the future of the fortress. The gunners and logisticians were equally of the opinion that the struggle could and should go on. Support was added by the navy. This unswerving commitment had placed Stoessel in a difficult position for he had already signalled the Tsar to the effect that: 'We cannot hold out more than a few days; I am taking measures to prevent a street massacre.' Stoessel made no mention of the signal but thanked those present: 'I am extremely grateful to all of you for coming to such a resolution.'

New Year's Eve is Japan's great day of celebration. Just after 10 a.m. they fired the series of mines under Fort Sungshu (Pine Trees), the sole surviving major fortress. The defenders surrendered at midday, but further progress by the Japanese was prevented by the depth of the defence. Barely could the good Russian regimental officers maintain their soldiers' spirit while the cancer of defeatism permeated downward from the very pinnacle of the leadership.

On 1 January Wantai fell. The Russian guns in the rear turned their attention to their former position but observers watching the fall of shot noticed a Russian officer riding towards the enemy carrying a large white flag. Someone jokingly said, 'He must be taking New Year's greetings to Nogi', but the contents of his briefcase were no joke. The message from Stoessel to Nogi, of which there are a number of versions, read:

> Being acquainted with the general state of affairs in the theatre
> of war, I am of the opinion that no object is to be gained by fur-
> ther opposition in Port Arthur, and so, to avoid useless loss of
> life, I am anxious to enter into negotiations for a capitulation. If
> your Excellency agrees, I would ask you to be so good as to
> appoint accredited persons to negotiate concerning the terms
> and arrangements for surrender, and to appoint a spot where
> they may meet my representatives.

The decision to send the message had not been referred to the council of war but had been decided upon between Stoessel, Fock and the Chief-of-Staff. Of this move, Smirnov was quite oblivious. The arrival of the message was a surprise to Nogi and his staff. While the Russian inner line was admittedly weak in places, they had steeled themselves to the prospect of a continuing and expensive assault. The surrender document, however, was ready. It had been meticulously prepared two years previously. There was no requirement for reference or reconsideration: 'The delegates are to be invested with full power to sign the capitulation, which shall take effect immediately after signing, without further approval'.

The news of the opening of negotiation for surrender was first released to Rear Admiral Wiren's office. Wiren sought confirmation, passing from office to office, calling on incredulous senior officers before confronting Stoessel, 'where the information of what had been done was confirmed'. Most of the ire was reserved for Fock, universally regarded as the evil influence over the weak Stoessel. Tretyakov reported, 'General indignation against General Fock was apparent and every kind of accusation was heaped upon his head'.

It was arranged for the delegates to meet at Sueshi village at midday on 2 January 1905. Despite Stoessel's orders to the contrary, beneficial ordnance was being destroyed and the echo of explosions from the harbour told of the final destruction of the remnants of the fleet. The chief Japanese negotiator objected and the senior Russian negotiator sent a Cossack to Stoessel asking that order be restored. Smirnov sent Kuropatkin a signal of protest: 'General Stoessel has entered into negotiations with the enemy for surrendering the fortress without informing me and in spite of my opinion and that of the majority of the commanding officers'. At 4.35 p.m. the terms of the capitulation were agreed and the Japanese forwarded a message to the Tsar from Stoessel:

> I was forced today to sign the capitulation surrendering Port Arthur. Officers and civil officers paroled with honours of war; garrison prisoners of war. I apply to you for this obligation.
>
> Stoessel

Jubilation swept through the Japanese lines. The humiliation of 1895 had been avenged.

Tretyakov was sitting down to dinner that night when the telephone rang. 'Arthur surrendered. The officers are allowed to keep their swords and return to Russia after giving their parole not to take any further part in the present war.' The officers' mess erupted in a commotion of indignation. In the wrecked town, Nojine witnessed the effect of the news upon the soldiers:

> Our men seemed suddenly to change their natures, all discipline went to the winds, and rioting commenced. Some, throwing their arms away, went straight down to the town, which became one vast scene of drunkenness and orgy. The shops and stores were looted, and wholesale robbery was the order of the day ... The officers, seeing that it was hopeless to try and cope with their men, hid from the maddened crowds.

Not all the officers shunned their men. In answer to his men's question as to whether they had to surrender, Tretyakov replied, 'Yes my lads. We have been ordered to surrender; but no blame attaches to the Fifth Regiment, and you can with a clear conscience tell each and every one that the Fifth Regiment has always looked death bravely in the face and has been ready to die without question for its Tsar and country.' He recalled, 'Many of them burst into tears, and I could hardly speak for the sobs that choked me'.

Stoessel was shaken by the rioting and the display against him. To him befell the humiliation of asking the Japanese to provide both him and his residence with protection. In the town, Nojine met an officer of the Japanese General Staff who greeted both him and a colleague in Russian. 'Ribnikov at once recognised him to be a man called Ito, who had been in Arthur for several years as a watchmaker. Small wonder they beat us!'

Decision time had arrived for the officer corps. The Tsar had replied to Stoessel's telegram:

> I allow each officer to profit by the reserved privilege to return
> to Russia under the obligation not to take part in the present
> war, or to share the destiny of the men. I thank you and the
> brave garrison for the gallant defence.
>
> Nicholas

Should they accept parole and return home or accompany their soldiers as prisoners of war to Japan? An immediate response would in all probability insist that officers should go into captivity with their men yet consideration should be given to the prevailing political situation in Russia. Some officers regarded voluntary incarceration as a pointless gesture as they would not be collocated with their men. A general shortage of officers existed and there was a real prospect of war in Turkestan. Additionally, there was in the air the unmistakable portent of revolution. Those officers who returned home believed it to have been their primary duty. Among those were Tretyakov and the officers of the Fifth Siberians.

When the Japanese checked the stores inventory of the Russians, they were astounded by the amounts that remained. It was not just that there was ample ammunition and food but the supplies of champagne and vodka also appeared inexhaustible. Surprise gave way to astonishment when the roll call revealed not only the 16,000 sick and wounded in hospital but also 868 officers and 23,491 men fit to march into captivity. The Japanese anticipated no more than 9,000 and believed that the Russians should have been honour bound to have continued their struggle. Many Russians would have agreed. The total number of casualties suffered by the Russians was 31,306 – less than a third of which had been fatal. The Japanese lost almost twice that number.

The conduct of many of the repatriated officers at the railway station lost them many friends and admirers. The joining of the trains for the journey home degenerated into an ill-disciplined scrum. Among the women elbowed out of the way were the widows of officers who had died in the battle. Stoessel's seat was guaranteed for he returned home to a hero's welcome and national and international awards. When the truth caught up with him, he, his Chief-of-Staff, Fock, and Smirnov were court martialled. All the prisoners were found guilty of a varying number of charges. Smirnov was unfortunate. His two charges arose from his loyal inaction relating to Stoessel's behaviour. Nevertheless, Fock and Smirnov were released and Stoessel was sentenced to be shot. The execution was never carried out and Stoessel remained in prison.

To the victor Nogi fell a deep-seated need to atone for his 'long display of military unskilfulness'. On 14 January he assembled all 120,000 of his soldiers before a shrine erected in honour of the fallen. Richmond Smith was present. 'In the form of a half circle, extending from the base of the hill far out onto the plain, was the victorious army, drawn up in divisions, brigades, regiments and companies, their fixed bayonets glittering in the sunlight.' Companies were brought forward in turn, to bow and enter into communion with their dead comrades. Nogi read the invocation, 'My heart is oppressed with sadness when I think of all you who have paid the price of victory, and whose spirits are in the great hereafter'. When the ritual was over, the army returned to its campsites to prepare for the journey northward.

CHAPTER TWELVE

FROM LIAOYANG TO MUKDEN

It had become clear at Liaoyang that the Russian span of command had grown too large for a single commander, hence the Tsar's decision to form the Second Manchurian Army. This act was seen by many as a snub for Kuropatkin. Yet, given his style of command – going through the pretence of consultation before imposing his plan in detail upon his subordinates – it should have come as no surprise. The justification for a separate, additional, higher command had increased with the arrival by mid-September of substantial reinforcements. These included the First Corps from Europe and the Sixth Siberian Corps, which was the basis for the Second Manchurian Army to be formed initially at Harbin and then destined for Tiehling, thirty miles north of Mukden.

Tiehling was selected by Kuropatkin for his next line of resistance after the 'prearranged retreat' from Liaoyang. The area here was more suitable for defence than the plains surrounding Mukden. Alexeiev interceded. He stressed to the Tsar his view that 'the continued retreat to Tiehling will not prove favourable to the morale of the army'.

It was true that Ivan's morale had evaporated. He accepted with his predictable stoicism what had become the by now routine withdrawals, believing and hoping that all this would end at the crucial battle forecast for Liaoyang. When that retreat also occurred, the bubble burst. The evidence of a demoralised army was clear to see. The Chinese were terrorised by marauding Russian troops, notably Cossacks. This in turn was to spur the Japanese advisors guiding the Hunhutze brigands to encourage numerous attacks upon the Russian rear areas. The trains, however, managed to get through, increasing to nine or ten daily. The major limitation was imposed by Alexeiev who forbade night movement lest his sleep be disturbed. Returning trains took the sick northward. Malingerers were closely vetted but dysentery was difficult to feign, as were the increasing numbers of self-inflicted wounds. Self-inflicted wounds of another nature were the numbers suffering from venereal disease, accounting for almost one-third of the casualties evacuated from the theatre.

One unusual aspect was the number of officers among the increasing ranks of drunkards and sufferers from gonorrhoea and syphilis. Here we find a good indication of the quality of the Russian officer. Kuropatkin berated these officers, as well as the many incompetents who had entrained for war, thereby alienating himself from his doubtful subordinates. The irony was that while he retained the respect of his soldiers, the worthy officers had lost confidence in their commander. The situation in and around Mukden was described by Sedgwick:

> Idle boasting and braggadocio, not by the rank and file but by officers, and those too in important positions, were common every-day occurrences. Among the higher leaders and the staff the spirit of cavilling at the actions of the Headquarters Staff and actions of equals was growing. The regimental officers were full of abuse of the leaders and their staffs. All ranks were heartily tired of the war.

The need for the Russians to go forward was as desirable strategically as it was to restore the morale of the land forces. Winter was held at bay by the rearguard action of an Indian summer, but shortly the armies would need to take to their winter quarters and accept the limitations imposed by the rigours of the Manchurian climate. Large-scale movement of troops would be precluded, offering Stoessel no prospect of relief by land and the probable loss of the haven of Port Arthur to Rozhdestvenski's fleet. The fall of Port Arthur would release General Nogi's Third Army, nullifying the numerical advantage so carefully nurtured by Kuropatkin. Port Arthur never ceased to provide a strategic rationale for the Russians to take action that could be described as unfortunate. 'Bear in mind', said Kuropatkin, 'the importance of victory to Russia, and above all, remember how necessary victory is the more speedily to relieve our brothers at Port Arthur'.

The Japanese also hoped that the Russians would advance southward. Hamilton wrote:

> It is the earnest hope of the Japanese that the Russians will soon
> sally forth and attack them again. The fact that Kuropatkin
> decided to come south and fight the last battle, instead of
> falling back and awaiting Oyama at Tiehling, north of Mukden,
> was the most splendid piece of good fortune that could possi-
> bly have happened to Japan.

A sometime proponent of the forward policy was the Tsar's nominee for command of the Second Manchurian Army, his aide-de-camp general, Oscar Casimirovitch Grippenberg. He was more a courtier, a political animal rather than a soldier. He had not seen service since the Crimea and his largest command had been a battalion. Now aged sixty-six, he was deaf and a hypochondriac. Although he was older than Kuropatkin he was none the less considerably junior. What Grippenberg was unable to bring to the battlefield in a military sense was outweighed by his recent experiences at St Petersburg where he had witnessed the increasing dissent, disorder and disobedience. A victory now, before winter brought down its curtain, could possibly stem the revolutionary tide at home.

While the pressure was growing for Kuropatkin to reappraise his situation, Marshal Oyama was methodically preparing for the next engagement. In Japan, the military law was modified to increase the length of service in the Kobi, or second reserve, from five to ten years and that in the conscript reserve from eight years eight months to twelve years four months. The burden of scarce manpower resources within the target age range was becoming a factor in Japan's ability to continue the war although lack of manpower would never be a reason for either side to seek peace. The new ordinance signed on 29 September would raise an additional 46,548 men to replace over one-sixth of the Japanese army that had fallen in battle.

The Japanese line of communication was further developed and diversified. The First Army continued drawing its supplies through Korea, although by early October improvements to the rail system into Liaoyang afforded the option of drawing from that city. Previously, the Japanese had relied upon carriages being pushed by coolie-power, but alterations of the gauge to accept Japanese rolling stock had the line fully operational by 3 October. The sea link was still functioning and the Second Army was supplied by sea and river until the latter means froze over. The major supply problem for the Japanese was in ammunition, much of which had been absorbed by the continuing action at Port Arthur.

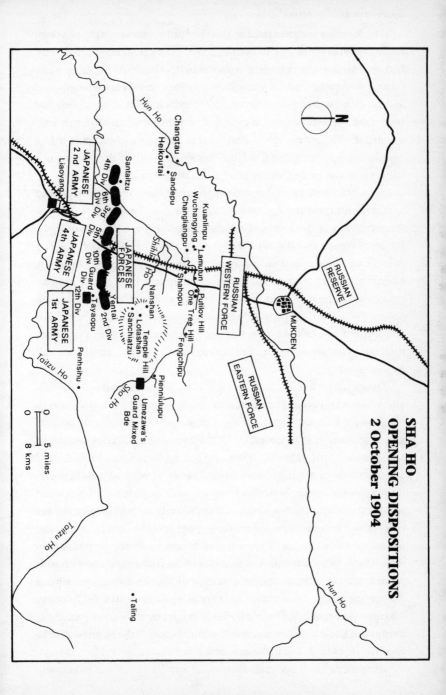

SHA HO
OPENING DISPOSITIONS
2 October 1904

N

Hun Ho
Heikoutai
Changtau

JAPANESE
2nd ARMY
Liaoyang

Santaitzu
4th Div
6th Div 3rd
Div Div
5th
Div

JAPANESE
4th ARMY

JAPANESE
FORCES

10th Guard
Div

JAPANESE
1st ARMY

12th Div
Tayaopu
Yentai
2nd Div

Penhsihu

Taitzu Ho

Sandepu

Kuanlinpu
Wuchangying
Changliangpu
Lamutun
Shahopu

Shihi Ho

Nanshan
Temple Hill
Sanchiatzu
Lotashan

Sha Ho

Piennulupu

Umezawa's
Guard Mixed
Bde

Putilov Hill
One Tree Hill
Fengchipu

RUSSIAN
WESTERN
FORCE

RUSSIAN
EASTERN
FORCE

MUKDEN

RUSSIAN
RESERVE

0   5 miles
0   8 kms

Taitzu Ho

Hun Ho

Taling

261

The Russians remained tied to their key rail communication although some new road building had been effected. On 29 September Kuropatkin had sent Alexeiev an optimistic report as to the condition of his men and state of his combat supplies although noting that 'there is not enough sugar and very little jam and other luxuries'. The 1904 harvest in Manchuria had been good and this fact took a great deal of pressure off an otherwise constipated railway system. As the days led into winter, the shortage of winter clothing obliged the general to issue an order permitting the wearing of a battle mufti comprising locally purchased Chinese padded clothing.

For whatever reason and due to whatever influences, Kuropatkin decided to take the initiative and go forward. During the gestation period of the planning, rumours of the proposed advance leaked through the region to the presses of Europe and ultimately to Oyama in Liaoyang. When Kuropatkin's orders came they contained a surprisingly limited objective. 'I order the Manchurian Army entrusted to my command to attack the enemy in whatever position he may be occupying having as the main object to gain possession of the right bank of the Taitzu river.' The attack was scheduled for 5 October and, deluged with clichés and homilies, the Russian army shook itself out of its torpor, determined now to settle its score with the despised 'yellow monkeys'.

Grippenberg, like much of his command, was yet to arrive in the theatre when Kuropatkin formulated his plan. Grippenberg's army was to comprise the Sixth and Eighth Siberian Corps, the Sixty-first Infantry Division and a division of Don Cossacks. In the meantime, Alexeiev permitted Kuropatkin the use of the Sixth Siberians subject to their not being divided and used only in a strictly limited area. There had been no significant reinforcement to replace wastage or battle casualties, although the sick and wounded discharged from hospital contributed to an improvement in the order of battle. Some of the veteran corps were severely under strength and part of the Fifth Siberian Corps was used to make up some of the losses in the First and Third Siberians. The strengths of the reinforcing corps had been eroded, among other things by desertion along the line of the railway. Kuropatkin recalls the arrival of the First Army Corps with a deficiency of 400 men per regiment. Despite these shortages, by the end of September Kuropatkin had the largest superiority in numbers over the Japanese that he had ever enjoyed: 261 battalions against 170.

After the battle of Liaoyang, Kuropatkin withdrew his forces to Mukden, which had been prepared for defence with a view to forming a bridgehead. Mukden shared the same general topography as Liaoyang. The Hun River, Hun Ho, runs north-east–south-west with, to the south, approximately a thirty-mile-wide strip of land before reaching the Taitzu. From the hills in the east flows the Sha Ho, around which most of the fighting was to take place. The railway, on a nine- to fifteen-foot-high embankment, ran north–south, parallel to the Mandarin road. To the west of these lines of communication the ground is flat and dotted with many villages. The houses were built of sun-dried bricks and had outer walls up to nine feet high and two to five feet thick. Shade was provided by clusters of trees. Most of the crossing places over the streams and rivers coincided with the location of the villages, leading to their fortification as a natural military expedient. The harvest had been brought in, leaving in the ground sharp stalks of *kaoliang* which limited the use of cavalry and was to cause much damage to the shoddy Russian boots. In certain areas fields of fire were as good as 1,000 yards but in others where the crops had been stacked to dry, some movement was possible without being seen.

The ground immediately to the east of the Mandarin road is the same as the west, but after a mile or two strikes random sandy knolls rising to precipitous mountains. Movement of infantry was confined to bridle paths, and other arms support was almost impossible.

Kuropatkin divided his army into a Western and Eastern Force, supported by a general reserve, two flank guards, two extreme flank guards and a rearguard. The Western Force was commanded by Bildering and comprised the Tenth and Seventeenth Corps supported by four regiments of Cossacks. Their line of advance was along the railway. The Eastern Force was commanded by the veteran Stakelberg and contained the First, Second and Third Siberian Corps with a division of Cossacks. They were to advance on a twenty-mile front through Pienniulupu to Penshihu. In the general reserve were the Fourth Siberian Corps and the First European Corps while the Sixth Siberian Corps formed the rearguard.

The bulk of the Russian front-line force was to the east of the railway, but to the west was the ground most favourable to the employment of their preponderance of artillery and cavalry. The ground to the east did not favour all arms co-operation and the Russians had consistently proved themselves inferior to the Japanese in the mountains. It was, however, in the east that Kuropatkin decided to make his main thrust. Here the Japanese right was overlapped and exposed. To what degree the element of surprise was intended as a deliberate ploy is not clear, but the plan was bold and could have worked.

The Japanese, reinforced now by a cavalry brigade, held a narrow position running from the Coal Mines at Yentai to Santaitzu. 'I wish', said Oyama, 'to concentrate as much as possible so as to be able to assume the offensive the moment an opportunity arrives.' On the left was Oku's Second Army, in the centre Nozu's Fourth Army, with Kuroki's First Army on the right holding his Twelfth Division in reserve to the right rear. At the time of this deployment the Japanese intelligence had not located the position of two of the Russian corps, yet Oyama held in general reserve in Liaoyang only three Kobi brigades and a field artillery brigade. High up in the mountains fifteen miles to the north-east of the main Japanese right flank at Pienniulupu was Umezawa's Kobi brigade. Some analysts, including the German General Staff history of the war, believe Umezawa was malplaced due to faulty maps. This was not just a problem that affected the Japanese. The Russians had the area from the south up to Liaoyang comprehensively mapped but had not bothered to survey the area to the north. Subsequent urgent requests for cartographers saw the thirty-five draughtsmen who arrived at the end of September absorbed into Alexeiev's burgeoning staff.

While we leave the Russians closing the gap from the north, marching toward the Japanese, it is worth examining the relative strengths. Kuropatkin had at his disposal eight and a half corps of which three were in reserve positions. Instead of both his force commanders being held responsible for their own flank security and protection, over-generous additional formations were assigned to that task. The function of the Western Force was to launch the vital holding attack, yet the two corps matched against the Second and Fourth Japanese Armies numbered between 40,000 and 45,000 riflemen while the Japanese strength would have been in the region of 65,00–72,000 riflemen. The main Russian assault force, the Eastern Force, consisted of seventy-three under-strength battalions numbering in all 50,000 riflemen. The First Japanese Army's strength would have been approximately 40,000 riflemen so that, given the nature of the country to be attacked, these were not reassuring statistics. Kuropatkin had again frittered away his numerical advantage before battle had been joined.

The first major contact of the battle was in front of Umezawa's position. Kuroki was convinced that this was the main Russian assault but Oyama could not be persuaded that Kuropatkin would choose such a course of action.

Fortune favoured Kuroki whose troops found on a dead Russian staff officer a copy of Kuropatkin's battle plan intended for Stakelberg. With this irrefutable evidence before him, Oyama decided not to await a general Russian attack but to pre-empt Kuropatkin and launch his own offensive.

The Russians were at their old tricks of advancing from one defended position to another. This slow progress enabled Umezawa to extricate his brigade from their exposed position on 7 October, retiring to Penhsihu without a shot being fired.

Cossacks and infantry had crossed the Taitzu but in order to claim any success the two back doors into Liaoyang, the passes and defiles at Taling and Penhsihu, had to be captured. Penhsihu was taken by the Russians but regained by the Japanese on 10 October, thereby securing the Japanese right flank and affording the worried Marshal Oyama much peace of mind.

To the east of the Yentai Mines, Hamilton had climbed a hill in the Second Division's area. Five miles to the north, as far as he could see, the ground was alive with Russians. He recalled the solid masses of cavalry, infantry and guns in formations he had seen in recent years only on the parade ground. The Russian progress he noted to be slow: 'long halts with very short advances'. Heavy storm clouds gathered over the massing troops, adding to Hamilton's gathering impression of foreboding:

> These dark masses began a stately deployment into long, continuous lines, which made my heart sink with an impression of resistless strength and of a tremendous impending blow. But now the long lines halted. Strange indecision! They remained motionless ten minutes; twenty minutes; and then I realised that they were entrenching out of range of the Japanese! In that one moment all anxiety passed away. I cannot explain the sensation or instinct which possesses me, but there it is, and I feel possessed of great calmness, and the full conviction that the Russians have by their failure to come on, parted for ever with that moral ascendancy which is the greatest of all the assets of an attack.

By 10 October the battle had been fully joined. In the west the advance of the Fifth Japanese Division was delayed for twenty-four hours by the resolute defence of one Russian regiment. The Second Japanese Army made slow progress over open country and without any real opposition since the

Seventeenth Corps withdrew before them. Before first light on the 11th, all the Russian troops in this sector were to the north of their new defence line, the fordable Shihli River.

The Russians formed a new Centre Group based on the Fourth Siberian Corps and Mischenko's Cossack Division to plug the gap that had opened up between the Eastern and Western Groups. The First Corps and the Sixth Siberian Corps were both brought forward, the former behind the Centre Group and the latter to the rear of the right of the Western Group. Meanwhile the key movements of the Eastern Group had bogged down, due as much to confusion as to poor communication, poor maps and over-caution on the part of Stakelberg. It was at this moment that Oyama issued his simple orders to attack. 'I desire to drive the enemy at present east of the Mukden highway towards the north east.' The intended execution was equally simple: the whole force, with the exception of the Twelfth Division and Umezawa's Brigade assigned to hold the right, were to advance northward sixteen miles to a new line Fengchipu to Kuanlinpu. The aim was to smash through the ad hoc Russian centre with the Second, Guards, Tenth and Fifth Divisions, the Fourth Army then wheeling right while the Second Army attracted the attention of the Russian right, thereby drawing in the reserves suspected to be in the vicinity of the road and railway.

The daylight hours of 11 October saw little real change to the situation as the battles swayed to and fro both in the mountains and among the defended villages on the plains. An unusual feature of the day was the effectiveness of Mischenko's Cossacks on the right and in the centre. The need for speed and resolute action in the attack had again been emphasised. The trend was underlined too that modern battles were not restrained by the hours of darkness. For the Russians, the need to fight the continuous battle was as much a reflection of their system of using reserves as it was of their lethargy in reorganising on the objective. The Russian tactic was to put lines of grey-coated soldiers down on a feature, sometimes shoulder to shoulder, with little by way of reserves in depth. Consequently, when the line suffered an attack, commanders screamed for assistance. The reinforcements would frequently come from the general reserve which would, under normal circumstances, be used for offensive action. So it was that reserves never knew where or when they were to be deployed and there were certainly no counter-attack or counter-penetration contingencies.

The Japanese demonstrated a flair for securing their newly won positions. A British attaché watching an attack had noted how 'the whole Japanese Army in front seemed to be underground'. Like the Russians they used the night attack to maintain their momentum but also to protect themselves from the domination of the Russian artillery. An important night attack, central to Oyama's orders for the Fourth Army to wheel right from its position, was that delegated to the Tenth Division on the night 11/12 October. Their objective was the enemy of Sanchiatzu.

At 1 a.m. a stack of *kaoliang* was set alight, signalling the attack to begin. The troops of the division moved forward in line with bayonets fixed. Control between the lines was effected by men carrying white flags. Each soldier was wearing his black greatcoat over his khaki uniform, with a white band round the left arm to distinguish friend from foe. In an earlier battle, there had been no time to prepare armbands and the brigade commander provided his soldiers with the simple formula which had been used before: 'Japanese are short, foreigners are tall. There are no foreign attachés with the Brigade tonight, so treat every tall man you come across as an enemy.'

The commanders had not been permitted rearward after orders, when their watches had been synchronised with the divisional commander's. The remaining hours of daylight were spent forward on ground orientation. This wise precaution was, on this occasion, largely nullified by the Japanese soldiers' enthusiasm for battle. The Russians had fortified a village en route to the regiments' objectives. From the walls a heavy fire fell upon the Japanese, wounding the brigade commander and killing a whole succession of colour bearers, including a commanding officer. Volunteers were sought to breach the walls of the village, some 200 setting off on a *'Kesshitai'* or forlorn hope. Most of the leaders were shot or bayoneted, but the sheer weight of what was by now almost the entire division, drawn from their own individual objectives into the vortex, was to win the night. In one of the houses the attackers found the regimental commander, tasting with his men their baptism of fire. He was so severely wounded that he could hardly stand, and was unimpressed by the information that a whole division was surrounding the village and that he should surrender. He refused, and although some of his soldiers saw logic in the Japanese demands many more fought on until they were killed.

The Japanese did go on to secure their objectives, but the night attack had been a technical failure. While the required wedge had been driven between the Russian Western and Centre Groups, it had been achieved at the expense of sixty officers and 1,250 men killed and wounded. These were the very men who, with the Fifth Division, were required to continue the right wheel into the heart of their enemy's position. Also that night Stakelberg made the last real attempt to breach the Japanese lines. His first effort to force the Taling Pass was easily swept aside for it had been well anticipated. The second attempt did succeed, but the Japanese were quick to counter-attack. The colonel of the regiment making the assault was at the head of the attacking group. No less than four colour bearers were shot down but the pass was soon back in Japanese hands. The Russians had again failed to secure their position and bring up reserves.

On 12 October the General with the overall superiority, Kuropatkin, handed over the initiative to Oyama because the Japanese Marshal was able to bring a superiority to bear at a given point. It was evident to Oyama that the casualties suffered by Ten Division, and also the need to bring the Fifth Division back into reserve, effectively ended any prospect of a major break-through in the centre. With great flexibility he rearranged his plan so that the main attack would fall on the Russian right wing, where the Seventeenth Russian Corps, numbering between 20,000–25,000, would be assaulted by three divisions totalling 32,000. It was the defeat of the Russian corps that was to be the turning point of the battle.

Up to this stage, Kuropatkin held an uncommitted reserve of 50,000 rifle-men and 250 guns. The main bodies of the Sixth Siberian Corps and First European Corps were untasked, as were the Second Siberians, held in limbo while Kuropatkin and Stakelberg engaged in a protracted long-range discussion. Oyama's sole reserve was his Fifth Division.

Kuropatkin patiently awaited news of Stakelberg's success in the east, for he knew that he faced only light opposition. It is true that Stakelberg had poor maps which showed contourless areas where in reality lofty mountains stood. Additional time was required for reconnaissance, yet the general's flair had been dulled by almost a year at war. He had become beset by the wariness that is so often the feature of the veteran. His decision to retreat from his position was due to the advance from the south of Prince Kanin's Second Cavalry Brigade reinforced by 1,200 troops from the lines of communication. Their skilful use of surprise, supplemented by their machine guns, forced the cavalry divisions of Samsonov and Liubavin to withdraw, thereby exposing the left of Rennenkampf's infantry on the north bank of the river.

In the west the Seventeenth Corps, reinforced by one brigade of the Sixth Corps under command, was exposed to the attacks of the Japanese Second Army. The Sixth Corps commander declined to assist, and Tenth Corps, which should have been under Bildering's orders as Western Group Commander, was being directed separately and without reference to him by Kuropatkin. The Seventeenth Corps, now severely defeated, was withdrawing along its front. In contrast to the wariness seen in the veterans, the newly arrived 219th (Yukhnov) Regiment, part of Sixth Corps but assigned to Seventeenth Corps reserve, moved surprisingly and eagerly forward. They marched into the attack in broad daylight over flat, featureless country, drawn up shoulder to shoulder in two lines. On the way they encountered the retreating men of the 139th and 140th Regiments who, not now surprised by anything, merely parted like a curtain to allow the unlikely counter-attack through. No one attempted to stop the Yukhnov Regiment.

On they marched, without changing formation and unsupported by artillery, towards a position occupied by six Japanese battalions and eleven batteries. The Japanese held their fire until the advancing Russians were within 600 yards. The Yukhnov Regiment's first experience of battle was to feel the full and devastating effect of the combined fire of sixty-six guns and several thousand rifles. Their serried ranks were blasted apart. An attempt was made to return the fire but there was no cover. The ranks wavered, broke and then fled rearward, leaving on the ground twenty-two officers and 832 men struck down in a matter of minutes. One-quarter had been lost but surprisingly, as future events would show, the regiment had not learned its lesson.

The dawning of 13 October confirmed that the Eastern Group was in retreat. The arrival that day of the Fifth Kobi brigade permitted Oyama to reinforce the depleted Twelfth Division. Her sister division, the Guards, was in serious trouble arising from a counter-attack by Stakelberg, but were saved when the Russians preferred to continue their retreat rather than pursue. Oyama despatched the Fifth Division, the last of his reserve, to restore the equilibrium and to assist Kuroki in an attempt to cut off the Russian Eastern Group.

In the centre the Lotashan, a bastion of the Nanshan mountain, fell to sustained Japanese pressure, confirming the Russians to be in retreat all along the line. In the west, Bildering's group had found respite due to the exhaustion of the Japanese Second Army. Oyama had no further reserves with which to gain an initiative, although the Eighth Division was in the process of detraining at Liaoyang. The Russians still held on the right flank their uncommitted guard under Lieutenant General Dembovski. Had this force been employed with flair and resolution, its twelve battalions, sixteen squadrons and thirty-two guns could have wreaked havoc among the exhausted soldiers of the Fourth Japanese Division. Herein can be seen the essential difference between an army whose aim is not to be beaten rather than one whose aim is to win. Accordingly, Oyama revised his orders, which had a new aim: 'to pursue the enemy as far as the left bank of the Sha river'.

The 14 October saw the tired, dispirited Russian force trudging the sodden tracks made almost impassable by the deluge of rain that had fallen during the night. The rain had been a godsend for the First European Corps, for the withdrawal of the Centre Group had placed the corps in a very dangerous position. Again, Mischenko's rearguard cavalry were to perform their duties with distinction. Tenth Corps had been placed in a similar position to that of the First. When the Thirty-seventh Russian Division was ordered to counterattack the Third Japanese Division, it was unable to comply due to the absence of many senior officers. One regimental commander assembled his regiment and marched it north over the Sha, leaving his position to be occupied by a grateful Japanese Eleventh Brigade.

At 7.20 a.m. Shahopu was lost by Tenth Corps. Over the river, frantic efforts were being made to gather together the Russian fugitives flooding north, with a view to forming a reserve. The left of Tenth Corps held part of the small Russian salient south of the river. They determined to withdraw but were prevented from so doing by Kuropatkin who sent forward ten battalions and gave orders for an attack to be launched southward. That night, Tenth Corps was to withdraw leaving only three points to the south of the river in Russian hands: the village of Lamutun, Putilov Hill and One Tree Hill. Prior to this situation, a counter-attack by Sixth Corps was launched against the Fourth Japanese Division.

The performance of the Sixth Corps was to suggest that their recently arrived troop trains had brought them to this modern battlefield from a bygone era. They were required to advance unsupported by either Dembovski or Grekov, Commander of the Western Group Cavalry, or Seventeenth Corps which was preoccupied with its own problems. For its second baptism, the Yukhnov Regiment was selected to advance with its sister regiment from Yepifan to Wuchangying and Changliangpu respectively. It was mid-morning, visibility was good and the plains flat and open. In full view of the

Japanese, both regiments were drawn up in the open order to be inspected by company and battalion commanders. Bands played and colours flew, all that was missing was Frederick the Great to take the salute. The mounted officers dismounted and at 11 a.m. the advance on the Japanese positions was resumed. Having moved for up to 300 yards in line, the Russians changed formation into single rank. They were permitted to come on before the Japanese unleashed their awesome firepower. The Yukhnovs lost almost 2,000 men and now ceased to exist as a regiment. The Official British History recalls: 'The whole operation was watched with breathless interest and amazement by the men of the Japanese Eighth Regiment, who had no difficulty in repelling, with heavy loss, the exponents of these bygone tactics.'

Oyama issued his orders for 15 October: 'I intend to reform the Japanese armies on the left bank of the Sha Ho, in order to prepare to advance to the line of the Hun Ho.' There was no possibility of Oyama wishing to cross the Sha at any point until everything was ready, his army reorganised and the few remaining Russian positions south of the river removed. That day Putilov Hill and Lamutun fell to the Japanese, but in that time Kuropatkin had gathered together a substantial reserve of between 25,000 and 30,000 riflemen.

Early in the morning of 16 October One Tree Hill was captured. General Gerngross commanded the ad hoc reserve formed from the East Siberian Corps. To him was entrusted the somewhat limited objective of capturing Putilov and One Tree Hills. These were not hills of great size, but rather mounds resembling double-yolked eggs sitting on the otherwise flat terrain on the southern bank of the Sha. Since the General's artillery was not expected to be ready for action until the afternoon, he decided to launch his attack that night.

Yamada, the Japanese Commander on the twin hills, sought reinforcement of his five battalions and two batteries but, since the Japanese staff believed the Russians would have deeper objectives for their counter-moves, including a counter-stroke along the Mandarin road, reserves were denied. At 5 p.m., when the Russian preliminary bombardment began, Yamada had already decided to withdraw.

The Russian plan was that General Putilov, a veteran of the Boer War who had fought the British, was to attack the hill that was later to bear his name. General Novikov, with three regiments of the First European Corps, was to attack One Tree or Novgorod Hill, while the Thirty-sixth East Siberian Rifle Regiment was to take the Japanese in the right rear.

The enthusiasm of the Europeans to take One Tree Hill saw them cross their start line early, catching Yamada before he had effected his withdrawal. The inexperienced Europeans were seen off, but the veteran Siberian Regiment rushed the hill and also attacked the echelon in the rear. The absence of liaison officers between the two Russian groups was a contributory factor to what followed, when the First Europeans accounted for many Siberians in the confusion that reigned during the two remaining hours of darkness. Four Japanese companies stayed on the hill, withdrawing before first light the next morning.

Putilov heard the sounds of battle raging away to his left and although his H-hour was still some way off, he ordered his two East Siberian Rifle Regiments to advance. The long grey lines moved silently across the river and were within 400 yards of the Japanese trenches when they were hit by a hail of gunfire. The Russians did not return the fire but quickened their pace until they were running the last few yards, whereupon they fell upon the defenders with their bayonets. Soon the hill was theirs.

The regaining of these two small hills went some way towards restoring some of the declining Russian morale. The price, however, had been high. The Russians lost 3,000 men, killed, wounded or missing, while the Japanese lost approximately 1,000. None the less, the good news was telegraphed to the Tsar, who declared that the western hill should be named after General Putilov and the eastern after Novgorod, the main garrison town of the Twenty-second Division.

The morning following the attack on the twin hills heralded the end of a week's continuous fighting. It heralded too the end of hostilities for the time being. The Russians recognised that they lacked the energy and resources for a counter-stroke and required further reinforcement from Europe. The Russian immobility suited Oyama. Although he could beat the Russians, the decisive victory had still eluded him. Now, as both sides dug in where they had halted, he was happy to bide his time until the troops released from Port Arthur gave him the reinforcements so vital to his future prospects. The supply situation on both sides was parlous. A report in *The Times* on 20 October stated: 'Victory may often rest not so much with the last man as with the last round and the last biscuit.'

Neither commander had secured his objective and the stalemate and advance of winter saw for the first time in modern warfare the construction of opposing lines of trenches, for the most part in open terrain. In some areas

only yards separated 200 miles of trenchworks protected by wire entanglements and mines. The design of the works reflected the military characteristics
of the two nations: 'Those of the Russians built solely for defence, their many
lines encouraging the inclination to retire; those of the Japanese were start-
ing points for another forward movement' (the Official British History).

The battle of Sha Ho can be described as indecisive. The casualties were
almost equal. The Russians lost 41,550 including 700 prisoners and the Japanese lost 39,769. While the outcome of the battle may have been indecisive, the
Russians lost a great deal. The opportunity to relieve Port Arthur had gone; so
too had the morale of the Russian army, buoyed temporarily as it had been by
the optimism as to the outcome of this battle. The German military observer,
von Tettau, considered this blow to the Russian soldiers' confidence and
enthusiasm to be so emphatic as to mark the battle of Sha Ho as their heaviest reverse of the campaign. Ivan proved himself equally as brave as the
Japanese, but he was let down again by poor tactical prowess and poor leadership. The Tsar sought to improve the top of the leadership pyramid by
recalling Alexeiev to St Petersburg and obscurity, leaving Kuropatkin a free
hand to plan the next move.

The Viceroy's final act before leaving Harbin on 25 October was to issue
an order that 'His Majesty today acceded to my request to be relieved of my
duties as Commander-in-Chief.' He departed, leaving Kuropatkin in an unenviable position. Now divested of Alexeiev's encumbrance, there could be no
further excuses concerning divided command. Kuropatkin had the need to
prove himself but had little by way of an opportunity. Winter brought with
it a fall in temperature to 14 degrees of frost; hardly the environment to raise
the morale of the army from the nadir to which it had fallen. The interest
in home reform grew among the shivering army, much of the information
being distributed by Japanese agents. A shortage of general supplies and poor
equipment made progress in any direction improbable. A senior officer at
the Staffka at St Petersburg reported:

> Messages to the highest quarters have been received from
> General Kuropatkin bitterly complaining of the tardiness of the
> commissariat department in sending supplies necessary to the
> soldiers, who are insufficiently clothed to meet the rigours of a
> winter campaign, and insisting that until there is better organi-
> sation military operations are impossible.

The news of the fall of Port Arthur followed what had been a new wave of optimism that the fortress might, after all, survive. The Mukden correspondent of the *Berlin Lokalanzeiger* recalled: 'The impression created was, therefore, that of a sudden disaster, which it was felt must inevitably influence the situation on the Sha Ho.' As 1904 gave way to the New Year, much of the local conflict had been represented by ongoing minor affairs. Prisoners brought in by the Russians showed that the Japanese were more severely affected by the weather than the Russians. For the time being, however, there was no prospect of the Japanese being able to turn one of the flanks of the 100-mile-long line of defence.

What was of most concern to Kuropatkin was the impending arrival of Nogi's Third Army on the Sha. The Russian reinforcement was proceeding well and the number of trains arriving had reached twelve daily. The trains, however, were bringing raw and under-strength units, not comparable with Nogi's veterans. During the course of the battle of Sha Ho, Kuropatkin had seen among his numerous cavalry evidence of a new sense of purpose and direction. Mischenko's rearguard action in the centre, for example, had been bravely conducted. So it was that a raid was planned through lightly defended areas, utilising the shock action of cavalry. Kuropatkin wrote:

> In order to induce the enemy to detach as many men as possible for their line of communications, and so weaken their front, to handicap their supply arrangements, and to stop the rail transport of Nogi's units to the front, a raid by a mounted force was organised against their line of communications.

Mischenko was selected to lead the 6,000-strong group of cavalry and six batteries of light guns. It was one thing to have lofty expectations of this worthy operation, yet quite another to provide logistic support given the climate and condition of the land. A letter in *The Times* revealed the true state of affairs: 'The country along the railway and for a wide radius has been utterly devastated. Nothing remains. The most populous and best cultivated section of Manchuria is a complete wilderness.' The essential, attendant, supply and forage train, therefore, was so massive as to restrict severely the mobility of the cavalry. On their first day, 8 January, they covered only twenty-three miles.

Mischenko's aim was to seize Newchwang station with a view to destroying the large stockpile of food there. The aim had two limitations: first, he was required to blow up the railway bridges and second, destroy a portion of the track between Tashihchiao and Kaiping. The pedestrian progress of the cavalry continued as subordinates allowed themselves to be diverted into minor skirmishes. Meanwhile, the Japanese were taking urgent steps to reinforce their vital supply depot near Newchwang.

On 12 January, the cavalry force approached the main stores depot which was normally guarded by 500 Japanese. Mischenko advanced along the railway, which had been cut behind him by his dragoons. It was four o'clock in the afternoon when the unwelcome noise of a fast-moving train was heard approaching from their rear. A train of sixteen trucks, each carrying thirty Japanese, steamed past the incredulous Russians who came under fire as the train swept by. The reinforcements swelled the number of defenders to 1,000, being well entrenched and ready in all respects to protect the depot from the cavalry onslaught. Three times the Cossacks charged but they were no match against the protected infantry. The Russian artillery fire did have some effect but the casualties were mounting and Mischenko withdrew, leaving behind him on the field sixty-two dead and six wounded.

The dragoons, who had been entrusted with the cutting of the vital railway line, had no concept as to how easily their half-hearted interference with the track could be rectified. It had taken the cavalry four days to reach their objective when two might have been considered reasonable in order to gain the best shock effect. What should have been a brilliantly executed raid, a much-needed morale booster, degenerated into a near fiasco. Mischenko's troops returned on 18 January, from which point the action at Sandepu will be described.

Grippenberg had arrived to take command of the Second Manchurian Army and was situated on the right of the Russian line. In the centre, under General Kaulbars, an extrovert of German stock, was the Third Manchurian Army. The left was held by the 'Siberian Wolf', actually a Polish Catholic named Linievich, who had been brought over from Vladivostok to command the First Manchurian Army. Grippenberg was pessimistic, showing some vacillation and inconsistency in his support for a new offensive in January. Eventually he fell into line to join a consensus to go forward, qualified by Kuropatkin 'on the condition that complete and direct touch was maintained between all three armies'.

The leaking of Kuropatkin's plan of campaign by the St Petersburg correspondent of the *Echo de Paris* led to speculation that the forthcoming action was political rather than military and that the harbinger of this movement was none other than Grippenberg. The 22 January had witnessed the massacres at the Winter Palace, 'Bloody Sunday'. *Cassell's History* hypothesised:

> It is not positively recorded that, as a result of that ghastly performance, the Tsar telegraphed to Kuropatkin at all hazards to take the offensive, but the fact that, three days later, the Russian Second Army was on the move lends a certain amount of colour to the suggestion.

The Grippenberg conundrum has never been satisfactorily resolved. In early January he had favoured an imaginative advance and right hook but by the middle of the month he was proposing a withdrawal to 'await a favourable opportunity to take the offensive'. It is possible that with Kaulbars and Linievich supporting a movement forward he was merely covering his tracks by endorsing a plan of action which would come to fruition with or without his support.

Kuropatkin's orders, issued three days before the massacres at the Winter Palace, declared: 'Our primary object is to drive the enemy behind the Taitzu River and to inflict on him as much damage as possible.' There has been further speculation that the Second Army was sent on what was intended to be merely a raid but that this was developed into a full-blown attack by the megalomaniac Grippenberg once he had crossed the frozen Hun River separating him from his immediate superior. This hypothesis is unlikely since while Kuropatkin's orders might appear limited had they been issued by a progressive general, issued by Kuropatkin and based on his performance to date, what he proposed was a total, unlimited offensive. The spectre of Nogi and the reinforcements that he would bring with him concentrated Kuropatkin's mind. One positive aspect of Mischenko's raid was that he was able to report that Nogi was not yet in the theatre. The time to move was now, the weather had deteriorated to 45 degrees of frost at night, a factor which was considered to be to the Russians' advantage.

Mischenko's raid and the *Echo de Paris* article had both served to highlight the vulnerability of the Japanese left flank to a turning movement towards Liaoyang. Grippenberg, for whom this was to be his re-baptism of fire, had been reinforced by the Tenth Corps as well as the First Siberians under Stakelberg in order to conduct the move the Japanese feared. Grippenberg's inexperience led to a grave breach of security which would have an unfortunate outcome on the battle. Major redeployments of troops on 14 and 16 January signalled Grippenberg's mission to the Japanese. Kuropatkin wrote: 'These movements, of course, at once disclosed our intentions, and information soon came in that the enemy had, in their turn, commenced moving their troops westward and fortifying opposite our new dispositions.'

The most southerly point occupied by the Russians was Changtau. Four to five miles to the south and thirty-six miles south-west of Mukden were the villages of Heikoutai and Sandepu, approximately two miles apart. Both were occupied and fortified by the Japanese, being described in *The Times* as a 'collection of farmsteads with a caravanserai for winter travellers'. The walls around the villages were high and three feet thick, dominating the surrounding countryside which was 'quite level and open, except for the villages and burial places, where there were groves of trees, which have now largely been burned for fuel'. The walls had been loop-holed giving the machine guns, of which the Japanese had a preponderance, good interlocking arcs of fire.

On 25 January the Russian general advance began. The weather was appalling. Only two days earlier *The Times* correspondent in Tokyo had expressed a view that the severe climatic conditions would prevent any movement for the time being. Grippenberg's army of 75,000 moved across the Hun, the bitterly cold prevailing wind blowing the snow before them into the faces of the Japanese defenders. Heikoutai fell to the First Siberian Corps after a tremendous struggle in which the Russians suffered horrendous casualties but the concurrent attack planned for Sandepu was permitted to be diverted elsewhere on what Kuropatkin declared to be a 'fool's errand'.

The Japanese had four divisions on their left flank facing the seven under Grippenberg and one of those Japanese divisions was the recently arrived and as yet unbaptised Eighth Division. Signs of confusion and failure to cooperate with Kaulbars's Army were evident within Grippenberg's command. On 26 January the Fourteenth Russian Division was sent against the one hundred-house, thatched village of Sandepu, garrisoned by the Japanese Fifth Division. Unfortunately the absence of maps, sketches and proper briefing resulted in the wrong village being shelled and occupied. A false report was despatched to Kuropatkin to the effect that Sandepu had fallen.

When Grippenberg realised his error he had already ordered his heavy guns away to support another task. His troops were exhausted and he asked permission to rest on the 27th. The rest area assigned to Stakelberg's corps was in Japanese hands and was being reinforced. Despite orders to the contrary, Stakelberg attacked the Japanese position before being obliged to fall back. He lost 6,000 men. Those who fell wounded froze to death during the night.

By the evening of 28 January the greater part of Grippenberg's army was separated from that of Kaulbars by the village of Sandepu. All efforts to take the fortified village had failed. Not only could the Japanese-held village deny co-operation between the two Russian armies, but it could also be used as a pivot for future Japanese counter-moves, particularly against the weaker Third Army. Grippenberg had enjoyed no success against a numerically inferior force, yet he insisted that he should go forward. Kuropatkin refused to reinforce his subordinate and ordered him to withdraw. This order coincided with Oyama's orders to force the Russians back over the Hun River. Grippenberg acceded to his orders with bad grace, falling back under a massive Japanese onslaught described by Oyama as follows: 'We attempted several attack movements but suffered heavily from the enemy's artillery, and especially from his machine guns, but all the columns continued the attack with all their might.' The failure of the Russians to take Sandepu emphasised the importance of Heikoutai as the key to their position which, if lost, would make their situation south of the Hun untenable. Oyama continued his account: 'Our forces charging into Heikoutai occupied the place firmly and entirely by half past nine.'

With none of his objectives secured, Kuropatkin had now to consider his next move, conscious of the fact that the Sandepu debacle had cost him over 20,000 men killed, wounded or missing. The Japanese casualties numbered 9,000. Over one-third of the Russian casualties were suffered by the First Siberian Corps for which their disobedient commander, Stakelberg, was removed from command. On 30 January Grippenberg, the commander of the First Manchurian Army for all of seven weeks, asked to be relieved of his command, giving as his reason his ill health. Kuropatkin wrote:

> This action of his set a fatal example both to those under him
> and to the rest of the army, and was most harmful to all disci-
> pline. The opinions, also, that he had expressed to the effect
> that the campaign was virtually over, and that we should retire
> to Mukden and Harbin, had a dangerously disturbing effect on
> our weaker members. It was in the long run more harmful than
> any single defeat of a portion of our force would have been.

When Grippenberg arrived in St Petersburg he gave the *Novoe Vremya* a highly embellished account of his own success and a damning criticism of Kuropatkin:

> Victory was in our hands, and I cannot tell you how anxiously I awaited men and authorisation to advance ... On the night of the 29th we retired, carrying away all our wounded men, and even picking up broken bayonets. The men retired unwillingly with tears in their eyes. I decided that it was impossible for me to remain any longer at the front, and the next day I reported myself to General Kuropatkin, asking him to relieve me of my command immediately.

Kuropatkin deserves some sympathy for, having at last rid himself of the interfering Alexeiev, he had the misfortune to acquire the buffoon Grippenberg. Here we have the hopeless situation of a country at war in Manchuria, simmering at home in revolution, and yet a senior general had the insensitivity to criticise the conduct of the war in the official newspaper. Soldiers in their tens of thousands had been killed in what many had viewed as a pointless war, the hospitals were unable to cope with the injured, maimed and dying, while in the trenches the demoralised subjects of the Tsar suffered the effects of a bitter and cruel winter. *The Times* encapsulated the plight of the rank and file:

> They had been told that they would beat the Japanese as soon as they had them on the plain. After Liaoyang they were told that they would beat the Makaki (leather-skinned dwarfs) as soon as the *kaoliang* was cut and the little tricksters had to fight in the open. After the Sha Ho they were told that the Japanese could not bear the cold, and that they would never stand their ground in a winter engagement.

Doubt had now been cast upon the one leader the soldiers most admired. Already rumours circulated among the soldiers concerning the cowardice of Stoessel and Fock at Port Arthur, while it was known that the two cavalry rivals, Samsonov and Rennenkampf, had brawled publicly on Mukden station. Seldom has any army deserved, or been in greater need of, inspired and charismatic leadership.

By February 1905, with the war a year old, the Russians maintained the same defensive posture on the Sha and around Mukden that they had adopted five months before. In one year of battle the whole size of the undertaking had dramatically changed. By comparison, the opening battle on the Yalu had been a mere curtain-raiser to what has been described as the first of the modern wars, with Liaoyang and the approaching conflict at Mukden considered to be the first of the modern battles.

The battle of Mukden was to be characterised by deception planning and tactical manoeuvre. The analogy of two generals opposing each other as in a game of chess is appropriate, but never before in the history of warfare had so many pawns been brought together to wage war. The Russian intention to hold Mukden was formulated as a pretence to the Chinese of guarding the tombs of the Manchu dynasty. But guarding them against whom? The Japanese were certainly not going to do anything untoward that would disturb the Chinese. The real strategic significance of Mukden was that if it should fall, Vladivostok would almost certainly become the next Japanese objective.

The trusty Trans-Siberian Railway had made good the Russian losses with more to spare. Under Kuropatkin's command were 275,000 riflemen, 16,000 cavalry and 1,219 guns. To their south, in Liaoyang, the city had grown with all the bustle and urgency of an ants' nest, with stores, *matériel* and soldiers being gathered for the next offensive. Again, Oyama was unable to match the Russian strength having 200,000 riflemen, 7,300 cavalry and 992 guns. Only in machine guns did the Japanese have a superiority; 992 against fifty-six.

In Japan, the manpower base of men of an acceptable standard had been severely taxed. The imminent arrival of Nogi's Third Army would bring together in the vicinity of Liaoyang virtually Japan's entire fighting strength. Cracks were now beginning to appear in the glaze of the Nippon military machine. The inability to beat the Russians comprehensively, the severe casualties, and now the privations brought about by the bitter climate all contributed their own dulling influences. In the financial markets of Europe and the United States the concern for Japanese ambitions grew apace. In Tokyo it was felt that the denial of further funds to pursue the war was very close. Rozhdestvenski's fleet was drawing nearer. The pressure developing on Oyama was therefore not just for another victory from which the Russians could again withdraw more or less intact, but for a complete victory with nothing less than the complete destruction of the Russian forces; in short a Sedan.

The Russian line to the south of Mukden was ninety miles long, having little depth and a general reserve centrally placed. On the right, in the plain, commanding the Second Manchurian Army was General Kaulbars who had replaced Grippenberg. His right rested on the Hun with his left exclusive of the railway. The railway and the Mandarin road were the right boundaries of Bildering's Third Manchurian Army with their left boundary including Putilov Hill. The rest of the terrain to the east as far as Shinking was under command of General Linievich and his First Manchurian Army. Two-thirds of the Russian cavalry, under General Rennenkampf, were on the extreme left of the line in the high mountains. The Russians had therefore adopted dispositions from which it would be difficult to execute effective offensive operations. The concentration of forces necessary for a blow or outflanking movement against the Japanese would surely telegraph the Russian intentions. Not that the Russians had at that stage clarified their intentions, which had been the subject of months of discussion and procrastination.

On 19 February, however, the Russian camp had decided to repeat on 24 February the Sandepu attack to be spearheaded by Kaulbars' Second Army. Meanwhile in Liaoyang Oyama was also planning to take the offensive. The Japanese staff had determined to strike at the moment when the worst of the bad weather had passed but before the thaw made the rivers impassable and mobility impossible. A premature thaw or unavoidable delays would of course frustrate these plans and could have left the attacking Japanese in a dangerous situation. As always, and unlike the Russians, they were prepared to take risks, for it is usually in that manner that battles are won. Their initial deployment incorporated a surprise.

A new Japanese army took the field to take the right of the line set against Rennenkampf through the high mountains. This was the Fifth Japanese Army, or the Army of the Yalu. Commanded by General Kawamura, the army was an army in name only, being much under strength and consisting of the Eleventh Division, veterans of Port Arthur, and a makeweight of reservists. To their left and to the east of the railway were the First and Fourth Japanese Armies with the Second Army on the left of line. A position in rear and to the west of Liaoyang had been reserved for Nogi's Third Army whose arrival would trigger the new offensive. *The Times* was impressed by the Japanese organisation and optimism:

> To launch, direct and support 400,000 [sic] men engaged at
> such a season over a front 100 miles in length, was one of the

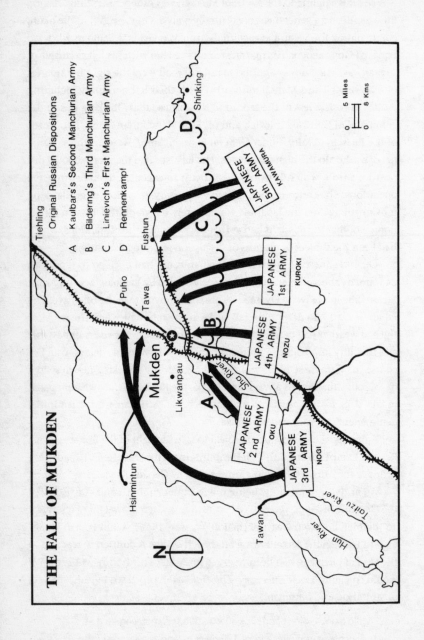

THE FALL OF MUKDEN

Original Russian Dispositions

A   Kaulbars's Second Manchurian Army
B   Bildering's Third Manchurian Army
C   Linievich's First Manchurian Army
D   Rennenkampf

Tiehling

Shinking

Fushun

Puho

Tawa

Mukden

Likwanpau

Hsinmintun

Tawan

Sha River

Hun River

Taitzu River

JAPANESE 5th ARMY   KAWAMURA

JAPANESE 1st ARMY   KUROKI

JAPANESE 4th ARMY   NOZU

JAPANESE 2nd ARMY   OKU

JAPANESE 3rd ARMY   NOGI

N

0   5 Miles
0   8 Kms

282

most remarkable tasks ever undertaken on the field of battle by
a modern staff. Wisely remaining at a point well in rear of the
army, but linked up with every column by telegram and telephone, Oyama, Kodama and their staff were uninfluenced by
the emotions of the battlefield, and were able to direct the
whole course of the battle with frigid precision and all the
desirable calm.

Nogi had been fortunate to avoid the pressures generating from Oyama's staff to have him removed for incompetence. None the less the future role and disposition of his army weighed heavily on Kuropatkin's mind. News of the movement of troops in the east, presumably Kawamura, was seen as a threat to Vladivostok. Although it is unimaginable that the Japanese would consider entering into a further siege so soon after Port Arthur, Kuropatkin reinforced Vladivostok. Kuropatkin had also responded to a successful Japanese cavalry attack upon his lines of communication. The Japanese detachment had left on 9 January and, after covering 300 circuitous miles, on 11 February reached its objective on the railway 160 miles north of Mukden. Here they blew up a bridge, saw off a Russian force and returned safely to their lines on 13 March. For their bravery the Japanese received a *Kanjo,* or unit cita-tion, while Kuropatkin reacted by sending to the rear areas a brigade and two regiments. The Japanese continued to play on Kuropatkin's ten-dency to react to every threat by a high level of misinformation which, when acting with the Russians' own self-deception, was to turn the battle to Japan's advantage.

Kuropatkin convinced himself that the Japanese would wish to avoid the plains where they were outmatched by the quality of the Russian artillery and the quantity of Russian cavalry. They had shown that they were more effective than the Russians in the mountains so, *ipso facto*, it was concluded that the main Japanese thrust would be through the mountains on their right flank. Kodama did his utmost to play on this illusion:

I had resolved to attack the Russians by enveloping them apparently in the east, so that they might despatch their main
strength thither while our main force was to be directed against
the Shaho–Mukden–Tiehling section of the railway, enveloping
them from the west.

Already, but understandably, Kuropatkin had overestimated the strength of Kawamura's 'army' but, when intelligence reported the confirmed appearance of Nogi's former division of veterans on the right flank, this was misconstrued as the presence of the Third Army also on the right. What was thought to be two armies therefore was in fact one regular division supported by reservists. In the meantime, Nogi's army had arrived in the theatre and sat behind the Second Army protected from the attention of indifferent Russian reconnaissance. A key factor in the Japanese plan was to convince Kuropatkin that the Third Army was ready and waiting on the right flank rather than sitting in hides in the west.

The advance of Kawamura's Army of the Yalu preceded by a number of days the general advance of the main Japanese army. It preceded by one day the Sandepu offensive planned for 24 February by Kaulbars' Second Manchurian Army. 'The object of the battle,' wrote Oyama,

> is to decide the issue of the war. The issue is not one, therefore,
> of occupying certain points or seizing tracts of territory. It is
> essential that the enemy be dealt a heavy blow. Since in all our
> battles hitherto pursuit has been very slow, it is imperative upon
> this occasion to pursue as promptly and as far as possible.

The move of Kawamura towards his objective of the Fushun mines prompted Kuropatkin to withdraw the First Siberians from under Kaulbars's command, and send them post-haste to stem what he perceived to be the main threat developing in the east. With that move, any prospect of a Russian offensive had evaporated. Given the linear dispositions, fortune favoured the army that made the first move and that, predictably, would be the Japanese.

Oyama's plan of campaign reminded a correspondent of tactics borrowed from the Zulu Wars: 'The five Japanese armies were to form a crescent whose cusps, over ninety miles apart at first, would gradually draw together, the western cusp however being finally and suddenly thrown forward so as to form a closed curve with the eastern.' The similarity of the Zulu *impi* can be drawn, whereby the horns close gradually until the enemy is completely surrounded to be dealt the *coup de grâce*: total destruction by the main body. Explicit in Oyama's plan was the avoidance of battle in the ancient city of Mukden. The Japanese had pursued a meticulously correct civil affairs policy and, ever the diplomat, Oyama had his eye clearly to the future. This positive 'hearts and minds' initiative, aimed at keeping the Chinese on-side, stood in stark contrast to the war of 1894–5 when, Chinese authorities claim, the Japanese murdered 10,000 non-combatants.

Gradually the advance of the main Japanese armies was taken up along the line. Kuroki's First Army moved off to fight through his front and to protect and link up with Kawamura's left flank. The two combined armies would find the Russian left much stronger than anticipated and casualties were heavy. Faced with an unacceptable delay, the irrepressible Kuroki wished to push on, yet a correspondent with his army recalled: 'Kuroki was ready to go on with the attack, but Oyama did not yet consider the sacrifices that this would entail would be warranted.'

On 27 February Nogi's Third Army left their bivouac area for a north-westerly course towards the Liao River. On the same day, the heavy Japanese artillery in the centre, including the feared 11-inch guns, opened fire on the well-protected Putilov and Novgorod Hills. The aim of the Japanese in this sector was to contain and hold the substantial Russian forces in the centre. The effect of the artillery fire was more mental than physical, for the Russians were to suffer few casualties. The appearance of the 'portmanteaux' among the demoralised army brought with each incoming, inaccurate round a sense of inevitability, the inevitability of further defeat. 'They must patiently lie on the cold ground under fire day by day. In most cases they might not even rise to a sitting posture to warm themselves by flapping their arms without being made the target for a dozen rifles.'

With the continuing transfusion of Russian troops from west to east came the first unwelcome news from the Cossacks on the right flank of the first sighting of Nogi's cavalry screen. Kaulbars assembled an ad hoc reconnaissance force to reconnoitre towards the Russian supply depot at Hsinmintun, thirty-three miles to the west of Mukden, to ascertain the size of the Japanese penetration. A second force of only two squadrons and four guns was assigned the task of driving the Japanese back over the Hun.

On 1 March the action in the east and centre was largely static. In the west Oku had made some advances but Nogi's army had reached Hsinmintun having made a highly dangerous and exposed, circuitous approach. Kuropatkin found himself in another dilemma. Without reserves he was unable to respond effectively to the movement of Nogi's army. All that could be mustered was one brigade sent forward in a counter-penetration role. The Japanese staff had assumed that the Russians would hold on one flank and attack on the other. Now it was clear that the Russians' intentions were to defend on both. No greater tactical advantage could have been so freely offered to the Japanese. Their offensive thereby had been greatly simplified. 'It also made the result of the battle far greater than had been anticipated,' said Kodama. 'It was never thought possible by us that we could surround the Russians and bring about a second Sedan.'

The 2 March witnessed the beginning of a new, transitional phase of the battle which was to last until the evening of 7 March. In the east, the Japanese continued to work away at the Russian defences. The Japanese commanders watched for the signs that Kuropatkin was responding to Nogi's threat by thinning out or withdrawing the troops in the mountains. On 7 March, the anticipated signs appeared when it was reported to Kuroki that the Russian trenches to his front had been evacuated. At that very moment he had been writing an order for one of his generals to launch an attack. He calmly crossed out the word 'attack' and wrote in the word 'pursue'. As usual, the co-operation between the Japanese armies was superb. Kuroki immediately sent a message to Nozu on his left flank enquiring whether he had noted any sign of weakening of the Russian-held positions. An investigation of the Russian defences showed that they had been abandoned and one more Japanese army commander amended his orders, not to attack but to pursue.

Meanwhile, the Russians had been destabilised. Lateral movement of troops to meet the threat of the moment was impeded by the withdrawal northward of the impedimenta of battle. In the rear areas, troops ran riot, crazed by the drunkenness arising from their unrestrained looting. Kaulbars's Second Army, which only a few days before had been intended as the hammer to strike at the Japanese, was now dispersed across the battlefield and could no longer operate as an effective formation.

Kaulbars was placed in command of the residue, which included the recently arrived, tired but not dispirited First Siberians. Their aim was to counter-attack the armies of Oku and Nogi who on 4 March had interlocked at Likwanpau. Unfortunately for the Russians, their counter-attack aimed at securing Mukden was uncoordinated and unconvincing. Kuropatkin considered Kaulbars's orders to be 'wretched'. Instead of a cohesive force, the Russians were hopelessly disorganised with troops intermingled in penny packets. *The Times* representative wrote:

> There were no less than sixteen detachments fighting isolated actions in this part of the field, many of them having received special instructions direct from army headquarters. Several

army corps commanders found themselves without troops and
unable to exercise any control upon the course of the battle.
This situation had been caused by the precipitate manner in
which attempts had been made to stem an attack against
which no antecedent precautions had been taken.

On 7 March Nogi's encircling movement progressed at a slow pace, so
much so as to annoy Oyama. The effect on Kuropatkin was somewhat different since, if Nogi was permitted to make his progress unhindered, he was
on course to seize the railway and cut the Russian lines of communication. As
a solution, Kuropatkin decided to lead personally a counter-stroke against
Nogi. In order to achieve his aim he needed to repeat the Liaoyang tactic of
withdrawing along his southern front to the Hun, to hold Mukden and to
use the surplus of troops withdrawn from the Sha in his counter-stroke force.

The orders given to Bildering and Linievich to withdraw during the night
of 7 March came as a bombshell. They had not been as aware of the consequences of Nogi's moves as their Japanese opponents. They were aware,
however, that for ten days, in the most appalling conditions, they had held
at bay the Japanese armies. They obeyed with quiet indignation, withdrawing at first in good order, but many soldiers wept as they left behind them
the frozen bodies of their unburied dead.

The Japanese, alerted to the withdrawal of Bildering and Linievich and
under no doubts as to Oyama's or Kuroki's or Nozu's orders, closed on the
Russians to maintain the momentum of their pursuit. In his new operational
orders Oyama wrote: 'I intend to pursue in earnest and to turn the enemy's
retreat into a rout.' Whereas at Liaoyang the passage of the Taitzu by the
Russians had been made in good order with an unfordable river obstacle to
their rear, this time the Hun was frozen over. That element of chance which
had so consistently favoured the Japanese and eluded the Russians was again
to come into play. The Japanese infantry crossed the river in the nick of time
before the ice broke up, necessitating the use of bridging pontoons, which
were well forward, to facilitate the passage of the guns. Thus the armies of
Bildering and Linievich were unable to enjoy that vital pause on breaking
contact. The Japanese continued at their heels, precluding recuperation or
reorganisation. Meanwhile the Russian position in the west had crumbled.
Oku had overwhelmed the Russian defences to the south-west of Mukden
and opened up a gap supported by Nozu on his right. Most ominous of all
and for the first time in the campaign, a significant body of troops under

Nogi had wrecked the railway to the north of Mukden and was now deploying to block the line of the Russian retreat. Kuropatkin's counter-stroke had become redundant, particularly since only twelve battalions could be found.

On 9 March a particularly violent dust storm blew into the faces of the frozen defenders while, in the much reduced visibility, the Japanese continued to close the ring. The storm continued into 10 March where the dust mingled in the air with smoke from burning supplies. At the station, the evacuation of the sick and reserve ammunition was accelerated, employing even the trains of the commanding generals. With the increasing noise of firing coming from the east, and with no prospect of victory, Kuropatkin ordered the retreat at 6.45 p.m. on 9 March.

In his orders, Kuropatkin detailed the Second Manchurian Army as the rearguard while the Third and First Armies were to withdraw along dedicated routes to Tiehling. Nozu's breakthrough over the Hun, however, forced on the withdrawing Russians an irredeemable situation whereby units were filtered and cross-fused on to the declining number of available routes. To the Second and Third Manchurian Armies had been assigned an axis of withdrawal along the line of communication, while Linievich, commanding the First Manchurian Army, kept to the east, thereby avoiding what was to become a debacle.

The Russian move northward along the line of communication was at first conducted in good order. The Japanese had pursued on a parallel course and were able from the railway embankment to pour heavy rifle and artillery fire into the close-packed Russian ranks. From that point, the retreat became a rout. Of the Second Manchurian Army, *The Times* correspondent wrote:

> All tactical control had been lost before the retreat began and
> the army followed the stream of fugitives in mobs and groups
> as best it might. The Russian Armies were scattered in the hills
> as sheep having no shepherd. Companies, battalions, regi-
> ments and even brigades disappeared from the ken of their
> commanders and from each other.

Kaulbars, the commander, was exhausted and dispirited, his shoulder in a sling to protect his collarbone broken in a fall from his horse. He paused for a rest when he overheard a liaison officer enquiring after the Seventh Regiment. 'The Seventh Regiment?' he interjected. 'I do not know what has become of my whole army and he asks me where my Seventh Regiment is!'

Some semblance of order was restored with the arrival on the scene of a number of generals who organised a rearguard to allow the retreat to continue before the Japanese had assembled sufficient strength for more emphatic and final action. All that was required, however, was for the Japanese to reappear, even in minimal strength, to re-instil panic and a complete breakdown in order. The wounded were abandoned and the whole route was strewn with the debris of war, broken wagons, rifles, saddles, cooking pots, food and dead horses. The terror which fuelled the Russian retreat was so intense that the relatively encumbered Japanese were unable to catch their enemy as they made for the supposed safety of the mountains around Tiehling.

Oyama signalled Tokyo: 'Today, at 10 a.m., we occupied Mukden. Our enveloping movement, which has been proceeding since several days, has completely attained its object.' If that object had been to destroy the Russian army then the object had not been attained. Oyama could win battles but he had not won the war. This had been no Sedan. At the final stage his troops had lacked the flair, determination and persistence which had been such a feature of earlier battles. They were a tired and cautious army whose quality had been diluted by the necessary infusion of a preponderance of reservists. At Mukden over a quarter of the Japanese troops engaged had become casualties, 15,892 officers and men killed and 59,612 wounded.

At Tiehling, Kuropatkin took stock of his demoralised army. Over one-third of his force did not report back for duty. Twenty thousand were killed or missing, a further 20,000 had been caught in the Japanese enveloping movement, and 49,000 had been wounded. Much of his combat supplies had been abandoned and the wherewithal to effect its distribution – wagons and horses – hardly existed. Fearing a rapid Japanese follow-up, Tiehling was put to the torch as the Russians embarked on a ten-day march northward to a new line of defence at Hsipingkai.

Mukden was Kuropatkin's last battle as commander for he was ordered by the Tsar to hand over to Linievich and return to Irkutsk. Kuropatkin recognised his shortcomings but, believing himself to be more efficient than some of his corps commanders, pleaded to be allowed to continue to serve in a subordinate position. Nicholas agreed and Kuropatkin and Linievich exchanged commands.

The Russians lost Mukden because Kuropatkin became beguiled by Oyama. There are two levels at which the detailed reasons for the Russian defeat can be examined. The first is found in *Cassell's History*:

> Yet by the employment of artifice, coupled by the most perfect
> co-ordination of his various armies, he [Oyama] was able, if not
> to envelop completely a force not appreciably smaller than his
> own [sic], at any rate to squeeze it out of a strong position and
> to damage it very seriously in the process. Without artifice,
> deceit, delusion, dust-throwing, or some such dissimulatory
> methods, the result of the Battle of Mukden might have been
> altogether different.

The final quotation from *The Times* military correspondent is an appropriate finale on which to draw the land battle to a close prior to examining the origins, progress and fate of Rozhdestvenski's Second Pacific Squadron:

> The crowning victory of Mukden was won, first and foremost
> because the statesmen of Japan had the spirit and the back-
> bone to declare war at their own hour; it was won because
> Japan was united in the attainment of national aims and shrank
> from no sacrifice to secure it; because the moral forces within
> the nation doubled and trebled material strength; because all
> was prepared, weighed, studied, known; because the short-
> comings of the enemy, which were many, were recognised and
> profited by; because a general staff, framed on the best existing
> model, was able to direct all forces to a common end; because
> each soldier and seaman knew and understood the part he had
> to play, and played it wholeheartedly for his country regardless
> of his own unimportant fate; and last, but not least, because
> the offensive in naval war was the beginning and middle and
> end of national strategy.

The small, victorious war his courtiers had promised the Tsar proved to be a long and disastrous war, a string of humiliating defeats. 'It is painful and distressing,' wrote the Tsar in his diary. But his pain and distress had not yet run their full course.

CHAPTER THIRTEEN

FROM THE BALTIC TO TSUSHIMA

Rear Admiral Zinovi Petrovich Rozhdestvenski, Commander-in-Chief of the Baltic fleet, now renamed the Second Pacific Squadron, awaited the Tsar's arrival on 9 October 1904 at Reval railway station (now known as Tallinn). The Tsar was coming for the final inspection prior to the fleet's sailing. The decision to despatch the force to the Pacific had been taken as long ago as June 1904. Rozhdestvenski had boasted to a reporter that the fleet would sail on 15 July, forecasting that he would have little to do in the Far East by September. The ships had left Kronstadt on 30 August but after many trials and tribulations had moved no further on their 21,000-mile voyage than the Gulf of Finland. Here the ragbag fleet, painted sombre black with canary-coloured funnels supplanted by a black circle, had been drawn up for the royal review. Under other circumstances and other reviews, it was not unknown for ships which formed part of the review to have only their shoreward side painted. It is a small point but underlines in a sense the poverty of the Russian navy in respect of both treasure and thinking and was emblematic of a country wherein the Potemkin Village had originated.

Whilst awaiting the arrival of the Tsar, Rozhdestvenski no doubt had an opportunity to reflect upon the circumstances which had brought him thus far in the course of an undertaking regarded by many as the ultimate in stupidity. He was a stern, handsome, bearded man aged fifty-six. He had already attracted international attention, principally due to what *Punch* described as his terrible name. Despite a reputation as one who was impatient, bad-tempered and fuelled by nervous tension, his Herculean efforts in working

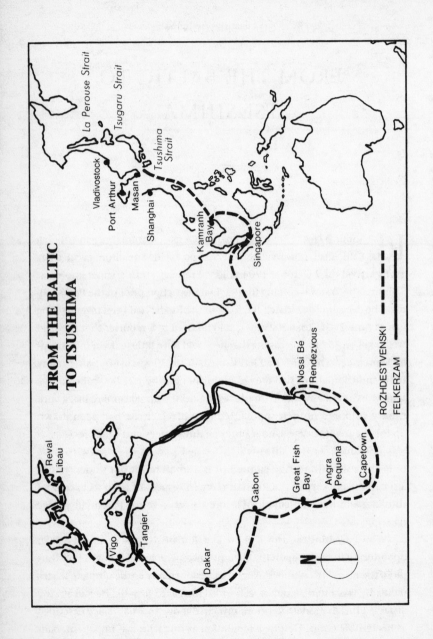

FROM THE BALTIC TO TSUSHIMA

La Perouse Strait
Tsugaru Strait
Tsushima Strait

Vladivostock
Port Arthur
Masan
Shanghai
Kamranh Bay
Singapore

Nossi Bé Rendezvous

Reval
Libau
Gabon
Great Fish Bay
Angra Pequena
Capetown
Vigo
Tangier
Dakar

N

- - - ROZHDESTVENSKI
—— FELKERZAM

eighteen hours a day for long periods were responsible for bringing a lethargic fleet and crew to its current state of preparedness. Even now, he had secret doubts as to the wisdom of this enterprise, inspired as it was by his own ego, megalomania and ambition. While in an unusually reflective, melancholic mood brought on by news of further delays in the dockyards, he confided his secret to one of his officers: 'We should not have started this hopeless business, and yet how can I refuse to carry out orders when everyone is so sure of success?' Despite his rarely shared misgivings, he was none the less determined that if the Second Pacific Squadron was to sail to confront the Japanese, then he was the person most suited to be in command.

It was quite unusual for a naval officer who was not a top-drawer, well-to-do aristocrat to have been elevated to such a responsible command position. It is true that many of his superiors had made it known that they would have nothing to do with the undertaking. As is often the case, however, luck had a great deal to do with the career development of 'Boyarin' (the Lord) Rozhdestvenski.

He had joined the Imperial Russian Navy at seventeen and specialised in what were the developing fields of torpedoes and gunnery. Promotion in peacetime was never dramatic, but the Russo-Turkish War of 1877–8 provided a catalyst to the languishing career of thirty-year-old Lieutenant Rozhdestvenski. He was employed as second-in-command to a fundamentally dishonest Captain Baranov. Their ship was an inconsequential little armoured steamer which cruised up and down the Black Sea. The chance meeting with a more heavily armed Turkish warship provided Baranov with the opportunity to write a highly embellished report of the little ship's alleged heroics. The report was opportune because it had the good fortune to coincide with St Petersburg's quest to identify and eulogise national heroes. The accounts in the press of little *Vesta*'s action, inflicting considerable damage on the heavily armoured Turkish warship, resulted in both officers being decorated for their bravery and being hailed as popular heroes.

Rozhdestvenski happily accepted the resultant promotion but his career became severely threatened when, at the end of the war, Admiral Hobart, British Commander of the Turkish navy, reported that the *Vesta* had fired a few long-range, ineffective shots and fled the alleged scene of battle. Rozhdestvenski admitted the truth to the press. Baranov left the service but Rozhdestvenski, apparently not having to justify his connivance, found his career to have been unimpaired by the scandal.

After the war, Rozhdestvenski assumed a gunnery appointment in Bulgaria before moving on in 1885 to London as the naval attaché. The mutual coolness between the British and Russians was evident but Rozhdestvenski could not help but admire the Royal Navy and its professionalism. In 1894 he had been promoted captain and commanded Alexeiev's flagship at Vladivostok. His association with the Viceroy-to-be did not provide a fillip to his career, for eight years later he was still a captain, commanding the Gunnery School at St Petersburg. It was this absence of patronage, coupled with the fact that he belonged to the lesser nobility, which seemed to conspire to keep him outside the circle of preferred or noble front runners.

On 24 July 1902 came the culmination of many weeks of gunnery practice and training aimed at demonstrating to the Kaiser the Imperial Russian Navy's prowess. To Rozhdestvenski this gunnery display was a labour of love. Although meticulously rehearsed and prepared, the display was sufficiently good to impress the Kaiser. As target after target was blasted, the Kaiser turned approvingly to the Tsar and said, 'I wish I had such splendid admirals as your Captain Rozhdestvenski in my fleet.' In the background, apparently calm and nonchalant, the ambitious captain exuded an impression of order and complete control. Only his deputy, Commander Clapier de Colongue, an efficient though effeminate officer of French extraction, knew of the tension and strain under which Rozhdestvenski was working. Nevertheless he carried the day, impressing both monarchs. Before the year had ended, he became an aide-de-camp to the Tsar and his promotion to rear admiral and appointment as Chief of Naval Staff provided the essential breakthrough into the inner naval circle. One of Rozhdestvenski's first acts as Chief of Naval Staff was to propose to the Minister of Marine the selection of a naval base other than Port Arthur. When the idea was relayed to Admiral Alexeiev, Commander-in-Chief in the Far East, it was ignored, the Admiral asking instead for additional ships to join those he was reluctant to exercise for fear of antagonising the Japanese. Faced with attitudes as negative as this, Rozhdestvenski came to the conclusion shared with General Kuropatkin that under such circumstances it was madness for Russia to go to war.

Some of those who knew Rozhdestvenski, however, while prepared to accept his ability to deal with the set-piece, doubted that he had the patience, flexibility and composure to cope with the vagaries and uncertainties of war. Witte was numbered among the ranks of the unimpressed. 'The Tsar,' he wrote, 'with his habitual optimism, expected Rozhdestvenski to reverse the war situation.' Strategically, Rozhdestvenski shared Makarov's concept of operations which envisaged the navy as an enabling factor in allowing the army to win the war, for which purpose the Russians required a sufficiency of naval power to keep the command of the Yellow Sea in dispute. Such a view was not shared by the St Petersburg strategists who believed the only course of action to be a decisive naval victory against the Imperial Japanese fleet. It is arguable whether their strategic argument was not influenced by considerations of national prestige and the imminent availability of four of the five battleships laid down in 1898 with the objective of war with Japan.

That the decision had been taken to send the relieving fleet with Rozhdestvenski as the commander was due in no small part to the influence of the naval correspondent of the semi-official journal *Novoe Vremya*. The correspondent was a serving naval officer by the name of Captain Nicholas Klado. When Port Arthur became isolated from Vladivostok, Klado was able to persuade the powers-that-be to release him from Vladivostok to join the naval expeditionary force being assembled at Kronstadt. Having been at war and decorated for bravery against Kamimura's squadron, Klado's philosophy, though simple, was regarded as authoritative. He believed that the armada should comprise anything that could float and should include ships still being built. Thus, he argued, the Japanese would be so swamped by the array of targets that their ultimate destruction by the Russian battleships would be assured. He wrote how the squadron 'must be powerful enough to inflict *alone* a serious check upon the *kernel* of the Japanese Fleet'. If fully adopted, the plan would have inflicted further delay and would encumber Rozhdestvenski with an unbalanced and unsuitable fleet. The Admiral strongly objected to this pseudo-Mahan concept, for he saw no benefit in taking to war small, slow vessels with small guns and voracious appetites for coal. Yet when Rozhdestvenski advanced towards Tsushima he kept his support ships with the main fleet, restricting progress to 9 knots and, in Klado's words, he 'terribly impeded the squadron in manoeuvres'.

The Admiral was only partially successful in leaving behind some of the 'galoshes'. Approximately a dozen cruisers and coastal defence vessels now in the Baltic had been sent back to Russia from the Pacific in the 1890s because they were obsolete and of no operational value. Klado's clever lobbying had won over Grand Admiral Alexis. Rozhdestvenski believed he was fully justified in loathing this forty-three-year-old who had become his own junior flag officer. Arguably, Klado did not deserve the admiral's disdain.

Of all the logistical problems facing the fleet's deployment, none was more critical than the problem of the supply of coal. Estimates had suggested that 3,000 tons of coal a day would be required to sustain the fleet at its best economical cruising speed. At full speed, 10,000 tons would be needed. This was not a new problem for the blue-water navies of the great powers. They had coaling stations on the way to and within their spheres of interest and influence. Russia had no such facilities. Of all the major European nations, she was the one country with no overseas colonies and was therefore the worst equipped to embark upon this proposed venture.

Under international law, neutral ports were forbidden to provide support to warships. Rozhdestvenski was to be bemused therefore by the attitude of France, friend of the predictably uncooperative British who were allied to Japan. In a not unusual example of *duplicité française,* France agreed to Russia having use of French colonial coaling facilities. Only sufficient coal was to be taken aboard to take the fleet on to the next port of call. Politically, France wanted Russia to cease her Far East adventure without delay in order to concentrate her power in Europe as a counter to the Kaiser's growing aspirations. Naturally, the commercial benefits of supplying the Russian fleet were not overlooked.

Grateful as the Russians were, the French gesture was insufficient. There were still gaps to be filled along the proposed route. The next country to come to Russia's aid was Germany. The Kaiser had already declared himself to be Admiral of the Atlantic and preferred to view the Pacific as where his Russian competitors' interest should be confined. Any move, therefore, which would take the Russian fleet out of his lake, and also over-commit that country, was a real political goal. Germany's colonies were widely spread but she did have the benefit of a comprehensive merchant fleet. The Hamburg-Amerika line was accordingly contracted to supply a fleet of sixty colliers to make rendezvous with the Imperial Russian fleet where required, whether at a benevolent neutral port or to transship on the high seas.

Rozhdestvenski flew his flag in the modern battleship *Kniaz Suvarov* of the same type as the ill-fated *Tsarevitch*. Also in the Second Pacific Squadron of this class were the recently completed *Orel, Alexander III* and the *Borodino*. These ships, comprising the First Battleship Division, looked impressive but were heavily overloaded. As with all the ships, every nook and cranny was filled with coal, supplies, water, vodka, champagne, clothing for both extremes of climate, and even cows, kept in special pens on deck. The battleship's intended displacement had been 13,500 tons but poor planning and after-thought had raised the tonnage to over 15,000 tons. The ships were dangerously top-heavy, all but two feet of the main armour plate was below the water, and the secondary armament could not be fired in high seas. Each ship carried 12-inch guns but the methods for control and firing were archaic. Engineers were embarked to fit telescopic sights while the fleet was en route, and instead of modern electrical firing mechanisms the Russian guns were still fired by lanyard. The new Marconi radio system was in service with most modern fleets but the *Suvarov* and her sister ships were fitted with second-rate, inefficient German equipment.

In the Second Battleship Division, commanded by Rear Admiral Felk-erzam, were three older, less well-armoured and slower battleships. The *Osylabya* flew the admiral's flag but that was all that distinguished this ugly battleship carrying 10-inch guns and an array of small but ineffective secondary weapons. She was supported by two old, slow 10,000-ton battleships, *Sissoy Veliky* and *Navarin*. Rear Admiral Enquist, commanding the First Cruiser Division, flew his flag in the decrepit *Dmitri Donskoi*. She had been built in the 1870s as an armoured frigate and had been rigged for sail. Under command was the speedy, hybrid and limited *Svetlana* as well as four fast modern cruisers, *Oleg, Izumrud, Zhemchug* and *Aurora*. The remaining significant warship was the twenty-year-old armoured cruiser *Admiral Nakhimov*. In support were nine 350-ton destroyers and a range of auxiliary craft among which was the fleet's albatross, the repair ship *Kamchatka*. Had the original squadron embarked upon its voyage to Port Arthur as intended before autumn, then it would have had a reasonable prospect of breaking through the Japanese fleet to form a junction with the fleet at Port Arthur. Alert to this danger, on 18 May 1904 Tokyo ordered General Oku to drive the Russians off the Nanshan feature and occupy Dalny as a matter of urgency. The Japanese however would discover that they had time to spare. It was after the capture of Nan-shan on 26 May that ships of limited capability such as *Sissoy Veliky, Navarin* and *Nakhimov* were added to the Baltic fleet.

The number of ships totalled forty-two. The need to find 12,000 officers and men to man the ships provided the Admiralty with considerable problems. Some were found from those who had rejoined the fleet from ships neutralised after the battle of the Yellow Sea. Among these was Semenov who became a supernumerary on Rozhdestvenski's staff. The shortfall of engineers was made good by impressing qualified men from the merchant fleet. Thirty-year-old Chief Engineer Politovski had completed the construction of the *Borodino* and was anticipating a reunion with his wife when he was ordered to report to the *Suvarov* as fleet engineer. He was to be kept busy not only with the older ships but also with those of the *Suvarov* class whose construction had been so rushed and altered. His experience in constructing the sister ship *Borodino* would be put to good use. While the preparation of the Baltic fleet made ponderous progress, news in September of the defeat at Liaoyang and at sea resulted in a conference being held to consider the whole point of sending a relieving fleet to the Far East. By now Rozhdestvenski insisted on leaving for Port Arthur with whatever suitable ships were available. Intelligence reports, however, indicated that Japanese warships had suffered only light damage and would be fully operational by the time Russian reinforcements reached the Far East. It was accordingly decided to postpone departure by a further month, not only to permit the inclusion of ships nearing completion but also to allow more time to negotiate the procurement of South American cruisers.

While the Black Sea fleet may have appeared a ready source for the supply of additional officers and sailors, the ongoing enmity with Turkey prevented any major reduction in that fleet's manpower. The quality and experience of the remaining pool of matelots in the Baltic and Kronstadt were impaired by the weather which reduced time at sea to six months of the year. There still remained a massive, quantitative shortfall which was to be made good by calling up raw recruits possessing not the slightest seagoing experience or tradition. As if to compound the problem, anarchists and revolutionaries who had decried and derided the unpopular war were also conscripted along with criminals and malcontents. The authorities hoped and believed that under Rozhdestvenski's stern and uncompromising command the undesirables might be transformed into good, loyal Russians. During the course of the long voyage to the Pacific, seamanship did quite naturally improve yet the political flashpoints aboard certain ships were undiminished in intensity. Aboard the *Orel*, as in many other ships, a revolutionary library was maintained, and eventually an engineering officer quite openly distributed literature throughout the ship. He was aided and abetted by the revolutionary Novikov-Priboy. A fire at St Petersburg had nearly prevented *Orel* from entering service, then she ran aground, and finally the engine-room cadre sabotaged her propeller shaft. The situation on board *Orel* was not dissimilar from that in other ships of the fleet. The ugly *Osylabya* was commanded with an iron rod and she was a most unhappy and disgruntled ship.

Now, after three months of frantic preparation, all was superficially ready for the Tsar's inspection. The ships of the Second Pacific Squadron looked pristine at anchor, having been scrubbed and polished by their complaining crews. 'Cleanliness became a mania,' wrote Novikov-Priboy. Rozhdestvenski was at the railway station awaiting the arrival of the royal train due at 9 a.m. Accompanying him were two of his divisional commanders. Dwarfed by his chief stood the second-in-command, the competent, smooth-faced but grossly overweight Admiral von Felkerzam. Alongside him, with the biggest, most flowing of white beards, was the equally short Admiral Enquist. They were an old, ridiculed pair who did not compare favourably with their presentable commander.

After lunch, the Tsar visited seven warships. It proved to be a chilly day with intermittent showers. Occasional sun patches provided the thousands of enthusiastic spectators lining the shore with a good view of the fleet until the smoke from the guns booming to herald the Tsar's arrival blotted it out. The Tsarina Alexandra found the weather not to her liking and remained in the warm with the precious Tsarevitch Alexei, born on 30 July 1904. She had brought with her chalices for the chapels on board the ships and these were distributed. As the Tsar moved between the ships on his itinerary, martial music played, flags cracked in the wind, and jingoism was in the air. Sailors in new uniforms contemplated their dinner as they braced themselves against the wind. The Tsar's ovation was stirring. He wished officers and crew a victorious campaign and a happy return to their native land. With cheers still ringing in his ears, the Tsar and his family departed, leaving the senior officers to a last banquet. That night, alone in his room at St Petersburg, the Tsar confided his deep thoughts of the fleet to his diary. 'Bless its voyage, Lord. Permit that it arrive safe and sound at its destination, that it succeed in its terrible mission for the safety and happiness of Russia.' In St Petersburg Bishop Feofan asked the Tsarina's favourite, the monk Rasputin, of the prospects for the Baltic fleet's success. 'Will its engagement with the Japanese be successful?' he asked. 'I feel in my heart that it will be sunk,' came the reply.

The following day, 11 October, Rozhdestvenski gave the orders for the vengeful fleet to sail. The beginning of this great undertaking was fraught and uncertain. The fleet hove-to for four days further down the coast at Libau before finally making for the high seas.

The movement of the Second Pacific Squadron through the Baltic was painful, like a funicular railway climbing from cog to cog each nautical mile towards its destination. There were delays for running repairs to ships, for taking on bread and fresh rations, coal, and ad hoc mine clearing in the narrows. The latter measures underlined a phobia, often repeated in the impressionable Chief Engineer Politovski's diary:

> We shall anchor off Bornholm, where I hope to repair the torpedo boat. Tonight there will be danger. We shall all sleep in our clothes and all guns will be loaded. We shall pass through a narrow strait. We are afraid of striking on Japanese mines in these waters. Perhaps there will be no mines; but considering that long ago, Japanese officers went to Sweden and, it is said, swore to destroy our fleet, we must be on our guard. This strait is eminently suitable for torpedo boat attacks or for laying down mines.

On all ships double watches were mounted and searchlights stabbed deep into the darkness. *Suvarov* had signalled, 'No vessel of any sort whatever must be allowed to get in amongst the fleet.' Some were warned off by shots and even the vessel bearing news of Rozhdestvenski's promotion to vice admiral was fortunate not to have been sunk.

That Japanese torpedo boats could have been expected to be operating unsupported 20,000 miles from their bases did not seem extraordinary to the muddled minds of the Russian navy. Months earlier, the Russian Captain Hartling had been sent to establish a counter-espionage cell in Copenhagen. He hired agents along the coastline to report suspect ship movements. They, in turn, to justify their keep, reported sightings in quiet creeks, off islands, on the high seas, building to a crescendo and swamping the Russian Admiralty just as Rozhdestvenski's fleet approached the Skaw. It was no mean compliment which the jittery Russians afforded to their foe in attributing to them a capability impossible to possess. The tensions and trepidations were not eased by more breakdowns. The torpedo boat *Prozorlivy* ('Clearsighted'!) ran aground and damaged her bows. 'Another mishap to the *Orel*,' records Politovski. 'At a most critical moment, when we were going through a narrow strait, her rudder was injured. She anchored. The damage is not yet ascertained. There is probably some scoundrel on board who has been trying all along to damage the ship.'

The fleet passed through the Skaw into the North Sea in a state of nervous tension and panic. Some deeper meaning was sought from the appearance of two harmless balloons. The sea was calm but the fog persisted, sirens were shrieking and maintaining position in the dark became impossible. The repair ship *Kamchatka* lost touch with the fleet until a contact report was received from her: 'Chased by torpedo boats.' Hearts leapt throughout the flotilla as thousands of sailors peered out over the rails into dark, calm sea. 'How many?' queried *Suvarov*, 'From which direction?' 'About eight from all directions,' came the reply. The desperately isolated repair ship radioed the *Suvarov* to reveal herself with her searchlight so that the lost vessel might orientate herself. Fearing a Japanese trick, Rozhdestvenski would have none of it and *Kamchatka* was directed to change course.

It had passed midnight on 22 October when throughout the fleet bugles sounded the alarm. Sailors stumbled to their posts, manning guns and searchlights while the terrified Politovski fled to a safe vantage point below decks. All hell broke loose as firing was taken up by ships throughout the fleet. Politovski, with hands held firmly over his ears, was quite amazed to observe: 'A small steamer was rolling helplessly on the sea. One funnel, a bridge, and the red and black paint on her side were clearly visible. First one, then another projectile from our ship struck this unfortunate steamer.' Then the cowering engineer saw other 'steamers'. 'They were, no doubt, fishermen,' concluded Politovski who added sagely: 'Now there will be a universal scandal.'

On the decks of the 100-ton, single-screw trawlers stood fishermen, turning their eyes away from the glare of the searchlights and holding aloft fish to show the nature of their trade. The boat which had caught Politovski's attention was the *Crane,* one of the Gamecock fleet out of Hull, fishing the traditional Dogger Bank. Young Joseph Alfred Smith was awoken by the fury of the firing. He ran up on deck to find his father and the third hand both headless in a pool of blood. Most of the remaining members of the crew had been wounded. The first hand stood on deck frantically waving a red lantern as the little boat was sinking beneath him. Three trawlers steamed through the fire to pick up the *Crane*'s dead and injured while on board *Suvarov*, Rozhdestvenski realised his error. The order to cease fire was given. Nearby, a 6-pounder continued to fire with enthusiasm. The enraged admiral stormed up towards the gun layer, pulling him away by his shoulder. 'How dare you?' he shouted. 'Don't you see the fishermen?'

By this time, most of the heavy-calibre fire had been lifted off the little fishing fleet, prompted by the sighting of cruisers. A fire fight developed between the opposing battleships and cruisers, hits being recorded on the latter. Enquist, the commander of the Russian cruiser squadron, should have been at least fifty miles away, but now he was returning his battleships' fire and reporting the engagement. That something was wrong occurred to Rozhdestvenski at the same time as he recognised the trawlers. Already *Orel* had loosed off 500 rounds and she was but one of the seven battleships to have engaged *Dmitri Donskoi* and *Aurora*. Fortunately, the accuracy of the fire was abysmal, hits being recorded only to the upper decks and superstructures. On board the *Aurora* the chaplain received mortal wounds, while a gunner was also wounded. When the news passed through the fleet there was much sadness and regret compensated only by the euphoria emanating from the pleasing victory over the Japanese torpedo boats which had sheltered so cowardly among the British trawlers. Only the chief surgeon of the *Suvarov* and the *Orel*'s paymaster's steward, Novikov-Priboy, author of *Tsushima*, appear to have believed that there never had been any such Japanese torpedo boats. Not pausing to pick up survivors, the great Russian fleet steamed southward on its journey. When the news was released in St Petersburg the man in the street read proudly that 'the lessons of the first days of the war have not been wasted, and the new treacherous attack by the Japanese had been met by the vigilant and pitiless eye of our Admiral and the straight fire of our guns'.

The battered little fishing fleet returned to the home port of Hull with the dead. News of the disaster had spread throughout the fishing town on the Humber with the earlier arrival of the wounded. A wave of indignation swept through the assembled crowd as they watched the coffins being taken from the rain-swept quay. That night, the town's MP left with a deputation for London where the presses of Fleet Street rolled out the startling news of 'The Dogger Bank Incident'. The editorial of the morning's *Times* was particularly scathing:

> It is almost inconceivable that any men calling themselves seamen, however frightened they might be, could spend twenty minutes bombarding a fleet of fishing boats without discovering the nature of their target. It is still harder to suppose that officers wearing the uniform of any civilised power could suspect they had been butchering poor fishermen with the guns of a great fleet and then steam away without endeavouring to rescue the victims of their unpardonable mistake.

The attack on the fishermen was seen as an attack upon Britain's status and dignity both as a seafaring race and as a great power. The King gave 200 guineas to the dependants' funds. He had been outraged by 'the unwarranted action', particularly since the Tsar had found the need only to 'regret' the incident rather than apologise to Edward. The Admiralty put the Home, Channel and Mediterranean fleets on a war footing. Crowds gathered at public meetings in Trafalgar Square, the Russian ambassador was booed, and among the worldwide messages of condolence came one from the mayor of Tokyo. War between Britain and Russia appeared imminent.

Rozhdestvenski was quite unaware of the furore his *faux pas* had caused as he passed under the cliffs at Dover lined with embittered spectators. Then part of the fleet had the effrontery to coal off Brighton's Royal Pier. Almost to a man, the Russians genuinely believed that they had successfully seen off an enemy attack. Even when they arrived to face the commotion at Vigo, their first port of call after the Dogger Bank Incident, there were few additional detractors from the belief that there had been a presence of Japanese torpedo boats and they, the Russians were in the best position to have known the truth. Twenty-eight modern ships of the Royal Navy, crewed by unarguably the most professional of the world's sailors, foregathered from diverse ports to await the order from London to destroy the Russian fleet.

The Russians had steamed 1,800 miles and bunkers were almost empty as the ships took up their stations in the wide, warm and welcome Vigo Bay. Rozhdestvenski and his staff had two matters of concern on their minds. The first was coal. Almost immediately orders were given for coaling to begin from the five pre-placed Hamburg-Amerika Line colliers. Before the order could be carried out Spain, prompted by Britain, reluctantly interceded. The admiral was informed that international law relating to belligerent warships would be upheld. The fleet would be welcome to rest and recuperate for twenty-four hours but the ships would be prevented from taking on stores, and that included coal. To enforce the decision, Spanish policemen boarded the warships to ensure that the order was carried out.

Rozhdestvenski exploded and sent his compliments to the port commandant, advising him to expect a personal visit that afternoon. Meanwhile his staff was collecting the press reports of the action which had taken place four days earlier. There were also messages from St Petersburg seeking clarification.

Rozhdestvenski's second problem was Nicholas Klado. The admiral's relations with Klado had become decidedly frigid. He had grown to respect the abilities of the sensible but unprepossessing Semenov but, of his staff, none was more highly valued, devoted and loyal than Clapier de Colongue. He had followed his leader from the Gunnery School to assume the appointment of Chief-of-Staff in the rank of captain. He was the man closest to the admiral. It was he who absorbed the shocks emanating from the temperamental outbursts; it was he who sponged up the ill feeling and fury; he was the essential link between an aloof and uncommunicative commander and the machine that had to translate those wishes into action. Tall, handsome and sensitive, it was not unusual for him to leave his admiral's presence with tears of exasperation in his eyes. Rarely has a subordinate been so loyal. His devotion and loyalty to his commander were to have a sad conclusion, as this tragic man's protection of his superior was to see him placed before a court martial and sentenced to be shot.

For the time being, Clapier de Colongue spent a while translating for his unbelieving admiral the world press reports of the Dogger Bank Incident. Even the partisan German press was hostile. It is not recorded how the unfortunate de Colongue fared with the following report from the *Berliner Tageblatt*: 'Rozhdestvenski is known to be an exceedingly nervous gentleman. He gets into a state of boundless excitement over trifles and it is all the more strange that he should have been entrusted with a post so unsuitable to a person of his type.' Nevertheless, Rozhdestvenski was not over-concerned by the welter of what he viewed as totally inaccurate reports. He regarded the Diplomatic Corps as being responsible for untangling these untrue fabrications. He had been heartened by a supportive message from the Tsar: 'While there may be temporary difficulties between Russia and a friendly nation, I have given my ministers orders to settle these differences as soon as possible. The eyes of Russia are on you and our hope and confidence accompany you.'

That afternoon a determined Rozhdestvenski set off to visit the port commandant. He passed near to HMS *Lancaster,* a token British cruiser from Beresford's cruiser division waiting outside the bay. The friendliness of the meeting with the Spanish representatives surprised Rozhdestvenski. He found them to be courteous and understanding. He was not surprised that they should relent and relax their earlier order allowing each ship to take on 400 tons of coal. While coaling got speedily underway, the tension began to relax as the warmth of the bay raised the sailors' spirits, aided by the issue of spirits more national in character.

On 1 November Admiral Sir John 'Jacky' Fisher wrote to his wife: 'It has nearly been war again. Very near indeed, but the Russians have climbed down.' Russia had found herself in a difficult position. She had no reason to disbelieve Rozhdestvenski but the aim of the exercise was not to wage war with Britain despite wishes to the contrary. Sir Charles Hardinge, British Ambassador in St Petersburg, reported the national mood: 'War with England would have been welcomed throughout Russia.' Within the fleet, similar views were held but for different reasons. Semenov overheard a junior officer gazing towards HMS *Lancaster* saying what a pity it had been that war with Britain had been averted. On being questioned, the officer replied: 'Because then they would have scattered us directly we had got outside. Now we have to go all that distance to meet the same fate.'

The Russian government found itself obliged to support its admiral for his orders had been to fire on any unidentified vessels which approached the fleet. In an unusually conciliatory and diplomatic mood Rozhdestvenski sent off a signal claiming that the attack on the fishing fleet had been accidental. There had been, he argued, two torpedo boats in the vicinity and every effort had been made to avoid the imprudent fishing boats. Significantly, he apologised and asked 'to express our sincere regret for the unfortunate victims of circumstances in which no warship could, even in times of profound peace have acted otherwise'.

Britain, believing that she had secured satisfactory guarantees, relaxed the pressure on Russia, although she was to discover once the Russian fleet was on the open seas that she had secured rather less than she had imagined. The Russians had undertaken to observe caution and avoid injury to neutral ships while en route to the Pacific. That was reassuring, but the optimistic British demand that the 'responsible officers' should be offloaded at Vigo to attend an international commission was ignored. Instead, Rozhdestvenski left behind mere eyewitnesses, officers he considered to be of no great import in the looming battle. The opportunity to rid himself of the turbulent Klado proved to be irresistible but unwise. As Klado departed in the pinnace to be *Suvarov*'s representative, an officer muttered: 'It is said that rats leave the ship before she sinks.'

From Semenov's accounts, which generally should be read with some caution, Klado did not witness the initial firing on the Dogger Bank and so was not a suitable eyewitness. He would not have been in a position therefore to applaud the 'brave sailors' who 'were not afraid at their peril to assume heavy responsibility by immediately opening fire on the unknown torpedo boats, taking no account of the presence of the fishing-boats (so-called neutrals)'. His selection to appear before the French-chaired International Commission into the Hull Incident which convened in Paris in December 1904 was due to his service and association with the French navy. Klado had served aboard the French cruiser *Latouche-Tréville*, one of the ships under the command of Rear Admiral Fournier who became President of the Dogger Bank Enquiry. Russia needed an honourable withdrawal from this embarrassing situation. If the findings had been too critical, St Petersburg would have refused to sign them. There is some suggestion of two reports, one published official report which the Russians signed, and a second, more honest report that was not published.

At 7 a.m. on 1 November the generously victualled Russian fleet weighed anchor and set course for Tangier. Despite the easing of tension the British cruiser squadron accompanied the Russians, watching the laborious, none-too-professional fleet meandering across the flat sea at 9 knots. The British presence caused resentment. The *Orel* broke down again, requiring the entire fleet to heave-to. Beresford responded by forming into battle order until the nature of the Russian move was discerned. A midshipman on the wallowing *Orel* watched the British cruisers: 'It's disgusting to treat us like this, following us about like criminals.' Politovski had gone aboard *Orel* and was stung by the same indignation: 'Horrid Folk! They are Russia's eternal enemy. They are cunning, powerful at sea, and insolent everywhere. How many impediments has this "ruler of the sea" put on our voyage? Every impediment has come from Britannia.' On board *Suvarov*, Rozhdestvenski nonchalantly watched the impeccable manoeuvring of the Royal Navy. Semenov, standing alongside, asked of the admiral, 'Do you admire this?' Rozhdestvenski's apparent indifference gave way to a strangled, almost sobbing reply: 'Those are real seamen. Oh, if only we . . .' He did not finish and, having regained his composure, departed the bridge.

On 3 November, as if to signify the end of the Dogger Bank Incident, Beresford's cruisers withdrew, permitting the Russians to celebrate freely the tenth anniversary of the Tsar's accession. The entire fleet, now reassembled after the political storm, anchored in the Tangier roadstead where officers and men talked briefly of exploits, plans, and the prospect of a run-ashore. The fleet looked impressive in the bright Moroccan light. The Sultan displayed his independence by affording Rozhdestvenski a warm welcome and a seventeen-gun salute. No limitations were placed on the Russians but the commander, now free of political considerations and his arrogant escort, wanted to push on.

The world's interest continued unabated. Not since Trafalgar had there been a major fleet engagement. From that time, the development of the battleship had been phenomenal but based on untested ideas. Sir George Sydenham Clarke wrote:

> It has, therefore, followed in this country especially, that the evolution of the warship had been frequently capricious, indicating the absence of any clear principles, and entailing an immense total expenditure upon vessels unsuited to our national requirements, but happily not forced to demonstrate their inutility.

It was to befall the hapless Rozhdestvenski to prove the inutility of his fleet in the only major battleship engagement since Trafalgar not influenced by underwater or air threats. Togo would emulate Nelson in what was, for good reason, to become known as the 'Trafalgar of the East'.

The Japanese strategic offensive in Manchuria was a typical joint Army-Navy operation. The Japanese army had defeated the Russians on their chosen ground of concentration at Liaoyang but had lacked the strength immediately to chase the Russians northward. The plan had of course been for the Third Japanese Army to provide the manpower and resources to give the Japanese the capacity for absolute victory, yet they were bogged down outside Port Arthur attempting to raise a siege with the wrong tactics. Meanwhile Russia's First Pacific Fleet was theoretically free to influence Japanese intentions both on land and at sea. It was only Japanese good fortune in ending the life of Admiral Makarov which nipped in the bud any offensive spirit the Port Arthur fleet might have possessed. That point was not apparent to Tokyo who viewed the continuing Russian naval presence at Port Arthur as a serious threat, a threat which it was realised could be extinguished through the occupation of 203 Metre Hill. From this observation point, artillery observers could pick off the Russian naval assets at Port Arthur as if removing goldfish from a goldfish bowl. The threat of the arrival of the Baltic fleet served to impose its own sense of urgency at the operational level at Port Arthur and strategically throughout Manchuria. The Japanese were aware of what their idol Nelson had done to the French navy and by implication to the French army by defeating the French fleet at the Battle of the Nile, 1 August 1798. Nelson's victory had effectively cut off the expeditionary French force in Egypt thereby ending any aspiration Napoleon had for an advance towards India. If the Imperial Japanese Navy were to suffer the same fate, her armies in Manchuria, starved of manpower and resources, would fall easy prey to a Russian army growing in strength by the day. The threat posed by the Second Pacific Squadron was therefore taken very seriously indeed. Admiral Togo concluded a signal he sent to Tokyo and General Kodama: 'I consider that now, when the Baltic fleet is on its way out here, the urgent necessity is to capture Port Arthur and to dispose of the ships there.' The need to destroy the Russian Pacific fleet henceforth took priority over the needs of the Japanese army in Manchuria. Intelligence reports conveyed information on Rozhdestvenski's progress to Admiral Togo but they were deemed insufficient and three cruisers were sent westward towards Singapore to provide early warning of the approach of the Second Pacific Squadron.

Rozhdestvenski's distrust and low opinion of almost all his officers led him to keep his own counsel. Rarely did the fleet know their next port of call, where coaling would take place, or have any inkling of the commander's intentions. At Tangier, the admiral decided to divide his fleet, supposedly because he believed the older ships would not survive the long journey around the Cape, being better suited to the Suez Canal route. To the latter route was assigned Admiral Felkerzam. He had been dispossessed of the *Osylabya* and now flew his flag in the *Sissoy Veliky*. Included in his division, whose orders were to make rendezvous at benevolent French Madagascar, were *Navarin*, *Svetlana*, *Zhemchug*, *Almaz* and a number of support ships.

The *Osylabya* joined the main fleet which set course for Dakar. The departure from Tangier in full view of the world's press was inauspicious. *Orel* broke down and *Suvarov*'s steering developed a fault causing her to come close to ramming *Kamchatka*. On weighing anchor, the *Amadyr* was surprised to bring up the telephone cable linking North Africa with Europe. Rozhdestvenski was not best pleased by this latest debacle and ordered the cable to be cut. Politovski reflected on the good fortune that it had been a French cable rather than British, for otherwise he believed there would have been hell to pay.

The main fleet's progress to the next port of call, Dakar, was reasonably uneventful. Here they made rendezvous with the ten colliers carrying among them 30,000 tons of coal. That quantity was far in excess of what the fleet, which had sailed south at 8 knots, could fit into the still partly stocked bunkers. The need to have sufficient coal to sustain operations meant that the bunkers were never emptied, coaling taking place approximately every five days. The admiral was aware that problems were anticipated at Libreville, and were certain at Great Fish Bay, a Portuguese colony. Portugal was conscious that she was Britain's oldest ally.

'Instructions for Storing Coal' were disseminated throughout the fleet. These orders had specific provisions for where additional bags of coal were to be stored. Officers' cabins, to the rank of commander, were not exempt. Coaling began immediately. Rozhdestvenski made no effort to justify his order. The *Suvarov*-class ships had a capacity for 1,100 tons of coal. They were ordered to load twice that amount.

The French admiral proved to be more sticky than anticipated. He told Rozhdestvenski that the coaling, by now underway, had to cease immediately. Already the temperature was 120 degrees F with humidity nudging 100 per cent. The climate, therefore, did not assist Rozhdestvenski's receptiveness of the Frenchman. 'I intend to take on coal unless your shore batteries prevent me,' shouted Rozhdestvenski defiantly. He knew the French had no shore batteries, and the visitor succumbed to amused acquiescence over a glass of welcome champagne.

This was the fleet's first taste of 'black fever' as the crews struggled in the heat to offload the colliers. There was insufficient water to satisfy their thirst or to free mouths and nostrils from the clinging dust which would be an unwelcome feature throughout the rest of their journey. Some fell over from heat stroke. Some died. Among the dead was the son of Nelidov, the Russian Ambassador to Paris. After twenty-nine hours the transfer of coal had been completed while the crew, exhausted by the heat and irritated by the dust, sought out liquid sustenance. 'We are tormented by thirst,' wrote Politovski, 'hot and unpleasant, but one drinks incessantly. I alone drank six bottles of lemonade today.'

Churchill wrote how the 'ordeal of coaling exhausted the whole ship's company. In wartime it robbed them of their brief period of rest; it subjected everyone to extreme discomfort'. While the Russo-Japanese War was being fought, naval ministries throughout the world argued over the merits of the transition from coal to oil. In 1904, the First Lord of the British Admiralty, Lord Selborne, wrote: 'The substitution of oil for coal is impossible, because oil does not exist in this world in sufficient quantities.' The truth was that the Royal Navy had coaling stations strategically placed throughout the world and had ready access to Cardiff coal while they had no guaranteed access to oil. Admiral Fisher disagreed with Selborne, having declared his hand in 1902. 'It is a gospel fact ... that a fleet with oil fuel will have an over-whelming strategic advantage over a coal fleet.' In 1904, the Liquid Fuel Board in the United States recommended the use of oil as a stand-alone fuel. The Russians leapt ahead of both the British and Americans in building a battleship fuelled by oil alone.

The overladen fleet set course on its training voyage to Gabon. The admiral publicly abused the captains whose ships did not respond to his immediate orders. 'You don't know how to command your ships,' he signalled to the captains of *Orel* and *Borodino*. As a punishment, they were made to steam to starboard of the flagship. The heat percolated through to the crew. The stokers in *Kamchatka* were mostly civilian and were sorely tried by the heat in the bowels of the ship. The threat of a strike was nipped in the bud, but throughout the fleet insubordination to officers increased.

Poor navigation resulted in the squadron sailing past Gabon, not helping raise the spirits or level of confidence of the fleet. The tug *Roland* was sent back northward to re-cross the Equator and locate the port. Eventually anchors were dropped four miles offshore. The colliers were not expected for two days and the wide-eyed, simple sailors were released to take shore leave in this tropical paradise.

The arrival of the Russian fleet had come as a surprise to the French governor-general. He was well disposed towards the Russians but none the less grateful that the coaling exercise was conducted outside his territorial waters.

The fleet sailed on, pausing briefly at Libreville before anchoring in international waters off Great Fish Bay. The Russian intentions had been made known to the commandant by the earlier arrival of three German colliers. Lisbon had telegraphed explicit orders that no facilities were to be offered to the Russians. With the three colliers now at anchor, the commandant signalled for naval reinforcement while the small gunboat *Limpopo* was prepared in order to execute the Portuguese government's wishes.

The little *Limpopo* was dwarfed as she came alongside the mighty *Suvarov*. Rozhdestvenski was not angered but rather amused by the captain who ordered the fleet to leave, otherwise 'drastic action' would be taken. Coaling continued in international waters while the *Limpopo* sailed off to summon assistance. The Russians were unconcerned because they knew that they would be well on their way before any outside assistance could be forthcoming. The next port of call promised to be more amenable. Angra Pequena in German South West Africa had been ceded to Germany by Britain who retained sovereignty over two offshore islands. From here, a British deputation endeavoured to intercede to prevent the coaling of the Russian fleet. The German governor remained unmoved by the British arguments.

Angra Pequena was the last port of call prior to the 3,000-mile voyage to Diego Suarez in Madagascar and the rejoining of the fleet. The port was to witness the biggest coaling exercise of the journey as each of the *Suvarov*-class ships required to take on 2,300 tons of coal. The colliers waited well out to sea, riding out a storm which was to last for two days. Rozhdestvenski's impatience, irritability and tensions spread throughout the fleet and discipline began to wane. Finally, in desperation, he called up the colliers. This move proved to be premature for the first collier to attempt to come alongside *Suvarov* was not under control as she pitched and rolled into the warship. After spearing the collier with the flagship's 12-inch guns, Rozhdestvenski reluctantly called the operation off and waited for the storm to abate.

As an interim measure, an efficient transfer of coal by launch had commenced from the colliers. It was not until 15 December that the intensity of the storm had died sufficiently for the colliers to come alongside to transfer their loads over the rails. On that day, the German governor came aboard the flagship to take lunch. He brought news of the fall of 203 Metre Hill. '203 Metre Hill, and what is that?' enquired Rozhdestvenski testily. He was more concerned with the maritime reports that he was receiving. The spectre of the Dogger Bank Incident was once more raising its head. With the governor had come a report that sailing schooners in Durban were being fitted with torpedo tubes to intercept and sink the Russian fleet. The admiral's ire was already raised by a message from London relayed through the Russian Admiralty that while passing through the established Durban fishing grounds he should avoid a similar incident to that which had occurred on the Dogger Bank. He sensed intrigue and sent a signal back to St Petersburg, in clear so that the message would be understood throughout the world. He said he would 'ruthlessly destroy all Durbanese fishing craft who attempt to break through my squadron or come within torpedo range'.

With bunkers, cabins, gangways and decks groaning with coal, the fleet took its leave of West Africa on 17 December. The lumbering ships steamed out awkwardly into the gathering swell praying that the weather would hold. Two days later, the wind increased as the falling barometer indicated a heavy storm ahead. The storm lasted for two days and tore through and at the fleet, dispersing it over a wide area. Had the squadron not been running before the storm the battleships would have surely capsized. Contact was lost with the *Roland* and the venerable *Malay* chose the height of the storm to suffer an engine breakdown. The *Kamchatka* took the opportunity to indulge in communication with the flagship concerning the quality of her coal. Then suddenly, surprisingly but unmistakably, she flashed the signal, 'Do you see the torpedo boats?' Despite the fact that even the large ships were struggling to remain afloat, it did not occur to the Russians that an attack by flimsy 300-ton torpedo boats might be improbable in the appalling sea and raging storm. Bugles and drums sounded action stations as sailors throughout the fleet struggled to their respective posts. Then came an apology from *Kamchatka*. The signalman had used the wrong code. What had been intended was, 'We are all right now'.

Both fleets celebrated Christmas according to the Russian calendar on 7 January at opposite ends of the island of Madagascar. The ships which had been lost or had broken down in the storm were rejoining the fleet. All that was required now was to link up with Felkerzam's squadron, refit and set sail without further delay for Port Arthur. Credit was due to Rozhdestvenski. He had proved both cynic and critic wrong. The deployment of his fleet, without loss or damage and without the benefit of coaling stations en route had been an epic seafaring achievement.

Meanwhile, the admiral impatiently awaited news of Felkerzam who had had the benefit of the shorter Suez Canal route, sustained by a British coaling contractor. Felkerzam should have been anchored at the rendezvous point of Diego Suarez but was not there. Ships were despatched to find him. Then, one morning, a collier arrived with news. St Petersburg had redirected Felkerzam to Nossi Bé, 600 miles distant, where he was overhauling his machinery. He would not be able to sail for two weeks. Rozhdestvenski, ever conscious of the need for speed, visibly exploded. 'I'll dig them out fast enough,' he declared as he sailed for Nossi-Bé.

Returning from her abortive hunt for Felkerzam, the tug *Rousse* brought information of a different kind. The news was to prove devastating, for it questioned the whole *raison d'être* of the fleet's mission. The message informed Rozhdestvenski that the fleet at Port Arthur had been destroyed and that the fall of the town was imminent. When that happened, the reinforcing squadron would be deprived of its only adequate base from which to engage the Japanese. The most significant factor was that without the support of Witgeft's fleet, even the most optimistic Russian protagonist would not have given Rozhdestvenski the slightest prospect of success. The solution to the problem had been offered and lobbied by none other than Captain Nicholas Klado. He had hoped to persuade the Higher Naval Board to assemble a Third Pacific Squadron from the Black Sea but since this was diplomatically impossible, the Third Squadron comprised most of the vessels previously rejected by Rozhdestvenski and they would not be in a position to leave Libau for at least a month. It was on Christmas Day that Rozhdestvenski had been ordered to await the arrival of cruiser reinforcements sent out as an 'Overtaking Division' when his own inclination was to press on immediately and get among the Japanese. At their end of November conference, the Japanese Naval Staff fully expected Rozhdestvenski's fleet to appear in the Formosan Straits early in January 1905. Rozhdestvenski's fury was unbounded. 'Telegraph to St Petersburg that I wish to be relieved of my command,' he instructed Clapier de Colongue and then disappeared for two days to his cabin.

While the admiral was occupied in enforced isolation, the news of the situation spread quickly through the fleet. To many, the case was hopeless. There was a feeling that they had been abandoned. It was Christmas, and their isolation was reinforced. The majority had never previously been away from their families. There had been no letters from home since the voyage began and no newspapers. At this point there was no strategic value in proceeding with the mission yet the politicians were being propelled at home by a press demanding retribution for the many affronts to Russia's dignity. Semenov wrote: 'If St Petersburg had grasped how utterly hopeless – not to say criminal – our adventure was, and if they had sent us categorical orders to come back, I should have said, "The Lord be praised".'

Christmas encouraged Rozhdestvenski out of both his depression and his cabin to make a rousing speech to the officers and crew of *Suvarov*. Such was the emotion and commitment on that Holy Day that Semenov wrote: 'Oh, if only we could go into action now.' But action was still months away. On 10 January 1905, the main fleet rejoined Felkerzam at Nossi Bé. The French had succumbed to Japanese and British pressure to deny the Russians use of the planned facilities at Diego Suarez, making available instead the equally good anchorage at Nossi-Bé.

While coaling was underway throughout the fleet, the divisional admirals met for a rare conference. Rozhdestvenski was never at ease with his subordinates and he was relieved after lunch when they returned to their own flagships. As to their commander's intentions, Felkerzam and Enquist were none the wiser after the meeting. Above the meticulously anchored fleet rose clouds of dust from the Cardiff coal, while the heat and humidity took its toll among the crew. Beyond the beach lay the tranquil scene of the white houses of the settlement in the shade of tall palm trees. The town had the unlikely but, as the Russians were to discover, inappropriate name of Hellville (named after the French Admiral Hell).

On board *Suvarov*, Rozhdestvenski read that the Admiralty had rejected his resignation. He was ordered to await the arrival of the additional cruisers and to use his combined force to cut the Japanese lines of communication and regain command of the sea. To achieve that aim the best prospect lay in speed, to strike before the Japanese fleet, which had been on constant operations for almost a year, could effect its essential refurbishments. In response to the Admiralty's request for Rozhdestvenski's assessment of the situation came the blunt reply:

> I have not the slightest prospect of recovering command of
> the sea with the force under my orders. The despatch of
> reinforcements composed of untested and in some cases badly
> built vessels would only render the fleet more vulnerable. In my
> view the only possible course is to use all force to break through
> to Vladivostok and from this base to threaten the enemy's
> communications.

The loss of the Port Arthur fleet meant that no longer was Rozhdestvenski's command a relief force but the main force which carried with it the high hopes of Tsar and country. Klado had the ear of the government and Rozhdestvenski was now expected to face the Japanese with nothing less than every available ship from the Baltic. A letter from one of his staff officers reflected their sense of despair at what was being asked of them:

> The personnel of the expedition, after hearing of the fate of
> Port Arthur and the destruction of our fleet had no longer any
> faith in the success of our enterprise. We shall never in this war
> gain the command of the sea; that is we shall never accomplish
> the task imposed upon us. What ought to be done? It is shame-

ful to acknowledge it, but I say, quite impartially, it is necessary
to put an end to the naval operations.

On 15 February the auxilliary cruisers of the Overtaking Division made
rendezvous and on 16 February news was received that the Third Pacific
Squadron under Admiral Nebogatov had left Libau.

Whereas Rozhdestvenski had been ordered via telegram 244 to await the
arrival of the Overtaking Division there seems to have been no categorical
order for him to await the arrival of the Third Pacific Squadron. It was an
implied requirement. If he was to take on the superior might of the Japanese navy, Rozhdestvenski requested of the Tsar that the Third Pacific Squadron
be reinforced by the Black Sea fleet, but in that approach he was no more
successful than Klado.

The *Novoe Vremya* bearing Klado's prophecies of doom circulated from
wardrooms to lower decks to be read assiduously by men with time on their
hands. Semenov, who disliked Klado intensely, observed that while Klado's
articles 'provoked a unanimous outburst of anger against him, and those
who inspired him, in the officers' messes, thus leading to still greater solidarity, the effect produced in the men was extremely unfavourable, not to
say dangerous'. This impression of unanimous wardroom antipathy against
Klado is misleading as is evident in a letter from a lieutenant aboard
the *Suvarov*. 'More power to Klado's elbow. The Ministry of Marine ought
to have had such a lashing long ago. Besides, he does not disclose the
hundredth part of the blunders of this department, which has ruined our
ill-fated fleet.'

Novikov-Priboy wrote of how widely and eagerly read was Klado aboard
the *Orel* and how he was:

> looked upon as a hero. From the comparison of the fighting
> strength of the respective fleets, Klado drew the inference that
> the Japanese outclassed the Russians by about two to one ...
> His arguments seemed irrefutable. As early as November, he
> had prophesied that Port Arthur would fall before our arrival
> and that the First Pacific Squadron could do nothing to avert its
> fate.

Klado's thoughts added more weight to the elbow of the revolutionary cell
aboard *Orel*. An Engineer Commander Kostenko spoke enthusiastically of
the strong impression Klado's writing had upon the messdecks. 'Klado has

shown himself to be a merciless critic. So much the better. But what we are waiting for is criticism still more daring. We want criticism of our whole social system.' Aboard the flagship, Politovski wrote: 'There are rumours here that after Klado's articles the public will demand the return of the fleet to Russia.'

As if to compound further the admiral's problems, the proximity to the war zones and Japanese threats to sink collaborating colliers was reflected in a declaration by the Hamburg-Amerika Line that there would be no further support east of Madagascar. For Rozhdestvenski this had been the last straw, and for the second time he was taken ill and retired to the confines of his cabin. Meanwhile, coaling had been completed and much fun was to be had ashore and solace found in an ample supply of champagne and vodka. For two weeks, while the admiral lay sick in his cabin, the crews ran riot in the town. The officers made little attempt to intervene. 'The officers, who usually went ashore in mufti, turned a blind eye to their inferiors' misconduct, being afraid that a reprimand would provoke insolent replies,' reported Novikov-Priboy. It required a formal complaint from the French Minister to rekindle the old fire in Rozhdestvenski who set about with renewed vigour the restoration of the fortunes of his fleet.

Shore leave was restricted and orders passed for the accumulated menageries in the warships to be put ashore. Monkeys, boa constrictors and even a crocodile received welcome repatriation. In this newly confined, oppressive environment, the revolutionary spirit generating at home was also to be seen within the fleet. Russian and foreign newspapers now percolated through. Not only did officers and crew read Klado's predictions of the fleet's impending doom but also, and more significantly, details of civil disorder, strikes, riots and the massacre at the Winter Palace. Revolutionary cells flourished in each ship but general, co-ordinated dissent was frustrated both by the movement restrictions and the depressive, enervating effects of the Madagascan weather. The first sign of trouble erupted aboard the poorly led *Nakhimov*.

The *Esperance*'s refrigeration plant had broken down and, as a result, the quality and variety of food had declined significantly. Each of the larger ships had their individual bakeries but no effort was made to spread this largesse among the smaller ships. The *Nakhimov*, for example, had received no fresh supplies of bread since leaving Libau and even the hard-tack biscuits were mouldering in the humidity. Crying out for fresh bread, the entire 400-strong crew threw the indifferent supper meal overboard and ignored orders to disperse. They reconsidered their situation when Rozhdestvenski trained the *Suvarov*'s guns on *Nakhimov* with the implication that if the mutineers did not disperse, then their ship would be sunk.

The admiral's subordinates had noted an inconsistency in his behaviour and contradiction in his orders. The man who had said, 'How can I intimidate men ready to follow me to death by condemning them to be hanged?', had no qualms in the arbitrary selection of fourteen of *Nakhimov*'s ringleaders to be shot. Courts martial became a common feature among all the ships to such a degree that their lock-ups were quickly filled. 'The temperature there is fearful,' wrote Politovski, 'and there is no ventilation. I do not think that a man could remain there long.' As a solution it was decided that the elderly *Malay* should return to Russia with the sick, insane and criminals, but not before she too was racked by her own mutiny.

Rozhdestvenski used his new lease on life to good effect. He was unexpectedly successful in persuading the representative of the Hamburg-Amerika Line to have a change of heart. With his coal supply assured, he turned his attention to retraining his fleet which had now enjoyed the benefit of a mechanical revival. The outcome of the spate of training did nothing to raise the sense of optimism within the fleet. On the contrary, there was insufficient ammunition for training and that which was used only served to confirm the poor state of gunnery. At least two ships were hit by projectiles and others narrowly avoided each other in their attempts to change formation. 'You men and your ships are a disgrace to the fleet,' raged Rozhdestvenski. By now, the admiral had made up his mind that he had to take leave of Nossi Bé before his command deteriorated completely. He was determined to try to make for Vladivostok before being encumbered by the reinforcing squadron whose position was deliberately kept from him by his cautious Admiralty.

The bad news from Mukden of the Russian army's comprehensive defeat there further emphasised the crucial importance of Rozhdestvenski's mission succeeding. In his view, the taking under his wing of the 'self sinkers' sent as a result of the plan of the despised Klado could only frustrate any glimmer of a prospect of success. When news came to hand on 15 March via the French that the Third Pacific Squadron was coaling at Crete, the Russian admiral decided to ignore his implied orders and find refuge in the long journey across the Indian Ocean. He told his staff to prepare to sail within twenty-four hours. When asked what the rendezvous point was to be, he said 'No! Nothing to no one.' All they were permitted to tell Petersburg was that he was proceeding east. There has been conjecture that Rozhdestvenski's failure to give a rendezvous point may have been intended to encourage the government to recall Nebogatov's squadron, allowing him to concentrate those assets already at his disposal and make best use of their mobility, but all that his sleight of hand appears to have achieved was to raise further the question of his suitability to command this enterprise. On 16 March the fleet set sail, its departure punctuated by breakdowns in the *Orel* and *Kamchatka*.

For three weeks the Russian fleet seemingly disappeared off the face of the earth. On 8 April a buzz of excitement spread through the island of Singapore as thousands of spectators lined the waterfront to verify rumours that a massive armada was shortly to steam by. Again, Rozhdestvenski had completed a magnificent feat of seamanship. His fleet had almost completed its 4,560-mile voyage, pausing no fewer than five times to take on coal on the high seas. So competent had the fleet now become at coaling that the world record was claimed by the *Suvarov* for taking aboard 120 tons an hour. The sight of the fleet impressed the world's correspondents as the ships passed within seven miles of the shore, their funnels belching out black smoke and waterlines noted by the following craft to be heavily festooned with long trails of seaweed. 'Unquestionably,' wrote D. W. Mitchell in his *History of Russian and Soviet Sea Power,* this had been 'one of the greatest logistic feats in the history of warfare'.

As the armada headed east from Singapore, the destroyer *Bedovi* picked up despatches from the Russian Consul's launch. The fall of Mukden and disarray of the Russian land forces were confirmed. Precise orders apparently required the admiral to await the arrival of Nebogatov's Third Pacific Squadron which was then at Jibuti and then, on arrival at Vladivostok, to hand over the fleet to the self-styled 'fighting admiral' Birilev. Needless to say, Birilev had never been in action. Rozhdestvenski wondered whether there would ever be an end to his personal torment. For a number of days he was to consider the situation and weigh up the possibilities of disobeying his orders. The appearance of in-passage British warships helped to make up his mind for he felt certain that his position would be signalled to the Japanese. Prior to setting course directly for Vladivostok he ordered his ships to advise their coal stocks. With the colliers empty, this check was a wise precaution. The *Suvarov-*

class ships all averaged the requisite 2,000 tons, that is with the exception of *Alexander III* still to reply. *Alexander III* had never previously been dilatory in matters of coaling, consistently winning the prize for the fastest coaling and continually flying the fleet's efficiency pennant. The delayed semaphore response hit the *Suvarov* like a bombshell; the *Alexander III* was 400 tons underloaded. The unbelieving Rozhdestvenski demanded confirmation: 'Have you made a mistake?' flashed *Suvarov*. 'No,' came back the reply.

There was no question of *Alexander III* being left behind. The opportunity for bold action and avoidance of the union with the 'flatirons' had now evaporated. Rozhdestvenski had been in half a mind to by-pass Kam Ranh Bay. 'Proceed to the coast as arranged,' muttered the melancholic admiral, who then retired to his cabin.

It was a bright morning on 14 April when the cautious Russian fleet entered Kam Ranh Bay. The admiral notified St Petersburg of his arrival from the shore station and asked for instructions. He was ordered to remain to await the arrival of Nebogatov. Later that same day the German steamer *Prinz Heinrich* en route for Singapore witnessed the Russian fleet in Kam Ranh Bay and the preparations to put a boom across its entrance. The *Prinz Heinrich* was far to the north of her proper course. On board were the Japanese Admiral Prince Arisugawa and his aide-de-camp. The Russian presence was relayed to Tokyo, from whence a protest was registered with the French ambassador. Shore leave was refused and the latent grievances again manifested themselves. Food was in short supply and the clothing stores were empty. There had been no mail or newspapers although spirits were raised by a rumour that the SS *Gortchakov was* carrying mail from Russia. When she arrived it was discovered she was carrying the mail the sailors had posted home from Nossi-Bé. Morale had never been lower. Daily the bodies of suicide victims would be found aboard and desertion on the inhospitable shore was to some a more reasonable option. The inevitable mutiny broke out on the *Orel*. Again Rozhdestvenski rose to the occasion and resolved the problem with firm discipline and a lashing tongue.

The French objected to the Russian fleet remaining longer than twenty-four hours. Rozhdestvenski humoured the half-hearted protest by moving his fleet within a small radius of the bay. He could not sail far because he awaited the arrival of four colliers of the Hamburg-Amerika Line. When they did arrive, coaling was completed by 18 April and the arrival of Nebogatov was now looked forward to with eager anticipation. Meanwhile Rozhdestvenski played a game of cat and mouse with French naval authorities who required that he move on – something he was unable to do.

Nebogatov, commanding the Third Pacific Squadron, faced a quandary in his attempt to make rendezvous with Rozhdestvenski who had done his level best to shroud his movements in secrecy. The Second and Third Squadrons might never have met had it not been for the guile and fortitude of a quartermaster by the name of Babushkin. Babushkin had been wounded at Port Arthur and was in the process of being repatriated via Singapore. The gallant Babushkin took an open boat and for three days waited out in open seas to intercept Nebogatov and convey details of what was known of Rozhdestvenski's movements. Despite the odds being heavily stacked against such a meeting, it did take place. Babushkin passed on the Consul's latest intelligence and, as a result, the two squadrons would be joined and consequently, according to naval historian Woodward, the scale of the Russian disaster 'became even more terrible than it would otherwise have been had Babushkin not been such a hero'.

While Rozhdestvenski awaited Nebogatov's arrival, Semenov complained: 'If this detachment did not exist, we should now be half way to Vladivostok.' But, in acknowledging that what he was writing defied logic, Novikov-Priboy recorded how the general response to the arrival of the Third Pacific Squadron on 9 May had led to 'a boost in morale'.

Nebogatov was surprised to end his reasonably amiable thirty-minute meeting with the admiral without having been given any tactical or operational orders. It was important, he was told, to paint the funnels of his ships yellow so as to conform with the rest of the fleet. In the meantime, he was instructed to start coaling so that the last leg of the voyage could be resumed without further delay. That concluded the first and only meeting between the two admirals. Neither would see each other again during the voyage. 'My first idea', explained Nebogatov before the Commision of Enquiry into the Causes of Defeat at Tsushima, 'was that the Admiral had no mind to disclose his plans in the presence of his Staff and that soon he would give me a private interview. We never discussed a plan of campaign.'

On 14 May the enlarged fleet of fifty-two ships steered an easterly course. Rozhdestvenski had signalled his Admiralty some days previously: 'I will not telegraph you again before the battle. If I am beaten, Togo will tell you. If I beat him I will let you know.' There was an air of grim resignation about the squadron. After all, Togo had commanded his fleet for eight years. Five of his vice admirals and seven of the rear admirals were his pupils who had served under his command and knew his ways. Semenov wrote:

> A fleet is created by long years of practice at sea in times of peace (cruising, not remaining in port), and, that a collection of ships of various types hastily collected, which have only learned to sail together on the way to the scene of operations, is no fleet, but a chance concourse of vessels. We could only regret our unpreparedness, and in the coming fight there was nothing for us to do but to make the most of what we had.

On 26 February the five commissioners published their report of the Dogger Bank Incident. By that time the heat had evaporated from the situation and the resultant whitewashing exercise was not unexpected. The Russians paid £65,000 compensation to the Hull trawlermen and escaped without too much damage to their prestige as a naval power. The commissioners concluded that there had been no torpedo boats present and that Rozhdestvenski's opening fire was unjustified. The report disapproved of the manner in which the trawlermen had been abandoned but, at the same time, the commissioners were able to find excuses for the Russian admiral's behaviour.

The importance of the report was as an indicator to an intelligence analyst, reflecting the state and condition of the Russian squadron. Japan refused to be swayed by the indicators as easily as other seafaring powers. The Japanese over-caution and over-emphasis of Russian naval strength was none the less valid, for the outcome of a naval battle is less predictable than one on land. Both nations had four sophisticated battleships. Accurate shots from the 12-inch guns of the *Suvarov*-class ships could be as decisive as Japan's fortune in accounting for Makarov and Witgeft in earlier conflicts. Togo had no doubt that the Russians were determined to fight and redress their catalogue of reversals. Besides, with the loss of Port Arthur, Rozhdestvenski had little option but to fight. On this occasion he brought with him a fleet to be fought as an entity rather than utilising ships piecemeal as had been the case earlier. Strategically he might have been wise to risk dividing his fleet so as not to introduce his total force in one package to the Japanese. The aim was to reconstitute a naval force in Vladivostok so the divided force option did have advantages to commend it.

It is true that the Japanese enjoyed a technological advantage over the

Russians in so far as they had electric firing mechanisms, superior ammunition and telescopic sights – force multipliers that a proactive Russian Naval Department might also reasonably have developed. The Russians had a slight advantage in the main 10- and 12-inch guns but a significant disadvantage in the secondary armament of 8- and 6-inch guns. Clearly it was in Russia's interest to fight the battle at the range of the 10- and 12-inch guns. One of the naval lessons of this war was the importance of these big guns and the consequent development of the Dreadnought-type battleships as suitable platforms yet, at Tsushima, much of the battle was fought between 2,000–4,000 yards, thereby affording Japan a significant advantage in the firefight. When to this is added the key factor of the speed of the Japanese ships (a point disputed by the American naval strategist A. T. Mahan) and the top-heaviness of the *Suvarov*-class battleships (which meant that much of the heavy armour was under water), the final outcome of the Battle of Tsushima should have surprised no one.

For his route to Vladivostok, Rozhdestvenski had to choose between going either east or west of the Japanese islands, either course then providing a further two options. This has become an oft-discussed subject among naval strategists and armchair theorists but the course the Russian admiral took – he chose the western course – was based on the best information available to *him* at the time. If the Russians had gone to the east of Japan they would have needed to pass through either Tsugaru or La Pérouse strait. The British naval historian Julian Corbett favoured the Tsugaru Strait for with Togo and his fleet waiting at Masan Bay on the south-east coast of Korea, the approach of the Baltic fleet would have been concealed until the strait was reached, leaving Togo with only sufficient time to intercept the passage to Vladivostok with his fastest divisions. It was argued that in those circumstances the Russians would have had the advantage of not being the inferior force, of being in open seas close to their base where the routinely frequent fogs might have obscured their presence. Most critics were of the same mind as to the desirability of the Russians having their engagement with the Japanese as near as possible to Vladivostok. The Tsugaru Strait however was reported by Russian agents to have been heavily mined and the Russian navy was by now acutely mine-conscious. Semenov wrote how the 'Tsugaru Strait could not be considered at all' due to it being a narrow, foggy strait with dangerous currents, a 'tortuous channel' and a torpedo guard.

The case in favour of La Pérouse was similar but the strait was more difficult to navigate and this was an important consideration. Semenov wrote in *Rasplata* of the difficulty in handling the Baltic fleet, of keeping it together. 'It only managed with difficulty to maintain something of a formation even in clear weather and in the most favourable navigation conditions.' La Pérouse was also the longer route of the two which would both have required further coaling after that of 23–26 May. The three ships which did reach Vladivostok via Tsushima had exhausted their coal so that anything over and above the main fleet contact could have so taxed coal stocks as to leave the Second and Third Pacific Squadrons dead in the water some way short of Vladivostok.

Of the two channels through the Korean Straits the western one was self-deselecting due to its narrowness and its proximity to two known Japanese bases. The eastern channel was furthest from these bases and once through the Tsushima bottleneck, opened up into the broad Sea of Japan, an important consideration in view of the limited Russian navigational and seamanship skills. Understandable though these considerations may have been, the final choice played into Togo's hands because the course to the west of Japan permitted the Japanese to use their destroyers in packs, the use of a convenient anchorage at Masan Bay from which to await the arrival of the Russian fleet and the convenience of fighting close to the Japanese coast.

The publication of the report of the Dogger Bank Incident coincided with completion of the refurbishment and refitting of Togo's fleet. As an interim measure, fast armed merchantmen had been patrolling the approaches to Japan. The retraining of the sailors was a high priority and they were worked to a high psychological pitch in anticipation of the inevitable battle. But the Russians had not come. They were still thousands of miles distant. The Japanese were not aware of the unwelcome prospect of months of vigilance.

Togo's appreciation of the situation had rejected as a course of action the Russian fleet sailing to the east of Japan to approach Vladivostok through La Pérouse or Tsugaru Straits. The distance of 1,500 miles could not be completed without coaling on the high seas. He would not have known that the operators of the Hamburg-Amerika colliers would most probably have declined to accept the risk, but as a sailor he knew the anger of the rough Pacific waters. He believed that the Russians could not avoid being detected, thereby becoming easy game for his generous supply of torpedo boats. Fortunately, Rozhdestvenski had come to the same conclusion. He did have a deception plan and despatched two steamers around the eastern seaboard of Japan. Both vessels were to reach Vladivostok undetected without having encountered any other ships en route.

There was no doubt in Togo's mind that the Russians would approach Vladivostok through the Straits of Tsushima. He had now reinforced his patrolling armed merchantmen with light cruisers. The whole expanse of the Korean Straits and the Sea of Japan had been divided into numbered squares, representing ten minutes of latitude and longitude just as in the game of 'Battleships'. Meanwhile, like a spider on the flank of her web, virtually the entire Japanese fleet lay in waiting in the sheltered Masan Bay on the south-eastern coast of Korea.

CHAPTER FOURTEEN

TSUSHIMA

The Russian fleet took a north-easterly course from Formosa hidden by the low visibility arising from persistent sea mist and torrential rain. The optimists aboard believed that given a share of luck they might pass undetected through the Tsushima bottleneck with the prospect of an open passage to Vladivostok. They did not know of the thick minefield laid by the Japanese around the port, but for many this was to be a factor of no great consequence. The weather improved on 26 May when the combined fleet exercised as a single unit for the first and last time. Signal flags from the *Suvarov* were easy to see in the bright and clear day. 'Prepare for action' was followed by 'Tomorrow, at the hoisting of the colours, battleflags are to be sent up'.

Six supply ships and colliers had been diverted to Shanghai the day before in preparation for the battle. Rozhdestvenski's fleet was deployed in two columns. In the starboard column was the bulk of his firepower represented by the seven battleships and the *Nakhimov*. The port column led by Nebogatov's *Nicholas I* consisted of all the other ships except for five reconnoitring cruisers. The whole fleet remained on radio silence as they neared the Korean Straits. The night came, bringing with it the welcome evening's mist enveloping them in its reassuring blanket. The Russian fleet remained undetected and was now within 150 miles of the Japanese islands. The gun crews had been at action stations for days but now the final preparations were being made. The moon shone through the heavily overcast sky, occasionally bathing the Russian activity in light. All superfluous equipment and furniture had been thrown overboard and wood that was likely to splinter was protected by

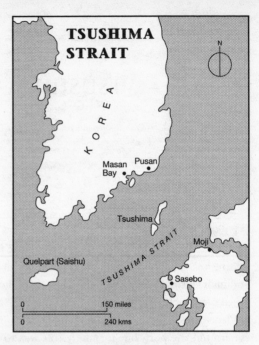

TSUSHIMA STRAIT

KOREA

Masan Bay

Pusan

Tsushima

TSUSHIMA STRAIT

Moji

Quelpart (Saishu)

Sasebo

0   150 miles
0   240 kms

canvas. First aid equipment was broken out and lifeboats filled with water.

Togo waited concerned and impatient in his lair. He was respected by his subordinates but not loved. Ten days without news of the Russian fleet made him decidedly unpleasant to those in his immediate vicinity. Perhaps this was understandable. The Russians had been defeated on land but they could still retire northward into Manchuria and Russia would never be entirely defeated by Japan. Almost the last of the trained Japanese reserves had been committed to the fray and it was known that foreign bankers were having second thoughts about further advances to what might be considered to be an undesirably strong Japan. It had been Togo's decision to gamble everything on the Russians passing through the Tsushima Straits. If he had been wrong, and somehow they had gone to the east of Japan, then the Japanese lines of communication would once again be threatened.

Self-doubt arose in the Japanese admiral's mind. There were rumours of a growing impatience among the Imperial Staff who were said to be on the point of ordering the repositioning of the fleet. He toyed with the idea of moving the fleet northward but instinct told him to remain at Masan for a further day. This was a wise decision for a signal arrived informing him that six

Russian auxiliaries had anchored at Shanghai. If the Russians had gone on the longer journey east of Japan they would not have detached a significant element of their support fleet which included the colliers.

The crackle of Japanese radio traffic could be heard emanating from the dimmed Russian radio offices. The mist persisted until it lifted momentarily to reveal the hospital ship *Orel* to the armed merchant cruiser *Shinano Maru*. It was 2.45 in the early hours of the 27th. The Japanese ship carried two 6-inch guns but although only a mile distant she turned away, disappearing into the swirling mist without further reconnaissance. Her message was relayed to Masan: 'The enemy sighted in number 203 section. He seems to be steering for the eastern channel.' The hospital ship *Orel* was bringing up the rear of the fleet on the starboard side which would have put the leading ship *Svyetlana* approximately twenty miles ahead. Togo received the news as a welcome omen, for his visit to 203 Metre Hill had left an indelible impression on him, particularly since the residue of the Port Arthur fleet had been destroyed by the land forces. Now the opportunity had arisen for him to make amends. At 5 a.m. the main Japanese battle force received the positive news of the sighting of the Russians and within ninety minutes the Japanese fleet had put to sea to intercept their enemy.

Daylight brought increased apprehension for the Russians who endeavoured in their various ships to celebrate the anniversary of the Tsar's coronation. The officers drank champagne while rum or vodka were issued to the sailors. There existed an ominous air of impending doom. On board the battleship *Orel* a Mass was being conducted on deck. 'The men's faces were sour and rigid as in a cataleptic trance,' recorded Novikov-Priboy. 'They crossed themselves as if flapping away flies.' The mist thinned to reveal the steep cliffs of Tsushima Island dominated by a twin mountain peak, 'the donkey's ears'. There could never have been a more appropriate endorsement of such an asinine project. Spiritual celebrations of both kinds were interrupted by the sounding of action stations, sending men hurrying to their places.

The mood aboard the closing Japanese ships provided a stark contrast. Each man had a tot of rum, and cigars provided by the Emperor were passed among the officers. Togo recalled that confirmation of the Russian fleet's imminent appearance had been 'received with enthusiastic joy by the whole fleet'. The shadowing of the Russians began at 7 a.m. on 27 May although proper observation was still made difficult owing to the mist. The first ship to show herself was the cruiser *Izumo*, to be joined later by three further cruisers and the venerable battleship *Chinyen*. All the while, reports were signalled to Togo of the state, condition and formation of the Russians. He had resolved to begin his attack after midday once the Russians had passed through the restrictive confines of the Tsushima Straits. Klado criticised the failure to deploy forward a cruiser scouting detachment and for allowing the *Izumo* to shadow the Russians unchallenged for four hours.

Throughout the morning the number of escorting Japanese warships increased. Four further cruisers were joined by a pack of destroyers. They were within range of the battleships but *Suvarov* made no orders. It appeared as though Rozhdestvenski preferred to believe that the shadows were not there. In exasperation the battleships watched *Suvarov* for the signal to open fire. None came. Captain Yung of the *Orel* decided to take the matter into his own hands and at 11.45 ordered the *Izumo* to be engaged. The firing was taken up throughout the fleet as the Japanese reacted by moving out of range. The admiral ordered the cease fire to conserve ammunition.

When the midday meal had been completed and the mist totally obscured the opposing forces, Rozhdestvenski ordered his First and Second Divisions to break away from the fleet's single line ahead by turning ninety degrees to starboard in succession and to increase their speed. It is probable that he anticipated the Japanese attack from the east. Just as the First Division completed the manoeuvre, the reappearance of Japanese cruisers caused Rozhdestvenski to change his mind. He ordered the Second Division, headed by *Osylabya,* to maintain their course while he swung the four battleships of the First Division back through ninety degrees so that they were sailing parallel to, but slightly ahead of, the main fleet.

While confusion reigned in the Russian fleet, the mist again lifted to reveal at 1.20 p.m. both fleets at a distance of seven miles. The Japanese were closing in on the Russians from the north and starboard. Rozhdestvenski was not dissatisfied with the Japanese position because by moving his ships to either port or starboard he believed he could 'cross the T' and hit the head of the Japanese fleet with broadsides. He had made a major misappreciation of the Japanese abilities.

The Japanese came on in line-ahead formation at 14 knots, a 3-knot advantage over the Russians. The *Mikasa* led the other three remaining battleships *Shikishima, Fuji* and *Asahi*. On the flagship's foremast flew a typically Nelsonian signal: 'The fate of the Empire depends upon today's event. Let every man do his utmost.' Following the principal ships came *Kasuga* and *Nisshin*, then Kamimura's armoured cruisers, *Izumo, Azuma, Tokiwa, Yagumo, Iwate* and *Asama.*

From this point, Togo seized and retained the initiative using the speed advantage to good effect. While still out of range, he crossed his fleet from starboard to port, north-west then west, in effect crossing the T ahead of the Russian parallel columns. Togo had conducted a similarly risky move during his first action off Port Arthur in February 1904. The Russians watched this precision and harmony of ships and men with amazement. Then they saw the Japanese reverse their direction, ships turning in single line through 180 degrees on the weaker flank being led by *Osylabya.* It is at this point that observations thus described in Corbett's *Official History* came into play: 'The tactical interest ended after the first few moves, and from the indiscriminate chase that consumed the rest of the day there is little professional profit to be gained'. The reconstruction of the Battle of Tsushima 'is wasted labour ... (which) ... could serve no useful purpose'.

Rozhdestvenski's response to the Japanese move was to order his four principal ships back into the head of the line. He failed to order the four battleships to increase their speed and similarly failed to order *Osylabya*'s column to slow down. Consequently the four rejoining ships had to shoehorn themselves into the van, causing chaos and concertina-ing in the rear. Nebogatov was to describe the scene later: 'One vessel had to turn to starboard and another to port so that there was absolute confusion. Mob is the only word literally to express our formation at this time.' Thereafter, Admiral Rozhdestvenski made no further orders of manoeuvre to his fleet.

While the Japanese were executing an extremely rash manoeuvre the Russians were in a state of confusion. Togo could have minimised the danger by ordering his ships to turn together but that manoeuvre would have prevented him from leading his fleet into action. While still in the process of turning some 7,000 yards from the Russians, accurate strikes were recorded on the *Mikasa* and *Shikishima.* Togo was disturbed by the surprising accuracy of the Russian shooting, particularly since he had now committed his twelve ships to turn on the same spot, a process that would take ten minutes. 'How rash,' commented a Russian officer. 'Why, in a minute we will be able to roll up their leading ships.' Russian fire intensified. Captain Pakenham aboard the *Asahi* watched the Russian fire follow *Mikasa* then return to concentrate upon the axis of the turn which took the twelve ships twenty

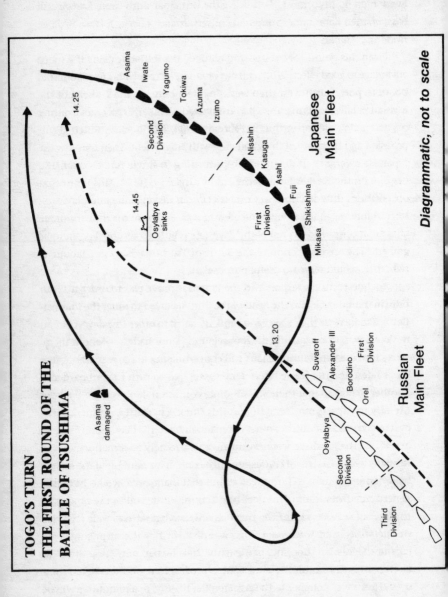

TOGO'S TURN
THE FIRST ROUND OF THE
BATTLE OF TSUSHIMA

Diagrammatic, not to scale

Japanese Main Fleet

Asama
Iwate
Yagumo
Tokiwa
Azuma
Izumo
Second Division
Nisshin
Kasuga
Asahi
Fuji
Shikishima
First Division
Mikasa

14.25

14.45
Osylabya sinks

Asama damaged

13.20

Russian Main Fleet

Suvaroff
Alexander III
Borodino
Orel
First Division
Osylabya
Second Division
Third Division

minutes to complete. The Japanese were unable to reply initially because they were masked by the other ships of the fleet. Each ship approached the crossing point and ran the gauntlet, suffering a spattering of minor injuries.

Once *Fuji* and *Asahi* had completed their turn, Togo ordered his fleet to open fire principally upon the *Suvarov* and *Osylabya* leading the two Russian lines. The danger had passed. Rozhdestvenski's hesitation and indecision had failed to take advantage of a winning situation presented on a plate so uncharacteristically by Togo. Those Russians who had doubted their admiral's qualities as a fighter had been right. Now the ships and sailors under the command of this burned-out man were to face the consequences.

The Russian Third Division, concentrating on the Japanese cruisers at the extremity of their range, had some success. *Yagumo, Asama* and *Nisshin* were all hit and *Asama* was forced out of line. Then the battle passed out of range of Nebogatov's division, which continued to make heavy going bringing up the rear in the rough seas. The division was extended to make 11 knots, thereby limiting the whole fleet to that speed. The Japanese approach was made at 15 knots. Pakenham's despatch to his Admiralty on 17 April noted: 'Speed is the factor of maritime efficiency least understood. The meeting fleets' promised difference in this respect sufficiently marked to demand careful notice should be given to its effect.' From their edge on speed the Japanese derived enhanced protection, while the Russians were to suffer as much from their overladen immobility as from the effects of superb gunnery.

The Japanese singled out for the attention of their 500 guns the flagships of Rozhdestvenski and his deputy Felkerzam. Admiral Felkerzam remained in his cabin as the first rounds hit *Osylabya* sending lightly armoured plates falling into the sea. He would play no part in the battle for he had died on 25 May and was now laid out in his coffin. Rozhdestvenski kept his death a secret and failed even to inform the next most senior admiral, Nebogatov.

On board *Suvarov* Semenov planned to take note of where the ship was struck but even he was overwhelmed by the accuracy and weight of the Japanese fire. 'I had not only never witnessed such a fire before, but I had never imagined anything like it. Shells seemed to be pouring upon us incessantly, one after another.' For the Russian part, their near misses outnumbered their hits, but then one-third of their shells failed to explode. Semenoff had spent six months in Port Arthur and the 'portmanteaux' were no longer a novelty:

> Shimose and melanite were to a certain extent old acquain-
> tances but this was something new. It seemed as if these were
> mines not shells which were striking the ship's side and falling
> on deck. They burst as soon as they touched anything – the
> moment they encountered the least impediment in their flight.

The Russian command centre was in the armoured conning tower perched above the ailing *Suvarov,* now alight from stem to stern from the effects of salvoes of 12-, 8- and 6-inch shells. Two rounds struck the conning tower and, although failing to penetrate the armour, they released from the inner wall splinters which tore around the confined space killing and wounding all but one of the tightly packed occupants. Rozhdestvenski struggled to lead his ill-trained fleet closer to the enemy in order to achieve striking power but then, at 2.35, the admiral was wounded for the first time. Five minutes later the *Suvarov* was turned four points to starboard away from the heat of the battle.

The Japanese shooting had a devastating effect upon the Russian crews; so much so that the returning fire became relatively indifferent and ineffective. The raw sailors were mesmerised by the slaughter of their comrades and such sights as the turrets of their main armaments being shaken and then snuffed out. Semenov rushed around endeavouring to arouse the sailors from their state of numbed shock to make them put out the fires. By 2.30 p.m. one funnel had gone, as had the main mast. Signalling was impossible. Then a salvo jammed the flagship's steering mechanism and she veered off to starboard, a sheet of flame and smoke.

All this was noted by Captain, later Admiral, W. C. Pakenham aboard the *Asahi*. He was still on board after fourteen months. He was regarded by the crew as something of a fixture as he sat in his cane deckchair on the quarterdeck taking notes while the battle raged around him. It is rumoured that after the war the Mikado ordered Togo to bring to him the bravest man in the fleet. Togo took Pakenham whom he greatly admired. This was a reciprocated admiration, for Pakenham's glowing reports of this confessed Anglophile admiral may well have been instrumental in Togo being awarded the British Order of Merit. 'Never, at any time, have his limits appeared to be in sight,' wrote Pakenham. 'He is indeed a noble man.'

Pakenham was most meticulously dressed in whites, in high collar, boots and a monocle in his eye. This was no fad and drew comment from Churchill after the First World War when Pakenham completed fifty-two uninterrupted months, impeccably dressed, aboard Royal Navy ships. Now he was aboard the fourth ship in line which had suffered more severely than the flagship *Mikasa*. With binoculars at hand Pakenham continued to take notes while, nearby, one of the ship's officers picked up the debris of mutilated feet, hands and bowels that had once belonged to the crew. Pakenham was stopped in his note-taking by a 6-inch shell killing the crew of the nearest 12-inch gun. As the gun crew was blown to pieces, the right half of a man's lower jaw, less the teeth, hit Pakenham, drenching him in blood. 'In spite of the quantity scattered, the amount of blood left on deck looked sufficient to fill a big cask,' recorded Pakenham. He put down his notebook and went below. At the scene of the butchery, oriental eyes met and the eyes alone spoke, wondering whether all this had at last been too much for the British captain. Five minutes later he returned in a clean, immaculate, white starched uniform, took his seat, and resumed his observation of the battle.

In the bowels of the fatally damaged *Osylabya* the senior and junior surgeons worked on. Unstemmable water roared through the ship, through the lower decks and into the magazine. As the list increased, the doctors with their deep crimson aprons proceeded with their unequal task among the waiting wounded, surrounded by amputated limbs. On the other side of the steel walls were the stokeholds and engine rooms where the crew worked under closed hatches. All the while the barrage continued and Kamimura, with a score to settle, took in six cruisers for the *coup de grâce*.

The ugly ship turned on her side belching smoke and flames over the rough sea's surface:

> The whole of the starboard side as far as the keel was laid bare, her bright plating looked like the wet scales of some sea monster; and suddenly, as if by command, all the men who had crowded to the starboard side jumped down upon those scales … Most of them were dashed against the bilge keel and fell crippled, into the sea. In the water they formed an imaginable mass … and the enemy's shell never ceased the whole time from bursting over them. A few more seconds and the Osylabya disappeared beneath the water.

Sailors had abandoned ship, some in such a hurry that they failed to take life-support equipment. The banging from the closed hatches fell on deaf ears. The captain shouted to his men to swim away from the ship which, with keel high, at 2.45 p.m. went bow first to the bottom with almost two-thirds of her crew. *Osylabya* was the first armoured battleship ever to be sunk entirely by gunfire. The speed differential between the Japanese and Russian ships and the accuracy of the Japanese fire became insurmountable force multipliers. A Japanese observer wrote: 'After the first twenty minutes the Russians seemed suddenly to go all to pieces, and their shooting became wild and harmless.'

By now the situation in the conning tower of the disabled *Suvarov* had become untenable. Rozhdestvenski had been wounded in a number of places but a head wound clouded even further his facility to make decisions. Clapier de Colongue decided to move the command centre to the aft turret and led the way through the wreckage, fire and debris. While on their way, a shell landed among the commander's group. A splinter tore into Rozhdestvenski's left leg, cutting the main nerve and paralysing the limb. He was dragged into the gun turret to be greeted by the amazed crew. The admiral turned to Colongue and demanded to know why the guns were not firing. The latest injury had rekindled some of his old phlegm and, not wishing to miss the opportunity, the Chief-of-Staff pleaded, 'Sir, we must shorten the distance, they're all being killed, they're on fire.' 'Wait a bit', queried the severely wounded admiral, 'aren't we all being killed also?'

While the flagship drifted eastward and out of control, the head of the line was taken up by *Alexander III*, now recovered from the confusion of following the out-of-control *Suvarov*. Captain Bukhvostov of *Alexander III* took Togo by surprise by charging 'for the middle of our squadron' and in so doing gained for the Russians an invaluable respite. Before long, she too was listing from a hole in her bows and the lead passed to the *Borodino*. It was not long before Chief Engineer Politovski's pride and joy was ablaze too, while *Orel* was in an equally bad condition. Nebogatov should have assumed command of the Russian fleet but he was equally unaware of whether Rozhdestvenski had transferred his command to another ship or that Felkerzam, the second-in-command, had died on 25 May. For three hours, no one was in command of the Russian fleet.

Togo's attention was caught by sight of the now stationary and devastated *Suvarov*. She was still being fought by the few crew remaining in the habitable areas of the ship. 'Her condition seemed infinitely deplorable. Smoke curling round the stern was rolling horizontally away on the wind. If the absence of funnels contributed much to her air of distress, the now extensive conflagration raging amidships showed its reality,' wrote Pakenham. Battleships do not have reserves, and of the 900 crew only a handful in the lower battery and windward embrasure remained alive. Of Politovski there was no sign. Perhaps he had sought refuge deep in the inner parts of the ship; perhaps he was already dead. He was not among the few survivors.[*]

After firing into the *Suvarov* at a thousand yards Togo sailed off to intercept the other battleships, making the way clear for Kamimura's cruisers and two divisions of destroyers. So intensely preoccupied had Togo become with sinking the gallant *Suvarov* that he lost sight of the big picture. According to a Japanese report, 'The enemy apparently altered course and disappeared in the fog.' When Togo turned northward in pursuit of the escaping Russians his flagship the *Mikasa* had been hit twenty-nine times. The little Russian destroyer *Buiny* dodged through the Japanese armada to come on to *Suvarov's* lee side to be threatened by what appeared to be a barrage of blow torches and jagged metal. De Colongue had risen to the occasion and directed the injured commander: 'Come on, sir, we haven't much time. There are some cruisers coming up.' The barely conscious Rozhdestvenski, his skull pierced by a shell splinter, protested in a barely audible voice. 'Command to Nebogatov – Vladivostok – course N.23°E.'

The admiral was carried gently towards the heavily pitching destroyer, now under fire from Kamimura's cruisers approaching from the east. At the right moment, the admiral's limp body was tumbled into the waiting arms on *Buiny's* packed decks. On board were 200 of *Osylabya's* survivors. There was no room for more than a chosen few from *Suvarov*. Among the dozen or so who joined the *Buiny* before she cast off from the flagship were Semenov and de Colongue. Those remaining on board continued to operate the workable guns under the direction of a midshipman until 7 p.m. Her executioner, Admiral Kataoka, wrote that:

> She scarcely looked like a man-of-war at all. Her interior was
> ablaze, and the holes in her side and gunports shot out tongues
> of flame. Thick volumes of black smoke rolled low on her deck,
> and her whole appearance was indescribably pathetic. She
> turned to starboard and port, as if seeking to escape, while the
> two or three stern guns, which were all that remained to her,
> kept up an heroic 'defence'.

[*] Politovski's journal, from which extracts here have been taken, was based on letters sent home to his wife. The last letters arrived on board the auxiliaries sent on to Shanghai just prior to the Battle of Tsushima.

Then, to relieve *Suvarov* of her torment, Kataoka released the destroyers of 11th Torpedo Division tearing through at 20 knots, the sea thick with the drowning sailors of the *Kamchatka*. Three of seven torpedoes detonated. One found her magazine and after that explosion she turned over. 'For a short time she floated upwards, and then at 7.30 lifted her bow high in the air and slid rapidly out of sight.' Of the *Suvarov* and her crew, Corbett wrote: 'If there is immortality in naval memory it is hers and theirs.'

At about the same time that *Suvarov* was destroyed with the loss of forty officers and 888 men, the Russians lost *Alexander III* with the loss of thirty officers and 806 men, as well as the repair ship *Kamchatka*.

Fuji was among the very last to fire as she put a 12-inch salvo into *Borodino* just as the sun was setting. The shells tore through the ship and detonated the magazines. All that remained was a 'dense cloud that brooded over the place she had occupied'. Of her crew of thirty officers and 823 men, only one man survived. 'The loss of the *Borodino*,' said an officer aboard *Oleg*, 'which happened before our eyes was so unexpected that we were stupefied, and, uncovering our heads, we gazed on the foaming grave of this heroic ship.'

Admiral Enquist, commanding the Russian cruisers, was not equal to the occasion. Under the cover of darkness he used his squadron's speed to break contact and take the *Aurora, Zhemchug* and *Oleg* into internment in Manila. He left behind to her own devices the old, slow *Dmitri Donskoi* which later became a target for the Japanese light cruisers and torpedo boats. She was to be blasted and eventually sank after every man aboard had been either killed or wounded. In addition to her own crew she had carried 270 men from the *Osylabya* and the destroyer *Buiny*. She had fought back valiantly, sinking two destroyers and damaging a third as well as damaging four cruisers. 'It was clear', Admiral Nebogatov told his Courts Martial, 'they were making a ring around us with a well defined radius which they were able to select owing to their superior speed.'

The attrition of the Russian fleet witnessed great contrasts in heroism and cowardice. By morning there was little left other than the remnants of Nebogatov's squadron with *Orel* under its wing. They were on course for Vladivostok which, at a speed of 9 knots and if not molested, they should reach in thirty-two hours. The first light of the cold morning revealed smoke on the horizon which developed into groups of ships until 9 a.m. when Nebogatov found himself surrounded by the entire Japanese fleet of twenty-seven ships. Togo stood off beyond the range of the best of the available

Russian guns and opened up with his own 12-inch guns. He showed no inclination to close the distance.

Unhurriedly, the 'portmanteaux' from the Japanese fleet landed among
the defenceless Russian ships. Nebogatov sought from his officers advice as to
what to do next. A consensus view was that it was pointless to fight. After a
moment's consideration, Nebogatov addressed his officers: 'Gentlemen, I
propose to surrender as the only means of saving our crews from destruction. Please give orders to run up the white flag.' A tablecloth was found and
run up the mast with the Japanese flag. *Izumrud* caused some confusion by her
refusal to surrender. Straining to all of her 24 knots, she passed through the
ring of fire to escape northward.

Meanwhile the Japanese main fleet continued to fire on the remaining
ships which had surrendered, *Nicholas I, Orel* and two coast defence vessels.
Togo was ruthlessly determined to destroy the Russians. This determination
to fight to completion was a decidedly British trait as evidenced in the behaviour of Nelson and Admiral Howe on the Glorious First of June. It was not
sufficient simply to defeat an enemy, it had to be done relentlessly. Elsewhere within his fleet, his admirals looked to the *Mikasa* for the signal to
cease fire. A staff officer drew the Japanese admiral's attention to the white
flags flying from the Russian masts. 'I will not cease fire until they stop their
engines,' came the reply. When the Russians understood the requirement
and stopped engines, an apparently disappointed Togo ordered firing to
cease. On board the *Orel* some sailors raided the liquor store and became
drunk.

Aboard the sea-tossed *Buiny* there was concern for Rozhdestvenski's health
among his staff. The ship's doctor had found that a sliver of bone from his
broken skull had pierced his brain. Any violent movement could kill him.

In the morning, with fuel virtually exhausted, the *Buiny* with her doomed
crew made a fortunate rendezvous with three small survivors of the battle
en route to Vladivostok. Rozhdestvenski chose to transfer to the destroyer
Bedovi which ran up the admiral's flag. Escorted by the destroyer *Groznyi*,
the admiral's flagship made her hopeful way northward while Rozhdestvenski slipped once more into a coma.

In the afternoon, the two Russian destroyers were intercepted by two
Japanese destroyers which approached at speed from the Straits of Korea.
The captain of the *Bedovi* asked de Colongue whether he should increase
speed to outstrip the closing Japanese. 'No', was the reply. Colongue knew

that there was a risk of killing the admiral if the little ship buffeted herself through the rough seas at high speed. When *Bedovi* ran up the red cross and parley flags, the *Groznyi* dashed away, drawing after her one of the Japanese ships in pursuit.

The captain of the Japanese destroyer came on board the *Bedovi*, cutting away the aerial as he approached de Colongue. He was informed of the admiral's presence and, after checking his identity and placing a sentry outside the cabin, took *Bedovi* under tow to Sasebo. The Russian destroyer entered harbour flying the Japanese flag, passing by Nebogatov's similarly attired fleet. Rozhdestvenski was taken to hospital where he was to recover prior to returning to Russia.

Admiral Togo selected as his aide for his visit to the wounded Rozhdestvenski a French-speaking lieutenant called Takano Isoroku. This officer had served aboard the cruiser *Nisshin* at the Battle of Tsushima, losing two fingers from his left hand. He therefore seemed an appropriate addition to the party intent on offering consolation to the injured Russian admiral. 'We fighting men suffer either way, win or lose,' remarked Togo. 'The only question is whether or not we do our duty.' As Togo took his leave he said to Rozhdestvenski: 'You performed your great task heroically until you were incapacitated. I pay you my highest respects.' The two Japanese officers departed.

The news of the one-sided, disastrous defeat percolated back to St Petersburg. At first there was a stunned, numbed despondency which gave way to a gathering uproar of anger and grief. As a result, there was a surge of rebellious outbreaks throughout the land. Of the thirty-eight ships of the Baltic fleet, all that reached Vladivostok were the pseudo-cruiser *Almaz* and two destroyers including the *Groznyi*. The Russians had suffered the loss of 4,830 men killed, 5,907 prisoners of war and 1,862 interned in neutral countries. The Japanese suffered 117 killed and 583 wounded. They had lost three torpedo boat destroyers and although other ships had been damaged they were repairable and rejoined the fleet. It required more of the Russians than the gutsy, brave display witnessed at Tsushima. Japan had prepared well for this event just as she would be well prepared for a future, more ambitious conflict of arms. As one observer remarked, it came down to the fact that 'well trained men, efficient ships, powerful guns won against peasants and convicts dressed as sailors, ancient or ill built ships and unsuitable armaments'. The blame therefore lies full square on the Naval Department at St Petersburg which had long been the target of the venom flowing from Klado's pen.

Responding to the mood of a restless public, the authorities in St Petersburg sought to identify a scapegoat to account for the national humiliation at Tsushima. Klado derided Admiral Rozhdestvenski, accusing him of defeatism and failing to employ properly the reinforcements which Klado had been so instrumental in sending. Appearing in 1906 before the court in civilian clothes, Rozhdestvenski explained to the judges, 'We were just not strong enough and God gave us no luck.' The issue before the court was the surrender of the *Bedovi*. The Commander-in-Chief of the Fleet, who had received a commiserative message from the Tsar, and his staff officer Semenov were exonerated on the grounds that they had not been informed of Commander Baranov's decision to surrender in order to save the admiral, his officers and the remainder of the crew. Despite Rozhdestvenski's insistence that the decision had been his, the court did not believe that his wounds would have enabled him to take a rational decision. Baranov, Clapier de Colongue and two other members on the Commander-in-Chief's staff were sentenced to death.[*] The Tsar intervened and those found guilty were dismissed the service and given varying periods of imprisonment. But these had not been major players in the battle. Someone more senior must be to blame. Rozhdestvenski had been exonerated, his deputy Felkerzam had died two days before the battle, so the next most senior was the commander of the decrepit but hard-hitting battleships, Admiral Nebogatov. Rozhdestvenski should be considered fortunate. His skill in bringing his ragbag fleet to within sight of Tsushima counted for little in relation to the mistakes made on the last leg. Naval strategists will continue to debate the issue as to which course he should have taken for Vladivostok but his significant failure was a failure to communicate. He never explained to his commanders his battle plan; the death of Admiral Felkerzam, the fleet's second-in-command, was kept a secret, which contributed to the Russian fleet not being under command for three hours at the height of the conflict, and Rozhdestvenski made only two, ill-considered, orders to manoeuvre – both before the conflict.

Nebogatov was tried under Article 354 of the 1899 Russian Military Maritime Law for surrendering his four battleships, now repaired and commissioned into the Japanese fleet. Legally and morally he should have been exonerated but it had become expedient that someone should be identified as having been guilty for the defeat of the Baltic fleet. The quest to find

---

[*] The sentences were later commuted to long periods of imprisonment.

a head was not extended to the corridors of Russia's Admiralty nor to the Tsar's noble advisers who had persuaded him to enter into this disastrous war in the first place. The court sentenced Nebogatov and his immediate subordinates to death, a punishment later commuted to ten years' imprisonment. In responding to the death penalty, Nebogatov addressed the court, concluding:

> According to the judges who have sentenced me to a shameful punishment, I should have blown the ships up on the high seas and caused the death of two thousand men in a few seconds. For what reason? Perhaps in the name of Saint Andrew's flag, symbol of Holy Russia? A great country must preserve her dignity and life of her sons and not send them to death on ancient vessels in order to hide her errors, intellectual blindness and ignorance of the most elementary principals of naval matters.

CHAPTER FIFTEEN

A NEW BEGINNING

The battle of Mukden had marked the virtual cessation of land warfare in Manchuria. While the Second Pacific Squadron was still making its ponderous progress towards Tsushima, the movement towards a peace initiative was well underway. Kodama had wisely perceived that there was no further advantage to be gained in being drawn deeply into Manchuria and Siberia. Certainly the Japanese forces had proved that they could beat their more numerous enemy but there was now a widespread conviction that a general defeat of the Russian forces was an impossibility. The Russians had not ceased their reinforcements and were to bring forward a further two corps from Europe. Japan was bankrupt. At the outbreak of war, her military skill was an unknown quantity and she had been subjected to almost penal international loan rates. Russia's in-theatre costs exceeded Japan's but Russia was in a better position to call upon German and French banks for extended loans. To that extent, Russia was in a stronger position to fight a long war. Fifty-three per cent of Japan's annual revenue was now devoted to the war effort. A consensus view was that peace would secure for Japan her due honour, suitable guarantees in Korea and Manchuria, and sizeable reparations from Russia to restore her empty state coffers.

At the commencement of hostilities President Theodore Roosevelt had openly favoured Japan but now, with the spectre of Japanese expansionism in Asia and the Pacific, he had adopted a more cautious view. After the fall of Port Arthur, Roosevelt wrote that if Japan 'tries to gain from her victory in the Russo-Japanese War more than she ought to have, she will array against her all the great powers, and however determined she may be she cannot successfully face an allied world.'

Clearly, Roosevelt remained troubled regarding the potential threat and challenge Japan posed to America's own increasing strength and power. While it is true that there were domestic reasons for sending the outspoken General Arthur MacArthur on an extended Far East tour, MacArthur's mission did have a strategic purpose. General MacArthur set off in 1905 accompanied by his wife and son, Lieutenant Douglas MacArthur. 'The purpose of our observations', wrote Douglas, 'was to measure the strength of the Japanese Army and its method of warfare ... But I had the uneasy feeling that the haughty, feudalistic samurai who were their leaders, were, through their victories, planting the seed of eventual Japanese conquest of the Orient.' Douglas MacArthur's *Memoirs* is neither the most reliable nor honest of autobiographies but the young Douglas would have noted that the Japanese amphibious landings in Korea in 1894 and 1904 were both conducted at Chemulpo, now known by its modern name of Inchon.

Roosevelt's willingness to act as mediator at a peace conference was telegraphed to Tokyo before Tsushima, an event which was to fuel further Japanese expectations as to the benefits to be accrued from the peace talks. The disaster of Tsushima had rekindled revolutionary fervour and zeal in Russia. Anarchists were already at work, having blown to pieces on 17 February 1905 the Tsar's uncle and brother-in-law, Grand Duke Serge Alexandrovitch, Governor General of Moscow. June was a bad month for St Petersburg. Riots and anti-war demonstrations were widespread and commonplace. The streets of Odessa were gripped by violence and bloodshed. The battleship *Potemkin* had been taken over by revolutionaries and sailed to Constanza, Rumania, and surrender. It is against such a scenario that the Russian peace initiatives should be seen. The common though erroneous view in Russia was that Japan had committed all her available manpower in the field. St Petersburg took the view that only mediation could save Japan from disaster. Yet Japan had offers of support from 700,000 additional volunteers pressing to join the colours. There was no comparable upsurge of nationalism or volunteers coming forward in Russia. The defining question was, would Russia run out of popular public support before Japan ran out of funds to sustain the war?

There was no question that Russia could permit herself to be humiliated. The domestic situation was highly volatile, yet in Manchuria the Russian generals were not universally in favour of discontinuing the war. They had seen the transition in the quality and fanaticism of their adversary and the Russian military strength was growing. After all, Russia had not lost any of *her* territory, but it was thought important to secure peace before that possibility came about. Japan had the capability to seize Russian Sakhalin but the question was, did she have the intention to do so in order to strengthen her bargaining position at the peace table? In July Japan invaded and won Sakhalin, posing an immediate threat to Vladivostok.

The prospect and imminence of peace encouraged a flurry of Japanese diplomatic movement which appeared to leave Russian initiatives wallowing. The Anglo-Japanese alliance was strengthened and extended for ten years and an accord with the United States gave Japan what was to be virtually a free hand in Korea. The cheering, joyful crowds which greeted the Japanese mission to the peace conference at Portsmouth, New Hampshire, seemed to underline the daunting task ahead for the Russians.

The Russian peace team was led by the large, untidy and unpopular Sergius Witte who, despite his appearance, was to fight a canny campaign, winning for Russia her sole claim to victory. He played deliberately upon American popular opinion, stressing that Russia was not beaten and could continue the war. He quietly spread abroad his views that the Japanese were greedy and avaricious with the aim of returning to Tokyo with as much loot as was possible. That was quite true; and it was therefore a very defensive Japanese delegation which met Roosevelt and their Russian counterparts on 6 August aboard the *Mayflower*.

Witte's brief was clear. The Tsar's position with regard to Korea had not changed since he had proposed abandoning his interest there before the war began. As for indemnity, the Tsar was adamant, Russia would not pay Japan a rouble.

Baron Komura, a graduate of Harvard, led the Japanese delegation. He was a diminutive man yet an accomplished career diplomat and former supporter of the war. His brief was wider than the Russians', whose requests seemed modest by comparison. The Japanese required that their interests in Korea should be absolute; that Russia should leave Manchuria; that the spoils of war be confirmed; the cession of Sakhalin; the granting of fishing rights along the Russian coast; and the payment of an indemnity to reimburse Japan for the cost of the war. Both sets of conditions were supposed to remain secret, yet somehow the Japanese draft proposals were leaked to the American press.

The conference was so arranged as to leave the difficult points until last, namely the cession of Sakhalin and the payment of indemnity. It appeared to the American public therefore that the God-fearing, Christian Russians were the epitome of virtue by abandoning claims on matters which, in any event, they could no longer control. On 15 August the two vexed questions of Sakhalin and indemnity were raised and for two weeks the heated discussions went to and fro while American public opinion swung itself behind the apparently reasonable Russians. Witte, briefed by the Tsar, had been implacably adamant. There was to be no payment for the return of Sakhalin and no indemnity, but it was stressed that there was a readiness in Russia to resume the war. Witte continued to stonewall.

The Tsar had told Waters that the strength of international opinion meant that he could not ignore Roosevelt's offer to open negotiations. Russia was well aware of Japan's financial distress and concluded that a demand for indemnity would be the main topic of discussion at the peace conference. 'This (the indemnity) would never have been entertained by him, and he had calculated that the Peace Conference would break down on this point, and the struggle be continued until Japan could raise no more money.' Roosevelt intervened, telling Japan that if she did not abandon her claims for an indemnity, the world would take the view that the war had been fought for financial gain. When Japan agreed and waived her demand for an indemnity, the Tsar admitted that it had been 'a great disappointment to him'.

On 5 September the peace treaty was signed. Under its terms, Russia agreed to 'the permanent political, military and economic interests of Japan in Korea'. Japan acquired the Russian lease on the Liaotung Peninsula, including Dalny and Port Arthur, the southern section of the Manchurian Railway, and the southern portion of inhospitable Sakhalin – the Russians gaining the north. The previous Russian rights in the ceded territories were transferred to the Japanese. It was further agreed that both nations would withdraw their troops from Manchuria. Of the affable hand-shaking bear Sergius Witte and his diplomatic coup the *New York Times* wrote:

> The judgement of all observers here, whether pro-Japanese or pro-Russian, is that the victory is as astonishing a thing as ever was seen in diplomatic history. A nation hopelessly beaten in every battle of the war, one army captured and the other overwhelmingly routed, with a navy swept from the seas, dictated her own terms to the victory.

Japan erupted. The tax burden, the loss of fathers and sons which had touched upon almost every family demanded compensation. The news that the army was to abandon Manchuria, that there was to be no indemnity and that the only tangible acquisition was half of frozen Sakhalin caused immediate, bloody, long-term rioting. Much of the anger was reserved for the United States and was to remain a feature of the relationship between the two countries. Symbolically, but accidentally, Togo's flagship *Mikasa* blew up on 11 September in Sasebo harbour killing 251 members of the crew. Shortly after, the prime minister and his cabinet resigned. Meanwhile in Russia the news of the successful treaty had little effect on a nation well on its way to revolution.

The Treaty of Portsmouth had been a watershed for the United States and served to establish her as a significant world power. In 1907 the United States demonstrated her power by despatching the Great White Fleet to Japan, but this only served to throw Japan closer to Great Britain with whom the alliance was renewed in 1911. Notwithstanding her disappointments at the peace table, Japan had become the focus of Asian aspirations. It is beneficial to recall a comment from Hamilton, a prosaic observation after the battle of Liaoyang: 'I have today seen the most stupendous spectacle it is possible for the mortal brain to conceive – Asia advancing, Europe falling back, the wall of mist and the writing thereon.' Throughout Asia the cry 'Asia for the Asians' was taken up.

Of the many questions deserving close scrutiny at the end of what had been an unique war, there are arguably two which stand out among the rest. For example, why precisely was it that on land and at sea the Japanese were consistently able to defeat the Russians? Why, also, was it that given the irrefutable evidence of the nature of what modern war was capable of becoming – trenchworks, barbed wire, pounding artillery delivering heavier shells over longer distances, machine guns and mining – were these lessons not readily identifiable in the doctrine, tactics and strategy of the combatants at the outbreak of the First World War?

To begin with, a response to the first question. It is not unreasonable to draw on two sporting analogies: the level playing field and the home fixture. Russia fought the war from a disadvantageous position. Had, say, the roles been reversed and Japan had to depend upon a 5,000-mile-long, single-track railway for her sustenance, and had Russia derived the benefit of being close to the seat of war, would Russia have beaten Japan? The answer is, an unequivocal *perhaps*. In terms of the family of available equipment, once the separate components are analysed in terms of plus or minus, one comes to a rough equivalence. There has to be, therefore, something additional here, something beyond head counts and numbers of artillery pieces, which acted as a force multiplier. The Russians did not fight this war badly but it is a fact that the Japanese fought better.

The Japanese officer provided the essential link between the men and their Emperor. The majority of junior officers were of peasant origin and had been educated in the tradition of the samurai and the school of Bushido. With very few exceptions, the Russian officer did not enjoy such empathy with his men because the men were of lowly origin. That in itself is no reason why, as Britain's armed forces proved in the twentieth century, they should not fight as an effective and harmonious whole. One reason why Russia's officer corps lacked the common standards and professionalism enjoyed by the Japanese officer corps was noted by a military observer: '… the remarkable number of Guards officers, who were either promoted to commands, or else were appointed to the staff. A few were good men in the field but family influence was usually the deciding factor, and the officers of the line – and Russia – suffered accordingly.' Another reason was the advanced years of many commanders, effectively blocking the progress of energetic, younger officers with new ideas.

The situation of the ordinary Russian, from where the basic soldier and sailor were taken, was described by another observer, Lieutenant Commander McCully:

> The root of all their disasters is found in the Russian character,
> of which the government is a natural consequence. Naturally
> simple, honest, and hard working, through apathy they have
> developed a government at the head of which is an autocrat
> whose will is expressed through bureaucrats, and administered
> by military satraps.

It was not just the urban proletariat that was now expressing dissatisfaction with the Tsar's regime. The Siberian peasants were also unsettled, principally due to acute land shortages. The groundswell of protest began to take hold in the country from 1890 and became most noticeable in the navy, spreading into the army on the back of continuing military failure in Manchuria.

Again, we have another contrast in the attitude of the Japanese, to their Emperor, the centre of the nation's military tradition and the samurai's instinctive need for authority. He had become cultivated as the focus for devotion and homage which historically had been diffused among feudal warlords. In his memoirs, the young Douglas MacArthur told the story of how General Oku's men were required to take dreadful-tasting pills three times a day to keep beriberi in check. They did not like the grim medicine and avoided taking it. As a way round the problem, someone had the inspiration to apply a printed text to the medicine tins: 'To prevent beriberi, the Emperor desires you take one pill three times a day.' MacArthur tells how the intended result was instantaneous. Not a pill was wasted. 'Nothing but death itself could stop the soldiers from taking the medicine.'

Both sides recognised that the Russo-Japanese war involved army-navy co-operation and so, by implication, the advantage would appear to fall to that nation best able to cultivate joint army-navy operations. There was little appreciable harmony between the Russian army and Russian navy. The navy, 'the darling of the Court', found greater favour because it was aristocratic, the purer of the two services, and there were fewer Germans in the navy. The fact that navy personnel were better paid did not help relations with the army. On the other hand, a Japanese newspaper explained to its readers: 'The army and the navy are distinguished nominally but, in truth, they are as the two wheels of a cart.' The London *Times* had more to add: 'Owing to the relative situation of the two Services in Japan, the command of the sea is regarded only as a means to an end, and not the end itself; the action of the navy is introductory and preparatory, and the decision is left to the land forces.'

All these factors added weight to the scales of advantage but collectively were unlikely to explain fully what the essential battle-winning ingredient had been. General Langlois spoke of the high Japanese morale as being one of three key principles or factors. Morale is also one of the British and Commonwealth principles of war, linked to offensive spirit and based upon universal confidence enhanced by success in battle. It is therefore not a constant but will reflect the military's mood and situation. Russia had observed the first hint of Japan's high morale during the 1894–5 conflict and asked Wanowski, the military attaché in Tokyo, for an assessment. He attributed the phenomenon to China's weakness rather than to Japan's strengths: 'It will perhaps be centuries before the Japanese army acquires the sort of morale on which the organisation of European armies is based.' But it was indeed morale or spirit which set the Russian and Japanese armed forces apart.

Tadayoshi Sakurai observed how the Russians 'did not believe in the Tsar's virtue', being 'oppressed and trampled upon by his ministers. They were therefore not at all anxious to support the government in this war.' Although he admitted to their strength and bravery, he found them to be lacking in what he believed to be the first requisite of a successful war-morale. Morale or *Damashii* was something the Japanese had aplenty. *Tamashii*, or spirit, when combined with the word *Yamato* (which came to mean Japan) becomes *Damashii*. The spirit of Bushido, a guide of ethical and moral principles, inculcated in the Japanese mind the golden rule never to turn one's back on an enemy. Hence, unlike the Russians, they thought only of going forward. 'We have inherited a temperament which knows no retreating even before sure death, and that inheritance has been made stronger by discipline,' wrote Sakurai. 'Our constant victory over the fierce enemy must largely be due to this characteristic of ours.'

The second question is, why had the land lessons of the Russo-Japanese War not been learnt and applied in time for the outbreak of the First World War in 1914? Many commanders were to express their surprise and horror at the deadly effect of artillery. It is an over-simplification to suggest that the observers had taken the view that the Russians had been too incompetent and the Japanese too fanatical to provide meaningful lessons. Apparently trivial yet profoundly important factors came into play to either dilute or to remove specific reports from the record. Observers would not always agree among themselves what lessons had been learnt, and this was not an entirely British phenomenon. The reporting of lessons learnt had become heavily layered in interest. Cambridge's Dr Philip Towle explained:

> The British armed forces tried harder to learn from the Russo-Japanese War than from any other foreign war before or since, as the number of officers sent as observers and the number of official histories clearly demonstrated. But each observer tended to draw lessons which reinforced his own belief and the interests of his regiment or corps.

Many enjoyed the patronage of their own senior generals keen that their protégés should bolster commonly held opinion and interest.

There was no uniformity in the circulation of reports emanating from the Russo-Japanese War. The fact that the Japanese were the allies of the British meant that the War Office was more than circumspect in the release of information on Japan's way in war. Reports were strictly controlled. There was no such sensitivity in relation to reports on the Russians' performance, which were freely available. This is not to say that because the Russian lessons learned were more readily available, this had a greater influence on what was given due weighting and attention. The valid observations of British observers attached to the Russians, in the matter of artillery and its contribution to the Japanese victory and also in enabling the Russians to keep in touch, was subordinated to the more conservative views originating from British observers with the Japanese. Had that not been the case, it is possible to speculate that the course of the First World War might have been different. There were elements in the British High Command who doubted the worth of artillery, believing it to be of value only against raw troops. The significance of heavy artillery as used against targets such as 203 Metre Hill was to be relearned, but not in time to prevent the British army beginning the First World War with the bulk of the artillery ammunition being of shrapnel nature.

The cavalry were foremost in the protection of their interests and they also had allies among other arms who maintained a nostalgic view of horse-mounted cavalry in warfare. It was an attitude which would take years to budge. At the time when the cauldrons of the Ruhr were spewing out the armoured plate upon which the Second World War's *Blitzkrieg* depended, a senior British general would insist, 'There is still a place for the horse in the British Army – albeit the well bred horse.' General Hamilton did not regard it as part of his charter to foster such sympathies. In one of his reports, duly censored, he wrote:

> For my part, I maintain that it would be as reasonable to introduce the elephants of Porus onto a modern battlefield as regiments of lancers and dragoons who are too much imbued with the true cavalry spirit to use firearms and too sensible, when it comes to the pinch, to employ their boasted *arme blanche* – willing to wound yet afraid to strike. The role they are condemned to play in 20th century battles is one deserving of the most profound commiseration.

In the First World War a cavalry corps of three divisions with all the attendant manning and logistical penalties was kept waiting on the Western Front for a classic cavalry counter-stroke that would never materialise. The failure to make a proper assessment of the value of the machine gun would cost the British and French thousands of lives in the First World War. The value of modern weapons, particularly to the defender, had passed largely unnoticed.

Clearly, therefore, reports could be – and were – censored, and other reports which survived and contained valid observations were ignored because they did not conform to conventional opinion. One such opinion was the unashamedly racist view that the Japanese could not possibly teach the West anything which was not already known.

Brigadier James Jardine, commanding the 97th Brigade, 32nd Division, in General Rawlinson's Fourth Army on the Western Front had been an observer with the Japanese First Army during the Russo-Japanese War. Immediately prior to the general offensive planned for the first day of the Battle of the Somme, on 1 July 1916, Rawlinson gathered together his formation commanders to discuss the plan of attack. Infantry and cavalry helped simulate the battle activity. Jardine wrote:

> It came to my turn and Rawlinson asked me had I anything to say, and I replied: 'The leading lines did not advance close enough to the barrage.' 'Oh,' he said, 'How close do you think they should be?' and I replied, 'Thirty to forty yards, Sir, and they must expect some casualties.' I could see that he did not like what I said for he replied, 'Oh, thirty to forty yards!!' 'Well Sir,' I said, 'That's what the Japanese did,' and his reply was, 'Oh the Japanese,' in a rather sneering way.

His recommendation summarily dismissed, Jardine decided nonetheless to employ the Japanese doctrine within 97th Brigade as best he could. One of his battalions, the 17th Highland Light Infantry, was able to leave its trenches in advance of the remainder of the division, following the artillery inexorably towards the German positions. Sebastian Dobson wrote:

> While many battalions along the front line climbed out of their trenches only to be mown down by German machine-gun fire, the 17th overran the enemy trenches in the Leipzig Salient before the opposing German infantry could emerge from their shelters, and made one of the few small gains of that terrible day.

Terrible indeed it was. At the end of the first day, 19,240 British and Empire soldiers had been killed, with a further 38,230 wounded or missing. When the battle ended in November, the total losses including killed, wounded and captured were 420,000 British and Empire, 194,000 French and 465,000 Germans.

Japanese confidence and assurance grew at an unstemmable pace. In 1914 she parted from her German military mentors in a most dramatic manner by declaring war on Germany even though she had never been involved in the origins of that war. The declaration also marked the beginning of the end of the relationship with Great Britain for, although allies, Japan had not fully consulted a miffed Britain as to her intentions. The parting was inevitable, since it would be an incongruous relationship for Asia's hero to retain links with the ultimate colonial power. Not that Japan herself was averse to colonies for she arbitrarily took over Germany's colonial interests in the Pacific and China.

Britain and the United States grew apprehensive as to Japanese aspirations. Their mutual suspicions were confirmed when, in 1915, Japan issued China with her notorious 21 Demands, a plan for the annexation of China. Japan was blocked for the time being, but there was reflection as to how long she could be kept down. The assistant British military attaché in Peking wrote in 1918:

> If Japan is not given a free hand in some part of the Far East,
> there is a danger that she might actually go over to the enemy.
> With Russia a prostrate neutral between them, Japan and Ger-
> many would form an extremely strong combination, which
> would threaten the whole of the allies' possessions in Asia and
> even in Australasia.

It had been in 1918 that a combined force which had included British, American and Japanese troops had gone to the assistance of the White Russians but, seeing the permanence of the revolution, Britain and America withdrew from the half-hearted intervention. Japan remained in Siberia until 1922 and did not return northern Sakhalin to Russia until 1925. (Russia acquired all of Sakhalin in 1945 as part of the agreement with the allies for her last-minute entry into the war against Japan.)

The interested powers had no intention of giving Japan a free hand in developing her power, and arranged at the Washington Conference in 1921 to impose conditions. Under this treaty the ratio of capital ship tonnages between Britain, the United States and Japan was set at 5:5:3. In 1923 the Anglo-Japanese alliance was abrogated and the London Naval Treaty of 1930 imposed further limitations upon the Imperial Japanese Navy. Anti-British feeling grew in Japan as pro-German sentiments increased. The technical exchange between Britain and Japan had ceased with the abrogation of the alliance. Since there was no prospect of support from the United States, with whom a fatal rivalry was now developing, Japan sought a new partner to supply essential technical expertise.

Britain's building of the Singapore naval base caused a furore in Japan where it was seen as an Anglo-American provocative measure to attempt to limit Japan's interests in the Pacific. In 1937, when the Sino-Japanese War began, relationships deteriorated further. Japan took full advantage of her time in China to develop and refine tactics and machinery. While the Stukas were being tested in Spain, a similar experience was being enjoyed by the Zeros in China. After the outbreak of war in Europe in 1939, Japan moved closer to Germany, culminating in September 1940 with the signing of the tri-partite pact. Japanese confidence had developed into Japanese over-confidence.

The attack on Pearl Harbor was a repeat performance of the attack on Port Arthur. As if to acknowledge that point, the lead carrier *Akagi* flew the same battle flag as Admiral Togo had flown on the *Mikasa* during Japan's pre-emptive strike on Port Arthur. What was surprising was that on 19 February 1942 a smaller *Akagi* carrier group would make a similar, successful, surprise attack on the airfield and ships at Darwin in what was to be described in Australia as 'a day of national shame'.

The writing of military history is concerned with the documenting of the preparation, execution and results of war. It seeks to study the political, intellectual, social, economic and geographical circumstances which conspired to bring armies into conflict. It analyses the strategic, tactical and logistical options that were available to the commander and considers the various factors which influenced the result. It would be wrong to believe that the simple expedient of learning from history will be infallibly beneficial, for selective study can be capable of justifying almost any opinion.

Liddell Hart wrote: 'If the study of war in the past has so often proved fallible as a guide to the course of the next war, it implies not that war is unsuited to scientific study but that the study has not been scientific enough in spirit and method.' One lesson from the Russo-Japanese War is the frequency with which different observers could view an event and come to totally different conclusions. A French summary of the war concluded: 'It is almost impossible for a front protected by really powerful weapons and field defences to be broken through even by troops of undaunted courage willing to sacrifice any number of lives.' A British view, however, stated:

> The war has certainly not demonstrated that frontal attacks are
> a sheer impossibility, as has so often been asserted. Where very
> large modern armies are concerned, attacks must be frontal,
> and that part of the enemy's front will be selected for the main
> attack, before which a large force can be concentrated quickly
> and secretly, and the attack of the infantry will be covered and
> supported by artillery and cavalry. No weak screen will be
> allowed to check such an attack. The fire of hundreds of quick
> firing guns will breach the line, and against the breach will be
> sent a mass of infantry to break the line. Through the break in
> the line will pour the cavalry divisions, to complete the victory
> and hamper the reserves from coming up to stop the breach by
> an offensive return, or to restore the battle by a counterstroke.

Some nations appear to have a tradition of not learning the lessons of history and while this was true in this war as it affected the land battle, the same was not the case when applied to naval design and development. Pakenham's observations as to the employment of battleships and suitability of tactics and equipment removed much of the guesswork from the research and development of a new generation of battleships. Admiral Fisher, the First Sea Lord, took careful note of Pakenham's recommendations, which were to be incorporated into the new design of Dreadnoughts. The irony of the new battleships was that their impact and effect were to be dulled largely by the emergence of the concurrently developing submarine as a weapon of war.

The Russo-Japanese War reconfirmed the benefits to be derived from the individual study of warfare. The Russians learnt at the end of their war of humiliation the need to design a structured operational force. The idea was conceptually sound but what was lacking were officers of the requisite quality to make it work. Waters wrote:

> 'When the Great War broke out it was impossible for me to
> believe, as so many experts, military and other, believed, that

> the incapable Generals of 1904 had been transformed into
> reliable commanders within the brief space of ten years ...
> No military genius will enable a Commander-in-Chief to gain
> victories unless he can rely on his subordinates to carry out his
> plans effectively.

In 1914, the Russian First and Second Armies were commanded by Rennenkampf and Samsonov, the former sparring partners at Mukden station in 1905.

Colonel Max Hoffman had been one of the German observers during the Russo-Japanese War and used the possibility of a breakdown in communication and co-operation between the two Russian generals to offer Ludendorff and Hindenburg a plan to divide the two Russian armies. When German signals intercept units picked up the Russian future intentions being sent in clear and not coded, Hoffman was able to persuade his doubting commanders that this was not a deception plan but rather sheer, unsurprising incompetence.

A more recent and telling example of learning from history is to be found in Field Marshal Slim's *Defeat into Victory*:

> We knew something of the Japanese intentions, but little of the
> dispositions of their reserves, and practically nothing about one
> of the most important factors that a general has to consider –
> the character of the opposing commanders. I had all the infor-
> mation I could obtain about Lieutenant General Kawabe, my
> opposite number, who as Commander-in-Chief, Burma Army
> Area, controlled all Japanese land and air forces in Burma, but it
> did not amount to much on which to build up a picture of how
> his mind would work. At this time, from what I had seen of his
> operations, I could only expect him to be, like most Japanese
> commanders I had met, a bold tactical planner of offensive
> movements, completely confident in the superiority of his
> troops and prepared to use his last reserves rather than aban-
> don a plan. Many years before, when I was working for the Staff
> College examinations, I had studied the Russo-Japanese War,
> and one thing about that campaign I had always remembered.
> The Russians never won a battle. In almost every fight they
> accepted defeat while a considerable portion of their forces, in

reserve, were still unused. On the other hand, the Japanese
were prepared to throw in every man, and more than once
tipped the scales of victory with their very last reserves. The
Japanese generals we were fighting had been brought up on
the lessons of that war, and all I had seen of them in this convinced me that they would run true to form and hold back
nothing. This was a source of great strength to them, but also,
properly taken advantage of might, in conjunction with their
overweening confidence, be a fatal weakness.

When the sound of war has passed away, the cigarette smoke of nervous delegates dispersed from untidy peace chambers, and armchair analysts
have embarked upon their safe investigation, it is left to the surviving soldiers – victors and losers – to return home to resume their life as best they
can. Those that were shot but did not die bear their scars, but few are able
to pass entirely through a war without being scarred in one way or another.
Suffering is not just the domain of the soldier for it reaches out to his general too. Kuropatkin was an exception. He survived both wars and was able
after the revolution to find compromise with the new proponents of the
classless society. The former Minister for War and commander of the then
largest army in the history of war assumed the various employments of clerk
and schoolteacher until his death in 1923.

Nogi, hero of Port Arthur and Mukden, took up a subordinate position in
Tokyo's great victory parade and, as if to show his complete humility, rode an
old nag. When required to give his report to the Emperor, Nogi, in the same
uniform that he had worn at Port Arthur, came forward but the words froze
in his throat and his eyes welled with tears. When he did eventually finish,
he pleaded to be allowed to die, to which the Emperor replied that he should
wait until the Emperor's death.

Nogi bided his time as principal of a Tokyo school. When the Emperor
died in 1912, Nogi felt free of his bond and prepared for the sacrifice contemplated all those years ago when he lost his regimental colours in the Civil
War. With both sons dead and tens of thousands of the soldiers who had
served under his command no more, he now believed that he had even
greater justification. Just as the Emperor's hearse was leaving the palace on 13
September, Nogi, in ceremonial uniform, plunged his sword into his stomach
to perform *hara kiri*. His wife had taken her own life a few minutes before.

The death of Nogi and his wife overshadowed the funeral of the Emperor and the end of the Meiji era. In feudal Japan it had been the tradition for the Samurai to follow his master to the new world but this tribute had been forbidden by law for many years. The irony of Nogi was that he was the least progressive of Japan's field generals, the one of the old school, the one least acquainted with the realities of modern war. It seemed that this, his final message to his countrymen, was recommending a return to the old Samurai virtues. In his death he became a god, a war god, and symbol of the new, ambitious and confident Japan, born out of the Russo-Japanese War.

Forty years after her humiliation in that war, Russia gained her revenge. After a hasty declaration of war against Japan on 8 August 1945, her long-contemplated invasion tore into and through northern China and Manchuria. The Japanese Kwantung Army had a given strength of 925,000 men but the veterans had long gone, replaced by reservists and 300,000 local troops. On 15 August 1945 the Emperor of Japan recognised that 'the war situation has developed not necessarily to Japan's advantage' and capitulated. Whatever *Damashii* still existed in the Kwantung Army up to that point had now evaporated, as the Russians continued their offensive after the surrender. When hostilities came to an end, the Russians were back in Dalny and Port Arthur. During the Red Army's offensive, one Army – the Sixth Tank Army – advanced an equivalent distance from Normandy's beaches to Milan, in eleven days.

EPILOGUE

The study of war ultimately returns to an all-consuming interest in those indivisible components, the soldiers and non-combatants who, in whatever manner, in a way big or small, experienced war and its wider implications. Understandably, it is to the man in uniform that our attention is first drawn and upon the curious 'kill or be killed' relationship which exists between anonymous opponents. But in war, for every man charged with the infliction of death or injury upon his enemy, there is a myriad of people in family groups praying for their own loved one's safe homeward return.

The literature of this war is no less replete than others with anecdotes, sentimental, sensitive or sad which prove that very point. One such was penned by the war correspondent Douglas Story. He reminds us that the boundaries of war's cruelty extend far beyond what we might at first expect and in so doing, emphasise the futility of war.

One evening I was pacing slowly to and fro athwart the station platform at Irkutsk, thinking regretfully, yet philosophically, of the thousands of gallant dead upon the plains of Liaoyang, when a woman's quick sob at my elbow pulled me out of my smug meditation into the reality of death and suffering. She was a poor woman, decently dressed in black, with a puling infant, swaddled in a shawl, close-huddled to her bosom. I followed her along the creaking platform, watching her as she passed through the glare from the windows of the buffet into the blackness of the intervening shadows. Creeping into the station hall she paused for a moment irresolute, with wide-open, dumb, imploring eyes, seeking for comfort yet expecting none. Seeing me she tendered a card she had carried in her tight-clenched mother's hand. It was a postcard with a gaudy representation in blue, and red, and yellow, of a giant Russian guardsman bayoneting a wizened Japanese. Beneath it were scrawled a few words in Russian. To me she murmured something in the language of the people, and I, for the thousandth time, murmured my stock phrase in reply: "I do not understand Russian."

'There was a friend of mine, a long-coated captain of artillery, clanking impatiently up and down the room. I led her to him and explained my inability to assist her in her trouble. He was a big, loud-voiced man, newly back from the bluster and brutality of battle. He glared for a moment at the woman who dared to interrupt his musing, but out of courtesy to me took the card and studied it. The heavy figures of peasants stretched upon the floor watched wonderingly. A railway official hurried about his business.

'The officer shifted uneasily, cleared his throat, rearranged his sword-belt. The woman stood patiently waiting. His voice had grown strangely soft when he answered in Russian that even I could understand: "Your husband was killed at Tashichiao on July the eleventh." The salt despair was welling out of the woman's eyes as he spoke. "Yes, my child – he has done his duty – to his Tsar."

'The officer crossed himself, and a broken figure in rusty black went tottering blindly down the steps into the fog and darkness of Irkutsk.

'My captain of artillery sought in his sleeve-cuff for his handkerchief, speaking angrily the while as though some one had insulted him: "She could not read. God! sir, it is like sentencing a man to be hanged to answer such a question. God help the women and children!"

'And he, too, strode into the darkness.'

Douglas Story, The Campaign with Kuropatkin

SELECT BIBLIOGRAPHY

Allen, H. N., *Korea: Fact and Fancy,* Seoul, 1904.

Anderson, J. H., *The Russo-Japanese War on Land 1904–1905,* London, 1909.

Asakawa, K., *The Russo-Japanese Conflict: Its Causes and Issues,* London, 1904.

Ashmead-Bartlett, E., *Port Arthur, the Siege and Capitulation,* London, 1906.

Ballard, Admiral G. A., *The Influence of the Sea on the Political History of Japan,* London, 1921.

Baring, M., *With the Russians in Manchuria,* London, 1905.

Bird, W. D., *Strategy of the Russo-Japanese War,* London, 1911.

Bodley, R. V. C., *Admiral Togo: The Authorized Life,* London, 1935.

Brooke, Lord, *An Eye-Witness in Manchuria,* London, 1905.

Cassell's History of the Russo-Japanese War, 3 vols, London, n.d.

Collier's Weekly, 'Russo-Japanese War, A Photographic and Descriptive Review', New York, n.d.

Cowen, T., *The Russo-Japanese War, From the Outbreak of Hostilities to the Battle of Liaoyang,* London, 1904.

de Negrier, General, *Lessons of the Russo-Japanese War,* London, 1906.

Ellison, Herbert J., *History of Russia,* New York, 1964.

'Footslogger', *A Short Account of the Russo-Japanese War,* London, 1925.

Fujisawa Rikitaro, *The Recent Aims and Political Development of Japan,* New Haven, 1923.

German General Staff, *The Russo-Japanese War,* 5 vols, prepared by the Historical Section, authorised translation by Karl von Donat, London, 1909–10.

Glasfurd, A. I. R., *Sketches of Manchurian Battlefields,* London, 1910.

Greener, William, *A Secret Agent in Port Arthur,* London, 1905.

Haldane, A. L., *Reports from British Officers Attached to the Japanese and Russian Forces in the Field,* London, 1908.

Hamilton, Lieutenant General Sir Ian, A *Staff Officer's Scrap Book during the Russo-Japan-ese War*, 2 vols, London, 1906.

Hardy, O., and Dumke, G. S., A *History of the Pacific Area in Modern Times*, Cambridge, Mass., 1949.

Hargreaves, R., *Red Sun Rising: The Siege of Port Arthur*, London, 1962.

Hart-Synott, Captain, *Reports from British Officers Attached to the Japanese and Russian Forces in the Field*, London, 1908.

Hildreth, Richard, *Japan As It Was and Is*, Tokyo, 1902.

His Majesty's Stationery Office, *The Russo-Japanese War, Reports from British Officers Attached to the Japanese and Russian Forces in the Field*, 3 vols, and 2 vols of maps, London, 1908.

Historical Section of the Committee of Imperial Defence, *The Official History of the Russo-Japanese War (Naval and Military)*, 3 vols, and 3 vols of maps and appendices, London, 1910–20.

Hough, Richard, *The Fleet That Had To Die*, London, 1958.

James, D. H., *The Siege of Port Arthur, Records of an Eye-Witness*, London, 1905.

Japan Times (Official Report), *The Russo-Japanese War*, Shimbashido, Tokyo, undated.

Klado, Captain N. L., *The Russian Navy in the Russo-Japanese War*, translated by L. J. H. Dickinson, London, 1905.

Kuropatkin, General A. N., *The Russian Army and the Japanese War*, 2 vols, New York, 1909.

Levine, I. D., *The Kaiser's Letters to the Tsar*, London, 1921.

McCormick, Frederick, *The Tragedy of Russia in Pacific Asia*, 2 vols, New York, 1907.

McCullagh, F., *With the Cossacks, Being the Story of an Irishman Who Rode with the Cossacks Throughout the Russo-Japanese War*, London, 1906.

Mahan, Captain A. T., *The Problem of Asia*, Boston, 1905.

Military Correspondent of *The Times*, *The War in the Far East*, London, 1904–5.

Morris, J., *Makers of Japan*, London, 1906.

Nojine, E. K., *The Truth about Port Arthur*, translated and edited by Captain A. B. Lindsay and Major E. D. Swinton, London, 1908.

Norregaard, B. W., *The Great Siege: The Investment and Fall of Port Arthur*, London, 1906.

Novikov-Priboy, A. S., *Tsushima: Grave of a Floating City*, New York, 1937.

O'Laughlin, J. C., 'The Russo-Japanese War', *Collier's Weekly*, New York, n.d.

Pakenham, Captain W. C., British Naval Attaché, *Admiralty Reports*, Public Record Office, London.

Palmer, Frederick, *With Kuroki in Manchuria*, New York, 1904.

Politovski, E. S., *From Libau to Tsushima. A Narrative of the Voyage of Admiral Rozhdestvenski's Fleet to Eastern Seas*, translated by Major F. R. Godfrey, London, 1906.

Rees, David, *The Defeat of Japan*, London, 1997.

Richmond Smith, W., *The Siege and Fall of Port Arthur*, London, 1905.

Rosen, Baron, *Forty Years of Diplomacy*, New York, 1922.

Ross, Colonel C., *An Outline of the Russo-Japanese War,* 2 vols, London, 1912.

Rowan-Robinson, H., *The Campaign of Liaoyang,* London, 1914.

Sakurai Tadayoshi, *Human Bullets,* Tokyo, 1907.

Sedgwick, F. R., *The Russo-Japanese War on Land,* London, undated.

— *1904 The Russo-Japanese War,* 2 vols, London, 1909 and 1912.

Semenov, Captain V. I., *Rasplata,* London, 1909.

— *The Battle of Tsushima,* translated by Captain A. B. Lindsay, London, 1906.

Steer, A. P., *The 'Novik' and the Part She Played in the Russo-Japanese War,* London, 1913.

Story, Douglas, *The Campaign with Kuropatkin,* London, 1904.

The Russo-Japanese War. Reports from Officers Attached to the Japanese Forces. 5 volumes. London and Tokyo, 2000.

Tretyakov, Lieutenant General N. A., *My Experiences at Nan-shan and Port Arthur with the Fifth East Siberian Rifles,* London, 1911.

US War Department, Office of the Chief-of-Staff, *Reports of Military Observers Attached to the Armies in Manchuria During the Russo-Japanese War,* 2 vols, Washington, 1906.

Villiers, F., *Port Arthur, Three Months With the Besiegers,* London, 1905.

von Tettau, Freiherr, *Achtzehn Monate mit Russlands Heeren in der Mandschurei,* quoted extensively in Sedgwick, *1904 The Russo-Japanese War,* 2 vols, London, 1909 and 1912.

Walder, David, *The Short Victorious War,* London, 1973.

Warner, Dennis and Peggy, *The Tide at Sunrise,* London, 1975.

Waters, Colonel W. H-H., *Reports from British Officers in the Field with the Russian and Japanese Forces,* London, 1906.

Westwood, J. N., *The Illustrated History of the Russo-Japanese War,* London, 1973.

Wood, O. E., *From the Yalu to Port Arthur,* Tokyo, 1905.

Wrangel, Count Gustav, *The Cavalry in the Russo-Japanese War,* London, 1907.

Wright, H. C. Seppings, *With Togo, the Story of Seven Months Under His Command,* London, 1906.

INDEX

Jutland 1916
Peter Hart
0 304 36648 X ☐
£6.99

Weapons of Mass Destruction
Robert Hutchinson
0 304 36653 6 ☐
£7.99

Eisenhower
Carlo D'Este
0 304 36658 7 ☐
£9.99

Enigma
Hugh Sebag-Montefiore
0 304 36662 5 ☐
£8.99

Fire from the Forest
Roger Ford
0 304 36336 7 ☐
£7.99

A Storm in Flanders
Winston Groom
0 304 36656 0 ☐
£7.99

Churchill's Folly
Anthony Rogers
0 304 36655 2 ☐
£7.99 ·

Rising Sun and Tumbling Bear
Richard Connaughton
0 304 36657 9 ☐
£7.99

All Orion/Phoenix titles are available at your local bookshop or from the following address:

Mail Order Department
Littlehampton Book Services
FREEPOST BR535
Worthing, West Sussex, BN13 3BR
telephone 01903 828503, *facsimile* 01903 828802
e-mail MailOrders@lbsltd.co.uk
(Please ensure that you include full postal address details)

Payment can be made either by credit/debit card (Visa, Mastercard, Access and Switch accepted) or by sending a £ Sterling cheque or postal order made payable to *Littlehampton Book Services*.
DO NOT SEND CASH OR CURRENCY.

Please add the following to cover postage and packing

UK and BFPO:
£1.50 for the first book, and 50p for each additional book to a maximum of £3.50

Overseas and Eire:
£2.50 for the first book plus £1.00 for the second book and 50p for each additional book ordered

---

BLOCK CAPITALS PLEASE

name of cardholder ....

delivery address
(if different from cardholder)

address of cardholder ....

....

....

....

....

postcode ....

postcode ....

☐ I enclose my remittance for £........................

☐ please debit my Mastercard/Visa/Access/Switch (delete as appropriate)

card number ☐☐☐☐☐☐☐☐☐☐☐☐☐☐☐☐☐☐

expiry date ☐☐☐☐   Switch issue no. ☐☐

signature ....

prices and availability are subject to change without notice